DYNAMICAL SYSTEMS
IN
SOCIAL PSYCHOLOGY

DYNAMICAL SYSTEMS
IN
SOCIAL PSYCHOLOGY

Edited by

Robin R. Vallacher
Department of Psychology
Florida Atlantic University
Boca Raton, Florida

Andrzej Nowak
Institute for Social Studies
University of Warsaw
Warsaw, Poland

ACADEMIC PRESS, INC.
A Division of Harcourt Brace & Company
San Diego   New York   Boston   London   Sydney   Tokyo   Toronto

This book is printed on acid-free paper. ∞

Academic Press, Inc.
525 B Street, Suite 1900, San Diego, California 92101-4495

United Kingdom Edition published by
Academic Press Limited
24–28 Oval Road, London NW1 7DX

Library of Congress Cataloging-in-Publication Data

Dynamical systems in social psychology / edited by Robin R. Vallacher,
    Andrzej Nowak.
        p.   cm.
    Includes bibliographical refrences (p.   ) and index.
    ISBN 0-12-709990-5
    1. Social psychology   I. Vallacher, Robin R., Date
II. Nowak, Andrzej.
HM251.D87   1993
302--dc20
                                                93-11325
                                                CIP

PRINTED IN THE UNITED STATES OF AMERICA
94 95 96 97 98 99   EB   9 8 7 6 5 4 3 2 1

CONTENTS

CHAPTER 1
The Chaos in Social Psychology

Robin R. Vallacher and Andrzej Nowak

CHAPTER 2
Dynamical Systems: A Tool for Social Psychology?

Andrzej Nowak and Maciej Lewenstein

CHAPTER 3

The New Statistical Dynamics: An Informal Look at Invariant Measures of Psychological Time Series

Arnold J. Mandell and Karen A. Selz

CHAPTER 4
New Mathematical Techniques for Pattern Recognition
Franklin E. Schweck Jr.

CHAPTER 5
Aggression, Love, Conformity, and Other Social Psychological Catastrophes
Abraham Tesser and John Achee

CHAPTER 6
Local and Global Dynamics of Social Relations
Reuben M. Baron, Polemnia G. Amazeen, and Peter J. Beek

CHAPTER 7

The Perception and Coupling of Behavior Waves

Darren Newtson

CHAPTER 8

A Family of Autocorrelation Graph Equivalence Classes on Symbolic Dynamics as Models of Individual Differences in Human Behavioral Style

Karen A. Selz and Arnold J. Mandell

CHAPTER 9

Toward a Dynamic Conception of Attitude Consistency and Change

J. Richard Eiser

CHAPTER 10

Attitudes as Catastrophes: From Dimensions to Categories with Increasing Involvement

Bibb Latané and Andrzej Nowak

CHAPTER 11
The Stream of Social Judgment
Robin R. Vallacher and Andrzej Nowak

CHAPTER 12
Toward a Dynamical Social Psychology
Andrzej Nowak, Maciej Lewenstein, and Robin R. Vallacher

CONTRIBUTORS

Numbers in parentheses indicate the pages on which the authors' contributions begin.

John Achee (95), Department of Psychology, University of Georgia, Athens, Georgia 30602

Polemnia G. Amazeen (111), Department of Psychology, University of Connecticut, Storrs, Connecticut 06269

Reuben M. Baron (111), Department of Psychology, University of Connecticut, Storrs, Connecticut 06269

Peter J. Beek (111), Department of Psychology, Faculty of Human Movement Sciences, Vrije University of Amsterdam, Amsterdam, The Netherlands

J. Richard Eiser (197), Department of Psychology, University of Exeter, Exeter EX4 4QG, England

Bibb Latané (219), Department of Psychology, Florida Atlantic University, Boca Raton, Florida 33431

Maciej Lewenstein (17, 279), Institute for Social Studies, University of Warsaw and Center for Theoretical Physics, Polish Academy of Sciences, 00-183 Warsaw, Poland

Arnold J. Mandell (55, 169), Laboratory of Experimental and Constructive Mathematics, Departments of Mathematics, Physics, and Psychology, Florida Atlantic University, Boca Raton, Florida 33431

Darren Newtson (139), Department of Psychology, University of Virginia, Charlottesville, Virginia 22903

Andrzej Nowak (1, 17, 219, 251, 279), Institute for Social Studies, Faculty of Psychology, University of Warsaw, 00-183 Warsaw, Poland

Franklin E. Schroeck Jr. (71), Department of Mathematics, Florida Atlantic University, Boca Raton, Florida 33431

Karen A. Selz (55, 169), Laboratory of Experimental and Constructive Mathematics, Departments of Mathematics and Clinical Psychology Center, Florida Atlantic University, Boca Raton, Florida 33431

Abraham Tesser (95), Institute for Behavioral Research, University of Georgia, Athens, Georgia 30602

Robin R. Vallacher (1, 251, 279), Department of Psychology, Florida Atlantic University, Boca Raton, Florida 33431

PREFACE

No phenomenon in science is more complex, spans a wider range of possible states, or is harder to predict than human social behavior. In even the most mundane interpersonal setting, there is an enormous wealth of information, expectations, and sensory stimulation impinging on a person, and this experiential barrage interacts with the person's capacities, prior experiences, and idiosyncracies to shape his or her thoughts, feelings, and overt actions. The awesome complexity of human social behavior has not gone unnoticed, of course, having engendered skepticism in some quarters that a complete understanding of social psychological phenomena can ever be attained. Within social psychology itself, voices are raised from time to time to decry the fragmented nature of social psychological theory and to express concern over whether the complex, dynamic nature of social phenomena will ever be fully captured in a parsimonious set of principles.

This book articulates a new vision for social psychology, one that is defined in terms of the very factors that promote skepticism among the field's critics and pessimism among its practitioners. In particular, the contributors to this volume take the idea that social psychological phenomena might be profitably viewed as dynamical systems as their point of departure. Broadly defined, a dynamical system is simply a more-or-less self-contained set of elements that interact in complex, often nonlinear ways to form coherent patterns. Even in a system consisting of very few elements, the nature of the feedback among the elements can promote complex dynamics and the repeated emergence of new order in the system. In principle, any phenomenon in nature can be viewed as a dynamical system, and indeed, in recent years just such a perspective has emerged as an integrative metatheory for many otherwise distinct domains of science, including meteorology, population biology, chemistry, statistical mechanics, economics, and cosmology. Treating natural science phenomena in this way represents a marked departure from Newtonian assumptions concerning reduction, determinism, and predictability and redirects the focus of science to the evolution and spontaneous self-organization of natural phenomena.

Our aim in this volume is to demonstrate what a dynamical systems perspective has to offer the field of social psychology. This perspective has already come to permeate other areas of psychology, for example, cognitive neuroscience, motor development, and language acquisition. It is our conviction that the subject matter of social psychology is ideally suited for theoretical formulations and research strategies explicitly concerned with complexity, feedback processes, and the emergence of coherent patterns. Beyond coming to grips with the complexity and temporal dependency of social psychological phenomena, the dynamical systems perspective offers promise of integrating an increasingly fragmented field. It has become fashionable over the years to take social psychology to task for offering a distinct theory for every topic. Principles of group dynamics, for instance, have little in common with principles of social cognition. Even within an area—say, social cognition—there seem to be all too few points of contact among different subtopics (impression formation, attribution, and others). When different domains of human thought and behavior are viewed as dynamical systems, however, their commonalities come into focus. Separate aspects of social psychology will always have their own specific mechanisms and laws, but they may achieve unity at a metatheoretical level by virtue of their respective manifestations of dynamical principles. This approach may promote integration within social psychology in much the same manner that it has exposed the deep invariants at work in different realms of science.

Appreciating the potential of the dynamical systems perspective is one thing; demonstrating its utility is quite another. To be sure, heuristic value is a useful commodity in science, particularly in an arguably preparadigmatic discipline like social psychology, but at some point it is necessary to go beyond metaphor to frame testable theories and to develop paradigms appropriate to such testing. This volume thus reflects an explicit concern with documenting specific applications of dynamical systems principles to social psychological phenomena. This concern is manifest in two ways. First, we invited several prominent mathematicians and physicists to develop in detail the nature of dynamical systems and the analytical tools with which the properties of systems are quantified and investigated. Equally important, we challenged these contributors to consider how these principles and tools could be applied to the investigation of everyday thought and behavior in interpersonal contexts—in other words, to the subject matter of social psychology. Second, we sought out social psychologists who have become professionally concerned with the application of dynamical systems concepts, principles, and methods to their respective phenomena of interest. Such psychologists are relatively few in number at this time, but we expect that their ranks will grow in the years to come as the dynamical systems perspective emerges as a major metatheory in the field.

Overview of Chapters

To a certain extent, dynamical systems theory exposes problems with existing approaches to social psychology and hence reinforces what various critics have had to say about the field. But it is also the case that this perspective redeems social psychology by showing that many of the seemingly intractable problems are actually consistent with what one would expect if one were to consider social thought and behavior in dynamical terms. In Chapter 1 we (Vallacher & Nowak) outline the special nature of social psychology, including those features that give many pause about the scientific maturity of the field and provide a sense of how the field might look if broached from a dynamical systems perspective. Attention is given in particular to complexity and time, which provide the focal points of dynamical systems theory and research, and to the manifestation of these concepts in various social psychological phenomena.

Chapters 2–4, each written by experts in dynamical systems, take up the banner by depicting pertinent dynamical concepts, principles, and methods and developing their implications for the subject matter of social psychology. In Chapter 2, Nowak and Lewenstein provide an overview of dynamical systems theory. Key dynamical concepts are defined and exemplified in the context of real-world social phenomena. In so doing, the integrative potential of the dynamical systems perspective is made explicit, as is the contrast between this general paradigm and traditional scientific theories and approaches. In Chapter 3, Mandell and Selz explore the application of basic time series measures in dynamical systems to social psychological phenomena. The focus in particular is on measures that capture the invariant properties of dynamic psychological processes, and on the commonalities underlying such properties. In Chapter 4, Schroeck argues that the key concern of any attempt to understand a dynamical system is the identification of patterns in the system's behavior. He then discusses various mathematical techniques for pattern recognition that may be of relevance for social psychology.

Chapters 5–11, each written by one or more social psychologists, apply a dynamical systems perspective to an established topic in social psychology. For purposes of exposition, we have organized these chapters according to a topical distinction commonly advanced in social psychology: social behavior (Chapters 5–8) and social cognition (Chapters 9–11). We do not wish to place a great deal of emphasis on this distinction, however. To the contrary, we feel that the boundaries traditionally maintained between social cognition and social behavior have had the unintended effect of promoting the fragmentation of the field. We hope that the application of common principles and paradigmatic guidelines to otherwise different topics will expose the deep invariants that find expression in the dynamics of both mind and action.

In Chapter 5, Tesser and Achee emphasize the sudden and dramatic changes in behavior that seem to characterize many social psychological phenomena. Concepts and principles of catastrophe theory—perhaps the first contemporary dynamical systems theory—are brought to bear on such topics as social influence and love. Their analysis suggests why traditional approaches commonly fail to capture the illusive and seemingly unpredictable nature of these phenomena.

The focus in Chapter 6, by Baron, Amazeen, and Beek, is the evolution of social relationships. They argue that a social dyad or group can be profitably viewed as a complex system that exhibits emergent properties reflecting the coupling of dynamics associated with the individual actors involved. This analysis is fleshed out by demonstrating how tools from nonlinear dynamics can be used to model the development of social relationships as diverse as marriage, ingroup–outgroup relations, and majority–minority relations.

Action is arguably the fundamental unit—the atom, as it were—in psychology. Yet, after decades of research there is very little consensus on what action is, let alone how best to measure it. In Chapter 7, Newtson tackles this problem head on, suggesting that action is indeed a measurable property that can be quantified from a dynamical systems perspective. Newtson's pioneering work in this regard is presented, and the application of this perspective and methodology to special topics in psychology is described.

In Chapter 8, Selz and Mandell discuss the important issue of establishing equivalence classes in human behavior. The advantages and disadvantages associated with different means of capturing the underlying commonalities in superficially distinct patterns of behavior are discussed. A paradigm specifically fashioned to establish deep equivalence is then introduced, and original data are presented to illustrate the potential of this paradigm for capturing invariant features of behavioral style.

In Chapter 9, Eiser argues for a radical revision of the concept of attitude, one of the oldest topics in social psychology. Drawing on connectionist principles in cognitive science, Eiser suggests that attitudes can be viewed as attractors in a multidimensional phase space, contrasts this perspective with traditional views of attitudes, and develops the implications of the dynamic perspective for such perennial issues as attitude consistency, stability, and change.

Latané and Nowak, in Chapter 10, also reexamine the attitude concept, but with emphasis on the internal structure of attitudes. They suggest that with increasing importance, attitudes tend to be represented in a bipolar, categorical manner rather than in a continuous, dimensional manner, so that when a change in a personally important attitude occurs, it tends to be catastrophic rather than incremental. Their chapter also develops the connection between attitudes at the level of the individual and the emergence of attitude clustering and polarization among members of social groups.

In Chapter 11, Vallacher and Nowak explore the idea that social judgment represents an underlying dynamical system that promotes internally driven changes in the conscious thoughts and feelings regarding a social entity. These changes occur in the absence of external instigations, can be reliably measured, differ systematically as a function of stimulus characteristics, and contain meaningful information about the underlying judgment system. A paradigm for tracking the intrinsic dynamics of judgment is introduced, and data attesting to the viability and relevance of this paradigm are presented.

In a concluding chapter (Chapter 12), Nowak, Lewenstein, and Vallacher discuss the implications of dynamical systems theory for a revitalized approach to social psychology. In drawing together the principles, methods, and analytical tools presented in the prior chapters, the authors provide concrete recommendations for empirical work and suggest how the host of topics and issues defining social psychology could be examined from a dynamical systems perspective.

Considered together, then, the various contributions to this volume show how social psychology generally can be recast to come into line with recent developments in the other sciences and illustrate how this approach can be applied to the specific domains that define social psychology. Thus, beyond making a case that the concepts, principles, and methods of dynamical systems theory signal a paradigm shift in social psychology, the book provides fresh insight into individual action, interpersonal behavior, social relations, close relationships, attitudes, and social cognition—in short, the major domains of theory and research within traditional social psychology.

Caveats

We add that this volume should not be viewed as the final statement on the applications of dynamical systems to the subject matter of social psychology. It was not our intent to produce a self-contained comprehensive text providing detailed algorithms for the application of dynamical models. Although several of the chapters do provide fairly detailed conceptualizations, others are somewhat more general and metaphorical in nature, reflecting the lack of precision that currently exists regarding the interface between dynamical systems theory and the social phenomena discussed in these chapters. The reader should not be surprised, therefore, that some of the highly advanced tools described in the "mathematically oriented" chapters are not exploited in the more topical chapters.

It was also not our intent to provide a unified picture of the field, as though there were a single set of conceptual and analytical tools that could be unambiguously applied to all topics in social psychology. To the contrary, the reader will discover that the chapters are quite diverse not only in their respective topics but also in the selection of theoretical and analytical methods used to understand these topics and even in some of their respective philosophy of science assumptions. Such diversity is inevitable at this early stage in the development of a new orientation and should be encouraged rather than frowned upon, as it is only through the expression of different approaches that a truly creative and effective synthesis can ultimately emerge.

What this volume is intended to do is portray the current state of the interface between dynamical systems theory and social psychology. Because the current state reflects diversity rather than consensus, we purposefully sought out scholars who would apply somewhat different conceptualizations and methods to substantive areas that had heretofore been explored by entirely different means. We also wanted to highlight some of the tools that natural scientists find useful but that have yet to find application in social psychology. In that sense, the book is intended to have heuristic value, pointing out some promising models and tools that may stimulate new lines of research in social psychology. In short, this volume should be viewed as introductory and generative rather than as comprehensive and exhaustive. It is our hope and our conviction that in the years to come, social psychology will come to embrace many of the leads advanced in the contributions to this volume.

Acknowledgments

We consider ourselves fortunate to have worked with a group of contributors representing such diverse yet compatible areas of expertise. In preparing this volume, the contributors not only fashioned and revised their individual chapters, but also graciously reviewed the chapters prepared by one another. This spirit of cooperation helped to reduce much of the redundancy and unevenness one typically finds in an edited volume, although of course such features can never be eliminated entirely in a venture of this kind.

We express our appreciation to those who helped the project in other ways. Several colleagues and friends commented on one or more chapters; they are duly noted by the respective contributors. Support for preparation of the volume was provided to Vallacher by the Max-Planck-Institute for Psychological Research in Munich, Germany, during the summer of 1992. Polish Government Grant KBN 1-1113-91-02 provided support to Nowak for his role in preparing the volume and for his research described in various chapters. We are grateful to Phyllis Merrill, who graciously volunteered her time and talent to help create the Author and Subject Indexes. We thank Nikki Fine, our editor at Academic Press, for her patience and encouragement during the various phases of this project. We also thank Sharon Hartley, the production editor, for her role in this project. Finally, a special thanks is given to Marcus Boggs, who saw the potential value in a volume such as this and provided the initial arrangement for its publication.

Robin R. Vallacher
Andrzej Nowak

CHAPTER 1

The Chaos in Social Psychology

Robin R. Vallacher
Department of Psychology
Florida Atlantic University
Boca Raton, Florida

Andrzej Nowak
Institute for Social Studies
Faculty of Psychology
University of Warsaw
Warsaw, Poland

I. Introduction

Social psychology is too big for its own good. Indeed, no other area of psychology presumes to cover so much ground. Over the years, everything from muscle movements and heart beats to juries and societies has become fair game for theory and research in spirited attempts to understand human thought and behavior in interpersonal contexts. Although such far-ranging eclecticism makes for an intellectually stimulating discipline, it also is a breeding ground for conceptual chaos. With no single level of analysis cutting across topical boundaries, and with the topical boundaries themselves encompassing virtually every feature of our daily interactions with the world, it is hardly surprising that there is little theoretical coherence in the field as a whole or that there is even less consensus regarding research paradigms. Such lack of theoretical, empirical, and operational integration has not gone unnoticed, of course. For many observers, the fragmented nature of the field has called into question the status of social psychology as a credible scientific discipline (cf. Gergen, 1985; Harre & Secord, 1972; Rosnow, 1981; Staats, 1991).

We suggest that despite the breadth and depth of the field, some degree of coherence is well within reach. This coherence will not be at the level of theory construction, however. As in any scientific discipline, different subtopics within

Dynamical Systems in Social Psychology

social psychology (e.g., person perception, group structure, intimate relations, and so on) ultimately must be understood in terms of their own phenomena, effects, and principles. The coherence we have in mind is at the level of metatheory—a set of concepts and assumptions from which to frame specific theories and broad paradigmatic guidelines for the generation of specific research methods. This metatheory, which has emerged in recent years to provide coherence for other areas of science (cf. Abraham & Shaw, 1982–1988; Glass & Mackey, 1988; Gleick, 1987; Haken, 1984; Prigogine & Stengers, 1984), is referred to as *dynamical systems theory*. A dynamical system can be informally defined as a more-or-less self-contained set of elements that interact over time in complex, often nonlinear ways. Before introducing this perspective and its potential for creating order out of the chaos of social psychology, we provide a brief overview of the current state of social psychology.

II. The State of Social Psychology

Social psychology does not suffer from a lack of empirical data. There are as many scientific journals devoted to the social context of human behavior as there are devoted to, say, microbiology, and each issue of each journal presents the results of numerous investigations that have passed muster with discriminating editors and tough peer reviewers. The problem is what to make of all the data being generated. Is it possible to incorporate the wealth of social psychological findings into broad, integrative theories? After all, it is theory, not data per se, that provides insight into long-standing issues (e.g., inner vs. outer determinants of behavior, the causal significance of consciousness) and allows us to generate definitive conclusions concerning important topics (e.g., group dynamics, intimate relations). By this criterion, then, what is the state of social psychology?

A. Theories, Issues, and Topics

There are several reasons to think that the answer to this question is not too flattering. To begin with, there are simply too many theories available to explain the same thing. Even with respect to relatively narrowly defined phenomena, there is often a host of competing theories stumbling over one another competing to provide the most convincing explanation. Intrinsic motivation, group polarization in decision making, attitude–behavior relations, self-presentation, and social facilitation, for instance, are hardly new concerns, yet each is currently open to several different theoretical interpretations, with little prospect of resolution in the near future. The theories that are advanced, moreover, typically have a narrow range of application (cf. Aronson, 1992), so that any insight provided into intrinsic motivation, for example, may have little if any relevance for group polarization, social facilitation, and the like. In effect, then, each topic has its own set of personal minitheories.

Worse yet, some theories are themselves open to interpretation. Schlenker (1992), for instance, noted that dissonance theory—arguably, the most successful social psychological theory to date—has derived much of its power and appeal over the years from its ability to assume whatever form various devotees wish it to take. Thus, depending on who you ask, dissonance is described in terms of consistency, ego defense, consistency plus ego defense, or a state of negative arousal that occurs when people feel responsible for aversive outcomes (cf. Aronson, 1969; Festinger, 1957; Scher & Cooper, 1989). In varying degrees, such theoretical elasticity can be said to characterize other theories as well (e.g., social comparison, exchange, equity, self-awareness, learned helplessness).

Even the topics that define the field are ill-defined and overlapping. Is attribution a topic, an assumption about mental process, or a theory of social cognition? Is self-perception a subset of social cognition, or does it qualify as a distinguishable phenomenon? Does it make sense to discuss motivation without discussing goal-directed action? Can attraction be discussed independently of person perception? Is there a rationale for distinguishing social cognition from social relations? Can either attitudes or prejudice be fully understood if they are treated as separate phenomena? Of course, separate treatments of topics like attribution, social cognition, self-perception, motivation, action, attraction, social relations, attitudes, and prejudice would make sense if the topics were ultimately integrated in some fashion. Thus, for example, basic principles of social cognition could be developed, and these principles could be invoked when other topics (e.g., social relations, group dynamics) are discussed.

Unfortunately, however, it does not seem to work that way. The work explicitly devoted to social relations, for instance, certainly must acknowledge people's feelings about one another, but such discussions typically bear little resemblance to the principles advanced in the literature on social cognition. Similarly, the literature explicitly devoted to attitudes has little in common with the literature on prejudice, as does the literature on motivation with that of goal-directed action, and so on. Such arbitrary boundary conditions become readily apparent on perusal of the table of contents in standard social psychology textbooks. Unlike physics textbooks, in which basic principles developed in an early chapter resurface in a later chapter to shed light on a macrolevel topic, social psychology textbooks invariably have a fragmented quality to them, jumping from one topic (e.g., attitudes) to another (e.g., social cognition or social influence) without the former being incorporated into the latter.

Because of the fragmented state of social psychological theorizing, the critical issues that generated all this attention in the first place remain to be resolved. Thus, surveying the field as a whole without adopting one theoretical stance at the expense of all its legitimate contenders leaves one wondering whether people are ultimately more concerned with pleasure, security, consistency, achievement, approval, justice, self-knowledge, or self-defense; whether people's actions spring from internal states (drives, values, self-images) or are largely responses to social, situational, or cultural forces; whether people's judgments and opinions are basically rational and driven by information or are basically irrational and driven by passion; whether human nature is fundamentally good, bad, or a *tabula rasa*; whether people's thoughts arise independently of overt behavior and come to direct it or are simply an epiphenomenal sideshow; whether people are capable of deep introspective self-knowledge or are merely observers unto themselves; and whether people are capable of living together in harmony or are destined for conflict, no matter how benign the circumstances.

B. Causation and Prediction

Setting aside the concern over fragmentation, one can question how successful social psychological theories have been in explaining their respective phenomena of choice. Do theories of social cognition, for example, account for people's impressions and judgments of one another? This question is typically answered empirically, by assessing how much variance in the phenomenon of interest is attributable to variation in the theoretically relevant independent variables under investigation. By this criterion, one could argue that social psychological theories by and large are not all that explanatory. It is not unusual for investigators to claim support for a theory based on a study in which the independent variables collectively account for less than 15% of the variance in the dependent measure. This means that even in the most carefully controlled (i.e., contrived) investigation, the lion's share of the variability among subjects has nothing to do with the theory being put to test.

In view of the notion of determinism in classical mechanics—which provides the basic paradigm in virtually all social psychological experimentation—this would seem to be a sobering state of affairs. After all, in a Laplacean world *all* the variance should be accounted for. Classical mechanics, as epitomized by Newtonian principles, holds that nothing is left to chance and that if all the initial conditions associated with a phenomenon were known, one could in principle have complete and precise knowledge of the phenomenon at any time, regardless of how far one looks into the future. By implication, the better the theory, the closer one should come to explaining 100% of the variance. From this perspective, accounting for a measly 15% makes one's theories look pretty inadequate.

Note the assumption here that determinism implies prediction. In the conduct of research, in fact, prediction provides the criterion by which one assesses whether the independent variables in a study have a deterministic influence on the phenomenon under investigation. Thus, the investigator mixes various levels of the independent variables (suspected causes) at Time 1 and then looks at the value of the dependent measure (the effect) at Time 2. Only if the dependent measure varies in the predicted manner as a function of the earlier manipulations does the investigator claim support for the theory being tested.

The relatively weak predictive power associated with social psychological theories thus suggests that these theories are correspondingly poor at specifying causation as well. To boost the apparent strength of a theory, of course, one need only increase the number of subjects in an investigation; the more statistical power, the less variance must be accounted for in order for the obtained effect to be statistically reliable (i.e., unlikely to have occurred by chance). But from the point of view of determinism in classical mechanics, such an approach does little to strengthen one's faith in the ability of social psychology to generate powerful deterministic theories.

C. Boilerplate Excuses

Social psychologists, of course, are aware of these complaints. Even the most adamant believer in the value of contemporary experimental social psychology would not deny that there is a surplus of theories, that these theories more often than not have a narrow range of application, that the topical layout of social psychology is based more on convenience and history than on an *a priori* natural category scheme, that fundamental issues have yet to be resolved, and that the predictive power of most theories is rather weak in an absolute sense. In the face of these problems, however, the erstwhile true believer has a number of ready-made explanations—or excuses, depending on one's perspective—with which to account for these seeming shortcomings. Three general explanations/excuses in particular are commonly advanced when critics press the point.

1. "Psychology Is Young"

This is probably the most common defense. Textbooks typically introduce the field as a young science—indeed, as the youngest science—and therefore as in somewhat of a preparadigmatic state. Most of the natural sciences can trace their roots back several centuries, which provides plenty of time for bad theories to be discarded and replaced with better ones. The first social psychology study, in contrast, was performed around the beginning of this century (Triplett, 1898). And whereas many of the basic paradigms and theoretical principles evident today in physics, chemistry, and biology have been in place for one hundred years or more, virtually nothing in contemporary social psychology was generated before World War II. By this logic, it is simply unreasonable to expect social psychology to be as mature, either in practice or in theory, as its natural science brethren. By implication, given enough time, social psychology too will have established paradigms, unequivocal principles, a clear topical agenda, and maybe even some resolved issues.

2. "People Are Complex"

This is a very compelling argument. Any given act can be seen as the net effect of the intersection of an untold number of factors, different sets of which correspond to different levels of analysis (Wegner & Vallacher, 1987). Greeting a stranger, deciding to go to college, running a red light, mailing a letter, getting drunk, washing one's hands after a meal, and standing in line can all be analyzed with respect to myriad potential genetic, hormonal, familial, situational, dispositional, and cultural causes. And given that different acts performed by different actors at different times represent different intersections of such causes, it is hardly surprising that precious little variance in behavior can be accounted for with recourse to any single set of theoretically derived factors. Because one simply cannot control or account for all possible past and present influences, either theoretically or empirically, there is necessarily a large degree of indeterminacy in thought and behavior (see, e.g., Meehl, 1978).

Note that this argument is based essentially on practicality, not principle. Presumably, if all the contributing factors *could* be identified and controlled, one would expect to account for 100% of the variance. And if one accepts the implicit equation of determinism with prediction in social psychology, once such a comprehensive theory is developed, the behavior of every person should be perfectly predictable well into the future. In other words, it is assumed that there is a deterministic landscape stretching toward the future that dictates our every thought and deed; if we fail to predict future thoughts and deeds, it is only because we do not have a good map of the landscape.

3. "People Have Free Will"

No one really says this in so many words, but those who hold that social psychology does not, cannot, or should not conform to the natural sciences come precariously close to making a case for free will (e.g., Gergen, 1985; Shotter, 1980; Simon, 1982). The basic point is that people are unlike physical objects in that they do not respond in a direct and invariant fashion to the forces surrounding them. Instead, people act on the basis of reasons (values, beliefs, wants, concerns, etc.). Reasons, of course, do not have a material substrate and thus are not directly responsive to material forces (e.g., gravity, heat) in the way that physical objects are. Nor are reasons direct and invariant consequences of exposure to specifiable social forces. The same influence attempt (e.g., ingratiation, threat, bribery) delivered to two individuals, for example, might engage a desire to conform in one but a desire to resist in the other. Even within the same individual, different reasons can rise and fall in relative salience over time and across settings in a seemingly unpredictable (and hence uncaused) manner.

From this perspective, attempts to impose universal, deterministic laws on human behavior are doomed to failure and miss the larger point about the special nature of human action. Variations on this view find expression in a number of specific approaches to social psychology, including hermeneutics, radical social psychology, and constructionism (e.g., Gauld & Shotter, 1977; Gergen, 1985; Harre & Secord, 1972). Although investigations into human behavior are called for in these approaches, the emphasis is on capturing broad themes that weave together the fabric of people's subjective interplay with the world around them, not on universal laws intended to predict specific behaviors under specific conditions.

All of these arguments have merit. The question is, what do we do with them? Assuming social psychology is young, do we simply adopt a patient attitude in the expectation that progressively more integrative and powerful theories will come to the fore? The emphasis on complexity, of course, suggests that we would have to be very patient indeed; the number of relevant factors is so staggering that it is unlikely anything even approaching a full accounting of human behavior will ever appear. Finally, if we adopt the free-will stance, all bets are off. The most comprehensive models imaginable, developed and tested with the aid of massive computing power, can never in principle dictate or predict how individuals will behave at a given time in a given instance.

In the face of these problems and their implications, most social psychologists tacitly adopt relatively modest expectations regarding theoretical integration. Although a grand unified theory is unlikely to appear on the horizon any time soon, if ever, we can certainly do better than we are doing right now, and there is reason to think that we will. The hope is that by sticking to our guns and working hard, we will gradually achieve an increasingly clear and integrated understanding of human thought and behavior. With maturity will come greater coherence, although perhaps not the degree of coherence attained in the natural sciences.

III. The Dynamics of Social Psychology

There is another way to think about the state of social psychology. We suggest that the problems identified thus far are not cause for abandoning a scientific approach to human thought and behavior but provide the very foundation on which new research strategies can be established. In particular, explicit attention to the complexity and seeming indeterminism of human behavior should enable theorists and researchers to capture the dynamics of social psychological phenomena. This orientation holds potential for fostering methodological and theoretical integration in social psychology and for bringing the field as a whole into better alignment with recent developments in the natural sciences.

A. Complexity

The complexity characterizing people is apparent on many different levels. At the level of brain function, there are approximately one hundred billion neurons, each of which is connected to hundreds, even thousands of other neurons. The number of possible patterns of neuronal firing is thus almost incomprehensibly large (cf. Sejnowski & Churchland, 1989). At the level of cognition, the number of specific thoughts, memories, images, and so on experienced by a given individual in even a mundane afternoon is again astronomically large, and the possible combinations of such cognitive elements renders it virtually impossible to capture all the nuances of someone's thought process. Formidable magnitudes of complexity can be seen as well with respect to such psychological phenomena as motor coordination (e.g., Saltzman & Kelso, 1987; Turvey, 1990) and group dynamics (e.g., Nowak, Szamrej, & Latane, 1990).

People are not the only complex phenomena in nature, however. In recent years, scientists have come to realize that virtually every phenomenon can be understood as a complex system (cf. Gleick, 1987). The weather on a given day, for instance, represents the intersection of many different local conditions (e.g., barometic pressure, humidity, wind direction and speed) as well as the influence of distal events and conditions (storms, tropical depressions, volcanos). None of these events and conditions—even something as seemingly insignificant as the flapping of a butterfly's wings in a different hemisphere—can be eliminated as contributing factors to current and impending weather conditions (Lorenz, 1963). More generally, many phenomena of interest to biologists (e.g., the immune system), ecologists (e.g., predator–prey relations), chemists (e.g., autocatalytic reactions), physicists (e.g., lasers), cosmologists (e.g., galactic evolution), epidemiologists (e.g., the spread of viruses), and economists (e.g., economic cyles) are viewed today as multidimensional systems that have certain general features in common. It may be fruitful, then, to consider social thought and behavior from this vantage point as well (cf. Vallacher, 1989, 1993).

Treating a phenomenon as a complex system does not simply mean that one's laws, models, theories, and research strategies have to incorporate many variables. The nature of complexity is such that the very nature of theory construction and theory testing differs from that associated with classical mechanics (cf. Davies, 1988; Gleick, 1987; Pagels, 1988). Perhaps the most basic point of departure concerns assumptions about causality and the relation between determinism and prediction. In the traditional model, it is assumed that specific factors can be isolated from one another and examined for their independent contributions to the phenomenon of interest. The systems perspective, in contrast, emphasizes the feedback among the relevant factors and the tendency of the system to become self-organized on the basis of patterns of such feedback. On this view, variation in any one factor is related in a nonlinear fashion to the behavior of the system as a whole; even a miniscule change in a given system element can, by virtue of its interactive feedback with other elements, promote dramatic, even qualitative changes in the functioning of the entire system.

Because each unique pattern of interactive feedback among system elements may be associated with a qualitatively different state of the system, and because the slightest change in the value of a single system element can make a profound difference in what state is observed, it is often impossible to specify exactly what the system will be doing at some distant point in the future. In classical mechanics, slight variation in initial conditions, or slight imprecision in their measurement, means only that there is a corresponding loss of precision in prediction. In marked contrast, the nature of complexity is such that variation or measurement imprecision can, under certain conditions, amplify into completely different solutions over time, thereby rendering even approximate predictions impossible. In modeling weather fronts, for example, Lorenz (1963) found that the slightest change in initial conditions—even a difference in rounding the initial ambient temperature and humidity—eventually led to entirely different patterns in his model weather system. More generally, anything short of infinite precision in one's knowledge of a system at one time can undermine knowledge of future states of the system. Because infinite precision is impossible, determinism is no guarantee of prediction.

One does not have to be a weatherperson to appreciate how nonlinearity can undermine prediction. Consider, for example, your birth. The odds against any one sperm among the millions in a given ejaculate fertilizing an egg are astronomical. Had your parents delayed for even a second during their pivotal coital encounter, your existence would be in serious doubt right now, and any effect you have on the future would thus be nullified. Indeed, had any event during the past four billion years been even slightly different, the ripple effects might have been such that you might not be here to read this book. The same case can be made for an auto accident, an event that can change people's lives irrevocably. Any accident represents not only split-second timing by the drivers, but also the precise confluence of events stretching back to prehistory. A collision in an intersection would not have occurred had one of the drivers experienced the slightest hesitation at an intersection three blocks earlier (or had one of them not been born).

B. Time

The distinctions between the classical mechanics and complex systems perspectives would probably go unnoticed if explicit consideration were not given to time in theoretical and empirical analyses. Indeed, it is only by tracking the evolution of a system's behavior on some time scale that the essence of a complex system can be identified (cf. Abraham & Shaw, 1982–1988). Such tracking reveals the hallmarks of dynamical systems, including attractors, phase transitions, hysteresis, critical fluctuations, and the emergence of macroscopic order from lower-level interactions (see Chapter 2). Because complex systems evolve and change in meaningful ways over time, assessing their nature at only a fixed point in time is as informationally impoverished as substituting a photograph for a motion picture (which, in turn, is an impoverished view of "real life").

Sometimes, of course, systems evolve toward a more or less steady state, so that useful knowledge of the system can be garnered from observing it at a single point in time (i.e., after reaching the steady state). The winding down of a pendulum, for instance, or the fall of an object to the earth represents instances of systems with fixed-point attractors—convergence of all the system elements to a fixed set of values. Even here, though, knowledge of the system's evolution toward its final state reveals important insight into the nature of the system; different kinds of pendulums wind down at different rates, after all, and differently shaped objects under different wind conditions fall to earth with different trajectories.

Beyond that, it turns out that a fixed-point attractor is only a special case of temporal evolution in complex systems. Many systems display instead periodic evolution, or limit-cycle attractors, in which there is oscillation among two or more different states in a rhythmic fashion over time. In certain chemical reactions, for instance, the respective concentrations of two or more chemicals reverse in a fairly regular manner over time (Prigogine & Stengers, 1984); in predator–prey relations, there tends to be yearly oscillations in the relative numbers of the respective species (May, 1976). In other instances, quasiperiodic behavior is observed in which the system oscillates over time but never returns to exactly the same state as visited before. The joint behavior of two coupled pendulums with incommensurate periods can be characterized in these terms (Thompson & Stewart, 1987).

Finally, some systems evolve in a chaotic fashion, with no apparent regularity. Beyond the lack of periodicity in their behavior, these systems display extreme sensitivity to initial conditions. Change the starting point ever so slightly, and the system will evolve in a dramatically different manner. The weather, as noted earlier, fits this criterion (Lorenz, 1963), as do such phenomena as fluid turbulence (Ruelle & Takens, 1971) and predator–prey ratios under certain environmental conditions (May, 1976). It is in chaotic systems, then, that the distinction between determinism and prediction becomes striking. Although such systems are completely deterministic, the algorithm needed to model them must be as complex as the phenomenon itself. Any attempt to reduce the phenomenon to simpler rules renders prediction worthless. The situation is somewhat akin to needing a road map as big and detailed as Texas to figure out how to drive across Texas.

It is also the case that systems can show phase transitions—sudden and dramatic changes from one pattern of temporal behavior to another. This occurs when some feature of the environment controlling the system's behavior changes in value. Kicking or otherwise "instructing" a horse to move faster, for instance, can produce a sudden transition from a trot to a gallop in the horse's gait. A trot and a gallop, of course, represent qualitatively different configurations of the horse's limbs that display different rates of oscillation (cf. Saltzman & Kelso, 1987). In like manner, the interval between water drops from a leaky faucet may change from slow periodicity to quasiperiodicity to chaos as the leakiness of the faucet changes (Shaw, 1984).

Although the information contained in the system's temporal evolution is important in its own right, it also can be used to infer properties of the system. The form of a system's temporal trajectory, for instance, can be used to infer the dimensionality of the system and the rules of interaction among the system's elements (Eckmann & Ruelle, 1985; Grassberger & Procaccia, 1983). To understand the nature of a complex system, then, it is necessary to observe the system unfold over time. From this perspective, structure and process provide complementary and mutually supportive means of describing a given phenomenon.

C. Dynamical Social Psychology

It is easy to appreciate both complexity and time in human thought and behavior. As noted earlier, complexity is apparent on (and has been investigated with respect to) many different levels of human functioning, from neural networks to social networks. It is also reasonable to assume that at each level there is a corresponding time scale for the associated function, although such correspondence has not been explicitly documented. Thus, very short time scales characterize neural transmission and neural networks, whereas somewhat longer time scales are probably associated with cognition and social judgment processes, and yet longer time scales are almost certainly displayed by more molar phenomena such as social relationships and group dynamics.

Beyond conforming to different time scales, various social psychological phenomena may display distinctive patterns of temporal evolution. From a cybernetic point of view, for example, one might expect many phenomena (e.g., attitude formation, goal-directed action) to be associated with fixed-point attractors. In such models, motivation arises from a felt discrepancy between a current condition and a desired endstate, with various mechanisms operating to reduce the discrepancy and restore motivational equilibrium (cf. Carver & Scheier, 1981; Miller, Galanter, & Pribram, 1960; Powers, 1973). As suggested earlier, the nature of evolution toward an endstate may be revealing about the system at work—a possibility that investigators have begun to explore. With respect to goal-directed action, for instance, there is evidence that the rate at which a particular discrepancy is reduced maps onto emotion, with more rapid rates associated with greater satisfaction and better mood (Carver & Scheier, 1990; Hsee & Abelson, 1991).

Fixed point attractors, however, represent but one type of temporal evolution, and it is tempting to consider how other types might be manifest in various social psychological domains. In particular, there is reason to suspect that limit-cycle attractors operate with respect to cognitive and behavioral processes, just as they have been shown to characterize certain biological processes (e.g., hormonal fluctuations, circadian rhythms). There seems to be certain rhythms to our moods, for example, and some form of periodicity may be inherent as well in our sentiments and judgments of others (see Chapter 11). The give and take in a social interaction might also be interpretable in terms of periodic evolution (see Chapter 7), as might the development and maintenance of long-term relationships (see Chapter 6). Our thoughts, interactions, and social relationships, in other words, may be dynamic rather than static, showing meaningful and measurable fluctuations over some time scale with respect to some key parameter of the process in question (e.g., evaluation, confidence, commitment).

It is also conceivable that whatever temporal patterns underly various social processes can themselves undergo change in accordance with dynamical principles. In physical systems, such change takes place when the system is destabilized by some nonsystem disturbance (perturbation) in the environment. An oscillating pendulum, for instance, can easily be destabilized by pushing the bob perpendicular to its trajectory. When this happens, though, there is a tendency for the motion of the pendulum to establish a new oscillating pattern in fairly short order. It turns out that this scenario captures an invariant feature of all dynamical systems. Thus, a system may resist or dampen perturbations up to a point, beyond which there is a rapid collapse of the attractor. The instability itself tends to be unstable, however, so that the system tends to become self-organized with respect to a new temporal pattern.

It is easy to envision this scenario being played out in a variety of social psychological phenomena. In interpersonal perception, for instance, the waxing and waning of feelings about someone may become temporarily disordered by the receipt of inconsistent information about the target, only to become reordered with respect to a new (or perhaps the original) temporal pattern as the information is assimilated, reinterpreted, or discounted. The give and take of conversation in a dyad, meanwhile, can become disrupted when the interactants discover that they are being observed or when an emotionally charged topic is introduced. After a period of instability, however, the interactants may establish a new pattern of give and take that accommodates the altered circumstances. On a somewhat longer time scale, the natural ebb and flow of passion in an intimate relationship can become seriously derailed when a baby is born or when an attractive stranger intrudes into the dyadic system. Eventually, though, the instability gives way to a new pattern of very close encounters (including, perhaps, a fixed point with zero values).

Unfortunately, these and yet other possible types of temporal evolution, not to mention the time scales on which they operate, are not well-represented in current social psychological theory. It is easy to see why. It is axiomatic in science that method shapes (and limits) theory (e.g., Kaplan, 1964; Kuhn, 1970), and this applies as well to social psychology (e.g., Gergen, 1973; McGuire, 1973; Rosnow,

1981). Although there is a wide variety of specific research strategies at the disposal of social psychologists, the majority of them share features that simply do not lend themselves to a dynamical systems perspective. For one thing, the predominant strategy, as noted earlier, is to select no more than three variables at a time for systematic manipulation, with all other potentially relevant variables controlled through randomization procedures. This is clearly at odds with the emphasis on identifying the qualitatively different states of a given system associated with particular patterns of interaction among all the system variables.

Perhaps more important, the dominant paradigms in social psychology are not equipped to identify the temporal trajectories of thought and behavior. In the prototypical experiment, the independent variables are manipulated at Time 1, and their (predicted) effects are assessed once, at some arbitrary Time 2. Beyond tacitly assuming that whatever process is at work converges on a stable state by Time 2, this approach is insensitive to the evolution of the process and thus cannot ask, let alone answer, a host of questions about the dynamics at work. Despite the abundance of work on impression formation, for instance, we do not know whether or to what extent people experience something akin to periodicity, quasiperiodicity, or chaos in their considerations of a target person in the process of forming a stable judgment of him or her. Similar gaps exist in our knowledge of such basic phenomena as social comparison, dissonance reduction, self-esteem maintenance, reaction to social feedback, conformity, and obedience.

This is not to suggest that contemporary social psychology is of little value or even that the experimental paradigms in place are inappropriate. Clearly, these paradigms have served us well, and we have learned a great deal about social thought and behavior because of them. Our point is that to generate a complete picture of human functioning, it is necessary to give explicit consideration to the complexity of social psychological phenomena and to the temporal patterns by which such complexity is revealed. Subsequent chapters in this volume suggest how this can be accomplished with respect to several diverse topics and provide testament to the benefit of doing so. In the final chapter, we summarize the methodological lessons of these chapters and suggest what remains to be done for a truly dynamical social psychology to emerge.

IV. Minitheory and Metatheory

Different phenomena must ultimately be understood on their own terms. Even within a given discipline, one should expect little theoretical commonality among different topics. In biology, for instance, the set of principles associated with photosynthesis, population ecology, and embryonic development are each fairly self-contained and disconnected from one another. From this perspective, it is unfair to criticize social psychology for spawning distinct theories for different topics. If the principles of attitude change turn out to be different from the principles identified for, say, impression formation, then that may simply reflect the separateness of these two topics. One could quibble, of course, as to whether the topical distinctions in social psychology (e.g., attitude change and impression formation) are as sharply drawn as those in biology (e.g., photosynthesis and population ecology) to justify separate theories. And serious questions, too, can be raised regarding the plethora of theories *within* a topic (e.g., attitude change). But in principle, at least, the mapping of different principles onto different topics does not by itself represent a fatal flaw for social psychology.

With this in mind, one should not hold out hope that a theory will someday emerge that cuts across topical boundaries to explain everything about social thought and behavior. What one can hope for, however, is a broad metatheory from which to generate topic-specific principles and a set of paradigmatic guidelines with which to test and refine these principles. Such a metatheory and its associated guidelines may be already available to us under the guise of dynamical systems. This orientation has come to play a metatheoretical role in the natural sciences, providing integration at a macro level for phenomena as disparate as weather fronts, cardiovascular function, galaxy formation, hydraulics, and evolutionary biology. The principles, concepts, and methods of dynamical systems seem particularly well-suited to capture the complexity and dynamism inherent in virtually all topics in social psychology.

In practice, a dynamical systems perspective will sensitize researchers to a variety of effects (e.g., phase transition and bifurcation, pattern formation, critical instability, hysteresis, intrinsic dynamics) that are currently recognized only implicitly, if at all, in different domains. Such sensitivity, in turn, would do much to integrate a fragmented field by showing the manifestation of common processes in otherwise different domains and by introducing common methodological and analytical tools to these domains. Yet, the dynamical systems perspective is sufficiently broad so as not to constrain independent lines of investigation and the search for topic-specific principles. So although a theory of social thinking, for instance, would have some critical features in common with a theory of intimate relations (e.g., periods of instability followed by emergence to a new pattern), the two theories may reflect very distinct principles and may be tested with equally distinct methods. A dynamical systems orientation, then, not only holds potential for generating fresh research questions but promotes a combination of high-level integration and low-level diversity that signals maturity in both lay and scientific understanding (cf. Kaplan, 1964; Piaget, 1971).

However, perhaps more important than the potential for integration within social psychology is the possibility that the field as a whole can become integrated with other areas of science that are being recast in terms of dynamical systems (cf. Abraham, 1990; Gleick, 1987). Psychology is commonly perceived as lagging behind the natural sciences in its approach to understanding. In a sense, though, the emergence of a concern with complexity, instability, pattern formation, and the like in such mature fields as physics and chemistry signals a lag in the reverse direction. Behaviorism notwithstanding, psychology has always appreciated the complexity and concomitant lack of prediction in human functioning and has been keenly aware of the deadends ultimately reached by overly reductionistic strategies. However, it has taken recent developments in the natural sciences to provide the conceptual tools necessary to frame coherent, testable theories and thereby legitimatize this perspective. Because this perspective resonates so well with psychology, it should be relatively easy for theorists and researchers to translate these tools into a set of concepts and operations appropriate for the study of the human system. Such a translation may provide a sense of what is truly basic to human experience, exposing the orderliness beneath the surface chaos of behavior.

Acknowledgments

Portions of this chapter were prepared while the first author was a visiting scholar at the Max-Planck-Institute for Psychological Research, Munich, Germany, in the summer of 1992. We wish to thank Roy Baumeister, Daniel Gilbert, Franklin Schroeck, and Daniel Wegner for their helpful comments on an earlier version of this chapter.

References

Abraham, F. D. (1990). *A visual introduction to dynamical systems for psychology*. Santa Cruz, CA: Aerial Press.

Abraham, R. H., & Shaw, C. D. (1982–1988). *Dynamics: The geometry of behavior*. Santa Cruz, CA: Aerial Press.

Aronson, E. (1969). The theory of cognitive dissonance: A current perspective. In L. Berkowitz (Ed.), *Advances in experimental social psychology* (Vol. 4, pp. 1–34). New York: Academic Press.

Aronson, E. (1992). The return of the oppressed: Dissonance theory makes a comeback. *Psychological Inquiry, 3*, 303–311.

Carver, C. S., & Scheier, M. F. (1981). *Attention and self-regulation: A control-theory approach to human behavior*. New York: Springer-Verlag.

Carver, C. S., & Scheier, M. F. (1990). Origins and functions of positive and negative affect: A control-process view. *Psychological Review, 97*, 19–35.

Davies, P. (1988). *The cosmic blueprint: New discoveries in nature's creative ability to order the universe*. New York: Simon & Schuster.

Eckmann, J. P., & Ruelle, D. (1985). Ergodic theory of chaos and strange attractors. *Review of Modern Physics, 57*, 617–656.

Festinger, L. (1957). *A theory of cognitive dissonance*. Evanston, IL: Row, Peterson.

Gauld, A., & Shotter, J. (1977). *Human action and its psychological investigation*. London: Routledge & Kegan Paul.

Gergen, K. J. (1973). Social psychology as history. *Journal of Personality and Social Psychology, 26*, 309–320.

Gergen, K. J. (1985). The social constructionist movement in modern psychology. *American Psychologist, 40*, 266–275.

Glass, L., & Mackey, M. C. (1988). *From clocks to chaos: The rhythms of life*. Princeton, NJ: Princeton University Press.

Gleick, J. (1987). *Chaos: Making a new science*. New York: Viking.

Grassberger, P., & Procaccia, I. (1983). On the characterization of strange attractors. *Physical Review Letters, 50*, 346–350.

Haken, H. (1984). *The science of structure: Synergetics.* New York: Van Nostrand Reinhold.

Harre, R., & Secord, P. F. (1972). *The explanation of social behaviour.* Oxford, England: Blackwell.

Hsee, C. K., & Abelson, R. P. (1991). Velocity relation: Satisfaction as a function of the first derivative of outcome over time. *Journal of Personality and Social Psychology, 60*, 341–347.

Kaplan, A. (1964). *The conduct of inquiry.* New York: Harper & Row.

Kuhn, T. S. (1970). *The structure of scientific revolutions* (2nd ed.). Chicago: University of Chicago Press.

Lorenz, E. (1963). Deterministic nonperiodic flow. *Journal of the Atmospheric Sciences, 20*, 130–141.

May, R. (1976). Simple mathematical models with very complicated dynamics. *Nature, 261*, 459–467.

McGuire, W. J. (1973). The yin and yang of progress in social psychology: Seven koan. *Journal of Personality and Social Psychology, 26*, 446–456.

Meehl, P. E. (1978). Theoretical risks and tabular asterisks: Sir Karl, Sir Ronald, and the slow progress of soft psychology. *Journal of Consulting and Clinical Psychology, 46*, 806–834.

Miller, G. A., Galanter, E., & Pribram, K. H. (1960). *Plans and the structure of behavior.* New York: Holt.

Nowak, A., Szamrej, J., & Latane, B. (1990). From private attitude to public opinion: A dynamic theory of social impact. *Psychological Review, 97*, 362–376.

Pagels, H. (1988). *The dreams of reason: The computer and the rise of the sciences of complexity.* New York: Simon & Schuster.

Piaget, J. (1971). *Psychology and epistemology.* New York: Viking-Compass.

Powers, W. T. (1973). *Behavior: The control of perception.* Chicago: Aldine.

Prigogine, I., & Stengers, I. (1984). *Order out of chaos.* New York: Bantam.

Rosnow, R. L. (1981). *Paradigms in transition: The methodology of social inquiry.* New York: Oxford University Press.

Ruelle, D., & Takens, F. (1971). On the nature of turbulence. *Communications in Mathematical Physics, 20*, 167–192.

Saltzman, E., & Kelso, J. A. S. (1987). Skilled actions: A task-dynamic approach. *Psychological Review, 94*, 84–106.

Scher, S. J., & Cooper, J. (1989). Motivational basis of dissonance: The singular role of behavioral consequences. *Journal of Personality and Social Psychology, 56*, 899–906.

Schlenker, B. R. (1992). Of shape shifters and theories. *Psychological Inquiry, 3*, 342–344.

Sejnowski, T. J., & Churchland, P. S. (1989). Brain and cognition. In M. I. Posner (Ed.), *Foundations of cognitive science* (pp. 301–356). Cambridge, MA: MIT Press.

Shaw, R. (1984). *The dripping faucet as a model chaotic system.* Santa Cruz, CA: Aeriel Press.

Shotter, J. S. (1980). Action, joint action, and intentionality. In M. Brenner (Ed.), *The structure of action* (pp. 28–65). New York: St. Martin's Press.

Simon, M. A. (1982). *Understanding human action.* Albany: SUNY Press.

Staats, A. W. (1991). Unified positivism and unification psychology: Fad or new field? *American Psychologist, 46*, 899–912.

Thompson, J. M. P., & Stewart, H. B. (1987). *Nonlinear dynamics and chaos.* New York: Wiley.

Triplett, N. (1898). The dynamogenic factors in pace making and competition. *American Journal of Psychology, 9*, 507–533.

Turvey, M. T. (1990). Coordination. *American Psychologist, 45*, 938–953.

Vallacher, R. R. (1989). Action identification as theory and metatheory. In D. W. Schumann (Ed.), *Proceedings of the Society for Consumer Psychology* (pp. 63–67). Washington, DC: American Psychological Association.

Vallacher, R. R. (1993). Mental calibration: Forging a working relationship between mind and action. In D. M. Wegner & J. W. Pennebaker (Eds.), *The handbook of mental control* (pp. 443–472). New York: Prentice-Hall.

Wegner, D. M., & Vallacher, R. R. (1987). The trouble with action. *Social Cognition, 5*, 179–190.

CHAPTER 2

Dynamical Systems: A Tool for Social Psychology?

Andrzej Nowak
Institute for Social Studies
Faculty of Psychology
University of Warsaw
Warsaw, Poland

Maciej Lewenstein
Institute for Social Studies
University of Warsaw
and Center for Theoretical Physics
Polish Academy of Sciences
Warsaw, Poland

I. Introduction

In the rapidly changing, turbulent, and unpredictable end of this century, the word *chaos* has suddenly become a fashionable term. This popularity does not simply reflect the fact that the social and political phenomena around us have become more complex, disordered, and difficult to understand. Rather, the fascination with chaos reflects a new meaning of the term, a meaning derived from recent developments in the natural sciences. Other keywords that have become popularized in the media and that reflect the same developments include *strange attractors, bifurcations, hysteresis, butterfly effect*, and *fractals*.

Dynamical Systems in Social Psychology

A. Dynamical Systems

Each of these terms is tied to the area of science that deals with so-called *dynamical systems*. The theory of dynamical systems actually has a long history, beginning with the rise of modern science. Newtonian mechanics, for instance, is a prototype paradigm for dynamical systems. For hundreds of years, dynamical systems have been used to describe simple phenomena like the motion of a pendulum or the revolution of the earth around the sun. During most of this time, it has been assumed that the complexity of the world is due to the large number of interacting elements. Only recently have we come to realize that even simple systems consisting of a few elements typically exhibit behavior of enormous complexity when the interactions among the elements are nonlinear. The rapid developments in dynamical systems theory in recent years is due to enormous progress in our understanding of nonlinear dynamics and to large-scale use of computer simulations. The enormous popularity of the mathematical theory of nonlinear dynamics reflects the fact that similar, even identical, models of dynamical systems apply to many diverse phenomena in science.

It is not surprising that dynamical systems are popular in mathematics (Arnold, 1983; Peitgen & Richter, 1986; Ruelle, 1989) and in various areas of physics and chemistry, such as mechanics (Arnold, 1978; Rasband, 1990; Zaslavsky & Sagdeev, 1988), hydrodynamics (Zaslavsky & Sagdeev, 1988), nonlinear optics (Haken, 1978), solid state physics (Haken, 1978), and the dynamics of chemical reactions (Othmer, 1986). Dynamical systems find practical applications as well in engineering (Moon, 1987; Thompson & Stewart, 1986), and meteorology (Lorenz, 1963). It may seem somewhat surprising, however, that the same dynamical systems theories serve to model various biological phenomena, such as "rhythms of life" (Glass & Mackey, 1988). Chaos in dynamical systems is also believed to govern some global aspects of information processing in the brain (Başar, 1990). And in recent years, the tools associated with nonlinear dynamics have been used in the psychology and physiology of motor behavior (Kelso 1981, 1984; Kelso & DeGuzman, 1988), economics (cf. P. W. Anderson, 1988; Batten, Casti, & Johansson, 1987), and genetics (cf. Sandefur, 1990). Nonlinear dynamical systems provide fundamental models in all areas of science that deal with population dynamics, such as ecology (May, 1981), demography and sociology (Weidlich & Haag, 1983), and epidemiology (R. M. Anderson & May, 1991). Dynamical systems are thus remarkably universal (Gleick, 1987), and for that reason they have spawned new interdisciplinary disciplines of science such as synergetics (Haken, 1978, 1983), catastrophe theory (Poston & Steward, 1978; Thom, 1975), and the theory of dissipative structures (Glansdorff & Prigogine, 1971).

A basic characteristic of dynamical systems is that they change and evolve in time. Think about an apple falling from a tree on a windless day. It starts moving, continues moving for some time, hits the ground, and finally stops moving. It is essentially the state of the apple at any instant (i.e., its position, velocity, angular momentum) that determines its state in the next instant. We can model and describe such motion using differential or difference equations. Such models of dynamical systems are deterministic in a Laplacian sense in that the future of the system can be fully predicted from full knowledge of the system's current state.

B. Dynamical Systems and Social Psychology

The concepts of *temporal evolution* and *determinism* are foreign to the dominant paradigms of modern social psychology. Time evolution is largely absent from most of the models in social psychology. Most research concentrates on trying to predict values of some variables from the knowledge of others. Changes are considered to be the immediate results of causes, so that their temporal variation is of no interest to researchers. Only on rare occasions is explicit attention given to internal dynamics (Tesser, 1978; Nowak, Szamrej, & Latané, 1990). One reason for this is the general belief that relations between variables have a strongly probabilistic character (Coleman, 1964). Sometimes it is even stated that in the social sciences, there are no relations without exceptions. Statistical analysis, based on traditional linear models, typically leads to very weak dependencies and correlations. Thus, social psychology has tended to reject formal dynamical models. However, there is a growing interest in and awareness of the potential usefulness of modern dynamical systems theory in social psychology. This volume exemplifies this trend.

What properties of nonlinear dynamical systems might be especially relevant for social psychology? The primary property is the capacity of dynamical systems to show amazingly complex behavior stemming from simple rules. Slight changes in such rules, moreover, frequently result in dramatic changes in the behavior of the system. Even "primitive" models are capable of producing behavior that looks random but is actually deterministic. Laplacian determinism is not particularly useful here, however, because chaotic behavior, although deterministic, is practically unpredictable!

The aim of this chapter is to introduce basic concepts of nonlinear dynamical systems to social psychologists. The plan is as follows. In Section II, we define dynamical systems more formally and introduce some basic concepts and notions. In Section III, we discuss various typical types of behavior that can be exhibited by dynamical systems. Section IV is devoted to a description of deterministic chaos and its properties. In Section V, we discuss patterns of change in behavior observed in dynamical systems, such as bifurcations, transitions to chaos, and hysteresis. Beginning in Section VI, we attempt to identify the signatures of nonlinear dynamics. Section VI,C, in particular, is devoted to the very fundamental problem of distinguishing random behavior from deterministic irregular behavior (deterministic chaos).

II. Dynamical Systems: Basic Concepts and Definitions

A. Dynamical Variables

To construct a model of a dynamical system, we have to specify first the state of the system at a given instant in time. Typically, we describe the state of the system by introducing dynamical variables. *Dynamical variables* are numbers that change in time and that characterize the relevant properties of the state of the system in a given instant. For the apple falling from the tree, the key dynamical variables are the apple's position and velocity. We do not try, for example, to represent quantitatively the color of the apple because for all practical purposes the color is irrelevant to its motion.

B. Order Parameters

Very often, models of dynamical systems are constructed to describe the behavior of complex systems consisting of huge number of elements. For instance, one may try to model the dynamics of gas molecules in a container of macroscopic size. Such an ensemble of molecules typically contains as many atoms as Avogadro's number ($N = 10^{23}$). No sane person would attempt to describe such a system by specifying the velocities and positions of all the particles. It turns out that the macroscopic properties of such systems are determined by a much smaller set of variables. It is clearly more efficient to introduce some global, macroscopic parameters that describe the state of the system. In the case of gas in a container, for example, a relevant macroscopic parameter may be the density of the gas or its temperature. Dynamical variables that play the role of macroscopic global parameters are often called *order parameters*. Unfortunately, for many complex systems it is not easy to identify appropriate order parameters. Finding appropriate order parameters is a big step in the construction of a successful theory (Landau & Lifshitz, 1964).

C. Phase Space

Let us assume that we have built a dynamical system in a form of a set of differential or difference equations (it may be a model of some real world system, although it is not always the case). Let us denote the values of the dynamical variables or order parameters by some numbers $x_1, x_2, \ldots, x_n$. The state of the system at time t is fully described by specifying actual values of the dynamical variables $x_1(t), x_2(t), \ldots, x_n(t)$. One way to follow the dynamics of the system is to look at these values and analyze how they change. There is, however, an alternative, geometrical method. The set of numbers $x_1(t),x_2(t), \ldots ,x_n(t)$ may be considered a set of coordinates of a point in an n dimensional space, called *phase space*.[1] In other words, the actual state of the system, described by the actual values of the dynamical variables, is represented as a point in this space. The dynamics of the system correspond to the motion of this point. This motion draws a curve[2] in the phase space, which is often called a *trajectory*. In other words, the trajectory is a set of points "visited" by the system during its time evolution. In the case of the falling apple, the most relevant dynamical variables are its position in the vertical direction (height) and its velocity in that direction. The corresponding phase space is thus two-dimensional, and the motion is represented as a trajectory, as in Figure 1. The motion starts at some initial height h_0 and 0 velocity. Over time, the velocity gradually grows in its absolute value and the height decreases. Velocity is negative at all points, which means that it represents downward motion.

It is worth stressing that dynamical systems may be realized either in discrete or continuous time. Each of these ways of description has its advantages and drawbacks and specific fields of application.

D. Discrete Maps

Dynamical systems that evolve in discrete time steps are called *discrete maps*. For discrete maps, the state of the system at time t determines the state of the system at time $t + 1$. In mathematical terms, this means that the values of the dynamical variables describing the state of the system at time $t + 1$ can be expressed as functions of the values that they took at previous time step t. For instance, the variable $x_1(t + 1)$ fulfills

$$x_1(t + 1) = F_1[x_1(t),x_2(t), \ldots ,x_n(t)], \tag{1}$$

the variable $x_2(t + 1)$ fulfills

$$x_2(t + 1) = F_2[x_1(t),x_2(t), \ldots ,x_n(t)], \tag{2}$$

and so on. Here, $F_i(x_1, x_2, \ldots ,x_n)$ for $i = 1, \ldots ,n$ denotes functions of n variables $x_1, x_2, \ldots x_n$. Equations 1 and 2 mean that by knowing the state of the system at time t (i.e., the values of $x_1[t], x_2[t], \ldots ,x_n[t]$) one can determine the state of the system at the next time step; that is, one can calculate the values of the variables $x_1(t + 1), x_2(t + 1), \ldots ,x_n(t + 1)$.

[1]In classical mechanics, the notion of phase space is used in a more narrow and specific sense (e.g., the number of dimensions is always even).

[2]In the case of discrete steps dynamics, it is a sequence of points rather than a curve.

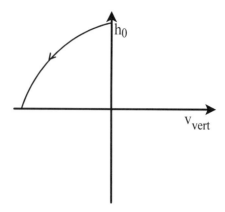

Figure 1 Phase space representing the fall of an apple. (The vertical axis represents the position in vertical dimension [height]; the horizontal axis represents vertical velocity).

E. Control Parameters

Generally speaking, functions $F_i(x_1, \ldots, x_n)$ depend additionally on some parameters that are constant in time or whose values are controlled by factors that are external to the system but that determine to a great extent the character of the dynamics observed. Such parameters are often termed *control parameters* because they represent conditions or influences external to the system itself. In the case of the Newtonian apple, such a factor could be the strength of the wind, which can completely change the character of the motion from vertical to almost horizontal. Another example is the magnitude of gravitational force. The velocity of falling of our apple would be much slower on the moon.

F. Example: Logistic Map

One of the most popular examples of a discrete map is the so-called *discrete logistic map*, which describes the dynamics of a single variable. Let us try to describe how many people eat lunch in a newly opened fancy restaurant per day. Let $x(t)$ denote the number of people that visit this restaurant on t-th day. In the beginning, very few people know about the restaurant. Those who visit it, however, are very satisfied and inform their colleagues about it, who decide in turn to visit it. As long as $x(t)$ is not too large, we may assume that

$$x(t + 1) = x(t) + \lambda x(t). \tag{3}$$

Here, λ is a control parameter, which can be interpreted as the mean number of newly informed persons by a person who has visited the restaurant. Equation 3 means that the number of people who visit the restaurant on a given day is equal to the number of those who visited it on a previous day plus the number of those whom they informed about the quality of the restaurant. Unfortunately, Equation 3 predicts the unlimited growth of the number of customers $x(t)$ in the course of time. Realistically, after a while the restaurant will become overcrowded. It will then not only stop getting new customers but also start losing old ones who become frustrated. The right-hand side of the equation must be modified by a factor that is roughly 1 when $x(t)$ is small and tends to 0 when the number of customers approaches the maximum number x_{max} that can be served each day. The simplest way of modeling such a factor is to choose it in a form of linear dependence, so that Equation 3 becomes

$$x(t + 1) = [x(t) + \lambda x(t)][1 - x(t)/x_{max}]. \tag{4}$$

From Equation 4 it seems natural to use as a dynamical variable the proportion of the actual number of people visiting the restaurant to the maximal number of visitors, $z(t) = x(t)/x_{max}$. Denoting $\Lambda = (1 + \lambda)$ as a total growth factor, we may rewrite Equation 4 to the "classical" form of the logistic map:

$$z(t + 1) = \Lambda z(t)[1 - z(t)]. \tag{5}$$

The logistic map has only one control parameter Λ, which controls the qualitative behavior of $z(t)$. In the course of time for some Λ values, the value of $z(t)$ may tend to static equilibrium, where the constant number of customers per day is a compromise between satisfaction and frustration. For other Λ values, the number of customers may exhibit regular or irregular fluctuations that reflect frustration—satisfaction cycles of different complexity.

G. Continuous Time Models

In many cases it is more appropriate to use continuous time instead of discrete time. Differential equations provide natural framework for describing continuous time dynamical systems. These equations express the rate of change of dynamical variables as a function of the state of the system (i.e., the values of these variables). Let the state of the system be described, as before, by dynamical variables $x_1(t), \ldots, x_n(t)$. The dynamics are governed, then, by the set of n differential equations that determine the rate of changes of each of the $x_i(t)$ variables for $i = 1, \ldots, n$,

$$\frac{dx_i(t)}{dt} = f_i(x_1(t), \ldots, x_n(t)), \tag{6}$$

where $f_i(x_1, \ldots, x_2)$ are functions specifying the interactions among n dynamical variables. These interactions depend in general on some additional coefficients—called, as before, *control parameters*. A prototypical example of continuous time dynamical systems is provided by Newtonian equations of motion, which describe rates of change in the positions and velocities of material objects. Among the simplest examples of nonlinear dynamical systems are models used in mathematical ecology to describe the dynamics of predator–prey populations (Lotka, 1925).

H. Predator–Prey Model

In presenting a possible social interpretation of the classical predator–prey model, we present a model of the dynamics of populations of pickpockets and naïve victims in a society. Let $P(t)$ denote the actual number of "predators" (i.e., pickpockets) and $N(t)$ denote the actual number of "prey" (i.e., victims) who naïvely fail to protect themselves from theft. If there were no pickpockets, the number of people with no protection would grow given that people who protect themselves would learn from those who do not protect themselves that there is no point in protection. For $N(t)$ that is not too large, the rate of growth would be proportional to the number of unprotected people,

$$\frac{dN(t)}{dt} = r_1 N(t) \tag{7}$$

where r_1 is a control parameter that describes the rate of growth per one unprotected person. Conversely, if the were no unprotected victims, the number of pickpockets would decay exponentially at a rate proportional to the actual value of P(t),

$$\frac{dP(t)}{dt} = -r_2 P(t) \tag{8}$$

where r_2 is a control parameter that describes the rate of decay per one thief.

In a freely interacting population, the number of contacts per unit of time between pickpockets and their victims that lead to theft is proportional to the product of $N(t)$ and $P(t)$. As a result of successful thefts, victims start to protect themselves and to convince others to do so. Thus, as a consequence of theft, the rate of growth of unprotected people decreases. Just the opposite is true for pickpockets. Success of pickpocketing would likely encourage others to engage in this activity. The dynamics of the two populations must thus fulfill a set of two coupled differential equations:

$$\frac{dN(t)}{dt} = r_1 N(t) - \gamma_1 N(t) P(t) \tag{9}$$

$$\frac{dP(t)}{dt} = -r_2 P(t) + \gamma_2 N(t) P(t). \tag{10}$$

In the above equations, γ_1 and γ_2 are control parameters that describe the rate of decay or the growth of populations per one victim and one pickpocket, respectively, as a result of theft. Over the course of time, populations $N(t)$ and $P(t)$ might tend to a constant equilibrium or to periodic oscillations (the *Lotka–Volterra cycle*). In such a cycle, the population of predators follows with some delay the dynamics of the population of prey.

III. Patterns of Behavior of Dynamical Systems

A. Conservative and Dissipative Systems

In mechanics, one often considers idealized systems without any frictional forces. Such systems are described as *conservative*. In such systems, some global properties such as energy do not change in time. The friction-free pendulum would swing with the same amplitude forever.

In everyday experience, we encounter more often *dissipative systems*, which lose some of their energy as a result of friction or other form of damping over time. Such systems eventually approach asymptotic states.

From a practical point of view, it is important that the possible trajectories of the evolution of a dynamical system exhibit (in a vast majority of cases) some universal patterns of behavior, independent of the specific functional form of Equations 1 and 2 or equations 9 and 10.

B. Attractors

Generally, when starting from the initial point $x_1(t_0), \ldots, x_n(t_0)$, we observe that after some time (transient regime), the trajectory tends to settle in a subset of the phase space; during its further evolution, the system explores only this subset or, more precisely, its closest vicinity. This subset of the phase space is called an *attractor*. Although attractors are only final destinations of dynamic systems, formally attainable only asymptotically in time (or when starting points already lie on them), one usually observes that when time elapses, trajectories come closer and closer to attractors, eventually becoming practically indistinguishable from motion on an attractor. All the trajectories of dissipative systems, regardless of their initial conditions, after some time converge on an attractor. We may say that an attractor attracts all the trajectories in the phase space. This phenomenon is sometimes described as a *loss of information* because the subset of space that may be visited during the time evolution of the system shrinks with time. When we know that the system is after some time close to its attractor, we need less information to specify the state of the system. In the extreme case in which the system evolves toward a single fixed point, we need no additional information to specify its state. No matter how strong we

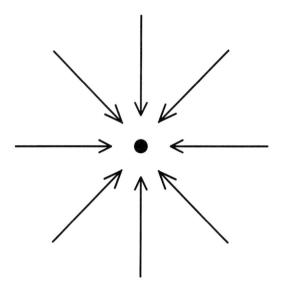

Figure 2   Stable-node attractor.

swing a pendulum, for example, after some time it will come to rest. Evolution toward attractors is a very general property of dissipative dynamical systems.

There are four classes of attractors of major importance (Eckmann & Ruelle, 1985; Sandefur, 1990; Schuster, 1984): fixed point, limit cycle, multiperiodic, and quasiperiodic.

1. Fixed–Point Attractors

A fixed-point attractor is also frequently called a *stable point*, a *stable node*, a *stable focus*, an *attracting point*, or a *point attractor*. For a system having only a single fixed-point attractor, all trajectories of the dynamical system in the phase space tend to a single point. Eventually, with the increase in t, the system settles to a stable equilibrium position that does not depend on the particular starting point. *Fixed point* describes a situation in which the set of all dynamical variables converges to some set of time-independent constant values. A stable node in phase space is presented in Figure 2. The arrows around it indicate the trajectories followed by the systems starting from various initial conditions. For fixed points that are called *stable nodes*, the approach is direct. Figure 3 depicts an example of time behavior of a dynamical variable for a system that approaches a fixed point. The example is taken from a *logistic map* of our previous restaurant example. The variable $z(t)$ representing the ratio of people that visit a new restaurant on a given day to the

Figure 3 Convergence on a fixed-point attractor.

maximal number of visitors tends to a constant value after a short transient period. It is worth stressing that this kind of behavior is observed for the logistic map independently of initial conditions when the control parameter Λ fulfills the inequality $1 < \Lambda < 3$. For higher values of the control parameter, the behavior is entirely different, as we shall illustrate.

Figure 4 shows two fixed points that coexist in phase space. Depending on the initial conditions, trajectories will be attracted by one of these points. Arrows indicate again the shape of trajectories in the vicinity of each fixed point. Each of these fixed points may be called a *stable focus* because the approach toward it is not direct but is combined with a circular motion.

2. Limit-Cycle Attractors

A limit-cycle attractor may also called a *periodic attractor* or a *periodic orbit*. In this case, the final state is a periodic one: The values of all dynamical variables

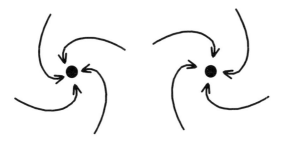

Figure 4 Two stable-focus attractors coexisting in phase space.

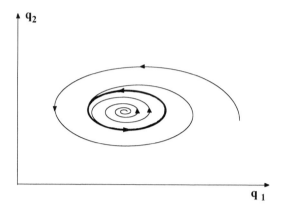

Figure 5   Periodic or limit-cycle attractor.

periodically repeat after time T, $x_i(t) = x_i(t + T)$, where T is the *period of the motion*. The periodic attractor is represented in the phase space as a closed trajectory (see Figure 5, thick line). The arrow on the attractor indicates the direction of the motion toward the attractor. The trajectories converge toward the limit cycle in the course of time. Two examples of such trajectories are drawn as narrow lines in

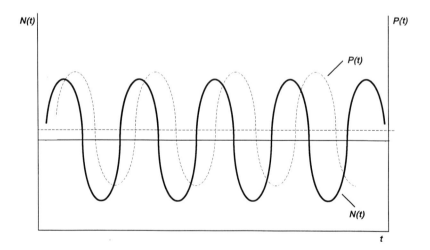

Figure 6   Number of pickpockets and victims as a function of time. (Solid line represents number of victims; dashed line represents number of pickpockets).

Figure 5. As before, there might be several periodic attractors coexisting in the phase space. In that case, the final limit cycle depends on initial conditions and may vary in size, period, and so on. Such a situation is characteristic of predator–prey models, where the amplitude of final oscillations of populations depends on initial data. Figure 6 shows the ratio of pickpockets and their victims as a function of time. Figure 7 presents the time evolution of $z(t)$ governed by the logistic map. For control parameter values $3 < \Lambda < 3.45$, $z(t)$ varies between two values. This behavior is called a *Period-2 Attractor*.

3. Multiperiodic and Quasiperiodic Attractors

A generalization of limit cycles occurs when each dynamical variable behaves as a combination of oscillations of several different periods. Such periods might be commensurate, (i.e., integer multiples of a single quantity—a basic period). In such a case, the motion is in principle periodic with the basic period, although its form might be much more complex than in the case of single-period oscillations in the form of sine or cosine. In the case in which different periods are incommensurate (i.e., they are not multiples of a single basic period), the motion is quasiperiodic. The system never returns to the same point in the phase space, although it can return arbitrarily close. The trajectory covers a larger region in a phase space, called a *torus*. Figure 8 shows a torus in some three dimensional phase space. The time dependence of a dynamical variable that undergoes quasiperiodic motion might be irregular and very complicated given that superimposition of waves of different length may create very irregular and quite complex shapes. In fact, any signal of a finite length may be approximated by combinations of some finite number of periodic waves of different frequencies. As we discuss later, however, a signal can be distinguished from deterministic chaotic motion.

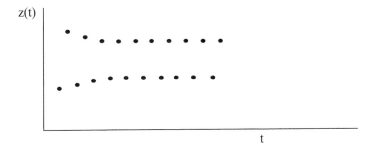

Figure 7   Period-2 attractor generated in a logistic map.

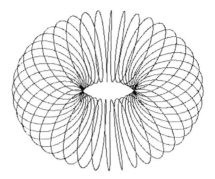

Figure 8   Torus in a three-dimensional phase space.

IV. Deterministic Chaos

A. Strange Attractors

Perhaps the most interesting asymptotic behavior is *deterministic chaos*. Most definitions of chaotic evolution include *sensitivity to initial conditions* and *mixing*. As the name indicates, the motion of the system in this case is completely irregular and seemingly chaotic. The trajectory tends to some subset of the phase space that is none of those mentioned in the previous section. It is neither a point, nor a closed line, nor a torus. Such a set usually has a very complicated geometrical structure, referred to as a *strange attractor*. In the continuous time case, it can occur as an attractor of a dynamical system only when the dimensionality of the phase space is large enough (i.e., $n \geq 3$). For the discrete time case, this limitation does not apply because discrete systems typically produce complex behavior much more easily than do continuous systems. Figure 9 shows the famous Lorenz attractor, which occurs in a set of three differential equations used for modeling in meteorology (Lorenz, 1963), hydrodynamics, and laser physics (Haken, 1982, 1983). Figure 10 shows a strange attractor that occurs in a simple two-dimensional discrete map, called a *Henon map*.

Figure 11 shows a typical example of chaotic time dependence of a dynamical variable obtained from a discrete map. Here, the evolution of $z(t)$ is obtained from a logistic map for control parameter value $\Lambda = 4$. Figure 12 shows a continuous time example of chaotic behavior: the evolution of one of the dynamical variables in the Lorenz model.[3]

[3]The chaotic nature of Lorenz attractor in not displayed by its overall shape, which seems quite regular, but rather by the dynamics of its time evolution and self-similar structure.

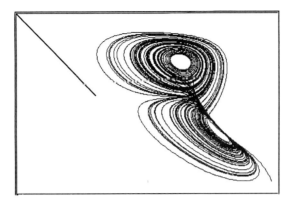

Figure 9   Lorenz attractor.

B. Sensitivity to Initial Conditions

All chaotic motion and motion on strange attractors exhibit the peculiar property of enormous sensitivity to initial conditions. This can be understood in the following way: If we start the motion from two very close points in a phase space (very similar initial conditions), the corresponding trajectories after some time will necessarily diverge from one from another. Figure 12 shows this phenomenon in the Lorenz model.

Sensitivity to initial conditions implies that the behavior of a chaotic system cannot be predicted in long time spans. In practice, it implies the breakdown of Laplacian determinism. Formally, the evolution of the system is deterministic in the sense that the behavior of the system is fully determined by differential or difference equations. In practice, the state of the system cannot be predicted over time. One reason is that we never know the initial data with infinite accuracy. Our knowledge always contains some rounding, errors, or uncertainty. All these inaccuracies are amplified by the dynamics. The second reason is that even the slightest and most momentary perturbation of the dynamics causes arbitrarily large effects after some time. This last effect is known as the *butterfly effect* (Lorenz, 1963) and is a major cause of our inability to do accurate long-term weather forecasting: Lorenz stated that even a butterfly flapping its wings in Brazil may cause a tornado some time later in Texas.

Sensitivity to initial conditions may be more precisely expressed in mathematical terms by means of *Lyapunov exponents*. Let us consider two points in the phase space that lie close together, $X_1(0), X_2(0)$, and let $d[X_1(0), X_2(0)]$ denote the distance between the two points. Let also $X_1(t), X_2(t)$ denote points in the phase space visited at time t by the trajectories initiated at the initial points $X_1(0), X_2(0)$. If

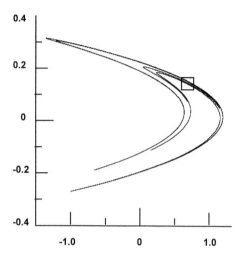

Figure 10   Henon map of a strange attractor in a simple two-dimensional discrete map.

initially the two points are close together, then for larger t the distance between them characteristically behaves as

$$d[X_1(t),X_2(t)] \simeq e^{\lambda t} d[X_1(0),X_2(t)], \tag{11}$$

where λ denotes the so-called *maximal Lyapunov exponent*, which can be explicitly expressed as

$$\lambda = \frac{1}{t} \ln \left\{ \frac{d[X_1(t),X_2(t)]}{d[X_1(0),X_2(0)]} \right\}. \tag{12}$$

The formula in Equation 12 holds strictly speaking when the initial distance

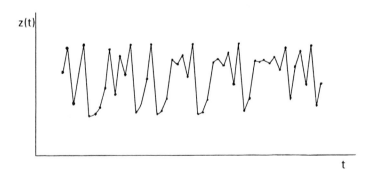

Figure 11   Chaotic evolution of a dynamical variable in a logistic map with the control parameter $\lambda = 4$.

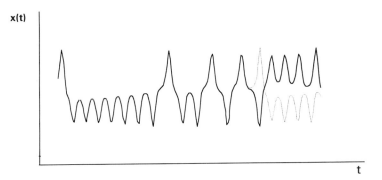

Figure 12 Chaotic evolution of a dynamical variable in a Lorenz model. (Note the eventual divergence of trajectories.)

between the points is sufficiently small and the time is sufficiently long. Obviously, the Lyapunov exponent is a local concept. It characterizes the divergence rate of two trajectories that originate close to a given point in the phase space. Thus, the Lyapunov exponent may vary from place to place. When two trajectories are attracted by a fixed point, the distance between them must decrease. λ is then negative, and both trajectories converge exponentially to the same point. In the case of a limit cycle, the maximal Lyapunov exponent is zero. Both trajectories become periodic oscillations in the course of time, but the distance between them remains finite. Finally, when motion is chaotic, the maximal Lyapunov exponent is positive. The two close trajectories diverge exponentially from each other, as shown in Figure 13. The time after which trajectories strongly diverge, thus making predictions impossible, is proportional to the inverse of the maximal Lyapunov exponent. It also increases logarithmically with the increase of the initial distance between the two trajectories (but only for sufficiently small initial distances).

$$d(t) = de^{\lambda t}$$

Figure 13 Exponential divergence of trajectories.

C. Mixing

Another important property of chaotic systems is *mixing*, which means that two points that initially were close together may be found after some time far apart, and some points that initially were far apart may be found close together. The spatial relations between points in the phase space are reshuffled in the course of time.

D. Fractal Nature of Strange Attractors

Strange attractors usually have a very complex geometrical nature. Typically, they are fractals, which means that their dimension is not a natural number but a fractional one. If we measure the size of standard geometrical objects with the stick of the size l, the result of the measurement behaves as l^d. For instance, a line of 1 m contains 10 dm and 100 cm. A square of the area of 1 m² contains 100 squares of the area of 1 dm. A cube of the volume of 1 m³ contains 1,000 cubes of the volume of 1 dm³ and so on. We can thus define the dimension of an object as

$$d = \frac{\ln S(l)}{\ln l}, \tag{13}$$

where $S(l)$ denotes the size of the object measured in the units of size l. For nonfractal objects, this measurement produces an integer value. For fractal objects, such measurement of the dimension leads to the result that d is fractional. The classic example comes from measuring the coast of Britain (Mandelbrot, 1982). If one uses a unit of measurement 10 miles long, many details of the coastline, like small bays or peninsulas, escape measurement. Decreasing the unit of measurement to 1 mile, in addition to the 10-fold increase reflecting simple change of the unit of measurement, captures much smaller details of the coastline that will increase the measurement by some amount. Decreasing the unit of measurement again, captures additional curvature of even smaller details, like rocks. The increase of the measurement for the coast of Britain grows approximately 1.31 power of the change of measurement scale. In general, the more curved and complex the shape, the higher its fractional component of the dimension.

Application of this measurement procedure produces a value between $2 < d < 3$ for the Lorenz attractor and $1 < d < 2$ for the Henon attractor. In general, the dimension of strange attractors may, and frequently do, depend on control parameters.

Fractals often have *self-similar structure*, which means that a magnified view of part of the object is similar to the whole object. An everyday example of this property can be seen in cauliflower, broccoli, and—last but not least—brocco-flower. In mathematical objects, selfsimilarity may be observed on an infinite range

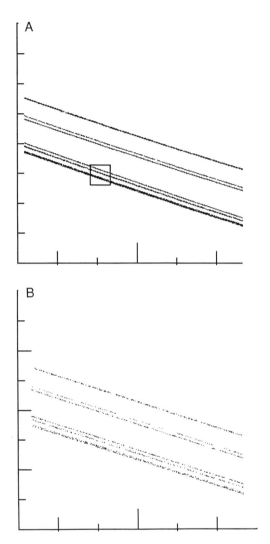

Figure 14　(A)Henon attractor. (Magnified view of the box in Figure 10). (B)Magnified box from the Figure 14A shows self-similarity of the Henon attractor.

of scales. In the real world, it will happen only on a few scales. Self-similarity of the Henon attractor is illustrated in Figure 14, which shows a magnified view of part of the attractor shown in Figure 10 and a magnification of the magnified part. (For a discussion of fractals, see Mandelbrot, 1982; Peigen, Jurgens, & Souppe, 1992; Peitgen & Souppe, 1988.)

E. Chaos in the Real World

The behavior of deterministic chaos is exhibited by many systems in the real world. Chaos frequently occurs in a system with a large number of dynamical variables. Prototypical examples include turbulent flows of liquids and gases studied in hydrodynamics, aerodynamics, and meteorology. As noted earlier, chaos may also occur in simple systems consisting of a few dynamical variables if the relations among them are nonlinear. Such low-dimensional chaos is observed in systems ranging from lasers to market economies to the human brain.

V. Patterns of Change in Behavior

A. Changes of Behavior—Bifurcations

In nonlinear dynamical systems, smooth and small changes in control parameters may lead to dramatic qualitative changes in behavior. Small and smooth changes of control parameters may lead to complete changes in the number, shapes, and types of attractors. In the analysis of nonlinear dynamics, it is often not sufficient to realize that changes take place; rather, it is more important to uncover the pattern of these changes. A simple change in the state of the system is not an indication of any external influence (e.g., an action of a causal factor) because the evolution in time is an intrinsic property of all dynamical systems. What is more crucial is detection of a radical change in the pattern of behavior. Radical change in the pattern usually follows from a change in control parameters and thus is an indicator of external influences (i.e., the appearance of important causal factors or stimuli). This important point is a basis of synergetics (Haken, 1978, 1982) and has been elaborated in the area of psychology by Kelso and his colleagues (Kelso 1981, 1984; Kelso, Ding, & Schoner, 1991). Changes in a pattern of behavior are called *bifurcations. Dynamical phase transitions* and *critical phenomena* are also terms sometimes used to convey this idea. It is worth stressing that changes in patterns usually follow well-defined routes. One can even speak of patterns of changes in patterns of behavior.

The theory of bifurcations is a very advanced and difficult branch of mathematics (Ruelle, 1989). The focus of catastrophe theory is the classification of bifurcations (Poston & Steward, 1978). Next, we discuss the most frequently observed bifurcations.

1. *Pitchfork bifurcation* is a bifurcation from a fixed point into two fixed points. This is probably the simplest kind of bifurcation. With the change of the control parameter, the fixed point divides into two fixed points that then diverge. Figure 15

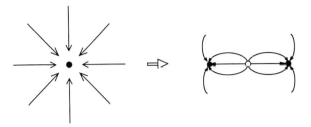

Figure 15   Pitchfork bifurcation

shows how the flow of trajectories change as a result of this bifurcation. Figure 16 shows the so-called *bifurcation diagram*, which shows the attainable values of the order parameter as a function of a control parameter. Such bifurcation occurs in many physical systems such as lasers or ferromagnets.

2. *Saddle-node bifurcation* is also a bifurcation from one fixed point to two fixed points. It is also called *fold bifurcation* or *tangent bifurcation*. At some values of a control parameter, before the original fixed point loses its stability, a new stable fixed point arises. The saddle-node bifurcation is usually followed by a so-called *inverted saddle node bifurcation*. Inverted saddle node bifurcation occurs for higher values of the control parameters when the original fixed point loses its stability so that the only stable fixed point is the new one. This type of bifurcation occurs often in real systems and is also called a *cusp catastrophe* in Thom's (1975) theory of catastrophes.

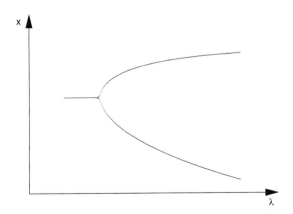

Figure 16   Bifurcation diagram of a pitchfork bifurcation. (Horizontal axis represents control parameter; vertical axis represents order parameter).

Figure 17   Hopf bifurcation

3. *Hopf bifurcation* is a bifurcation from a stable focus into a limit cycle. The changes in the flow of trajectories in the phase space are shown in Figure 17. Such bifurcations are believed to be responsible for starting and stopping various biological rhythms (Kaplan & Glass, 1992).

4. *Bifurcations from a limit cycle* may have various manifestations, such as a bifurcation from a limit cycle into two coexisting limit cycles, as shown in Figure 18. Bifurcations frequently take the form of a change from a simple periodic orbit into a multiperiodic or quasiperiodic orbit. In the latter case, we deal with the bifurcation from a limit cycle to a torus. Figure 19 shows a particular example of a bifurcation of a limit cycle into two dimensions into a limit cycle in three dimensions.

5. *Period-doubling bifurcations* occur when a limit cycle of period T becomes unstable and is replaced by a new limit cycle of period $2T$. Figure 20 shows a trajectory of a so-called *Duffing oscillator* immediately before and after a period-doubling bifurcation in the phase space. Figure 21 compares the dynamics of a logistic map with Period 2 for $\Lambda = 3.5$ and with Period 4 for $\Lambda = 3.55$. The period-doubling bifurcation in this case occurs when the control parameter

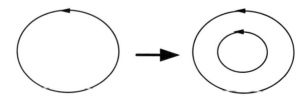

Figure 18   Bifurcation from a limit cycle into two coexisting limit cycles.

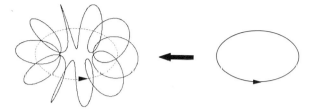

Figure 19 Bifurcation from a limit cycle in two dimensions into a limit cycle in three dimensions.

$\Lambda \simeq 3.54$. Obviously, bifurcations from limit cycles to other limit cycles and tori can be generalized to cases of bifurcations from tori to other tori.

B. Bistability and Multistability

The cases in which an attractor bifurcates into two or more coexisting attractors is termed *bistability* or *multistability*, respectively. In such a case, some of the

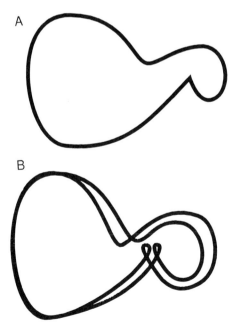

Figure 20 Trajectory of a Duffing oscillator before (A) and after (B) a period-doubling bifurcation.

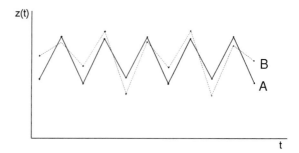

Figure 21   Logistic map with Period 2 (A) and with Period 4 (B).

initial points in the phase space will be attracted by the first attractor, some by the second, and so on. Regions of the phase space attracted by a given attractor are called its *domains of attraction*. The domains of attraction may have very complex structure–fractal boundaries (Peitgen & Richter, 1986).

C. Hysteresis

One of the most fascinating phenomena that occurs in bistable or multistable systems is *hysteresis*. This phenomenon refers to the fact that when we gradually change a control parameter, the state of the system depends on the history of these changes.

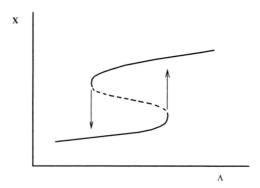

Figure 22   Hysteresis. (The arrows indicate the path followed by the system with change in the control parameter in different directions. Dashed line corresponds to unstable equilibrium.)

We illustrate the hysteresis phenomenon for the case of a simple saddle-node bifurcation in Figure 22, which shows the bifurcation diagram (i.e., the values of fixed points as a function of a control parameter Λ). Suppose we start changing the control parameter from very low values. The system remains in the original fixed point (i.e., it follows a lower branch in Figure 22). At the point of the inverted saddle-node bifurcation, the original stable point loses its stability and the system suddenly jumps to the upper branch of the bifurcation diagram. The situation is reversed when we then decrease the control parameter. The system will remain on the upper branch much longer—until the control parameter is decreased to the value at which the saddle-node bifurcation takes place. Only then does the system return to the original fixed point.

Hysteresis is a very frequent signature of nonlinear behavior and occurs in a variety of systems such as ferromagnets, optical and electronic bistable devices, human motor behavior (Kelso, 1981, 1984, 1988), and love relationships (see Chapter 5).

D. Roads to Chaos

Finally, it is worth stressing that there are universal roads or scenarios according to which dynamical systems become chaotic. Such scenarios typically consist of specific sequences of bifurcations as the control parameter is changed.

1. *Landau–Hopf scenario.* As noted earlier, a fixed point may bifurcate into a limit cycle by a Hopf bifurcation. The first frequency then appears in the system. Such a limit cycle might later bifurcate into a torus (the second frequency appears). Landau and Lifshitz (1964) suggested that this process may be continued. More and more new frequencies appear as tori bifurcate into tori in higher and higher dimensions. The dynamics become increasingly irregular. Note that such a scenario may be realized only when the phase space has a very large number of dimensions.

2. *Ruelle–Takens scenario.* Ruelle and Takens (1971) showed that in low dimensional systems, the bifurcations from a two-dimensional torus to a three-dimensional one typically do not occur. As soon as a third incommensurable frequency occurs in the system, the motion becomes chaotic and follows a strange attractor. We stress, however, that in many experiments the transition from two-dimensional to three-dimensional periodic motion is quite often observed.

3. *Period-doubling scenario.* Often, chaos is reached by means of a sequence of period-doubling bifurcations. The system makes transitions from a limit cycle of Period 2 to one of Period 4, then 8, then 16, and so on. The period tends to infinity at some finite value of the control parameter. Above this value, the motion is chaotic.

4. *Intermittency scenario. Intermittency* is a term coined by Pomeau and Manneville (1980) to describe a situation in which dynamical variables undergo periodic oscillations that are from time to time interrupted abruptly by "bursts" of chaotic behavior. As the control parameter is increased, the bursts occur more frequently and the duration of regular behavior decreases. Intermittency may occur, for instance, in systems that are close to saddle-node bifurcations when a new fixed point appears.

E. Transitions in the Presence of Noise

In real dynamical systems (as opposed to idealized mathematical models), the dynamics of the system are usually influenced by external or internal factors that can be regarded as random influences (or in other words, *noise*). What are the effects of noise on nonlinear dynamics and bifurcations? First, noise leads to minor quantitative changes and changes of the values of control parameters at which bifurcations occur (cf. Haken, 1983; Kelso et al., 1991). Second, noise may lead to qualitative changes of the structure and stability of the attractor. In general, it "smears" the structure of attractors. In the case of strange attractors, it erases the structure on the shortest scale. Stable attractors of very high periodicity and strange attractors may even cease to exist. Usually, only the rougher structures are preserved in the presence of noise. In experiments, for instance, usually only the first few steps of a period doubling sequence can be detected. Finally, in the case of multistable systems, the noise may cause random jumps between coexisting attractors. This property may be applied to the control of the behavior of dynamical systems, such as neural network models (Lewenstein & Nowak, 1989).

VI. Signatures of Nonlinear Behavior

When we observe a system that changes in time, we can ask the following question: Is the behavior of the system governed by the laws of nonlinear dynamics? The simplest way to answer this question is through visual observation. We should look for typical types of behavior of nonlinear dynamical systems. Convincing evidence for nonlinear dynamics is supplied by the presence of bifurcations, by characteristic changes in patterns of behavior, and by hysteresis. If we can identify patterns of behavior and observe that those patterns change and if the changes of patterns follow bifurcation rules, we can infer that we are observing a nonlinear dynamical system. For instance, a strong indicator is period doubling or bistability in the system. Naked-eye observation, however, is not a very precise means of analysis. It is therefore very important to develop more precise means of observation and detection of patterns of behavior.

A. Autocorrelation and Cross-Correlation Function

A typical empirical data set consists of a discrete time series of one or more dynamical variables. Evaluation of the corresponding autocorrelation function can be done using the time-series analysis of standard statistical packages, such as Statgraf or SPSS. The autocorrelation function $C(\tau)$ for the variable $x(t)$ is a function of a time lag τ. It measures the magnitude of correlation between two values of a dynamical variable $x(t)$ and $x(t + \tau)$, separated by the time lag τ and averaged over all the possible choices of t. If a system randomly fluctuates around a fixed point, the autocorrelation function reflects the properties of the noise only and tends to zero for times larger than a, the so-called *noise correlation time*. If the system undergoes nontrivial dynamics, it is usually reflected in the autocorrelation function. For periodic or quasiperiodic dynamics, the autocorrelation function is periodic or quasiperiodic, respectively. For chaotic motion, the autocorrelation function is similar to that of purely random noise; it decays to zero on a time scale called a *correlation time*. The correlation time is not determined by the properties of noise but by the properties of the underlying nonlinear dynamics. It decreases with the efficiency of mixing and with the magnitude of the Lyapunov exponent. Note that the autocorrelation function alone is not a good tool for distinguishing between deterministic and random noise.

The cross-correlation function has very similar properties to those of the autocorrelation function except that it describes the magnitude of correlation between two different dynamical variables. For this reason, it may be used do detect statistical and dynamical interrelations between two variables for a given time lag τ between them.

B. Fourier Analysis

This technique, also referred to as *spectral analysis*, may be applied to any time series using standard statistical packages. Fourier analysis is based on the fact that each signal is a linear combination of simple oscillations of fixed frequencies. Fourier analysis is used to find these frequencies and the corresponding amplitudes of oscillations. In a typical approach, Fourier analysis consists of the calculation of a so-called *Fourier transform* of the autocorrelation function. This Fourier transform is a function of the frequency, takes positive values, and is called a *spectrum* or a *power spectrum*. The power spectrum shows the contributions of various frequencies to the signal.

When a system randomly fluctuates around a fixed point in phase space, its spectrum consists of a single peak at the frequency zero. In the absence of noise, that peak would be infinitely narrow; in reality, it has always some width that is

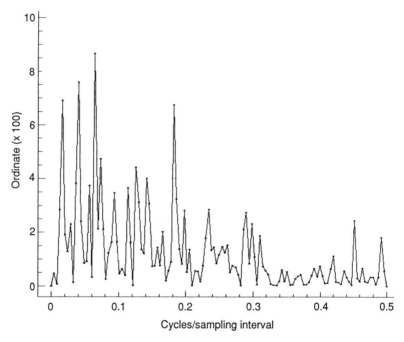

Figure 23   Power spectrum from Lorenz model. (Horizontal axis represents frequencies; vertical axis represents power).

proportional to the inverse of the noise correlation time. In the case of limit-cycle attractors of a given frequency, the spectrum has a peak at this frequency. Usually, it also contains peaks at the so-called *harmonic frequencies*, which are multiples of the basic frequency. In the case of period-doubling bifurcations, a new feature of the power spectrum arises: It starts to contain *subharmonic frequencies* equal to half of the basic frequency, quarter of the basic frequency, and so on. In general, subharmonics are a fraction of the basic frequencies. Figure 23 shows a power spectrum obtained from the Lorenz model at some value of the control parameter containing harmonics, subharmonics, and multiples of subharmonics. In experimental situations, the width of the peaks of the spectrum is determined by the properties of the noise. Structurally, a very similar situation takes place for quasiperiodic attractors. The only difference is that the peaks in the spectrum correspond to frequencies that are incommensurate. The characteristic property of chaotic motion is that the spectrum becomes broadband. This is illustrated in the Figure 24. The spectrum has a form of a function that decays slowly when the frequency ω grows from zero to infinity. On top of this slow decay are remnants of a peak structure. In principle, the spectrum visible in Figure 24 can be interpreted as a spectrum of purely random

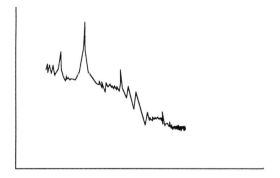

Figure 24 Broadband power spectrum indicating chaotic motion.

motion with a short correlation time. Again, we face the problem of distinguishing between deterministic chaos and random motion.

C. Distinguishing Deterministic from Random Chaos

The problem of distinguishing deterministic chaos from random chaos is of major importance for practical applications. In social psychology, most data have a very irregular character; therefore, the models are usually of a stochastic character. Although there may be no logical reason that stochastic models are unavoidable, when we are dealing with a deterministic system, that knowledge is of great importance. It allows us to look for a deterministic model to explain the irregularities.

1. Takens's Theorem

In experimental situations in general, and in social psychology in particular, we almost never know what many of the appropriate dynamical variables are. We often monitor the time evolution of a single dynamical variable, having no idea of what all the other relevant dynamical variables are. Takens's (1981) theorem tells us how to reconstruct the original shape of an attractor using the time evolution of only a single variable from a dynamical system. The basis for this idea is that in a dynamical system the influence of all the dynamical variables can be observed in the history of each of the dynamical variables. We can thus treat different moments in the evolution of a single variable as indicative of the values of other dynamical variables in the system. According to Takens, we should start from a sequence of values of a single dynamic variable equally spaced in time $x(t)$, $x(t + \tau)$, $x(t + 2\tau)$, . . . , $x(t + n\tau)$. Each of the time-delayed values of the dynamical variables is an inde-

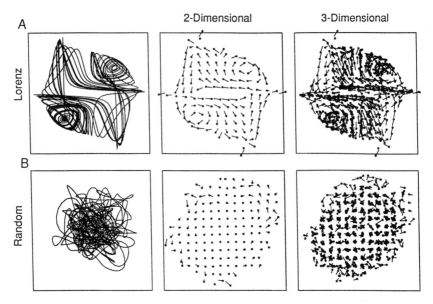

Figure 25   (A) Two- and three-dimensional embeddings of the dynamics of a single variable of a Lorenz model. (B) Two- and three-dimensional embeddings of a purely random signal. (Power spectra for A and B are identical. From "Direct Test for Determinism in a Time Series" by D. T. Kaplan and L. Glass, 1992, *Physics Review Letters, 68*, p. 427–430. Copyright 1992 by American Physical Society. Reprinted by permission.)

pendent coordinate of the phase space. Each sequence of values $x(t), x(t + \tau), x$ $(t + 2\tau), \ldots x(t + n\tau)$ defines a point in the phase space. The dimension of this phase space is the number of coordinates (i.e., the number of time delays). As t changes, the corresponding point in this phase space follows a trajectory. Takens has proven that an attractor of the motion defined in such a phase space has the same dimension as and a similar shape to the original attractor of the dynamical system.

Without knowing the nature of the original dynamical system, of course, we do not know the dimensionality of its phase space. This implies that we should try out different dimensionalities and choose the one that gives us the most satisfactory results. If we just plot the points of the trajectory in the manner described above and any regular shape appears, it suggests that we are dealing with a deterministic system. For random systems, however, we get shapeless blobs. The upper left panel of Figure 25 shows the two- and three-dimensional embedding of the dynamics of a single variable coming from the Lorenz system, constructed according to Takens's rules. The lower left panel of Figure 25 has been constructed as a two- and three-dimensional embedding of a purely random signal. The difference between the two panels is obvious. Later, we present more sophisticated methods than visual observation for the analysis of attractors reconstructed in this way. For both methods we discuss, we can in principle use the values of the original dynamical variables of dynamical systems. The cases in which we know the values of all the dynamical variables in a system, however, are rare in reality. We thus present these methods as applied to attractors reconstructed according to Takens method.

2. Direct Test for Determinism in a Time Series

Kaplan and Glass (1992) proposed a new method to determine if the dynamics is generated by deterministic rather than stochastic process. The method is based on the observation that the tangent to the trajectory generated by a deterministic system is a function of position in a phase space. That means that all the tangents to the trajectory in a sufficiently small region of a phase space will have similar orientation.

Suppose that we are measuring a time signal describing the evolution of a single variable $x(t)$. We may embed this signal in two-dimensional phase space by considering as dynamical variables $x(t)$ and its delayed companion $x(t - \tau)$. The motion in this two-dimensional phase plane is illustrated in the upper left panel of Figure 25. It shows a trajectory obtained by plotting $x(t)$ versus $x(t - \tau)$ for the deterministic Lorenz attractor. Note that the Lorenz model is three-dimensional and that its trajectories do not cross in three dimensions. As upper three panels of Figure 25 indicate, they do cross when projected onto a two-dimensional plane. In the next step, one divides the phase plane into a coarse-grained grid. In the upper panels, the plane was divided into 16×16 boxes. Each time the trajectory passes a box of number j, it generates a vector of length 1, called the *trajectory vector*, $v_{k,j}$. The subindex k denotes the number of subsequent visits to the j-th box. The direction of this vector is determined by the vector joining the point where the trajectory enters the box with the point where it leaves it. This vector gives the average direction of the k-th pass through the j-th box. Finally, we form an average vector for each box, adding all the vectors for this box and dividing the result by their number. In mathematical terms,

$$V_j = \sum_k \vec{v}_{k,j} / n_j, \tag{14}$$

where n_j is the total number of passes through the box j. In regions of the phase space where the trajectory vectors are all aligned, the resulting averaged vector will have a length close to 1. In regions of phase space where trajectories cross in various directions, the length of resulting averaged vector will be close to zero. The averaged vectors are presented in the upper middle panel of Figure 25; as one can see, most of them have unit length. Their length is reduced only in the region where many crossings of the trajectory occur.

The same procedure may be repeated in three dimensions. To this end, we consider three variables $x(t)$, $x(t - \tau)$, and $x(t - 2\tau)$. Trajectories in the phase space with such coordinates do not cross. We can divide again such a phase space into small cubes and construct averaged trajectory vectors in three dimensions. This is done for the same Lorenz model in the upper right panel of Figure 25. Kaplan and Glass (1992) used a $16 \times 16 \times 16$ grid and drew a projection of averaged vectors V_j onto the plane of $x(t)$ and $x(t - \tau)$.

These results are compared with the results of the same analysis obtained for purely random motion. To make a fair comparison, Kaplan and Glass (1992) constructed a random noise that had the same autocorrelation function as the deterministic motion on the Lorenz attractor considered before. In the lower left panel of Figure 25, a typical trajectory for such noise in two dimensions is plotted. The lower center and right panels show averaged trajectory vectors for two-dimensional and three-dimensional embeddings, respectively. Comparison of results for the deterministic and the random case shows obvious differences.

Kaplan and Glass (1992) provided yet another measure of the difference between deterministic and random chaos. They calculated average length of the vectors V_j for all those boxes that had been visited a given number of times k. The resulting average length $\bar{L}_k^n$ depended on the number of passes k and the embedding dimension n. For purely random motion, the sum of k random vectors of length 1 has, according to the central limit theorem, typically a length of $1/\sqrt{k}$. The results are presented in Figure 26. $\bar{L}_k^n$ *clearly drops as* $1/\sqrt{k}$ for the random motion and remains close to 1 for deterministic chaotic motion, both in the case of two- and three-dimensional embeddings.

3. Determining Attractor Dimension

Determining attractor dimensions may be achieved using the Grassberger–Procaccia method (Grassberger & Procaccia, 1983). The goal of this method is to estimate from the measurements of a single variable sequence equally spaced in time the dimension of the attractor of the underlying dynamical system. The attractor dimension is an important characteristic that allows one to characterize the dynamics of the system without specifying the equations characterizing its time evolution. The dimensionality of a fixed-point attractor is zero, and the dimensionality of periodic motion is 1; for quasiperiodic motion, it is equal to the number of incommensurate frequencies present in the motion. As we mentioned, strange attractors usually have dimensions of fractal values. Random motion is infinitely dimensional. From knowledge of the dimension of the attractor of a dynamical system, we can thus infer whether the system is random or deterministic (where a finite dimension means that we are dealing with a deterministic system). For deterministic systems, we can also determine the number of variables necessary for the description of their time evolution. This number corresponds to the dimension of the attractor. For strange attractors that have a fractal value, the num-

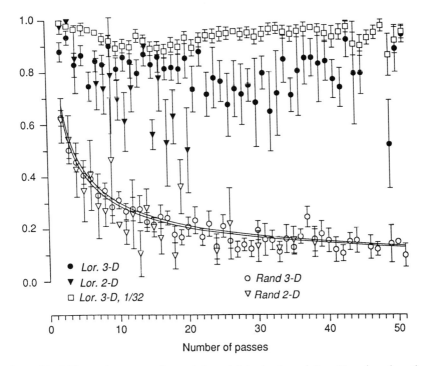

Figure 26 Difference between random and deterministic chaotic evolution. (Error bars show the standard error in the estimation of the mean. The lines show the theoretical values computed for random flights in two and three dimensions. "Lor" denotes Lorenz attractor embedded in two and three dimensions; "Rand" denotes random evolution in two and three dimensions, respectively. The open squares represent a three dimensional embedding with finer resolution. (From "Direct Test for Determinism in a Time Series" by D. T. Kaplan and L. Glass, 1992, *Physics Review Letters, 68*, p. 627–630. Copyright 1992 by American Physical Society. Reprinted by permission.)

ber of variables needed is the lowest integer higher than the dimension of the attractor.

To apply the Grassberger–Procaccia method, we first use the Takens method to embed the time signal $x(t)$ in an n-dimensional space. The points of the trajectory in this phase space have coordinates $x(t + \tau)$, $x(t + 2\tau)$, ... $x(t + n\tau)$. For each pair of points from this trajectory at times t_i and t_j we can calculate the distance between them in the phase space, which we denote as d_{ij}.

Note that all the points lie on the attractor. Let us construct a kind of spatial correlation function that measures how often a trajectory visits regions of an attractor separated by the distance R. In mathematical terms, we define this correlation function as

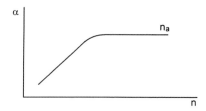

Figure 27 Plot of attractor dimension α versus embedding dimension in the Grassberger–Procaccia method.

$$C(r) = \frac{1}{N^2}\sum_{d_{ij}\leq R}1, \tag{15}$$

where N denotes the total number of accessible measurements. The formula in Equation 15 means that $C(R)$ is equal to the number of pairs of points on the trajectory whose distance does not exceed R.

It is obvious that for small values of R, $C(R)$ should vanish given that even when the trajectory visits very close points many times, it is not very probable that measurements are being made at this special instants. Moreover, for small R, $C(R)$ behaves typically as

$$C(R) \propto R^\alpha. \tag{16}$$

The exponent α is a function of the embedding dimension n. Let n_{max} denote the actual dimension of the underlying phase space in which dynamics takes place. When the embedding dimension n is smaller than n_{max}, the trajectory in n-dimensional phase space fills up a region in this space rather than producing a nontrivial shape. The exponent α depends then on the embedding dimensionality and is roughly equal to it. As we increase n, the exponent α grows until it stabilizes and attains the value of the actual dimension of the attractor n_a. n_a is smaller than n_{max} and may even take fractional values. In practice, to calculate the dimension of the attractor, we start with the low embedding dimension n and observe how the obtained α changes with the growth of n. For random signals, we observe linear growth of α with n. For deterministic signals, α stabilizes for values of n greater than the attractor dimensions n_a and takes the value n_a. To identify the attractor dimension, one typically uses graphical analysis of the plot of α versus n, as shown in Figure 27.

It should be stressed that the Grassberger–Proccacia method may also be applied to systems that undergo a combined influence of deterministic dynamics and small noise. This is the typical situation encountered in experiments and with empirical data. The main result of small noise is that it "smoothes" the structure of

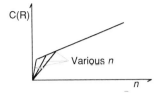

Figure 28 Plot of logarithm of C(R) versus embedding dimension n in the Grassberger–Procaccia method applied to data with noise.

attractors on small scales. In these "smoothed" areas of the phase space, all points are accessible for trajectories. As a result, the correlation function $C(R)$ for very small R is always proportional to R^n. However, for larger R, it crosses over to the dependence R^α, where the exponent α, as before, carries the information about the attractor dimension. To determine α as a function of n, one uses graphical analysis as presented in Figure 28.

VII. Conclusion

In this chapter, we have presented a very basic overview of nonlinear dynamical systems and their typical behavior. The theory of dynamical systems, although based on strict mathematical rules, allows for the use of less rigorous, intuitive, and qualitative methods. Dynamical systems show complex patterns of behavior such as chaos and rapid changes of a qualitative character. This kind of behavior is often encountered in social psychology. Social scientists have used examples of such behavior as arguments for the lack of determinism in the social sciences. However, from the perspective of modern dynamical theory, these arguments are not sound. This does not imply that in the future we will be able to write down an equation that describes completely the behavior of humans. We may, however, make use of the theory of dynamical systems in a qualitative way without evoking any specific dynamical equations. We can just look for similarities between different properties of dynamical systems and people behaving in social contexts. Still, we can learn a lot from such a perspective. In the last chapter of this book, we discuss implications for social psychology that stem from the theory of dynamical systems.

References

Anderson, P. W. (1988). *The economy as an evolving complex system* (Vol. 5). Santa Fe, NM: Santa Fe Institute. Studies in the Sciences of Complexity Proceedings Volumes No. 5, New York, Addison-Wesley.

Anderson, R. M., & May, R. M. (1991). *Infectious diseases of humans: Dynamics and control.* Oxford, England: Oxford University Press.

Arnold, V. I. (1978). *Mathematical methods of classical mechanics.* New York: Springer.

Arnold, V. I. (1983). *Geometrical methods in the theory of ordinary differential equations.* New York: Springer.

Başar E. (1990). *Chaos in brain function.* Berlin: Springer.

Batten, D., Casti, J., & Johansson (Eds.). (1987). *Lecture notes in economics and mathematical systems: Vol. 293. Economic evolution and structural adjustment.* Berlin: Springer.

Coleman, J. S. (1964). *Introduction to mathematical sociology.* New York: Free Press.

Eckmann, J. P., & Ruelle, D. (1985). Ergodic theory of chaos and strange attractors. *Review of Modern Physics, 57,* 617–656.

Glansdorff, P. & Prigogine, I. (1971). *Thermodynamic theory of structure, stability and fluctuations.* New York: Wiley.

Glass, L., & Mackey, M. C. (1988). *From clocks to chaos: The rhythms of life.* Princeton, NJ: Princeton University Press.

Gleick, J. (1987). *Chaos: The making of a new science.* New York: Viking-Penguin.

Grassberger, P., & Procaccia, I. (1983). On the characterization of strange attractors. *Physics Review Letters, 50,* 346–350.

Haken, H. (1978). *Synergetics.* Berlin: Springer.

Haken, H. (Ed.). (1982). *Order and chaos in physics, chemistry, and biology.* Berlin: Springer.

Haken, H. (1983). *Advanced synergetics.* Berlin: Springer.

Kaplan, D. T., & Glass, L. (1992). Direct test for determinism in a time series. *Physics Review Letters, 68,* 427–430.

Kelso, J. A. S. (1981). On the oscillatory basis of movement. *Bulletin of the Psychonomic Society, 18,* 63.

Kelso, J. A. S. (1984). Phase transitions and critical behavior in human bimanual coordination. *American Journal of Physiology: Regulatory, Integrative and Comparative Physiology, 15,* R1000–R1004.

Kelso, J. A. S. & DeGuzman, G. C. (1988). Order in time: How cooperation between the hands informs the design of the brain. In H. Haken (Ed.), *Neural and synergetic computers* (pp. 305–310). Berlin: Springer.

Kelso, J. A. S., Ding, M., & Schoner, G. (1991). Dynamic pattern formation: A primer. In A. B. Baskin & J. E. Mittenthal (Ed.), *Principles of organization in organisms* (pp. 397–439). New York: Addison-Wesley.

Landau, L. D., & Lifshitz, E. M. (1964). Statistical Physics. Oxford, England: Pergamon Press.

Lewenstein, M., & Nowak, A. (1989). Fully connected neural networks with self-control of noise levels. *Physics Review Letter 62,* 225–229.

Lorenz, E. (1963). Deterministic nonperiodic flow. *Journal of Atmospheric Science, 20,* 282–293.

Lotka, J. A. (1925). *Elements of physical biology.* Baltimore: Williams & Wilkins.

Mandelbrot B. B. (1982). *The fractal geometry of nature.* New York: Freeman.

May, R. M. (Ed.). (1981). *Theoretical ecology: Principles and applications.* Oxford, England: Blackwell Scientific Publications.

Moon, F. C. (1987). *Chaotic vibrations.* New York: Wiley.

Rasband, S. N. (1990). *Chaotic dynamics of nonlinear systems.* New York: Wiley.

Nowak, A., Szamrej, J., & Latané, B. (1990). From private attitude to public opinion: A dynamic theory of social impact. *Psychological Review, 97,* 362–376.

Othmer, H. G. (Ed.). (1986). Lecture notes in mathematics: Vol. 66. *Nonlinear oscillations in biology and chemistry.* Berlin: Springer.

Peitgen, H.-O., Jurgens, H., & Souppe, D. (1992). *Fractals for the classroom: I. Introduction to fractals and chaos.* Berlin: Springer.

Peitgen, H.-O., & Richter, P. H. (1986). *The beauty of fractals.* Berlin: Springer.

Peitgen, H.-O., & Souppe, D. (1988). (Eds.). *The science of fractal images.* New York: Springer.

Pomeau, Y., & Manneville, P. (1980). Intermittent transition to turbulence in dissipative dynamical systems. *Communications in Mathematical Physics, 74*, 189–197.

Poston T., & Steward I. (1978). *Catastrophe theory and its applications.* Boston: Pitman.

Ruelle, D. (1989). *Elements of differentiable dynamics and bifurcation theory.* New York: Academic Press.

Ruelle, D., & Takens, F. (1971). On the nature of turbulence. *Communications in Mathematical Physics, 20*, 167–192.

Sandefur, J. T. (1990). *Discrete dynamical systems.* Oxford, England Clarendon Press.

Schuster, H. G. (1984). *Deterministic chaos.* Vienna: Physik Verlag.

Takens, F. (1981). Detecting strange attractors in turbulescence. In D. A. Rand & L. S. Young (Eds.), *Lecture notes in mathematics:* (Vol. 898, pp. 366–381). New York: Springer.

Tesser, A. (1978). Self-generated attitude change. In L. Berkowitz (Ed.), *Advances in experimental social psychology* (Vol. 11, pp. 289–338). New York: Academic Press.

Thom, R. (1975). *Structural stability and morphogenesis.* New York: Addison-Wesley.

Thompson, J. M. T., & Steward, H. B. (1986). *Nonlinear dynamics and chaos.* New York: Wiley.

Weidlich, W. (1991). Physics and social science: The approach of synergetics. *Physics Reports 204*, 1–163.

Weidlich, W., & Haag, G. (1983). *Concepts and models of quantitative sociology.* Berlin: Springer.

Zaslavsky, G. M., & Sagdeev, R. Z. (1988). *Vvedenye v nyelinyeynuyu fizyku.* (Introduction to nonlinear physics). Moscow: Nanku.

CHAPTER 3

The New Statistical Dynamics: An Informal Look at Invariant Measures of Psychological Time Series

Arnold J. Mandell
Laboratory of Experimental
  and Constructive Mathematics
Departments of Mathematics,
  Physics, and Psychology
Florida Atlantic University
Boca Raton, Florida

Karen A. Selz
Laboratory of Experimental
  and Constructive Mathematics
Departments of Mathematics
  and Clinical Psychology Center
Florida Atlantic University
Boca Raton, Florida

I. Statistical Properties of Nonlinear Dynamical Systems
II. Is There a Single Dynamical Invariant Measure?
References

I. Statistical Properties of Nonlinear Dynamical Systems

The utility of formulations involving abstract dynamical mechanisms has become increasingly evident in a range of clinical and applied fields over the past few decades. They may now be fruitfully applied to the study of a wide range of psychological phenomena. In Chapter 1, Vallacher and Nowak provided a thoughtful and thorough justification for their use in social psychology.

The theoretical context of a new *statistical dynamics*, beyond those based on the central limit theorem, for the behavioral and brain sciences arises from a century of research involving the problems associated with finding solutions to a class of nonlinear differential equations whose solutions depend nonlinearly on parameters and time (Hirsch & Smale, 1974). Nonlinear systems, unlike the more familiar and tractable linear variety, do not demonstrate proportional stimulus–response relations. For example, they allow discontinuitous jumps ("bifurcations") to new kinds of solutions as the result of surprisingly small changes in parameters or initial conditions, as well as large parameter changes that yield no apparent change in the

Dynamical Systems in Social Psychology

observable (Gilmor, 1981). Their solutions are best described by means of the qualitative geometry of their orbits in phase space (Thompson & Stewart, 1986) using statistical measures unique to the "ergodic theory of dynamical systems" (Ruelle, 1989) and density distributions that are usually associated with variously constrained random processes (Lasota & Mackey, 1985). An intuitive example of nonlinear behavior is the effect of increasing the parameter of relevant information on a personal opinion. Our opinions generally do not change smoothly and in proportion to our knowledge of their objects. Instead, they mature in leaps and pauses, may reverse themselves any number of times with increasing or decreasing variability in response to increased receipt of information.

Sensitivity to initial conditions (STIC) is typical of the nonlinear dynamic systems of interest in neuroscience and psychology and is the property of these systems that would seem to make scientific prediction and control impossible. But, although it is certainly true that the specific path of the orbit in the phase space of a nonlinear equation may be impossible to predict, it is equally true that, given a set of parameters for a particular equation, it is often possible to obtain less directly observable "invariants of the motion," which are (on the average) systematically parameter sensitive within some range. Even though the system may generate very different specific orbital trajectories within the parametric region, the manifest statistical properties may be independent of a relatively broad set of initial conditions.

This chapter addresses the question, When and by what computational means may we say when one "messy" and "misbehaving" data source is like another? It hopes to prepare the reader to think about his or her data in the context of the new statistical dynamics.

Defining categories of equivalence among nonidentical sets is a difficult problem shared by the behavioral sciences and the mathematics of nonlinear dynamical systems. The behavior of psychologically relevant systems, like that of their representative equations, is sensitive to small changes in parameters and initial conditions. Breakthroughs came in mathematics when the topological properties of systems in motion on abstract surfaces (e.g., nearness, continuity, and sequence) were substituted for metric similarities like length or area. Imagine, for instance, that we can reversibly map the features allowing identification from a normal rabbit to one that is 7 ft tall and 1 in. in diameter. It is still generally recognizable as a rabbit. Statistical properties such those derived from partitions of divergent behavior in brain can also be used to construct such equivalence relations (Selz & Mandell, 1991a). That is, we can call two systems behaviorally equivalent (with some constraints) if we can smoothly deform the observable of one into that of the other, leaving rank or relative position invariant. (See Chapter 8 for a more detailed treatment of this topic.)

Because the relevant equations are not solvable using analytic methods (so specific solutions cannot be compared), it is through the use of interactive computing that some techniques for determining similarities between apparently different dynamical objects have emerged (see Baker & Gollub, 1990 and Devaney, 1990 for some useful computer algorithms in this area). The use of unobvious, global invariants "of the motion" of a system or system of equations or human subject under observation is not unknown to phenomenological psychology (e.g., in psychopathology).

Bleuler (1911) identified "dynamical invariants of the behavior" in a definable set of schizophrenic patients: autism, ambivalence, flattened affect, and associative abnormalities. Bleuler claimed these deep properties could be inferred from clinical behavior across large individual variations with respect to the more dramatic "secondary" symptoms such as hallucinations, delusions, uncontrollable excitement, and catatonia (i.e., more superficial observables).

Although the popular writing on the subject of chaos has emphasized the "butterfly effect" (i.e., STIC) of the Lorenz equations about weather (i.e., even a butterfly's perturbation of conditions amplified through the system's chaotic dynamics markedly reduces the predictability of weather systems), the remarkable aspect of such systems is their stability with respect to a definable set of deep quantifiable properties. The issue of representativeness of global description is usually dealt with under the aegis of stability and genericity (typicalness) in nonlinear differential equations (Arnold, 1983). Orbital equivalence is regarded as too strict a requirement, whereas dynamical categories based on statistical properties, such as the average directional divergence rates of nearby initial conditions, appear to be useful.

Psychological, psychometric science works at being insensitive to superficial variation in just this way. Again, using psychopathology, the compulsive hand washer may not wash all the time; in fact, he may do so only intermittently. Whether he will be scrubbing next Tuesday at 2:00 P.M. is anybody's guess. We come to know the persistent, statistical, dynamic properties of the system that withstand its time-dependent, unpredictable details. We then, implicitly and explicitly, base our hypotheses and experimental examinations on these deep (higher-order) characteristics.

We will discuss four such unobvious, statistical properties of dynamical systems, give examples of each from basic and clinical neurobiological science, and then argue that all of them may be aspects of one very general and important characteristic, the system's entropy. A rather surprising set of theorems from the mathematics of complex systems suggests that there may exist only one invariant of a system like the brain, which generates information continually, although its expression may take a number of (nonindependent) forms (Ruelle, 1978, 1989). Although rigorously defined, both in the language of abstract dynamics and computer algorithms, intuitive ideas about these measure-theoretic entropies of the brain and their equivalents may be a more fundamental property than the better-known, cross-disciplinary ideas in brain and behavior such as "arousal" (Gray, 1987; Hebb, 1955), "attention" (Adrian, Bremer, & Jasper, 1954; Spitzer, Desimone, &

Moran, 1988), "psychic energy" (Brenner, 1955), and perhaps clinical description of the flexibility and/or rigidity of personality (Kets de Vries & Perzow, 1991).

A. The Decorrelation, Relaxation Time, τ

An example of a deep property, quantifiably inferable from the behavior of a complex system, is its characteristic *fluctuation and relaxation time*. We label a system's characteristic time using the abstract label τ rather than some specific t because there is no single time t across the disciplines of the brain sciences. The relevant time in brain and behavior is determined by the local clock. Interspike intervals may be in milliseconds, and the half-life of brain proteins can range from minutes to months. A variety of statistical physics research programs have shown that τ in all of its forms (including the [auto]correlation function, $C[\tau]$), is an important invariant of a nonlinear system (Reichl, 1981).

What we mean by *fluctuation and relaxation time*, τ, is, in the time metric appropriate to the system, how long it takes for the system to settle down to its average value in the presence of its spontaneous motions (fluctuations) or (roughly) its equivalent after perturbation. In passing, we note that this idea led to the successful demonstration of the similarities between the "wave length," *t*, of the electroencephalographic voltage fluctuations and a characteristic time, τ, of auditory or visual evoked potentials in the same human subjects (Başar, Durusan, Gouder, & Ungan, 1979).

In the context of this invariant property, Lennox, Gibbs, and Gibbs (1942) concluded that the individual difference characteristics of the time-dependent wave form distributions of the electroencephalogram (EEG) were more reliable than IQ, as reliable as weight or height, and nearly as reliable as fingerprints in determining the ovularity of twins. Although the biophysical mechanisms in the generation of the EEG remain conjectural (Nunez, 1981), the relations between the time structure (inverse frequencies) of the brain wave patterns and global states of consciousness in both sleep and awakeness are beyond debate. Brain wave patterns as "brain times" are good examples of a global dynamical pattern being reliably characteristic in the absence of knowledge of the generators or their mechanisms.

If we had a time series of observables, ΣO_{tn}, such as interpersonal contacts or skin conductance, we could ask the question, How big must *n* be such that the mean value and/or the average deviation from the mean value "settled down," $\tau = f(n)$? Here, the central limit theorem, requiring the statistics be done on a series of independent events, fails because nearest neighbors in a sequence have relations in nonlinear, highly coupled systems, such as those studied in psychology and the neurosciences. Slowly converging or nonconverging density distributions may be found as a result (Lasota & Mackey, 1985). It is in this way that statistical methods with the assumption of the central limit theorem may fail.

A major lesson that the study of deterministic dynamics with chaotic behavior has taught us is that apparently random behavior can have unapparent low-dimensional structure that supports (noisy) long-range correlations (Ottino, 1989). This is not true for the idealized but not physically realizable chaotic attractor (called a *horseshoe* for technical reasons) that is so thoroughly mixing (i.e., disordering in the series of sampled points in a recurrent orbit when compared with a sequentially ordered periodic process) that its correlation functions decay exponentially in a way that is indiscriminable from a purely random process.

Real psychological and biological behavioral systems, with nonuniform velocities across different sections of the observation period (imagine the behavior of the individual contributions of several participants involved in a conversation), mix nonuniformly so that the (auto)correlation function $C(\tau)$ decays not exponentially but rather as a fractional (fractal) stretched exponential, e^{-tB} ($0 < B < 1$) or even slower, as a fractional exponential power of time, t^{-B}, (n^{-B}) (Shlesinger, 1988). The quantity, B, describing a convergence rate slower than that seen in a random system, is a stretching exponent or fractional power of time and serves as an invariant of the dynamical system, $C(\tau) \cong 1/B$. (See Chapter 8 for an experimental example.) Fourier (power spectral) transformation of autocorrelation functions from EEG time series demonstrate a hierarchy of modes consistent with this power law decay of correlations (Mandell & Selz, 1992).

The loss of a hierarchy of times in brain function with the emergence of a single characteristic τ may have implications for the "health" of the system. Studies of normal postural tremor generate power-spectral distributions (i.e., frequency histograms) with a hierarchy of times (with amplitudes inverse to frequencies; Musha, 1981), whereas the $\cong 4$ Hz tremor in the Parkinson syndrome establishes a single dominant τ. Also, the change in the EEG with epileptic syndromes is from a hierarchy of brain wave frequencies to domination by a single periodic rhythm. Moreover, there is similar loss of a multiplicity of characteristic times in cardiac interbeat interval in some syndromes of sudden cardiac death (Goldberger, Bhavgava, West, & Mandell, 1986). Similarly, the onset of paranoid states is marked by the transition from multifrequency, large variations in thought content to the single frequency, finite time limit cycle or fixed point of perseveration in rigid, delusional thoughts (see, e.g., Millon, 1981).

B. The Dispersion and Mixing Rate, $\overline{\lambda}$

Imagine a handful of initial conditions as nearby dots dropped at the bottom of a hill and a function f pushing them up and down a hilly terrain in which the slope of the hill(s) defines the velocity of the dots' motion. We can imagine that in going up a hillside with a gradually decreasing incline, the velocity of the dots would decrease, $f'' < 0$ and they would bunch up. Let the tendency for points to converge on each other be symbolized by $\bar{\lambda} < 0 = \bar{\lambda}(-)$. On the other hand, going down a hillside with a gradually increasing slope, the dots would increase their speed, $f'' > 0$, and spread out, $\bar{\lambda} > 0 = \bar{\lambda}(+)$. Most of us have seen this happen when we follow a line of big trucks (with a limit on their functional energy) through a chain of mountains. Because the velocity is never constant, $f' \neq 0$, the second derivative, f'' (the rate of change of the velocity or the acceleration), goes from negative to positive and back again, passing through zero, $f'' = 0$, at what is called a *critical point*, $\bar{\lambda} = 0 = \bar{\lambda}(0)$, at this locus of dynamical instability. Perturbing a system when it is speeding up does not change the fact that it is speeding up; perturbing a system when its slowing down is also stable against an induced change in the direction of acceleration. It is at the points where the second derivative is zero, however, that small perturbations may be translated into large changes in the dynamics as a result of the possibility of forcing a change in the sign of the acceleration, $f'' = 0 \rightarrow < 0$ or > 0 (e.g., Jordan & Smith, 1977).

A definitional property of nonlinear systems is their nonuniform response to the same force or stimulus, their behavior being a function of their location and velocity in phase space when encountering the influence on their motions. These systems move along their orbits on a manifold (an at least locally Euclidean surface) with uneven velocity, like the trucks. In some regions, the orbit may accelerate so fast under the action of a episodic external influence as to almost jump to a new position, spreading out nearby points as it goes, resulting from the action of $\bar{\lambda}(+)$. In other regions, they may be seen to slow down and clump up under the action of $\bar{\lambda}(-)$ in the neighborhood of the critical point.

In these critical regions, the "saddle" points of the system are subject to the simultaneous influences of $\bar{\lambda}(+)$ and $\bar{\lambda}(-)$ as generalized Lyapounov exponents, describing the characteristic expanding actions on the unstable manifold, $\bar{\lambda}(+)$, and the contracting actions on the stable manifold, $\bar{\lambda}(-)$. What started as a single file, well-ordered set of moving points "curdles" as the orbits slow down and gather together around unstable fixed points of conflicting influence. They wiggle, shuffle, mix, lose their order, and then break lose on their journey toward another unstable fixed point and another episode of shuffling. It is obvious that two labeled points starting out together could come to be very far apart when studied over many journeys through the system. It is this "mixing property" that leads to STIC and the orbital indeterminacy that has made the unpredictability aspect of dynamical systems so prominent (Ruelle, 1989).

There is another and equally psychologically relevant side to this story, however. Although the point-mixing process is going on along with global "stretching and folding," the latter so as to put the orbit back onto the bounded manifold, a thin ribbon of mixed points is being shaped into a many-looped invariant structure as the influence of $\bar{\lambda}(-)$ "irons down" the shuffle-wrinkled orbit onto the $\bar{\lambda}(+)$-stretched, unique geometry that we recognize as the "unstable-manifold" attractor of chaos, each with a signatory structure. Mixing of sequential order leaves invariant the geometric structure (the *attractor of initial conditions*). The existence and stability of this and similar kinds of dynamical objects may turn out to be a major contribution of mathematical physics to the fields of behavior and brain.

Of major interest with respect to behavioral sciences is the apparently paradoxical fact that the expanding, disorganizing influence, $\overline{\lambda}(+)$, becomes the stable geometric structure of the system and statistical dynamical measures of $\overline{\lambda}$ (and τ) on it are invariant with respect to initial conditions. $\overline{\lambda}(-)$, meanwhile, becomes invisible, observed only indirectly through its smoothing influence on the orbital bundle of the attractor, generated by $\overline{\lambda}(+)$. (See Moon, 1987, for an accessible treatment with many physical examples and Ottino, 1989, for helpful pictures.)

Increased apparent randomness (i.e., mixing) in the form of increased "arousal" is associated with improved and more reliable perceptual, motor, and integrative task performance to some point (usually an inverted U shaped relation) and has been demonstrated repeatedly in psychological and psychophysiological studies over the decades (Duffy, 1962). We argue that the long-lasting problem of measurement with respect to "diagnosing arousal" from a time series of psychophysiological or behavioral observables might benefit from the four measures discussed in this chapter. The globally stable, yet locally mixing patterns of $\overline{\lambda}(+)$ dynamics can be viewed as a better search algorithm for "broadening" attentional stimulus-dependent tasks (Bergen & Julesz, 1983; Spitzer et al., 1988) and a randomizing eraser for irrelevant solutions (i.e., "narrowing"; Moran & Desimone, 1985). In these contexts of the cognitive neuropsychology of visual perception, the attentional variables associated with brainstem–neocortical arousal states have been demonstrated to have both effects.

The absence or impairment of mixing dynamics would then be expected to lead to loss of neurobiological relaxation and, in fact, can be shown to result in a global tendency for behavioral preservation, which Geschwind called *stickiness* in his temporal lobe epileptic patients (Benson & Blumer, 1975). That is, the dominant τ extends, becoming protracted and potentially maladaptive. Equally troublesome is a dominant short τ, with little or no memory. This sort of impairment in disengaging attentional focus has been reported following thalamic (pulvinar) damage in monkeys, as reflected in delays in attention-switching tasks (Petersen, Robinson, & Morris, 1987).

The more technical name for $\overline{\lambda}$ is the *(Lyapounov) characteristic exponent.* (See Chapter 2 for a more formal treatment of $\overline{\lambda}$.) As usually computed on real data, it represents the logarithm of the average rate of divergence of nearby orbits (Grassberger & Procaccia, 1983; Landa & Rosenblum, 1991; Wolf, Swift, Swinney, & Vastano, 1985). Determined globally by both the influences of the stable, $\overline{\lambda}(-)$ (converging to a fixed point or orbit), and unstable, $\overline{\lambda}(+)$ (diverging from a fixed point or orbit), tendencies of the motion, the resultant $\overline{\lambda}$ is an invariant of the system with respect to initial conditions. The simultaneous influences of stabilizing, $\overline{\lambda} < 0$, and unstabilizing, $\overline{\lambda} > 0$, with no $\overline{\lambda} = 0$, is called *hyperbolic stability.* This new concept has replaced that of feedback-regulated homeostasis and has played an important role in understanding how systems that mix their sequential order can manifest invariants of motion as well as stable, recognizable phase space geometries (i.e., attractors). We have measured $\overline{\lambda}$ from time series of neuronal interspike intervals (Selz & Mandell, 1991b), and several studies have used these measures on the EEG (Babloyantz & Destexhe, 1986; 1986; Mandell & Selz, 1992; Rapp et al., 1989).

Again, recalling that the characteristic time, τ, is lengthened in systems with correlated sequences, that is, with slower than random decay of $C(\tau)$, then it follows naturally that the greater the mixing as reflected in the $\overline{\lambda}$ measure of STIC, the smaller will be the τ. In fact, with a pure, physically unrealistic, uniformly hyperbolically mixing system, the behavior on a $\{0,1\}$ partition over the range of values cannot be discriminated from the behavior of a fair coin and is called a *Bernoulli process*, with autocorrelations that decay exponentially. In other words, if we recode our sequence of events into any binary code (e.g., {on,off}, {high,low}, {open,close}), then uniformly expanding deterministic behavior cannot be distinguished from the random binary sequence of a coin toss. That is, uniformly hyperbolic behavior can be modeled by Poisson processes, for example. We have found generally, however, that neurobiological systems are not uniformly hyperbolic, are not uniformly expanding, and can be discriminated from random systems even though they have small positive values for $\overline{\lambda}$ with, generally, $\overline{\lambda}(+) \cong 1/\tau$ (Eckmann & Ruelle, 1985). We have used deviations from a Bernoulli process (and therefore from exponential relaxation) as a measure of the amount of nonuniformity in the dynamics of single-neuron discharge patterns (Selz & Mandell, 1991a).

It has been a major theme in our work (Mandell, 1981; 1987; Mandell & Shlesinger, 1990; Selz & Mandell, 1992) that the decrease in the value of $\overline{\lambda}(+)$ in a behavior or brain-regulated system indicates a loss of STIC and often reflects resulting defects in adaptive flexibility. Habituation and desensitization in an array of psychological and neurobiological systems is associated with a loss of the randomizing influence of $\overline{\lambda}(+)$. Emergent dominant periodicity in the resting record and reduced responsiveness to perturbation (i.e., loss of adaptive flexibility) seem to be correlated in many behavioral systems. The difference between nearly periodic, circadian behavior and periodic behavior in a psychologically or biologically relevant observable may be the difference between health and disease.

C. Generating Dynamical Complexities, H_T and H_M

It is not too far from intuition to imagine a division of the rate of creative action in a system between generating new possibilities (trajectories) of behavior, H_T, and (re)distributing the membership (probabilities) among the already existing ones, H_M. H_T is called the *topological entropy*, and H_M is called the *metric entropy*.

Intuitively, with respect to brain and behavior, they mean somewhat different things. A reported sequence of thoughts that tended to expand into new ideas and creative insights might be described by a dynamical system with $H_T > 0$. One might already guess that one estimate of H_T is $\log \overline{\lambda}(+)$. (See Alekseev & Yakobson, 1981; Ruelle, 1989) for the clearest explication of these issues.) A reported stream of consciousness that maximized H_M, on the other hand, would sort through already existing possibilities, spending about as much time with each or visiting each about as often as any other, avoiding the emergence of a dominant one or the exploration of new ideas. Again, drawing on pathological behavior, we might imagine that the free-wheeling thinking of mania would show an elevated H_T, whereas the depressive thought style would show increased H_M and decreased H_T with respect to thought contents.

These ideas emerged from the great Russian mathematician, Kolmogorov (1958), whose solution to a measure theory problem involved invariants of systems that were generating complexity. The original unsolved question was innocent sounding enough: In a sequence of coin tosses, prove which would lead to a more random series, a two- or three-sided coin? Kolmogorov invoked the Shannon entropy expression, $H = -\Sigma p_i \log p_i$ (the minus is in front just so H will come out positive). Assuming both coins were fair, he simply computed that $(.5 \times \log .5) + (.5 \times \log .5) = 0.398$, whereas $(.333 \times \log .333) + (.333 \times \log .333) + (.333 \times \log .333) = 0.434$. Thus, the three-sided coin would generate a "more random" (i.e., higher entropy) sequence. We can also infer that generally, H, (H_T), increases with the number of possibilities (as the number of additive $p_i \log p_i$ terms increases), and, with a little computation, we can show how equal distribution of probabilities among a given set possibilities leads to the highest values of H_M. Said another way, equating complexity with entropy, we could say that complexity decreases with decreases in possibilities and increases with the equipartitioning of probabilities among a given set of possible categorical states of the system. It is also clear that a maximal (supremum) estimate of H is H_T, and an infimum estimate is H_M; $H_M \leq H \leq H_T$. (See Katok, Kneiper, Pollicott, & Weiss, 1990, for recent results and references.)

The applications of measures of loss of complexity such as H_T and H_M appear promising. We have recently related this kind of entropy decrement to the neurobiological aging process due to the loss of desynchronizing neurons from the reticular formation and biogenic amine systems, and we suggest that drugs may place the whole system into a parameter region of greater $\overline{\lambda}(+)$ such that cell loss might be compensated for by a global increase in the complexity of the dynamics (Mandell & Shlesinger, 1990). Selz (1992) reported personality-related and demographic differences in H_M in the context of simple, computer-gamelike tasks.

Intuitively, it is easy to imagine a decrease in complexity measures in the EEG in cases of epileptic spiking, a decrease in complexity of the motions of a dominant resting tremor in Parkinson's disease, and (more abstractly) a decrease in the pathogenic aspects of stereotyped and compulsive reductions in behavioral complexity in a wide variety of disorders. Chronicity, for example, seems to bring entropy decrement in most relevant observables.

Paulus, Geyer, Gold, and Mandell (1990) used the H_T and H_M measures on the patterns of exploratory behavior of rats. They used these techniques to discriminate among an array of amphetamine congeners, with the number of behavioral events per time unit held constant. They used the rat paths themselves to generate the divided pattern on the floor of the observation cage into i partitions and used a variety of ergodic measure-theoretic techniques to compute temporal-spatial measures of H_T and H_M. This program currently involves the systematic measurement of the complexity generation or reduction by a variety of psychopharmacological agents and has become a quite subtle discriminator of drug family subtypes. The partition of the space of observables is critical because this can powerfully influence the measure-theoretic entropies.

D. Nonuniformity, $\overline{\mathfrak{A}}$ in Complexity Generation

A common characteristic of a time series of observables in living systems has been called *bursting*. The distribution of interspike intervals of neurons, for instance, demonstrates "shorts" and "longs," and the time series may manifest "runs" of shorts followed by irregular series of shorts and longs before another run of short interevent times starts again. Dopamine, norepinephrine, and serotonin containing cells of the brainstem manifest different characteristic patterns of bursting behavior (Selz & Mandell, 1991a). Patterns of hormone release from pituitary cells in perifusion systems also demonstrate what dynamical systems researchers call *intermittency* in the healthy cells and emergent periodicity in similar tumor cell preparations (Guillemin, Brazeau, Briskin, & Mandell, 1983).

As mentioned, a characteristic property of deterministic, intermittent systems is the growth of the variance of the interspike intervals with n. This is a demonstration of the failure of the central limit theorem. A Poisson random process may be discriminated from a deterministically intermittent one with the knowledge that the random single-parameter distribution converges such that the mean $\cong$ variance in the random process but diverges in the intermittent one. One might argue that intermittency is a more natural pattern of behavior in signal-sensitive psychological and biological systems than either randomness, which is difficult or impossible to achieve, or periodicity, which we have argued indicates desensitization and, often, pathology.

Once we have observed that a system's behavior is intermittent, we must adjust our predictions about its future behavior away from those implied by the finite variance on which we can no longer count. It is counterintuitive but generally true that the observation of an extreme value in a (nonlinear) intermittent system is more likely to be followed by another extreme value of the observable than the usual "regression toward the mean" anticipated of independent, random systems with an attractive central limit. (See Montroll & Badger, 1974, for clear and relevant descriptions of density distributions with long and even nonconvergent tails.) One way to think about this is that if a complex, cooperative system has come together to produce an unlikely event at a particular time, its neighboring times will be dense in this event as well. An absence of such an event would suggest that neighboring times will be missing it as well. As described above, bursting may occur as a pattern of activity riding on the slow fluctuations in cooperativity in the underlying elements at the next time scale. This constitutes a theory of the source of the hierarchical frequency composition of the power spectra of complex systems (see Scher, Shlesinger, & Bendler, 1991, for a nontechnical development).

Alcohol and drug abuse and compulsive gambling may come in binges before becoming chronic and have been definitively associated with the syndromes of mood disorder (see this clearly developed in Goodwin & Jamison, 1990). Other aspects of comorbidity syndromes such as character disorder and psychopathic behavioral decompensation appear intermittent as well, as predicted by the confluence of disorders on several time scales. Generally, the pattern of occurrence of what might be called *high amplitude, rare events* may deserve more attention with respect to characterizing a system. What may be called the *rhythm of finger drumming* may be a more common natural neurobiological rhythm than is generally acknowledged.

Measures directed toward the characterization of intermittent behavior have been of serious interest to physicists and engineers studying hydrodynamic turbulence. Although, at first glance, the statistical dynamics of turbulence (Tennekes & Lumley, 1972) appears far afield from psychology, we have found that it is generally the best of the available physical metaphors for the complicated, sometimes unpredictable systems of interest. That is, the ability of an "infinite" dimensional system to self-organize under the influence of a single generalized parameter, such as flow velocity or complexity, into relatively stable patterns might help explain humans' rather impressive functioning, as well as supply us with models of global failure to function.

It was long a mystery how water flowing at a constant rate past a rock (or at fixed parameters in laboratory experiments) could generate vortices intermittently, either singularly or in batches. Why, with no change in parameters, would the system demonstrate periods of quiet flow alternating irregularly with periods of turbulent flow? Of the statistical measures, the fourth moment, called *kurtosis* (the flatness of the distribution indicating the presence of symmetrical outliers), is commonly used as a descriptor of this sort of system. We have recently made use of the kurtosis and the growth rate of the longest run (in a binary partition over n) to differentiate the interspike interval patterns of bursting neurons of different types

(Selz & Mandell, 1991a). The statistical pattern of intermittency has alternatively been studied in physical systems as anomalous diffusion (Geisel & Nierwetberg, 1984; Shlesinger & Klafter, 1987).

A deeper treatment of intermittency involves a quantification of the difference between the maximum and minimum entropies given that, by definition, maximal entropy for a partition must be closer to uniform occupancy of the possibilities than the minimum. We have been somewhat successful in our use of $|H_T - H_M| = \overline{\mathfrak{A}}$ to characterize nonuniform dynamics in neuronal firing patterns, as well as the variance of the distribution of intermediate values in a Lyapounov computation, $\rho(\overline{\lambda})$, (Nicolis, Meyer-Kress, & Haubs, 1983), to capture the intermittent, nonuniformity property of dopamine and serotonin neurons (Mandell & Kelso, 1991).

II. Is There a Single Dynamical Invariant Measure?

Questions about the "globality" of arousal-like psychophysiological and biochemical observables in relation to behavioral states have been researched and discussed from the days of James (1884) and Pavlov (1927). In this case, debates involving intensity versus specificity have gone unresolved (Duffy, 1962; Gale & Edwards, 1983; Schacter & Singer, 1962). An analogous problem exists with respect to the relation between the four measures discussed earlier when applied to real brain and behavioral observables. In even abstract and idealized mathematical systems, it is a difficult (and as yet incomplete) job to formally prove relations between the four deep characteristics of nonlinear dynamical systems' time series described here (Katok, 1980; Katok et al, 1990; Ornstein & Weiss, 1991).

It is, however, pleasingly intuitive to use the episodic "shuffling property" (i.e., conflict in the vicinity of an attractive, repelling fixed point) as a metamechanism to demonstrate how it might be that the augmentation of this property increases $\overline{\lambda}(+), H_T$, and H_M and decreases τ. The nonuniformity of the shuffling of orbital points in phase space would determine $\overline{\mathfrak{A}}$. One might think about growing $\overline{\mathfrak{A}}$ as the beginning of organization in a strong shuffling system that previously produced an independent set of random observables. The first signs of its organization would be a reduction in the rate of shuffling and the resulting "curdling" of point-set organization and would result in intermittency in the time-dependent observables (Mandelbrot, 1982). That is, $\overline{\lambda}$ and H would decrease, and τ would increase as the system curdled into the slowly decaying episodic order of intermittency. Islands of (complexly) ordered phenomena around less-ordered behavior in a nonrandom, but difficult to predict deterministic pattern may be more natural than trigonometric functions describing periodicity in the modeling of psychological phenomena.

Acknowledgments

The authors wish to acknowledge the support of the Office of Naval Research, sections on Biological Intelligence and Systems Biophysics.

References

Adrian, E. D., Bremer, F., & Jasper, H. H. (1954). *Brain mechanisms and consciousness.* Springfield, IL: Charles C Thomas.

Alekseev, V. M., & Yakobson, M. V. (1981). Symbolic dynamics and hyperbolic dynamic systems. *Physics Reports, 75,* 287–325.

Arnold, V. I. (1983). Geometrical Methods in the Theory of Ordinary Differential Equations (pp. 87–141). New York: Springer-Verlag.

Babloyantz, A., & Destexhe, A. (1986). Low dimensional chaos in an instance of epilepsy. *Proceedings of the National Academy of Science U.S.A., 83,* 3513–3517.

Baker, G. L., & Gollub, J. P. (1990). *Chaotic dynamics: An introduction.* Cambridge, MA: Cambridge University Press.

Başar E., Durusan R., Gouder A., & Ungan P. (1979). Combined dynamics of EEG and evoked potentials. *Biological Cybernetics, 34,* 21–30.

Benson, D. F., & Blumer, D. (1975). *Psychiatric aspects of neurologic disease.* New York: Grune & Statton.

Bergen, J. R., & Julesz, B. (1983). Rapid discrimination of visual patterns. *IEEE Trans. Systems Man. Cybernet., 13,* 857–866.

Bleuler, E. P. (1911). *Dementia praecox or the group of schizophrenias.* New York: International Universities Press.

Brenner, C. (1955). *An elementary textbook of psychoanalysis.* New York: Anchor.

Devaney, R. L. (1990). *Chaos, fractals, and dynamics: Computer experiments in mathematics.* Reading, MA: Addison-Wesley.

Duffy, E. (1962). *Activation and behavior.* New York: Wiley.

Eckmann, J.-P., & Ruelle, D. (1985). Ergodic theory of chaos and strange attractors. *Review of Modern Physics, 57,* 617–655.

Gale, A., & Edwards, J. A. (1983). Psychophysiology and individual differences. *Australian Journal of Psychology, 35,* 361–379.

Geisel, T., Nierwetberg, J. (1984). Statistical properties of intermittent diffusion in chaotic systems. *Z. Phys. B., 56,* 59–68.

Gilmore, R. (1981). *Catastrophe theory for scientists and engineers.* New York: Wiley.

Goldberger, A. L., Bhargava, V., West, B. J., & Mandell, A. J. (1986). Some observations on the question: Is ventricular fibrillation chaos? *Physica, 19D,* 282–289.

Goodwin, F. K., & Jamison, K. R. (1990). *Manic–depressive illness.* New York: Oxford University Press.

Grassberger P., & Procaccia, I. (1983). Measuring the strangeness of strange attractors. *Physica, 9D,* 183–208.

Gray, J. A. (1987). *The psychology of fear and stress.* Cambridge, England: Cambridge University Press.

Guillemin R. C., Brazeau P., Briskin A., & Mandell A. J. (1983). Evidence for synergetic dynamics in a mammalian pituitary cell perifusion system. In E. Bazar, H. Flohr, H. Haken, & A. J. Mandell (Eds.), *Synergetics in the brain* (pp. 365–376). New York: Springer-Verlag.

Hebb, D. O. (1955). Drives and the conceptual nervous system. *Psych. Rev., 62,* 243–254.

Hirsch, M. W., & Smale, S. (1974). *Differential equations, dynamical systems, and linear algebra*. New York: Academic Press.

James, W. (1884). What is emotion? *Mind, 9*, 188–205.

Jordon, D. W., & Smith, P. (1977). *Nonlinear ordinary differential equations*. Oxford, England: Clarendon.

Kolmogorov, A. N. (1954). General theory of dynamical systems and classical mechanics. In *Proceeding of the International Congress of Mathematics* (pp. 315–333). Amsterdam: North Holland.

Katok, A. (1980). Lyapounov exponents, entropy and periodic orbits for diffeomorphisms. *Publ. Math. Inst. Hautes E'tudes Sci., 51*, 137–173.

Katok, A., Kneiper, G., Pollicott, M., & Weiss, H., (1990). Differentiability of entropy for anosov and geodesic flows. *Bull. Am. Math. Soc., 22*, 285–294.

Kets de Vries, M. F. R., & Perzow, S. (1991). *Handbook of character studies: Psychoanalytic explorations*. Madison, CT: International Universities Press.

Landa, P. S., & Rosenblum, M. (1991). Time series analysis for system identification and diagnostics. *Physica, D48*, 232–254.

Lasota, A., & Mackey, M. C. (1985). *Probabalistic properties of deterministic systems*. Cambridge, England: Cambridge University Press.

Lennox, W. G., Gibbs, F. A., & Gibbs, E. L. (1942). Twins, brainwaves and epilepsy. *Arch Neurol Psychiat., 47*, 702–723.

Mandelbrot, B. B. (1982). *The fractal geometry of nature*. San Francisco, CA: Freeman.

Mandell, A. J. (1981). Statistical stability in random brain systems. *Adv Subst Abuse, 2*, 299–341.

Mandell, A. J. (1987). Dynamical complexity and pathological order in the cardiac monitoring problem. *Physica, 27D*, 235–242.

Mandell, A. J., & Kelso, J. A. S. (1991). Neurobiological coding in nonuniform times. In J. A. Ellison & H. Uberall (Eds.), *Essays on classical and quantum dynamics* (pp. 203–236). New York: Gordon & Beach.

Mandell, A. J., & Selz, K. A. (1992). Period adding, hierarchical protein modes and electroenchephalo-graphically defined states of consciousness. In S. Vohra, W. L. Ditto, M. F. Shlesinger, & L. Pecora (Eds.), *First experimental chaos conference* (pp. 175–193). Singapore: World Scientific.

Mandell A. J., & Shlesinger M. F. (1990), Lost choices: Parallelism and topological entropy decrements in neurobiological aging. In S. Krassner (Ed.), *The ubiquity of chaos* (pp. 000–000). Washington, DC: American Association for the Advancement of Science.

Millon, T. (1981). *Disorders of personality DSM–III Axis II*. New York: Wiley.

Montroll, E. W., & Badger, W. W. (1974). *Introduction to quantitative aspects of social phenomena*. New York: Gordon & Breach.

Moon, F. C. (1987). *Chaotic vibrations*. New York: Wiley.

Moran, J., & Desimone, R. (1985). Selective attention gates visual processing in the extrastriate cortex. *Science, 229*, 782–784.

Musha, T. (1981). 1/f Fluctuations in biological systems. *NBS Special Publication, 614,*

Nicolis, J. S., Meyer-Kress, G., & Haubs, G. (1983). Non-uniform chaotic dynamics with implications to information processing. *Z. Naturforsch., 38a*, 1157–1169.

Nunez, P. L. (1981). *Electric fields of the brain*. New York: Oxford University Press.

Ornstein, D. S., & Weiss, B. (1991). Statistical properties of chaotic systems. *Bulletin of the American Mathematics Society 24*, 11–116.

Ottino, J. M. (1989). *The kinematics of mixing: Stretching, chaos and transport*. Cambridge, England: Cambridge University Press.

Paulus, M. P., Geyer, M. A., Gold, L. H., & Mandell, A. J. (1990). Ergodic measures of complexity in rat exploratory behavior. *Proceedings of the National Academy of Science, 87*, 723–727.

Pavlov, I. P. (1927). *An investigation of the physiological activity of the cerebral cortex*. New York: Dover.

Petersen, S., Robinson, D. L., & Morris, J. D. (1987). Contributions of the pulvinar to visual spatial attention. *Neuropsychologia, 25*, 97–113.

Rapp, P. E., Bashore, T. R., Martinerie, J. M., Albano, A. M., Zimmerman, I. D., & Mees, A. I. (1989). Dynamics of brain electrical activity. *Brain Topography, 2,* 99–118.

Reichl, L. E. (1981). *A modern course in statistical physics.* Austin: University of Texas Press.

Ruelle, D. (1978). *Thermodynamic formalism.* New York: Addison-Wesley.

Ruelle, D. (1989). *Chaotic evolution and strange attractors.* Cambridge, England: Cambridge University Press.

Schacter, S., & Singer, J. E. (1962). Cognitive, social and physiological determinants of emotional state. *Psychological Review, 69,* 379–399.

Scher, H., Shlesinger, M. F., & Bendler, J. T. (1991). Time scale invariance in transport and relaxation. *Physics Today, 43,* 26–34.

Selz, K. A. (1992). *Mixing properties in human behavioral style and time dependencies in behavior identification: The modeling and application of a universal dynamical law.* Unpublished doctoral dissertation, UMI.

Selz, K. A., & Mandell, A. J. (1991a). Bernoulli Partition equivalence of intermittent neuronal discharge patterns. *International Journal of Bifurcation and Chaos, 1*(3) 717–721.

Selz, K. A., & Mandell, A. J. (1991b). Critical coherence and characteristic times in brain stem neuronal discharge patterns. In T. McKenna, J. Davis, & S. Zornetzer (Eds.), *Single neuron computation.* New York: Academic Press.

Shlesinger, M. F. (1988). Fractal time in condensed matter. *Annual Review of Physical Chemistry, 38,* 269–290.

Shlesinger, M. F., & Klafter, J. (1985). Comment on accelerated diffusion in Josephson junctions and related chaotic systems. *Physics Review Letter, 54,* 2551.

Spitzer, H., Desimone, R., & Moran, J. (1988). Increased attention enhances both behavioral and neuronal performance. *Science, 140,* 338–340.

Tennekes, H., & Lumley, J. L. (1972). *A first course in turbulence.* Cambridge, MA: MIT Press.

Thompson, J. M. T., & Stewart, H. B. (1986). *Nonlinear dynamics and chaos.* New York: Wiley.

Wolf, A., Swift, J. B., Swinney, H. L., & Vastano, J. A. (1985). Determining Lyapounov spectra from a time series. *Physica, 16D,* 285–317.

CHAPTER 4

New Mathematical Techniques for Pattern Recognition

Franklin E. Schroeck, Jr.

Department of Mathematics
Florida Atlantic University
Boca Raton, Florida

I. Introduction

There is presently a great interest in the social sciences in introducing very new and sophisticated mathematical techniques into the field. The excitement in this is a consequence of two things: the paucity of results using older mathematical methods on the complex situations arising in the social sciences and the surprising power and range of applicability in unexpected areas of methods of mathematics that have recently evolved. This same phenomenon is also occurring in psychology, neurobiology, physics, computer science, and engineering. Catchwords include *dynamical systems, nonlinear systems, coherent states, neural networks, wavelets,* and *chaos.* Also coming into vogue in the social sciences and psychology is a much older mathematical technique termed *Fourier analysis.*

With this myriad of new methods available, the nonmathematician with some mathematical talent, when exposed to the beauties of one of these subjects, is likely to work very hard within his or her own field to show how that single method may be applied. The problem is that if this single method is advocated by

Dynamical Systems in Social Psychology

a sufficiently powerful authority, then it may dominate the field, even when it is far less appropriate than alternative methods for specific applications.

Of course, this situation has always existed in some form or another. Those familiar with the history of science will recognize that Aristotelian philosophy and its accompanying epicycle theory of planetary motion took centuries to displace, at severe cost to better thinkers, Galileo included. One reason for the longevity of the epicycle theory was that any new experimental data disagreeing with the old theory could be "fixed" by adding one more epicycle. Eventually, the theory lost its appeal and support for lack of simplicity. A less familiar example concerns Fourier analysis, which has dominated in engineering and physics for the past century. Only recently has the error in this exclusionary domination been realized. But there is much inertia in the system, with many established engineers and physicists preferring to ignore the new methods because the old ones have seemed "good enough."

The phrase "good enough" like this has puzzled biologists, psychologists, and social scientists for decades. When attempting to apply mathematical methods used in physics and engineering to their own fields, the results were either of too narrow a use, or failed altogether. Certainly, no global understanding occurred in social science in contrast to the apparently successful mathematical description of, say, physics.[1]

In the past decade, researchers in the so-called "soft sciences" have discovered that nonlinear systems theory, neural networks, and the like, do give remarkably good descriptions of some of the phenomena in their fields. The result is understandable—a major embracing of these methods like children with new toys at Christmas. (Perhaps the social scientists should study this sudden evolution!) A danger is that the social sciences are now vulnerable to locking into one or two narrow approaches, the choice depending on which authority espouses which method. The purpose of this chapter is to give an introduction to and overview of a variety of new mathematical methods currently available, as well as to indicate how they may be applied in social psychology. I also specify circumstances in which they may be inappropriate and therefore should be avoided. Because this volume contains chapters on chaos, dynamical systems, and nonlinearity, I will be less than thorough in the treatment of these subjects.

---

[1]In fact, the description of physics also suffered many difficulties and paradoxes arising from logical internal inconsistencies within the framework of quantum theory, problems of interpretation of quantum theory arising from the improper use of the language of classical mechanics in the quantum framework, and incompatibility of the formulations of quantum theory and relativity. But the successes *seemed* so good that the flaws tended to be rationalized one by one, resulting in a modern version of the epicycle theory. The new mathematical techniques described in this chapter are being successfully used to remedy this situation. The effort, however, is overwhelming because of the inertia of the establishment in physics. The social sciences do not have this inertia built in yet, and I hope that this chapter may help prevent this.

In all these considerations, we should bear in mind the central problem—finding the method of mathematical analysis for problems arising in social psychology that is best suited for discerning patterns of behavior. By *pattern of behavior* I mean a reoccurring sequence or continuum of events with time as the parameter (i.e., a regularity). The pattern is not assumed to always occur with any particular regularity or with a constant duration—it may be stretched out over time on different occasions and may have onsets determined by external events. Because the best pattern recognition device presently known is the right side of the human brain, we should pay attention to the division of labor in the brain. The left side is specialized for analyzing in a sequentially logical manner and is therefore usually associated with "mathematical" thinking. However, this side of the brain is not so useful when one is trying to imagine a new theorem, a new area of mathematics, or the transference of an old method to a new arena. The right side of the brain is associated with these activities, including pattern recognition. If I only tell you here of ways to have some machine discern patterns using some automated sequential logical process, I would not be giving you the most powerful techniques. What I will describe are new mathematical methods to obtain data in a form more suitable for feeding to a good pattern-recognizing device (such as the brain).

The organization of this chapter is as follows: Section II discusses the distinction between linear and nonlinear systems and more generally indicates the essential properties of a range of new mathematical methods. Section III discusses briefly the properties of the specific type of linear analysis usually called *Fourier analysis*. Section IV discusses coherent state analysis. In Section V, neural networks are defined, and coherent state analysis is placed within that framework. I will refrain from using excess mathematical notation and jargon whenever possible. Instead, I will illustrate the concepts with examples that come primarily from the social sciences, psychology, and biology.

II. Linear or Nonlinear?

Suppose we do an experiment of whatever variety in which two properties of a system are related. For example, suppose we relate time with the number of people in a population who have heard some "it" (news/rumor/joke). Such properties may be assigned numerical values, and we may plot the results. Suppose the results look like Figure 1 over a short time scale. Such a plot is fairly well approximated by a straight line. If we know that deviations from a straight line are due only to a random statistical error of measurement, then we may use *linear* statistical regression theory to determine the best fit straight line to the data.

Almost all types of experimental results show approximately linear behavior over sufficiently short intervals. Such phenomena are termed *differentiable* in the

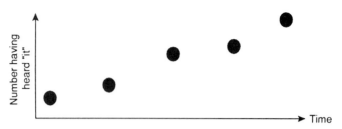

Figure 1   (Approximately) linear behavior.

language of calculus. We are more interested here in identifying phenomena that are linear over large intervals.

We could also have taken data so as to relate the percentage of the population per unit area having heard "it" as a function of time and location. To graph this would require at least three dimensions, three if we record only distance along one direction for location. Now it is possible for the resulting graph to appear as points on some plane, tilted at some axis (and perhaps also inexact because of the presence of some random statistical error). Again, if one knew that the points ideally did belong on a plane, linear regression could be used to determine the "best fit" parameters of such a plane.

Any time a "mathematically flat" object such as a line or a plane (or higher dimensional version of a flat object, called a hyperplane) can be fit precisely to the data in the absence of error, the properties are said to be *linearly related* or *affinely related*. One should observe that by statistical analysis of correlations, correlations of ±1 require that the properties are linearly (affinely) related, except perhaps for statistically rare events that may be neglected in practice. However, if the correlations are only "close" to ±1, it is problematical but common to conclude that the properties are (statistically) linearly related. The presence of noise for which the distribution is independent of the system parameters will preserve correlations; however, even slightly nonindependently distributed noise will result in a perturbation of the correlation coefficient away from ±1. This makes interpretation difficult. As an example, the graph of the data may have a gentle curve. Extrapolating such data with a straight line or a flat plane could be very dangerous. But is the slight curve a "real" phenomenon or just noise? How can one tell? In experiments in the social sciences, linear relations are very rare, and correlations are rarely anywhere near +1 or −1.

Relations that are not linear are said to be *nonlinear*.

If one computes the correlation between two properties and the correlation is near zero, one can conclude that the two properties are not (statistically) linearly related. A major logical error, which is ubiquitous, is to conclude that the two

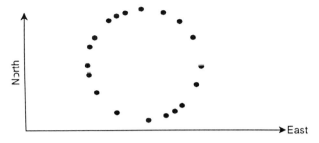

Figure 2   Spread of "it."

properties are not related. In reality, they are not *linearly* related. As an example, Figure 2 represents the boundary of the region over which "it" may have spread after some fixed time. It would be ridiculous to conclude that no relation existed between the variables, and yet the correlation is zero. The existence of a clear (reproducible) pattern proves that there is a relation. Of course, we could argue for a theory in which the pattern of this boundary is a circle and then use nonlinear regression based on circles to best fit a circle. Such nonlinear regression requires prior knowledge of the shape (pattern) to achieve the best fit. Because it presupposes a theory, it is more difficult to apply in the "real world" and is rarely used because of the complexity unless an established theory already exists.

Finally, suppose we analyze as we did in the case for Figure 2 but instead obtained Figure 3. Would we concoct some weird theory to fit the data? Suppose we had overlooked the fact that the population was confined to live in a valley. What may have happened is that a simple, perhaps otherwise linear theory, is being confined to a nonflat surface, and the results no longer look simple. Inclusion of the geographical topography as a variable may restore the simplicity of interpretation of the graph at the expense of introducing more dimensions. And this is the crux of one problem occurring in the social sciences, in psychology, in biology, and

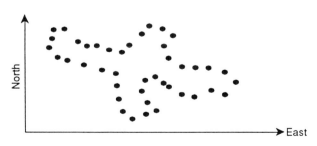

Figure 3   Spread of "it."

even in physics and engineering: By not considering sufficiently many appropriate variables, simple theories in large dimension may appear as complicated theories when ignoring essential variables. This is exacerbated if we do not know how to guess what variables might make the theory simple, and this may be another reason why one has to deal with such complex theories in social science.

Figure 3 also illustrates a second consequence of considering too few variables. One may have interpreted the raggedness of the boundary as a statistical error, computed the standard deviation, and so on. But the data may, in fact, be exact! Considering an incomplete set of data may result in an interpretation of variations as (statistical) error in measurement when there is no error. Even the neglect of one important variable can cause this effect. Thus, "simplification" of an analysis by restricting it to fewer variables than necessary can cause an effect the opposite of simplification.

Situations that do occur in the social, biological, and psychological contexts that are never linear are those situations in which feedback mechanisms play an essential role. Presumably, nonlinearity is predominant in most "complex systems." But there are degrees of nonlinearity. A linear (affine) equation between two variables x and y takes the form

$$y = ax + b,$$

where a and b are constants. An equation of the form,

$$y = ax^2 + bx + c,$$

where a, b, c are constants, is said to be *quadratic*; that is, an exponent "2" appears in the equation. Situations in which only exponents of "1" or "2" appear in the equations are no longer linear and thus are no longer susceptible to purely linear analysis (matrix theory, linear differential equation theory) but may be susceptible to *coherent state analysis*. This is the case in quantum mechanics (a highly successful theory of physics) and more generally in any field in which the data, expected values, or the like appear as some form of cross-correlation or auto-correlation. Coherent state analysis is specifically a method used to find patterns, even if embedded in noise, using sets of correlations as input. (Factor analysis is a special case of coherent state analysis from this viewpoint.) The coherent state method is useful in some analyses of signals, of simple-cell vision in cats, and perhaps of bat echolocation processes in the auditory cortex of the bats (for a review, see Schroeck, 1990). In all these situations, the data occur in the form of a correlation of the signal mixed with a fixed-test signal that is then squared and integrated; hence, it is quadratic in the signal, and the data have a nice mixture of linear and quadratic terms. The evolution of the system may or may not be linear, but the data must alway have this quadratic structure. This quadratic structure is provably preserved under linear evolution. This will be discussed in detail in Section IV. For now, we may think of coherent states as patterns that naturally and frequently appear in quadratically behaving systems and for which the evolution may be described in a simple (read "linear") manner.

Of course, there are many other types of equation than the linear and qua dratic ones—as many as the different types of functions that one can imagine: higher polynomials, exponentials, logarithms, trigonometric functions, and worse. Such situations lead us into the general field of nonlinear dynamics. Of course, a quadratic system is nonlinear, but as we shall see, it is one susceptible to special techniques that give results strong enough to justify special treatment.

Perhaps I should explain what a mathematician means by the statement "This theory gives strong results." In general, the wider the range of models to which the theory can be applied, the fewer things the theory can tell you about the models. This is evidenced by fewer theorems or theorems with little "punch." A theory is "strong" if it has a lot of theorems with a lot of "punch." We have this situation here. General nonlinear theory should be reserved for cases in which neither linear nor coherent state methods work because the latter give stronger results. Coherent state methods should not be used in linear situations because the results of linear analysis are even stronger. Unfortunately, in the social sciences, linear analysis rarely applies. However, if linear analysis does not apply, one should not rush immediately to general nonlinear analysis if coherent state analysis can be used. One should first check to see if the system has coherent states (fundamental patterns) determined from auto- and cross-correlations.

We are concerned here with the dynamics of a system, that is, the motion of bodies within the system (the time development of the system) when the system is under the influence of "forces." These "systems and forces" occur in a social context but are analogous to those in the usual physical and engineering context. Techni cally speaking, a system possessing a known dynamics is called a *dynamical system*. There are special types of dynamical system that incorrectly, but by common use, carry the general name. This can be a source of confusion if not explained; I shall discuss one such case presently.

Before that, a few words should be said about *chaos* and *chaotic systems*. A major difficulty is defining *chaos*. At the start, let me say that just because one does not see any pattern in a system does not make it chaotic. Furthermore, a system need not be chaotic simply because it is governed by probability, rather than being deterministic. In fact, there are both deterministic as well as stochastic systems that are chaotic and others that are not. So, where do we begin? The *Webster Dictionary* definition of *chaos* is "a state of things in which chance is supreme" or "a state of utter confusion." Now, if we are utterly confused, we can offer *no* analysis of the system. Furthermore, "chance" need not mean "complete randomness." For ex ample, a standard embarrassment to the scientific community was the publication of a table of supposedly "random numbers." As it turned out, it was not so random after all, although it was successfully used as if it were for many years. I conclude with the observation that situations that seem utterly confused from one standpoint may seem rather simple and orderly from another.

The best definition of *chaos* that I know has to do with the behavior of correlations in the system and how fast these correlations decay with time. In a chaotic system, the distance between two states that are initially near each other tends to grow at least exponentially with time; conversely, two states that are initially widely separated may converge exponentially or faster. In linear systems, one or the other may occur; in chaotic systems, both occur. For example, consider the "baker's transformation" of taking a piece of dough for making raisin bread, rolling it out, cutting it in half, putting one half on top of the other, rolling it out again, cutting, and so on. Two raisins that are initially close may separate (sometimes drastically fast, by the cutting process), and separated raisins may rapidly become near to each other. This is an example of a deterministic but chaotic system. Such a system is said to be *mixing*. Nonetheless, there is structure in this chaotic system: Notice that throughout this process, the total volume of the dough is constant. In mathematical lingo, this transformation is "measure preserving." Conclusion: Even chaotic systems may have nicely preserved structures. (For a nice discussion of chaos, see Jurgens, Peitgen, & Saupe, 1992.)

I present two possible approaches that one may take when faced with analyzing an apparently chaotic system. The first suggests that a considerable amount of work be done to develop a kind of "encyclopedia" of systems; the other requires a truly involved right brain:

1. Take a nonchaotic social system, add noise in some statistically (i.e., "stochastically") regular way, and store the results. In this way, build an encyclopedia of models. Then see if any model corresponds to the supposedly chaotic system. (The mathematics of stochastic differential equations falls in this category.) If the comparison is good, then at least some average properties will behave simply; this provides a means for testing the applicability of this method.

2. Change one's perspective of the situation altogether. This is a right-brain activity given that one is trying to see a system in a way that does not logically follow from systematic sequential analysis. It is consequently not a subject that I or anyone can describe by some systematic logic! But I can try to give a hint of what is happening by means of some examples. On the one hand, one could look for new quantities to be measured, these quantities being drastically different from the "standard" ones that have now proven to be less than useful. Along with this, change the way the new and old quantities are measured. For example, the inclusion of the topography in Figure 3 brings order out of apparent chaos (and shows that the system was in fact hardly chaotic in any sense). What we are doing is switching perspectives until we see a pattern emerge. This is definitely a right-brain activity. For another example, suppose that we study the behavior of couples in their habits

of going out to eat. A standard analysis we could use might be computing the average frequency with which each couple dines out. We could also use Fourier analysis to try to discern any periodic behavior in their eating habits, like going out each Friday night. These are standard systematic methods of analysis. On the other hand, we could attempt to observe nonperiodic patterns of eating out (a left-brain activity). For example, suppose that a couple follows the pattern of first going out for pizza and beer in the evening, followed by a diet of asperin the next morning, followed by something mild like Chinese food for either lunch or supper. The onset of such a pattern may be caused by the arrival of a paycheck, a tax refund, or the like, thus the pattern is not necessarily a periodic one.

How do we decide which patterns to attempt to discern? The heretofore standard method of discerning patterns has been to stare at the data and hope that the right brain can find a pattern, say while we are asleep. If we could discern such a pattern, then the analysis of the system would reduce to simply finding the time of onset of occurrences of the pattern, or the length of the pattern, or both. Coherent state analysis provides us with a way to present data so that they are potentially in a more suitable format for presenting to the right brain or any other pattern-recognition system. This will be seen to be an immediate consequence of the method of data aquisition required by and present in the coherent state analysis of systems.

In spite of all the discussion of Approaches 1 and 2, if either approach "works," then I would be inclined to say that the system was "nontrivial" rather than "chaotic." If neither worked, I would say, "Keep working." Truly chaotic systems are hard to analyze (see Jurgens et al., 1992).

Finally, I turn to a special type of dynamical system that sometimes is termed a *dynamical system* without reference to its special nature. Suppose we have a system described as a function of time, t. Frequently, we can describe such a system with a differential equation. Now make the approximation that time is discrete and write the differential equation in the approximate form: the system at $t + 1$ equals a function, f, of the system at t and of other variables, $v(t)$, at time t:

$$s(t + 1) = f[s(t), v(t)].$$

We suppose that the variables $v(t)$ are known for each time t. (They are commonly taken to be constant.) Then, given an initial value of the system $s(0)$, by substitution into f one obtains $s(1)$. Substituting again gives $s(2)$ and so on. Zillions of hours are now spent on computers doing this iterating, watching the plotted results develop, and getting enthralled by the complexity or simplicity of these plots. A function is not declared to be "interesting" if it is linear. The intrigue comes when the function is not linear. In this way, one obtains "attractors," "fractals," and other interesting figures.

I claim that the question for social scientists should not be, Which plots fit a given application in social science? but rather, Which function f is appropriate to a given application in social science? Why do I say that it is f that is to be justified? Because different fs can yield the same or very similar plots, and slight changes in f can yield drastically different pictures. Furthermore, keeping the same f but using different initial states of the system, $s(0)$, can also yield drastically different plots in nonlinear systems. For example, for the system described with the time-dependent parameter $y(t)$ that obeys the differential equation

$$\frac{dy(t)}{dt} = 2t[y(t)]^2,$$

any initial condition at $t = -10$, $y(-10) < -\frac{1}{100}$, yields a system that cannot evolve past $t = 0$ because it goes to negative infinity as time approaches zero! If $y(-10)$ is between $-\frac{1}{100}$ and 0, the system initially goes more negative until $t = 0$; then as time increases further, the system rises to zero. If, however, $y(-10)$ is positive, the system y initially decreases, remaining positive, and then rises, going to infinity in finite time. This system is, therefore, highly sensitive to slight changes in or inaccurate knowledge of the initial state of the system at $t = -10$. Moreover, the change to a slightly different equation, namely

$$\frac{dy(t)}{dt} = 2t\{[y(t)]^2 + 10^{-30}\},$$

leads to a system that has an infinite collection of times at which the system diverges to infinity. Nonlinear systems may behave drastically differently under very small changes.

To make matters worse, one can prove that there are only a few basic building-block structures (some say three such basic structures) that can occur in these dynamical systems. It seems unreasonable, however, to think that there are such a paucity of structures describing the vast array of social systems.

III. On Fourier Analysis

Consider any system for which the pattern of purely periodic behavior has been recognized. For example, consider the annual post-Christmas depression, the seasonality of leisure activities, or the monthly changes in prominence of mental instability ("lunacy"). Phenomena such as these are common enough to have caused a significant following of astrology in almost all cultures. Such phenomena are easy to recognize because of the regularity of recurrence over many cycles occupying long time periods. Likewise, one may tune a stringed instrument by comparing the regular vibration of any string with harmonics of another string over an arbitrarily long time. Just as for strings, some of the periodic aspects of societal behavior may be understood by "harmonically" decomposing the activity into its different temporally periodic components, each component being labeled by its frequency of regular occurrence. This decomposition is termed *Fourier analysis* or *harmonic analysis*. A well-established formalism (Fourier transform theory) exists to carry out the harmonic decomposition.

Stationary societies may exhibit such regular, nonconstant phenomena. An example is the annual price of turkeys in London during the holiday season: Over a period of many decades in the 17th and 18th centuries, the price from year to year alternated between high and low. Apparently, when the price was high, many people decided to raise turkeys for the next year, driving the price down; then, having taken a financial beating, fewer people raised turkeys for the next year, so the price rose. This continued for a very long time until someone recognized the pattern and realized the potential for profit (see also Goldberg, 1958, pp. 176–184). The situation persisted for such a long time solely because periodic patterns had not previously been recognized in economic situations. You can be sure that such opportunities are now well-understood by big investors, and chances for similar economic windfalls are now slim. Similarly, in the social sciences, it is unlikely that any important patterns with regular periodic structure have not been observed and discussed already. In the words of a disappointed researcher, "the easy cases have already been done."

Engineers and physicists exploited this type of mathematics and it worked well for systems that exhibited regular behavior for many periods (stable systems). But in recent years, as the methods were applied to systems over ever shorter time spans, the results became less efficient and more cumbersome.

As a prime example, consider analyzing the sound of a symphony. You could record the intensity of sound as a function of time only (as if you were tone deaf) and try to identify the symphony. Identification might be very difficult. Then one could perform the Fourier transform to determine the intensity of sound as a function of frequency only (see Figure 4). Even with both sets of data, with hundreds of thousands of data points, it would be difficult, if not impossible, to identify

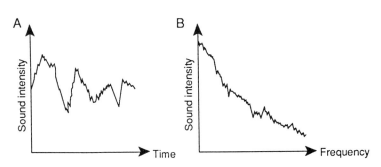

Figure 4   (A) time series; (B) frequency spectrum.

the symphony (see Bennett, 1976, p. 401). This typifies one penalty for trying to use Fourier analysis in inappropriate places. Fourier analysis would be more appropriate for identifying instead of "99 Bottles of Beer on the Wall" because it does have essentially a regular repeating pattern over many periods. Identifying this song is, for all practical purposes, a "stationary signal analysis" problem, whereas identifying the symphony identification is a problem in "nonstationary signal analysis." The question raised here can be taken to its ultimate logical extreme:

1. From the data in Figures 4a,b, is it possible at all, whether practical or not, to determine *uniquely* the sound that made it?
In case the answer is yes, we would say that the data is *informationally complete*. To be precise, a set of properties that is observed is said to be informationally complete if and only if it (the data set) consists of these properties that uniquely determine the "signal" (used in the generic sense).

We may show that, even for stationary signal processes, the set of intensities obtained through Fourier methods is not informationally complete. For example, "Row, Row, Row Your Boat" sung over and over would appear to be a good candidate for Fourier analysis; however, it could not be distinguished from "Row, Row, Your Row Boat" (the order is scrambled) sung over and over because the two would have the same intensity/frequency spectrum as well as the same intensity/time spectrum. To summarize, we have just proven that the set of sound intensities as a function of time only plus the set of sound intensities as a function of frequency only for a signal is generally informationally incomplete.

There are even greater drawbacks concerning the misuse of Fourier analysis than discussed so far. Several more questions that arise naturally are the following:

2. If the sound (signal) has noise superimposed on it, can the noise be separated from the signal?

3. If the signal is slightly modulated, say by playing a recording of the sound on a machine that runs at an incorrect or erratic speed, do the displays as in Figure 4 change slightly or enormously? (If slightly, we say the analysis is *stable* or *insensitive*; if enormously, *unstable* or *sensitive*.)

4. What are the consequences of a temporary loss of signal, such as the "lost 18 minutes of tape recordings" famous in the Watergate scandal investigations or cutting off the corner of a photo?

For both stationary and nonstationary processes, joint time–frequency analysis (as in a music score or a tone distinguishing ear) is far better for identification purposes (see Grossmann, Kronland-Martinet, & Morlet, 1989, p. 18, Figure 14). In pattern recognition devices used for speech recognition of primates (Bauers, 1989) the signal is electronically divided into frequency ranges and time intervals simultaneously (by use of coherent state techniques, it turns out). Such data can be shown to be a sampling from an informationally complete set of data.

The advantage of joint measurement may be understood by an analogy with "dependent random variables in probability theory." There are sets of random variables that have different joint distributions but identical marginal distributions. More information is contained in the joint distribution than in the two marginal distributions combined. As long as we have a pattern recognition device that is receptive to the joint distribution, it will be a better pattern recognizer when analyzing joint data than when analyzing marginal data. The auditory center in the right brain is certainly jointly time and frequency receptive. Likewise, the visual cortex is jointly spatial and wavelength sensitive. The obvious conclusion is that we should find methods for providing the results of joint measurements to whatever pattern-recognizing device we choose to use. Preferably, we should feed an informationally complete set of joint data to the device.

From the analogy with probability, we say that time and frequency are not independent. This analogy is a rigorously valid one and points out a potentially weak method of data analysis that can arise anywhere, social psychology included: When analyzing a social system, taking marginal data rather than joint data for dependent properties admits loss of information and potential ambiguity in interpretation of data. In other words, one needs to test for the interactions of the different variables, and not tacitly assume that they are independent, when designing the method of data aquisition.

In the signal example discussed, this dependence does not arise solely because there is a simple (Fourier) transform relating time and frequency. I will show presently that the specific joint time–frequency distribution obtained as data depends inextricably on properties of the measuring device used to obtain those data. Consequently, the effect of the experimental procedure has to be understood from the start. I will also show that this involvement of the measuring device is not only possible but advantageous when exploited.

There is a common misconception about signals (and quantum mechanics and other physical theories) that we should face here. The "signal" one observes on a heart monitor or seismograph or oscilloscope is a graph of the intensity of the signal as a function of time; it is not the graph of the signal as a function of time. The signal possesses a structure that is jointly dependent on both time and frequency. If one attempts to represent the signal as a function of time only, the function cannot be simply a real-valued function of time but must instead be given as a complex-number-valued function of time; that is, the representation of the signal has two components, the real part and the imaginary part. That this is possible at all is a consequence of the area of mathematics called "group representation theory," which I will refrain from reviewing here, except to say that the role of the Fourier transform relating intensity/time representations with intensity/frequency representations comes out naturally from it. That it is reasonable to us is simple to justify: We need *two* components to encompass both the intensity/time and the intensity/frequency properties. We are so used to visualizing the intensity/time graphs that we tend to forget this complex structure of the signal. The actual signal has twice as many degrees of freedom as we "see" on the monitors.

If we know the complex representation of the signal for all times (or for all frequencies), then we indeed uniquely determine the signal. Intensity as a function of time, however, is informationally incomplete, as is intensity as a function of frequency, or even both of these sets of information. This has nothing to do with the practical matter that we do not sample the signal at all frequencies or at all times but only at a discrete subset of them; the informational (in)completeness results hold even when sampling at all values. However, if we are really obtaining data on the full complex signal, then the Nyquist theorem tells us that we can still retain informational completeness when sampling at a discrete set of times (or frequencies) as long as we sample "often" (see O'Neil, 1991 p. 1122). The theorem also tells us how often we must sample. This is rarely useful because we seldom sample anything other than intensity.

On the other hand, there is a way to represent the signal as a real-valued function of time and frequency jointly (which I will discuss in detail). Certainly, we would have no difficulty visualizing these joint data if they were presented graphically. And such data are informationally complete.

The question of noise removal is connected with informational completeness in the following way: If the data taken correspond to an informationally complete set, if the noise is "fixed" (of unchanging character), and if the data for just the noise can be obtained either before or after the phenomenon to be studied is introduced, then those data uniquely characterize that noise. Therefore, when the data for the desired signal plus noise are taken as a joint function of time and frequency, the effect of the noise may be removed by simple subtraction of the intensity distribution for noise from the total intensity distribution, without significant damage to the intensity distribution for the desired signal. That the noise is characterized with known intensity distribution over an equivalent of joint regions of time/frequency space is the basis of the most modern method of (white) noise subtraction (i.e., "wavelet analysis"), which is one type of coherent state analysis. Removal of the noise without severe effects on the desired signal is not possible if one lacks informational completeness. For example, in Fourier analysis, subtraction of the noise data from the combined data tends to degrade or destroy the signal data.

As an example, we are all familiar with the weather radar on the evening news. If the radar station is based in a city, the pattern on the screen shows a characteristic bright region in the center due to reflection of the radar signal off nearby buildings. Because these radar systems are usually developed to run using Fourier analysis, this annoying effect cannot be simply subtracted off without damage to the overall picture. In particular, such a radar is incapable of detecting a tornado just outside a building! In the next section, I show how this problem can be circumvented.

In the social sciences, there are many processes intertwined in most situations, and just as in the case of noise intermixed with a signal, Fourier analysis methods are not suitable for separating their various effects. In general, the same problem persists for any type of linear analysis, and not just Fourier analysis.

It is also disappointing that Fourier analysis is generally unstable under small perturbations. For example, a small break in a signal can cause a much larger ringing effect, called *Gibb's overshoot phenomenon*, when using Fourier analysis. In other words, a disturbance tends to get amplified. In the next section, I show that coherent state analysis is much more stable in this regard. Let me give one visual example to illustrate the point. In cutting off the corner of a photograph, you lose all information about that portion of the object in the picture. If instead you cut off the corner of a holograph, you still retain a picture of the entire object but with some loss of clarity. Furthermore, the holograph encodes *three-dimensional* information! Holography is an example of (informationally complete) coherent state analysis. If one persists in visualizing a signal as a function of just frequency or just position, then the hologram records the full complex signal. I find it easier to think that a holograph records the intensity of the signal as a function of all the variables jointly.

Holography also illustrates the difference between local analysis (the photograph encodes only local information) and nonlocal analysis (the holograph apparently encodes information about the entire object in each region of the holograph). Another type of local analysis is based solely on derivatives at a point (Taylor expansions). In general, one can prove that any type of local analysis is informationally incomplete! One must thus moderate one's expectations when using local analysis.

In spite of the drawbacks of Fourier analysis, it is remarkably good in situations in which it is appropriate, that is, in situations exhibiting stationary periodic behavior of their dominant properties (see, e.g., Chapter 7). Many such situations in social science have been observed and analyzed. I have mentioned several already, but others include the weekly (weekend) mayhem on the highways late at night, the cycle of marital disputes and good times in a family (reflecting the biological cycles of the individuals), annual cycles of unemployment, and annual increases in (summer) teenage problems. These phenomena are fairly well-understood. Outstanding unsolved problems in social science are probably not of this nature, and methods in addition to Fourier analysis are likely to be useful.

In situations not exhibiting regularly occurring patterns, it would be better to try to recognize irregularly occurring but characteristic patterns with analysis based on nonperiodic but appropriate patterns. This is the essence of coherent state analysis. In human development and biology in general, one possible explanation of the pattern recognition capability in the right brain is that an animal is first "imprinted" (to set the pattern) followed by subsequent efficient recognition of the pattern even in noisy environments (e.g., young birds recognizing their mother's call in a large bird colony). For another example, consider a sequence of sounds emitted by stumptailed macaques for communicating a specific message (Bauers, 1989). Suppose that this sound always follows the same pattern but is initiated at irregular intervals. For analyzing such a signal, Fourier analysis is useless because the patterns are not periodic.

In summary, then, Fourier analysis is useful when

1. the system is known to possess periodic behavior,
2. the system is not embedded in a highly noisy background, and
3. the cost of acquiring many data points is not prohibitive.

Fourier analysis is not useful when

1. the system does not possess regular periodic behavior,
2. attempting to separate the effects of interdependent processes,
3. the system is susceptible to perturbations that can cause instabilities in the Fourier transform,
4. nonlocal properties are the dominant ones, or
5. one wishes to minimize the amount of data handled (data compression).

If Fourier analysis effectively identifies the patters sought, use it; if it does not "work," there may still be regularities to be discovered, but other tools will be needed to find them.

IV. Coherent State Analysis

Consider any system that produces some type of output in the form of a function of time. List all the operations that one could perform on an output and obtain another valid output. For example, take a pattern of behavior; one may shift it in time, lengthen it, shorten it, and so on. If one had, instead, a picture for an output, one could also rotate it. The set of all such operations forms a *group* in mathematical lingo. Now take a single output (the "test pattern") and perform all allowed operations on it to obtain a family of patterns. This family is called a *family of coherent states*. Under some rather general conditions, one can show that the data obtained by correlating any output with the members of this family constitute an informationally complete set of data (Healy & Schroeck, 1993). Coherent state analysis is the mathematics that allows the reconstruction of the output from this set of correlations. For us, it is enough to know that the set of correlations is informationally complete because then we may use the imprinting method for pattern recognition, bypassing any reconstruction computations.

Just as linear analysis and Fourier analysis have good points and drawbacks, so does coherent state analysis. Coherent state analysis seems to be immune from the drawbacks discussed in the previous section. The first drawback that coherent state analysis has is that one must know *which* group of operations on the system leads to the informationally complete set of correlations and how one efficiently obtains these correlations as data. The second drawback can be minimized by appropriate experimental design, which explains the great recent interest in these methods. To illustrate the key points, I begin with the example of bat echolocation (see Simmons, Howell, & Suga, 1975; Suga (1990).

A bat emits a sound consisting of a relatively pure tone (i.e., with a narrow frequency range), followed by a continuous drop in frequency over a short time (a "chirp") at the end of the emission. Let us call these Pattern 1 and Pattern 2, respectively. The same "instructions" that determine the emission also generate an internal signal (the test pattern). Simultaneously with the emission of the vocal signal, this internal signal is sent to the auditory cortex of the bat in the following way: The auditory cortex appears to be split into a number of different levels, and the emission is transferred to each level with slightly different time delay for each level. This process is repeated until an echo is received. When the echo is sensed, Pattern 1 is extended in time so that there is a long period when the echo is received in the ears and transmitted to the auditory cortex. In this way, the echo and the emitted signal, with various time delays, overlap for a significant amount of time, and the intensities of the combined signals are felt. Those of you who have heard a train whistle as it passes have noticed the change in frequency (pitch) of the whistle (higher as the train approaches, lower after it passes). This is called the *Doppler shift*. The bat uses the same effect to tell the velocity of the object reflecting Pattern 1 of its own emission. The physiology is easy to explain. When two signals of different frequency are mixed, the intensity of the mixture is composed of three intertwined components: the first input (of constant intensity in time), the second input (of constant intensity in time), and the cross-correlation, which oscillates in time (called *interference fringes* in physics). The latter may be separated from the first two components if one has a sequence of copies of the mixture with the two inputs separated by a corresponding sequence of small time differences. This principle has been used in science and engineering for about a century. Apparently, bats automatically process signals this way through use of the different levels of their auditory cortex, and they have been doing this for millenia. Bats isolate the intensity of the cross-correlation. From it, the velocity of the target can be determined with great precision. And if the target has wings beating, this is also detected as a spread in the velocity of the target.

This is far from enough for a bat because, at this stage, it has absolutely no idea of the location or texture of the target. Bats prefer to eat soft fuzzy things rather than rocks. They also have no appetite for tennis balls (which I personally have confirmed will initially fool a bat). So, the bat also is interested in the size, shape, and texture of the target. It must also get all this information from the echo.

After the bat receives an echo, it does a clever thing with its next emission: It drops the frequency! Now, what can one determine with reflected signals at two frequencies? It can determine the distance, it turns out, as well as get some information about the size, shape, and texture of the target. But pure tones are not efficient for determining the latter three properties. The chirp (Pattern 2) is efficient for that and is used in modern radar technology for similar purposes.

In summary, the bat isolates and analyzes the patterns of intensity of the cross-correlations between a test pattern and the pattern to be analyzed as a function of the time delay t and the frequency shift ν of the test pattern. Call this function $C(t,\nu)$.

Each cross-correlation intensity $C(t,\nu)$ is nonlocal in the pattern; that is, the entire pattern is needed to obtain the intensity. (Actually, only the "significant" [intense] part of the pattern is needed.) Recent work of the authors, Healy and Schroeck (1993), proved that the set of these cross-correlations $C(t,\nu)$ for all (t,ν) is informationally complete. Thus, the reflected signal, and hence the target, can be uniquely identified, and, furthermore, fixed background noise can be separated from the desired signal. This latter point is extremely important because bats hunt in groups of up to several thousand, and any bat must distinguish reflections of its own signals from the multitude of signals coming from other bats. Because the voice boxes of bats of the same species are extremely similar, the differences in signal from one bat to another in the group are very small. Thus, the bats must be very efficient. There is a theoretical limit to this efficiency, first derived in quantum mechanics in which it is called the *uncertainty principle*. Experimentally it has been shown that bats operate at this quantum limit!

I remark that the specific signal processing that isolates the cross-correlation intensities $C(t,\nu)$ actually isolates data that are quadratic in the complex-valued representative of the signal. Before leaving this example, I also emphasize that the change from the test signal to the signal shifted by t and ν is a linear change.

Using this example, I now outline the principal input for a system of coherent states suitable for our purposes:

(a) We have a group, G, of operations that act on a basic pattern s_0 with the result denoted $U(g)s_0$ for each g in G. The set of all patterns of the type $U(g)s_0$ is called a set of coherent states. g here is the generic name for the variables. In the example of bats, $g = (t,\nu)$.

(b) For any other state s, the set of correlation intensities, denoted

$$[C(g) = |<s, U(g)s_0>|, g \in G],$$

must be such that s can be recovered from this set (informational completeness).

Bats do a good job using small subsets of this set of correlations. It is very important to observe that they select from an informationally complete set; so, there is a hope to still get complete information from a subset. This is unlike Fourier theory in which one does not even begin with an informationally complete set. In this sense, Fourier analysis is less powerful for pattern recognition compared with coherent state analysis. Also, I emphasize that only magnitudes of $<s, U(g)s_0>$ are to be used given that one always obtains real numbers (here, intensities) as measurement results; $<s, U(g)s_0>$ is generally complex because the signal s is taken to be a complex signal. Nonetheless, $<s, U(g)s_0>$ is usually the object analyzed with Fourier analysis.

Property B may be deduced as a theorem from the properties under some technical conditions on the group, on s_0, and on the space of all allowed states. (Healy & Schroeck, 1993.)

As long as Property B holds, we know we can uniquely identify the unknown pattern s. This is not the same as being able to reconstruct s. For this purpose, "reconstruction formulae" have been derived for certain classes of groups. But this is not our objective here. The bat is happy enough to identify the pattern of a known edible target; the bat does not have to reconstruct a "visual" picture of the target (mentally). Similarly, this joint time/frequency analysis is usable in identifying speech patterns in macaques (Bauers, 1989). This simplification for pattern recognition can be of utility in social psychology generally.

I now give other examples of coherent state analysis in "the real world." A large class of examples can be found in patterns of individual behavior. These situations frequently have the property that they are not periodic behavioral patterns in the sense of occurring with regular frequency (not susceptible to Fourier analysis) but follow the same complicated pattern whenever they do occur. For example, a mass murderer may strike at irregular intervals but with a similar pattern during each episode. Of course, this same type of fixed pattern at irregular intervals may occur for both normal and abnormal behaviors. When these patterns occur over long time intervals, if the individual or those around the individual are aware of the pattern, then at the onset of the behavior, the pattern can be broken. For example, certain misdirection plays by an individual in a marriage or a social group can be recognized by the spouse or the group members after several occurrences, after which the behavioral pattern becomes ineffective. Undetected or with no response, such patterns tend to repeat at perhaps irregular intervals.

The duration of these patterns of behavior sometimes might be stretched or shortened so that the pattern is really a family of patterns differing only by this time dilation and time of onset. As a word of warning, the time dilation considered here is one that is uniform; time dilations that dilate time with different dilations in different intervals of time perturb the "signal" in a way that cause this analysis to fail. In summary, the family of patterns considered here is precisely a family of coherent states with respect to the group of time translations and (uniform) dilations. (This group is called the *affine group*, and the coherent states for this group are called *wavelets* [see Daubechies, 1992].)

Coherent states may also appear in the context of the dynamics of interacting populations. For example, there are patterns of crowd excitation. Certain speakers are well-known to know just how to control crowds and become the well-known entertainers, rabble-rousers, and the like. Thus, not only do the patterns exist, but they can sometimes be excited to occur. It is still an art form to be able to teach someone how to capture a crowd; that is, we do not yet understand it fully. On the other hand, police are taught how to disperse a crowd; that is, to detect the pattern and disrupt it efficiently.

To summarize, if Fourier methods fail to identify patterns, try coherent state analysis. To apply coherent state analysis

1. Identify the group of transformations of patterns relevant to the problem under study;

2. Pick a basic pattern (test pattern) and apply the elements of the group to it to obtain a family of coherent states, or select a finite subset of this family either by a known sampling theorem or on some other principle;

3. Obtain the cross-correlations between the signal to be analyzed and the coherent states, or at least the intensities of these cross-correlations (thus, the data are a sequence of intensities of correlations);

4. Present this data, which is informationally complete, to a pattern recognition device. This device may operate on known principles, such as template matching, or may work, as in the right brain, without our understanding how it works. The proof is in the product.

If this process fails to identify patterns, then proceed on to general dynamical systems analysis.

I close this section by recognizing three other methods that have some features in common with coherent state analysis.

a. For coherent states, as we have discussed, *all* states obey a linear evolution. In general nonlinear dynamical systems, there also may be some fixed patterns that tend to move without (serious) change in the pattern. These are termed *solitons*. Certain ocean waves act as solitons; others behave as coherent states. Solitons differ from coherent states in two ways: (i) In coherent state systems, all patterns evolve with a linear operator; in nonlinear systems, the general evolution is nonlinear, only the rare solitons evolving with a dynamics that may also be described with a linear operator. (ii) Solitons do not interfere to reveal the interference fringes necessary for the coherent state analysis. Two solitons tend to move through each other almost as if each were transparent to the other. This is unlikely to be the case as one coherent state of prolifers moves through another coherent state of prochoicers, for example.

b. *Queueing theory*, which I do not describe here, can have simple structures (that propagate simply) embedded in complicated systems. These also are not coherent states. Queueing theory belongs to the realm of linear analysis.

c. Some patterns tend to form and then grow in size because of complex interactions with the population as a whole. This is an example of *synergy*, wherein the energy of the large system is collected by some complicated dynamics into a growing, moving pattern. For an intense discussion of this, see Weidlich and Haag (1983).

V. Neural Networks

The concept of neural networks arose some years ago. The idea was to modify pattern recognition techniques and computer programming to reflect ways in which the brain was assumed to work. In particular, the idea that each tiny segment of the brain was dedicated to a single task became totally discounted. Instead, entire regions or the entire brain were thought to behave in some coherent manner for each task. With this paradigm in mind, simple memory devices were composed of a small bank of processors equipped with connections between the individual units that could be made stronger or weaker during a pattern-learning period. With such devices, robot arms with stereooptic sensors were rapidly taught to sense spatial location of target objects to be procured (Kuperstein, 1988, 1989). Other devices, again with only a small number of components, learned to read character sets in a variety of fonts (Cerf, 1989). The important ingredient that makes these devices work is the feedback between components, so that they recognize global patterns in a coherent way. In a similar fashion, the feedback between different individuals or segments of society can organize the society into coherent action. If the resulting states have correlations of long duration, coherent state methods may apply, whereas if the organized collective notion grows in size, a synergetic system may result.

To be a bit more careful about this, let me give a mathematician's definition of a neural network. I warn the reader that the term *neural network* is used by many in a pedestrian, nonexact manner. There is no universally accepted definition presently. According to most definitions, a neural network is a signal processor that

1. Is nonlinear in the signal,
2. samples the signal nonlocally,
3. can process nonstationary signals,
4. is adaptive or capable of learning, and
5. is stable under small changes of input and in the presence of noise.

We see that coherent state analysis, as discussed, possesses all these properties. In fact, we see that bats most likely use this coherent state analysis in their auditory cortex; so coherent state analysis is neural processing in our sense of the word!

VI. Summary

We have explored a variety of different types of mathematical analysis that may be applied to social phenomena. The simplest is linear analysis, which is mathematically powerful but is either not encountered in sociology or is not relevant to the remaining interesting problems. Next most powerful is coherent state analysis in which we attempt to identify patterns in correlations that may appear in the context of sociology. To use this analysis, one needs knowledge of which groups of transformations of the patterns are relevant. In the most general nonlinear situation, patterns appear as solitons. It is worth while spending the time to differentiate this case from coherent state analysis, which has stronger results than general nonlinear analysis.

References

Bauers, K. A. (1989). *The role of vocal communications in the intra-group social dynamics of stumptailed Macaques.* Unpublished doctoral dissertation, University of Wisconsin—Madison.

Bennett, W. R., Jr. (1976). *Scientific and engineering problem-solving with the computer.* New York: Prentice-Hall.

Cerf, G. (1989). *Mapping multilayered neural networks for pattern recognition onto multiprocessors.* Paper presented at the Second Annual Neural Systems Symposium, Miami, FL.

Daubechies, I. (1992). *Ten lectures on wavelets* (Conference Board of the Mathematical Sciences: 61). Philadelphia: Society for Industrial & Applied Mathematics.

Goldberg, S. (1958). *Introduction to difference equations with illustrative examples from economics, psychology and sociology.* New York: Wiley.

Grossmann, A., Kronland-Martinet, R., & Morlet, J. (1989). Reading and understanding continuous wavelet transforms. In J.-M. Combes, A. Grossmann, & P. Tchamitchian (Eds.), *Wavelets, time-frequency methods and phase space* (pp. 2–21). New York: Springer-Verlag.

Healy, D. M., & Schroeck, F. E., Jr. (1993). On informational completeness of covariant observables and Wigner coefficients. Hanover, NH: Dartmouth College.

Kuperstein, M. (1989). Adaptive hand–eye coordination. Presented at the Second Annual Neural Systems Symposium, Miami, 1989. See also Proc. Am. Control Conf., Atlanta, 1988, 2282–2287; Proc. IEEE Internat. Conf. Automat. Robotics, Philadelphia, 1988, 140–144; *Science, 239,* 1308–1311.

Jurgens, H., Peitgen, H. O., & Saupe, D. (1992). *Chaos and fractals.* New York: Springer-Verlag.

O'Neil, P. V. (1991). *Advanced Engineering Mathematics* (*3rd Ed.*), Belmont, California: Wadsworth.

Schroeck, F. E., Jr. (1990). Unsharpness in measurement yields informational completeness, implementations in quantum signal processing and natural biological systems. In P. Lahti & P. Mittelstaedt (Eds.), *Symposium on the foundations of modern physics, 1990* (pp. 375–399). Singapore: World Scientific.

Simmons, J. A., Howell, D. J., & Suga, N. (1975). Information content of bat sonar echoes. *American Scientist, 63*, 204–215.

Suga, N. (1990). Biosonar and neural computation in bats. *Scientific American*, Vol. 262(6), 60–68.

Weidlich, W. and Haag, G. (1983). *Concepts and models of a quantitative sociology: The dynamics of interacting populations.* New York: Springer-Verlag.

CHAPTER 5

Aggression, Love, Conformity, and Other Social Psychological Catastrophes

Abraham Tesser
Institute for Behavioral Research
University of Georgia
Athens, Georgia

John Achee
Department of Psychology
University of Georgia
Athens, Georgia

Our intention in this chapter is to provoke thought about how social psychologists think about modeling. In attempting to understand phenomena of interest, psychologists tend to think in ways that have been so well ingrained that they are rarely questioned. Yet, these canonical approaches appear to be questionable on both intuitive and empirical grounds. After laying out a couple of such assumptions, we present a mathematical model, catastrophe theory, that incorporates solutions to some of the questions raised. We then show how this formalism can be mapped onto the social psychological constructs of "personal disposition" and "situational pressure" to integrate predictions about behavior that a number of disparate other perspectives also make. After a quick, selective review of the literature, we offer a preliminary study that provides some encouragement and invites additional work.

Dynamical Systems in Social Psychology

I. Canonical/Normal Social Psychology

A. Smoothness/Proportionality

It is widely assumed that causes and their effects are proportionally, or at least, "smoothly" related. If you push on a ball slightly, expect only a slight movement in the ball. As the strength of the push increases, expect the ball to roll progressively farther. With a strong push, expect lots of movement. Similarly, if someone is mildly annoyed, expect them to act mildly aggressive. As they become more angry, expect their behavior to become progressively more aggressive. If they become exceedingly angry, expect lots of aggression.

Although the assumption of proportionality is plausible, its universality is questionable. Consider the following scenario. An important church leader approaches us at a church picnic and begins to openly criticize us. Because of the situational pressures that we would presumably feel in such a predicament, we may be unlikely to respond aggressively to her attack, even if it angers us. If she continues with her aggressive behavior, perhaps if she even escalates it, we would certainly become more angry and upset, but we might still behave nonaggressively in this situation. Finally, at some point, like the straw that broke the camel's back, one additional criticism or aggression leads to an explosive display of anger and aggression on our part. In short, large increases in provocation resulted in little or no changes in behavior, whereas only a very small increment resulted in a very large, disproportionate shift in aggression.

Now imagine that our antagonist's level of provocation starts to decrease. Would we reduce our aggressive stance proportionally? Possibly, but we may also maintain our level of aggression in this situation. After all, we just openly attacked a church leader in front of the church members themselves, and we do not want to believe that we were aggressive for no reason. Such a commitment to aggression may be difficult to reverse at this point.

This example illustrates that not all changes in behavior are smooth functions of their causes. Sometimes, behavior change is discontinuous, as if the smallest change in a cause leads to some threshold being exceeded. In the example above, our own aggressive behavior did not smoothly "track" the aggression we were exposed to, nor did it track our anger or frustration. Rather, at some point, we exploded. The change in our behavior was abrupt, not smooth. And, when our aggressor became conciliatory, our behavior did not smoothly follow this deescalation in hostility but maintained itself at a "disproportionately" high level.

B. Unimodality

The expectation of unimodality is another assumption that we believe is worth questioning, at least under certain circumstances. Most social psychological models predict that only a single value of the dependent variable(s) will exist (excluding random disturbances) for any single level (or combination of levels) of the independent variable(s). For example, we might predict that aggression will be a function of the sum or average of one's anger and the situational pressure or an interactive combination (i.e., product) of anger and pressure. In either case, there is only one predicted value for any set level of anger and pressure. The same level of aggressive behavior may be observed for different levels of the causes (e.g., high levels of anger combined with moderate levels of social pressure against aggression may lead to the same moderate level of aggression as may moderate levels of anger combined with weak social pressure), but only one level of aggression will be associated with any single combination of causes.

However, in our example, different levels of aggression occurred as results of the same combination of causes. Prior to the aggressive outburst, anger was increasing, yet aggressive behavior was at a low level. After the outburst, aggression was apparent at the same level of anger that previously manifested no aggression. People confronting exactly the same moderate level of provocation may be quite aggressive (those who have already displayed anger) or not aggressive at all (those whose threshold had not yet been passed). Thus, when there is strong social pressure against aggression and moderate provocation, we would not expect unimodal but bimodal responding.

As the previous example illustrates, there are instances when the traditional assumptions of social psychology do not hold. On the other hand, it is not difficult to generate nontrivial examples of important psychological phenomena that exhibit discontinuities and bimodalities using traditional social psychological theory.

Consider a high school student contemplating his first encounter with alcohol. Presumably, his tendency to have that first drink will depend on his desire to try alcohol—the more he wants to try it, the more likely it is that he will do so. However, what if he faces considerable social pressure against drinking (e.g., parental pressure, pressure from church members)? It is possible—and consistent with social psychological theory—that he will conform to the social pressure and avoid alcohol, regardless of his predisposition to try it. It is also possible—and consistent with social psychological theory—that he will react against the social pressure and try the alcohol regardless of his predisposition. In fact, it is certainly plausible that the same constellation of disposition toward trying alcohol and social pressure against doing so would lead to one or the other of these outcomes for different people, resulting in a bimodal distribution.

Furthermore, imagine that our student's initial disposition toward trying alcohol is relatively low. In combination with social pressure against trying alcohol, it would appear highly unlikely that he would take that first drink. But, what if his desire to try alcohol increases? Given that social pressure against drinking is still high and given that he has a history of not drinking, then he still may be expected to be unlikely to have a drink. Eventually, though, if his desire to try alcohol continues to increase, we may expect him to reach a point at which the smallest increase in his desire to try alcohol leads to a somewhat sudden change in his behavior as he "gives in" to his desire and tries his first drink. To take a drink when one's religion, family and friends are against drinking is to "take a stand" in the face of adversity. A single drink seems hardly worth the effort of facing down such substantial pressure and enduring the social recriminations. So, the first drink is likely to be associated with a substantial amount of drinking.

Moreover, once having declared one's independence with regard to alcohol, it will be difficult to give alcohol up. To say "I was wrong" about alcohol when family, friends, and Bible are there to say "I told you so" is very difficult. So, our adolescent is likely to continue drinking even if his disposition or desire to do so decreases. Indeed, his desire would have to decrease substantially for him to decrease his drinking. And, in the face of continued social pressure, when the decrease comes, it is likely to be associated with a sudden jump to abstinence.

In sum, it is clear that there are instances when traditional assumptions operating within social psychology do not hold. Behavior will not always be a smooth function of its causes; rather, smooth changes in causes may lead to discontinuous "jumps" in behavior. Furthermore, a single combination of causes may lead to more than a single outcome. Is there a model that can incorporate these insights?

II. Catastrophe Theory: A Model That Goes Beyond the Canonical

In 1972, Rene Thom, a French mathematician, proposed such a model. The model, known as *catastrophe theory* (Thom, 1972), has a number of intuitively appealing features, but most working scientists are not trained in topology, the branch of mathematics from which the model originated. Yet, catastrophe theory quickly caught the attention of scientists in a variety of disciplines, including the behavioral sciences. Indeed, by 1978, an entire issue of the journal *Behavioral Science* was devoted to the topic.

This increased interest in catastrophe theory was due, at least in part, to Zeeman (e.g., 1976), who made the theory accessible to nonmathematicians by prolifically publishing highly visible, nontechnical accounts of the theory along with compelling examples of how the theory could account for interesting behavior. However, given that the adoption of scientific innovations often follows a discontinuous (catastrophic) trajectory, it is not surprising that, within five years of its introduction, applied catastrophe theory met with a series of devastating critiques. According to Kolata (1977), the attacks were of two varieties: The applications had little or no data or there were some mathematical inconsistencies in the application assumptions and their mapping onto the "pure" mathematics.

Although the critiques' immediate results was to put a halt to the bandwagon effect, there currently appears to be a small but active cadre of investigators in psychology using catastrophe theory, and the model again seems to be on the cusp of wider acceptance. We believe that this can be attributed to several factors, including the development of a variety of methods to test catastrophe hypotheses (e.g., Cobb, 1978, 1981; Gilmore, 1981; Guastello, 1982, 1992); a strong surge of interest in dynamical models related to catastrophe theory, such as chaos and fractals (e.g., Gleick, 1987); and finally, the initial accumulation of data that validate our intuitive feeling that the model describes significant behavioral phenomena (e.g., van Geert, 1991).

The Cusp Catastrophe

So far we have been talking about catastrophe theory the way Werner Earhart talks about "it" in his growth lecture series. However, although vagueness may sell growth seminars, it does not go very far in selling scientific models. Some time ago we (Tesser, 1980) published a concise description of the model that we explore in this chapter. We quote extensively from that description:

There are four elementary catastrophes which describe all possible cases of discontinuity in a single dependent or *behavior* variable with anywhere from one (the "fold catastrophe") to four (the "butterfly catastrophe") independent or control variables (Zeeman, 1976). We will be concerned only with the case of two control variables and one behavior variable—the "cusp catastrophe." To illustrate the properties of this catastrophe, we will consider the behavior of "*dating/mating*" (D/M), an individual's behavior or involvement in a *romantic relationship* as a function of two control variables—*love* for the partner and social pressure *against* the partner.

The *cusp* catastrophe model is illustrated in Fig. 1. The model is three dimensional. The horizontal plane is called the *control surface* and is defined by the two control dimensions, in this case, love and social pressure. These are the independent variables. The vertical dimension is the *behavior* dimension, e.g., D/M, and the top with the fold *curve* in it is called the *behavior surface*. Assuming that the behavior surface is translucent, if one were to shine a light directly above the figure, there would be a shadow cast on the control surface directly below and conforming to the shape of the fold curve (in two dimensions). The cusp shaped area the shadow defines is called the *bifurcation set*.

To make predictions from the model, find the point on the control surface defined by the particular levels of interest on the control dimensions. The level of the behavior surface directly above this point is the predicted behavior. Note that there are two behavior surfaces, i.e., the fold, above the bifurcation set. In this case, the behavioral prediction is *bimodality*.

The back of the figure represents very low levels of social pressure. If we restrict ourselves to the back slice of the control space and move from right to left or left to right, it can be seen that the behavior surface is a smooth function: As love increases D/M increases. Now suppose that the partner is a member of some out group, e.g., "wrong" religion or race, and there is a strong social pressure against romantic involvement. Now, we are at the front slice of the cube. At low levels of love, we predict low levels of D/M. Moving to the left on the control space, we continue to predict low but slightly increasing amounts of D/M until we reach the bifurcation set at point (a). Since the fold is above the bifurcation set, there are two [not counting the unstable fold] behavior surfaces above the set and thus two predic-

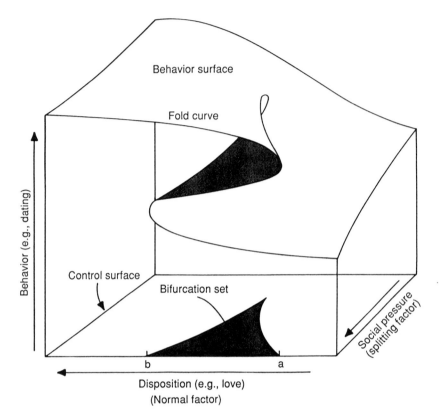

Figure 1   Cusp catastrophe model showing social pressure as a splitting factor, love as a normal factor, and dating/mating as the behavior.

tions for each point on the control surface. With high social pressure and relatively high levels of love, the prediction is that some people will engage in low levels of D/M and some people will engage in high levels of D/M, but few people will engage in moderate levels of D/M. Thus, the model specifically builds in bimodality. Bimodal distributions are predicted for each point in the bifurcation set and unimodal distributions for all other points on the control surface.

The dynamics of the model allow predictions of who will be high and who will be low on the behavioral dimension when there is a bimodal distribution. Consider the case of an individual exposed to a potential partner of another race. Assuming low love and strong social pressure against a romantic involvement, D/M is minimal. Suppose, as time goes on, love feelings for the partner steadily increase. Still there would be little increment in D/M. When love reaches a high enough level, just a small increment in love will exceed the threshold and result in a large and sudden increment in D/M, i.e., catastrophic change in behavior. The model predicts that just beyond point b, the fold on the behavior surface, there is a catastrophic jump from the lower to the upper surface. To review, the individual started on the front, right section of the behavior space. Social pressure was constant at a very high level, but love was increasing steadily so the individual was moving from right to left on the behavior surface. Notice that he stayed on the lower surface in the area on the bifurcation set. However, as he passed through the area of the bifurcation set, he reached the left-hand fold and there was no more bottom surface. Since changes in the control variable continued moving him leftward beyond the fold, there was a catastrophic jump to the upper surface—the only surface that exists left of point b.

Still assuming strong social pressure, let us examine the case of love at first sight. When we enter the system, love is very high and D/M behavior is also quite high. Now let us assume that over time love decreases. As this happens, our hypothetical suitor moves from the front left area to the right. He continues at relatively high levels of D/M behavior and is on the upper level of the behavior surface over the bifurcation set. As love continues to move rightward, he will come to the fold (above point a) beyond which the upper surface will cease to exist. Further movement will cause a catastrophic jump to the lower surface. Assuming no change in social pressure, he will remain on the lower surface even if love goes up again. Only if love goes up sufficiently, i.e., beyond point b, will there be a return to the upper surface.

In general, in the area of the bifurcation set, whether a person is on the upper or lower level of the behavior surface depends on his recent history. If he enters the area of the bifurcation set in the neighborhood of the upper level, he will stay on the upper level; if he enters in the neighborhood of the lower level, he will stay on the lower level. The bifurcation set, as noted above, defines the area of bimodality. Its edges are the threshold set for catastrophic jumps. Movement inside of or into the bifurcation set will not cause catastrophic changes in behavior. Also, movement out of the set on the same side as entry into the set will not cause a catastrophe. Changes in control factors that cause an individual to pass through the bifurcation set, i.e., enter on one side and leave on the other, will produce catastrophic jumps in behavior upon leaving. Note also that jumps from the top to the bottom levels take place at a different location than jumps from the bottom level to the top level. This effect is known as *hysteresis*.

What happens if love is held constant and social pressure is varied? Very little, if love is held constant at very high or very low levels. On the other hand, at moderate levels of love, changes in social pressures do make a substantial difference. At very low levels of social pressure and moderate love, the model predicts moderate D/M, i.e., back center region of the figure. As social pressure increases and we move forward on the control surface into the bifurcation set, the corresponding behavior surface bifurcates. The model predicts that with the moderate levels of love, increasing social pressure will divide the sample, producing divergent behavior. That is, some persons will show increased D/M, while others show decreased D/M. Very slight differences in love in the middle range will result in very large differences in response to change in social pressure.

In our example, both love and social pressure have been called control factors but clearly they do not function in the same way. Increases in social pressure, in the middle range of love, leads to divergence—both increasing and decreasing D/M. This kind of control factor is called a *splitting factor*. On the other hand, when the splitting factor, social pressure, is held constant, increases in love are always associated with monotonic increases in D/M. Sometimes the changes in D/M are very small and sometimes they are very large and catastrophic, but they are always monotonically related to love. In this case, love is a *normal factor*. The control surface need not always be defined in terms of a normal and a splitting factor, but in this paper, however, we will be concerned with the cusp catastrophe with a control space defined with a splitting and normal factor.[1]

Another way to conceptualize the behavior surface of the cusp catastrophe in a way that is in keeping with the theme of this volume is as an attractor of a dynamic system. That is, the behavior surface is a region of stability or equilibrium of a system defined by the two control parameters—the splitting factor and the normal factor (social pressure and love, respectively, in our previous example)— and the behavioral parameter (e.g., closeness). As the control parameters change,

[1] From "When Individual Dispositions and Social Pressure Conflict: A catastrophe" by A. Tesser, 1980, *Human Relations, 33, 393–407.* Copyright 1980 by Plenum Press. Reprinted by permission.

the system tends towards the equilibrium condition defined by the behavior surface.

Recall that, in the area referred to as the *bifurcation set*, the model predicts bimodal behavior. That is, for the same combination of control parameters, two modes of behavior are expected. On the surface, this seems to contradict the idea of stability or equilibrium. After all, what is stable about a system that is in equilibrium at more than one point? Actually, the model is indeed stable—or bistable—in this area. In fact, the dynamics of the system strictly determine which of the two stable surfaces above the bifurcation set is the equilibrium surface at any given time. As noted earlier, the equilibrium condition when the combination of control parameters sends the system into the bifurcation set is determined by the point at which the bifurcation set is entered. That is, when the area is entered along the lower surface (e.g., high social pressure and initially low but increasing love in the previous example), the lower surface above the bifurcation set will be the equilibrium surface. Conversely, when the area is entered along the higher surface, the higher surface above the bifurcation set will be the equilibrium surface.

III. The Conflict between Personal Dispositions and Social Pressure: Toward a Psychological Model

Our general hypothesis maps the cusp catastrophe, a mathematical abstraction, onto abstractions with empirical indicants in the social psychological realm. In general, we propose that any behavior is likely to map onto the surface of a cusp catastrophe when one's disposition to engage in that behavior is in conflict with social pressure against that behavior. The D/M example used to describe the cusp dynamics was not fortuitous. It also illustrates our psychological hypothesis (i.e., what happens to dating behavior when a personal disposition to date, i.e., love, comes into conflict with social pressure against dating).

Because this is a relatively unexplored model, we have opted for definitions that are relatively nonrestrictive; as theoretical insight and data accumulate they will, no doubt, force us to become more specific. By *behavior*, we simply mean any overt or covert action that, from the point of view of the actor, is interpreted as being relevant to the focal disposition and social pressure. The model applies only to those behaviors that engage both a disposition and a conflicting social pressure. By *disposition*, we mean any controllable preference for a class of behaviors that, from the point of view of the actor, is seen as having an internal origin and expressing some aspect of the self (e.g., an attitude, a personality disposition). Finally, *social pressure* refers to the perceived presence, again from the point of view of the actor, of social forces that are opposed to the performance of the relevant behavior. The strength of the force is determined by its importance to the individual and would be influenced by factors such as the closeness of the people in opposition to the behavior, the number of others in opposition, and the strength and clarity of the feelings of the opposition.

A. The Elephant and the Blind Men

Catastrophe theory is a mathematical formalism. It is not a psychological theory. Our application of this formalism has appealed to the reader's intuition about the shape of unfolding behavior as circumstances change. Here, we try to breathe psychologically meaningful theoretical life into this formalism. The theoretical life form turns out to be a composite. Some social psychologists have already been working on the tail; others, the nose; and still others, the legs. Like the Indian parable about the three blind men and the elephant, these workers do not appear to realize that, although their descriptions are accurate, they are but parts of a larger, integrated whole. Furthermore, when the parts are juxtaposed, there are interesting aspects of the composite that were not obvious before.

Now let us put the elephant together. According to Gilmore (1981), there are a number of flags or signs that identify behavior as being consistent with catastrophe theory. In social psychology, there is a lot of theoretical and empirical work that produces results that are consistent with two of these signs: divergence and hysteresis. The work on conformity (Asch, 1956) and reactance theory (J. W. Brehm, 1966, 1972) is related to divergence; work on cognitive dissonance theory (Festinger, 1957), commitment (Brickman, 1987; Kiesler, 1971), and order effects in impression formation (Anderson, 1974; Asch, 1946) demonstrates hysteresis.

Divergence refers to differing effects of the splitting factor on behavior. Sometimes increases in the splitting factor increase the behavior, and sometimes they decrease behavior. In this social psychological application, the splitting factor is social pressure. There is a substantial amount of work on conformity (e.g. Asch, 1956) suggesting that when social pressure increases, behavior tends to change in the direction of the pressure. Introductory social psychology texts provide well-developed theoretical reasons for conformity effects: The responses of others provide information about the appropriateness or correctness of one behavior or another; going along with others increases the probability of obtaining acceptance and other social rewards controlled by those others. So, social pressure generally yields behavior consistent with it. But not always.

J. W. Brehm (1966, 1972) suggested the presence of a motive to maintain one's freedom to behave as one wishes. This countermotive to conformity is termed *reactance*. There is now a substantial body of literature documenting the operation of this motive (S. S. Brehm & Brehm, 1981). In one study, for example, Heilman (1976) gave subjects on the streets of New York the opportunity to sign a petition for an issue that they mildly endorsed. In the course of the interaction, some of the subjects learned that someone else believed that people should not be allowed to sign such petitions. This latter group of subjects was more likely to sign the petition than were subjects who were not exposed to this social pressure. So, sometimes social pressure encourages contrary behavior.

Taken together, the work on conformity and reactance do a nice a job of documenting divergence: Sometimes social pressure increases conformity; sometimes it decreases conformity. Each literature has documented the presence of a number of factors that moderate the focal effect (i.e., conformity or reactance). The present model suggests that level of disposition may be a crucial determinant of which effect is obtained. At low levels of disposition, social pressure should produce conformity; at high levels of disposition, social pressure should produce reactance.

B. Hysteresis

A change in behavior is not always reversible; sometimes history counts. Therefore, exactly the same set of current circumstances can produce very different behaviors. Returning to Figure 1, we can see that, at high levels of social pressure, both increases and decreases in love produce discontinuities, although the discontinuities occur at different places. If love and behavior start out low, there is a tendency for the behavior to remain low even though love has increased substantially; if love and behavior start out high, then behavior tends to remain high even though love has decreased substantially. (This "sticking" tendency is known as *hysteresis* in physics.)

This property of the model also seems to capture some of the psychological substance of what we have been doing for years. Dissonance theory provides a very nice psychological model for hysteresis. Assume that one's disposition is consonant with engaging in the behavior and that undergoing negative social pressure is dissonant with engaging in the behavior; one's disposition is dissonant with not engaging in the behavior, and the presence of negative social pressure is consonant with not engaging in the behavior. If one starts out high on the behavior in the face of strong social pressure, then as one's disposition decreases, dissonance increases. To reduce the dissonance, one will look for additional cognitions to support the behavior. Hence, the behavior will tend to remain high even in the face of a decreasing disposition. On the other hand, starting with strong social pressure and low levels of behavior, increasing one's disposition will increase dissonance. To reduce the dissonance, one will look for additional cognitions to support not engaging in the behavior. Hence, the behavior will remain low even though the disposition is increasing. The net result? Hysteresis.

A similar analysis can be drawn for commitment. For example, behavior taken in the face of adversity such as negative social pressure is known to increase commitment (Brickman, 1987; Kiesler, 1971). Commitment makes the behavior more resistant to change. This, also, would explain hysteresis.

We can see pieces of the elephant. Each piece is associated with a well thought out explanation and empirical support. We have focused on only two pieces here, divergence and hysteresis. However, a more complete perusal of the social psychology literature yields evidence for even more "flags," such as bimodality and discontinuity (See Tesser, 1980). From our perspective, the beauty of the catastrophe integration is not that it provides greater psychological insight but that it unites realms of research into a meaningful whole in a way that is unique and has some valuable heuristic properties. Next, we describe an attempt to demonstrate that heuristic value.

IV. A Test of the Model

A. The Conformity Pilot

Reardon and Tesser (1982) designed a study intended to look at hysteresis and discontinuities. These phenomena are likely to be observed under high social pressure. Hysteresis depends on history (i.e., subjects starting from different psychological states facing the same situation will behave differently). Thus, some of the subjects were induced to conform on a prior trial, whereas the remaining subjects were induced to resist conforming. The dependent variable or behavior was resistance to conformity on a subsequent trial. Disposition to resist conforming was manipulated by selecting a topic on which the subjects' own belief strength varied.

Here are some details. We started with 88 female undergraduates who had previously indicated the extent of their agreement or disagreement with a number of sociopolitical items. Subjects were scheduled in groups of four and seated, separated by partitions, in front of a Crutchfield (1955) apparatus, facing the experimenter. They were told that to stimulate the discussions to follow, they were to share their opinions on each item by means of the apparatus before them. Each subject's Crutchfield console was arranged so that single agree and disagree response buttons were available. Above the response buttons were three pairs of lights, "to indicate agreement or disagreement by the other three group members." Actually, these pairs of lights were tied only to the experimenter's master console. Each subject was led to believe that she was Person B. This allowed the experimenter to simulate Persons A, C, and D. On item one, Person B was asked to respond second, and her console was programmed to display total agreement with her pretest position. On item two, Person B responded first. To avoid suspicion, her console displayed two-thirds agreement with her pretest position on this item.

The two independent variables, prior conformity and disposition to conform or attitude strength, were manipulated in Items 3 and 4.

B. Initial Conformity/Nonconformity

Person B was asked to respond last on Item 3 and was confronted with unanimous disagreement with her pretest position. For subjects assigned to the initial conformity group, this was an item on which they had very weak feelings; for subjects assigned to the initial nonconformity group, this was an item on which they had very strong feelings. It was expected that subjects holding a strong position would resist conforming to the group pressure when making their responses. Subjects holding a weak position were expected to conform.

C. Disposition to Conform

The behavior of interest is conformity on Item 4. Item 4 was topically related to Item 3. Again, Person B responded last and faced a unanimous disagreeing majority. For Item 4, however, subjects varied in their disposition to resist. The four levels of disposition corresponded to the following belief strengths reported on the pretest rating scales: "very strongly," "strongly," "moderately," and "slightly."

D. Results

What do we expect? Social pressure was high, so we are looking only at the front slice of Figure 1. People who had conformed in the past entered the situation on the upper surface of the figure, whereas those who had not conformed entered on the lower surface. Strength of current disposition to disagree should have produced discontinuities in conformity for both groups. Furthermore, the jump down for the prior conformity group should have come at a higher level of disposition than should the jump up for the prior nonconformity group.

Of the 59 subjects assigned to the prior conformity group, 48 actually conformed; of the 25 assigned to the prior nonconformity group, 20 did not conform. The anomalous subjects were dropped. (An additional 4 subjects were dropped because they expressed some suspicion of the procedure.) Figure 2 presents the plot of percentage of subjects who conformed on the focal trial as a joint function of prior conformity and current disposition. Although these results should be considered preliminary at this point, they are encouraging and provide a good illustration of the sort of results that support an underlying catastrophe.

As we mentioned, subjects in the prior conformity group had already conformed in the face of pressure to conform; thus, they entered the focal trial on the upper portion of the behavior surface. On the focal trial, we saw high levels of conformity except for those subjects who had a very strong disposition not to

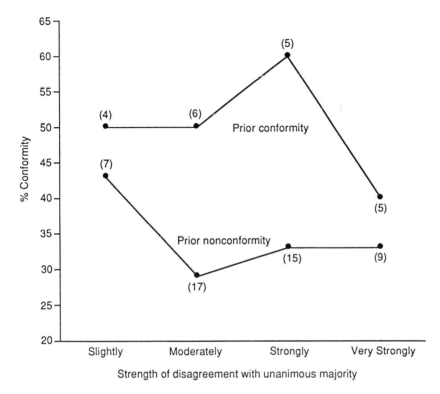

Figure 2 Percentage of subjects conforming as a function of prior conformity and strength of disagreement with a unanimous majority. (Numbers in parentheses indicate number of subjects in each condition.)

conform. These subjects conformed at a rate approximating that of the prior nonconformity group. Thus, it appears that a discontinuity occurred for the prior conformity group in the area of strong to very strong disposition not to conform. Beyond this point, a relatively low level of conformity was found, as if subjects had dropped to the lower portion of the behavior surface.

Similarly, subjects in the prior nonconformity group who did not conform in the face of pressure to do so entered the focal trial on the lower part of the surface. On the focal trial, we saw low rates of conformity except for those subjects who had a weak disposition not to conform. These subjects responded at a rate approximating that of the prior conformity group, suggesting a discontinuity for the prior nonconformity group in the area of moderate to weak disposition not to conform. Beyond this point, a relatively high rate of conformity was found, as if subjects had jumped up to the higher portion of the behavior surface. It is important to note that the points of discontinuity differed for subjects depending on prior conformity or nonconformity (i.e., depending on which part of the behavior surface was occupied), as the model requires.

V. Recapitulation

We have used this chapter as a vehicle for questioning the canonical assumptions that psychologists tend to make about causal relations. These questionable assumptions are that causes and their effects are proportionally (or smoothly) related and that for any unique psychological situation there is likely to be a single modal response. The cusp catastrophe model was introduced as an example of a model that includes smooth and discontinuous causal relations and unimodal and bimodal responding. In this connection, the concepts of divergence (the notion that a single cause can push behavior in opposite directions depending on the state of a third variable) and hysteresis (the notion of behavioral "sticking") were introduced. We argued that the catastrophe formalism can be used to describe the results of conflicts between personal dispositions and social pressure. A preliminary study intended to test these ideas produced some tentative support for the approach.

Acknowledgments

Work on this chapter was facilitated by National Institutes of Mental Health Grant 41487-07, National Science Foundation Grant DBS-9121276, and a fellowship to the Center for Advanced Study in the Behavioral Sciences. Comments should be directed to Abraham Tesser, Institute for Behavioral Research, University of Georgia, Athens, GA 30602.

References

Anderson, N. H. (1974). The problem of change of meaning (Technical Report No. 42). La Jolla, CA: Center for Human Information Processing, University of California.

Asch, S. E. (1946). Forming impressions of personality. *Journal of Abnormal and Social Psychology, 41,* 258–290.

Asch, S. E. (1956). Studies of independence and conformity: A minority of one against a unanimous majority. *Psychological Monographs, 70,* 416.

Brehm, J. W. (Ed.). (1966). *A theory of psychological reactance.* New York: Academic Press.

Brehm, J. W. (1972). *Responses to loss of freedom: A theory of psychological reactance.* Morristown, NJ: General Learning Press.

Brehm, S. S., & Brehm, J. W. (1981). *Psychological reactance: A theory of freedom and control.* New York: Academic Press.

Brickman, P. (1987). *Commitment, conflict, and caring.* Englewood Cliffs, NJ: Prentice-Hall.

Cobb, L. (1978). Stochastic catastrophe models and multi-modal distributions. *Behavioral Science, 23*, 360–374.

Cobb, L. (1981). Parameter estimation for the cusp catastrophe model. *Behavioral Science, 26*, 75–78.

Crutchfield, R. S. (1955). Conformity and character. *American Psychologist, 10*, 191–198.

Festinger, L. (1957). *A theory of cognitive dissonance.* Stanford, CA: Stanford University Press.

Gilmore R. (1981). *Catastrophe theory for scientists and engineers.* New York: Wiley.

Gleick, J. (1987). *Chaos: Making a new science.* New York: Viking.

Guastello, S. J. (1982). Moderator regression and the cusp catastrophe: Application of two-stage personnel selection, training, therapy, and policy evaluation. *Behavioral Science, 27*, 259–272.

Guastello, S. J. (1992). Clash of the paradigms: A critique of an examination of the polynomial regression technique for evaluating catastrophe theory hypotheses. *Psychological Bulletin, 111*, 375–379.

Heilman, M. E. (1976). Oppositional behavior as a function of influence attempt intensity and retaliation threat. *Journal of Personality and Social Psychology, 33*, 574–578.

Kiesler, C. A. (1971). *The psychology of commitment: Experiments linking behavior to belief.* New York: Academic Press.

Kolata, G. B. (1977). Catastrophe theory: The emperor has no clothes. *Science, 196*, 350–351.

Reardon, R., & Tesser, A. (1982). "Is conformity a catastrophe?" University of Georgia, Athens, GA. Unpublished raw data.

Tesser, A. (1980). When individual dispositions and social pressure conflict: A catastrophe. *Human Relations, 33*, 393–407.

Thom, R. (1972). *Structural Stability and Morphogenesis.* New York: Benjamin.

van Geert, P. (1991). A dynamic systems model of cognitive and language growth. *Psychological Review, 98*, 3–53.

Zeeman, E. C. (1976). Catastrophe theory. *Scientific American, 4*, 65–70, 75–84.

CHAPTER 6

Local and Global Dynamics of Social Relations

**Reuben M. Baron and
Polemnia G. Amazeen**
Department of Psychology
University of Connecticut
Storrs, Connecticut

Peter J. Beek
Department of Psychology
Faculty of Human
   Movement Sciences
Vrije University of Amsterdam
Amsterdam, The Netherlands

I. Introduction

There is growing recognition in social psychology of the need to enrich the sociality of our enterprise so that *social* means more than defining our stimuli and responses as referring to people. One can see this empirically in the rapid expansion of the field of interpersonal relations (Gilmore & Duck, 1986) as well as in the reemergence of groups (Paulus, 1983) and intergroup relations (Turner & Giles, 1981) as active problem areas. Metatheoretically, there is also increasing concern with concepts such as mutuality (Levinger, 1980) and interdependence (McClintock, 1988). What appears missing, however, is a principled approach to integrating the phenomena that we take to be social in the sense of relational. Perhaps one of the reasons for this state of affairs is the lack of consensus about what constitutes a social system and what the aims of social analyses should be. We claim that what ties social problems together qua relational problems is that

Dynamical Systems in Social Psychology

they all implicate social coordination as a complex phenomenon; that is, it is a phenomenon that incorporates processes and components at different time scales and levels of aggregation and, by virtue of this property, exhibits functionally stable dynamics as well as qualitative changes in functional behavior. In short, social systems are complex systems, not only intuitively but also in the technical sense of the word. Qua complex systems, social systems exhibit macroscopic or global dynamics that arise from the often nonlinear interactions of subcomponents, but once the global dynamics is established, it affects the local dynamics of its constituent components. Thus, the achievements of social systems involve an interplay of local component dynamics and global dynamics. They have the properties of nonlinear dynamical systems and can, so we claim, in principle be modeled accordingly. In this chapter, we develop the theme of local and global dynamics in a social context. Because we cannot assume common background knowledge, we begin by reviewing basic concepts and simple coupling phenomena, after which we address more complex dyadic and group-type problems in social coordination.[1]

II. Basic Concepts

In defining relevant dynamical concepts that might be applicable to social theory and research, we start with the basics: After using dynamics to describe purely physical events, we then progress to using dynamics to describe biological movements. Finally, we address the question of how this approach might be applicable to social psychology, citing instances in which the gap between the scientific domains is being bridged in experiments designed to study the social coordination of biological movements.

A. The Dynamics of Physical Systems

In the past decade, a dynamical systems perspective has been adopted by ecological psychologists to study the self-organizing aspects of biological systems in the context of movement coordination (e.g., Beek, 1989; Kugler & Turvey, 1987; Schmidt, Beek, Treffner, & Turvey, 1991; Schmidt, Carello, & Turvey, 1990; Turvey, Schmidt, & Rosenblum, 1989). The application of dynamics to biological systems was anticipated by von Holst (1939/1973), whose ideas will be discussed together with the more current position. Contrary to a third-party perspective in

[1]Although we see the dynamical systems approach as especially well suited to extending Gibson's (1979) ecological perception analysis to issues of social coordination (Beek & Hopkins, 1992), both the present analysis and dynamical models in general are potentially relevant to a wide range of theoretical frameworks (as attested to by the breadth of the chapters in this volume).

which the various subcomponents of the biological system are necessarily organized and driven by some outside source (i.e., an executive or external timekeeper), an autonomous dynamical systems perspective posits that relatively stable, new behavior patterns can emerge at a system level (global dynamics), that is, from system properties alone. For example, starting in the purely physical, nonbiological realm, given a set mass and a set length, a pendulum in free oscillation will have a particular frequency, called its *eigenfrequency*. Although the pendulum might be a compound pendulum with various subcomponents, each with a different mass and length (e.g., a handle at the top, a rod or a string for length, and a bob at the end), we can always treat the more complex, compound pendulum system as a simple pendulum with its entire mass located at a particular distance relative to the center of oscillation. This distance is called the *simple pendulum equivalent length of the compound pendulum* (Kugler & Turvey, 1987). The gravitational frequency corresponding to the simple pendulum equivalent length is the compound pendulum's eigenfrequency and is completely specified by the compound pendulum's distribution of mass relative to the center of oscillation. In other words, the behavior of the oscillating pendulum is not guided by an outside physical or cognitive force. It is emergent from the natural component properties of the pendulum itself. It is an autonomous system.

B. The Dynamics of Biological Systems

The application of dynamics to purely physical systems may be self-evident. It is interesting, however, that concepts in dynamics apply equally well to biological systems. Similar to how we see the pendulum, we may view animals as autonomous agents that are dynamically coupled to their environment. The length of one's walking stride, for example, can be determined in much the same way as one calculates a pendulum's swing. People have a preferred stride length because the proportion of their legs to the rest of their body and the mass distribution of their bodies (for example) allow them to walk most efficiently with a set size leg swing. The preferred stride length, in combination with the preferred stride velocity, produces a preferred frequency of walking that is proportionate to the eigenfrequency of the leg. Taller people have longer legs and therefore most comfortably take larger steps; short people tend to have shorter legs and so their step length is necessarily shorter. Similarly, people with different leg lengths will prefer stairs of different heights because they can most easily climb steps that have a .25 ratio of riser height to their leg length (Warren, 1984). Warren's work showed that not only could individuals consistently and uniformly perceive which stair height would be most suitable for them, but when asked to climb stairs of differing heights, they expended the least amount of energy on the stairs that were most dynamically suited to their movement. Once again, as in the pendulum example, there is no executive machinery responsible for guiding the leg movement. The properties of the movement (and the properties of the perception for movement) arise naturally from properties of the leg's components.

If we were to look at each joint as having a certain number of degrees of freedom of movement, we would see that as we take more joints into consideration (as we must do if we are to consider a walking leg), the number of ways in which each joint can move is lawfully constrained; in other words, there are fewer degrees of freedom for each joint individually as we involve more and more joints in the system (for a more detailed argument, see Turvey, 1990). Eventually, although many movements are possible for each joint individually, there are only a limited number of movements lawfully possible for each joint given the fact that all joints are moving together. Any other combination of joint movements is impossible for the system. These statements about the constraints operating on joint movements should not be read to refer solely to the mechanical constraints that follow from the human body's architecture. They also refer to the informational constraints that follow from neural control principles. The latter type of constraints are particularly crucial because they are responsible for the ability of movement systems to self-organize, that is, to show qualitatively new forms of behavior and to lawfully harness cooperation from many local components. Put in the terms of our example of a moving limb, the local dynamics of each individual joint both guide and give way to a more global dynamic that in turn guides the movement of all joints in the system; the system as a whole feeds back to those components of which it is constituted (F. D. Abraham, Abraham, & Shaw, 1990). We consider this the self-organizing aspect of the system.

C. Linking Systems: Coordination

The coordination of joints is a microexample of biological dynamics and one that leads us in the direction of more complex coordination, specifically, the coordination of our limbs and coordination within and between two people. Interlimb coordination works in much the same way as does interjoint coordination. The increased constraints placed on the system by additional components cause a decrease in the degrees of freedom of movement. If we were to think back to the pendulum example, imagine two different sized pendulums swinging freely. They would exhibit different frequencies, each according to its own component properties. Each would have a certain number of degrees of freedom of movement. If they were joined by a spring, however, the two pendulums would exhibit what von Holst (1939/1973) called both a *maintenance tendency* and a *magnet effect*. Although the two pendulums would maintain their own frequencies to an extent (the maintenance tendency), each would be constrained (or entrained), by means of the spring connection, to move with a frequency similar to that of the other pendulum (the magnet effect). In other words, the two pendulums would have fewer degrees of freedom of movement than the sum of their individual degrees of freedom. A person's legs work the same way. Given that they are connected to each other by the person's body, each cannot move freely without being constrained in some way by the other.

Let us now consider walking and some characteristic properties of it: Most people have legs that are similar to each other in length and proportion; therefore, the most efficient movement they can produce for locomotion is that of alternating footsteps (e.g., as opposed to jumping with both feet touching the ground at the same time or stepping twice with one foot and once with the other) so that the two legs are usually exactly opposite to each other in their stride. Because the stride is cyclical (i.e., the leg returns to roughly the same position at the end of each step), we shall consider each stride to be a full 360°, like a circle. Considering the situation in which both feet touch the ground at the same exact time as 0° relative phase (i.e., they are in the same position in the cycle), we would consider walking behavior to be normal when legs have a relative phase difference of 180°. Because both legs move most comfortably at the same frequency, they are spaced equally and exactly opposite to each other, or 180° apart out of a possible 360°, in the stride cycle.

Most people have legs that are just slightly uneven, and this does not drastically affect the spacing of their legs during walking, but consider now the situation in which a person's legs are grossly uneven in length. Although people who have this biology alternate their footsteps in order to locomote, their legs are not usually 180° out of phase. Instead, the longer leg has a naturally longer stride than the shorter leg, the two legs are not exactly opposite to each other in the stride, and their relative phase will be less than or greater than 180°. This is an interesting situation to analyze because the two local components, the legs, are not equivalent to each other. Consequently, it would seem that some compromise must be reached between the two to settle on a stride length that each can achieve. As mentioned previously, the system exhibits both a maintenance tendency and a magnet effect; the maintenance tendency, or competition, is exhibited to the extent that each leg can only move within given parameters, but the magnet effect, or cooperation, must occur for the person to locomote. Walking behavior, therefore, emerges from the properties of the local components but constrains the behavior of each local component as well.

1. Models for Coordination

Considering the special situation of two uneven legs encourages us to look into models for interlimb coordination that allow us to manipulate the local components of a system more specifically. Although walking experiments that use people's natural limb length have been conducted, they are more difficult to monitor and understandably more difficult to manipulate (e.g., Valenti, 1989). Earlier, we discussed how a pendulum has an eigenfrequency, dependent on the characteristics of its components. If we were to substitute pendulums for a person's limbs, we would have a more flexible and more easily manipulable object of study. Indeed, a person who is asked to coordinate the swinging of two hand-held pendulums displays a coordination of two limbs, the arms, in much the same way that he or she displays a coordination of the legs during normal walking behavior (e.g., Kugler & Turvey, 1987; Schmidt et al., 1991; Turvey et al., 1989). Because we can modify the length and mass distribution of the pendulums, we have the ability to manipulate the components of the system and therefore to see how various manipulations of the local components affect the system as a whole. Because the pendulums themselves, rather than the limbs, are now the local components, the same frequency and amplitude are displayed by all individuals who swing those pendulums. This is one of the great strengths of this model: The observed behavior is systematic and consistent across individuals and thus betrays its lawful dynamical basis.

For example, if a person is asked to swing two pendulums of equal mass and length (e.g., two pendulums that have the same eigenfrequency), then the system automatically self-organizes into one-to-one phase-locking behavior, where each pendulum swings at the same frequency and each covers one cycle swing in the same time. The frequency at which they swing together, the eigenfrequency of the coupled system, is the same as the frequency at which they swing when separate because there is no difference to begin with. In terms of relative phase, the system will either swing at 180° relative phase, as in walking, or at 0° relative phase, which is the more stable solution in pendulum swinging but not in walking.

On the other hand, if the pendulums are of different lengths or masses, they have different eigenfrequencies, and so we have a situation similar to that in which a person is walking with uneven legs. The eigenfrequency of the coupled system is no longer the same as the eigenfrequency of each pendulum separately nor is it an average of the two, but it is a function of properties of the local units. Kugler and Turvey (1987) demonstrated the calculations of the eigenfrequency of the coupled system, which is more simply understood as the frequency with which a single simple pendulum would swing, given the properties of the two separate pendulums. Swinging two pendulums with different local properties at a particular phase relation is revealing of the joint influence of the maintenance tendencies and the magnet effect. Increased deviations of the eigenfrequencies from each other will produce greater instability in the phase relation between the pendulums, so that just like the case in which a person has uneven legs, it is more difficult to maintain a stable walking period, and the relative phase is likely to be slightly higher or lower than the intended 180° (or 0°) (Rosenblum & Turvey, 1988; Schmidt et al., 1991).

So we see that two hand-held pendulums swinging independently each have an eigenfrequency that is dependent on the joint properties of their own individual components; however, when they are joined together in the within-person inter-limb coordination system, they themselves are the components in a larger system. They oscillate at the eigenfrequency of the coupled system and they are a certain relative phase with respect to each other, the most stable of which are 0° and 180°. The more their individual eigenfrequencies deviate from zero, the less stable the system. Under particular conditions, sudden jumps from an out-of-phase mode of coordination to an in-phase mode of coordination may be observed. For instance, when two short pendulums are swung at a relative phase of 180° and the common frequency of oscillation is gradually increased, an abrupt shift to a relative phase of 0° may be induced. Prior to such an abrupt shift or phase transition, the variability in relative phase may get very large. This phenomenon is called *critical fluctuation* because it signals the onset of a different mode of behavior (Haken, 1977; Turvey, 1990). We will discuss it later when we present the concept of attractors. All of these phenomena are in line with what can be expected from a dynamical system; therefore, we consider interlimb coordination to be dynamical in nature.

2. The Dynamics of Socially Coordinated Biological Systems

Intuitively, movements coordinated between people are more complicated to understand than movements coordinated within a person. Although two people who are coordinating their movements can be considered to be a single system, this system is quite unlike the systems discussed thus far in that the moving segments are not joined by any type of biological tissue and their behavior is often considered to be cognitively geared. However, it is interesting that when two people are asked to coordinate the swinging of their legs, they demonstrate the same type of phenomena as demonstrated in purely biological (i.e., nonsocial) systems, including phase transitions (Schmidt et al., 1990), the maintenance tendency, and the magnet effect (Schmidt & Turvey, 1992); in other words, although each individual has a preferred leg swing, a compromise (the eigenfrequency of the coupled system) emerges at the level of the system. Furthermore, their legs most commonly assume a relative phase of either 0° or 180°, a phenomenon also observed in social walking studies (Valenti, 1989). Thinking back to our initial discussion, the emergence of the global behavior is a function of properties of the local components alone and not some third executive power. Despite the lack of a physical connection, coordination between individuals behaves according to the most fundamental rules of a dynamical system.

3. Personality as a Constraint on Coordination

What happens when we introduce more social variables, such as personality, to the coordinating system? Christianson (1992) used the pendulum paradigm as well as a shortened version of the Riggio Social Skills Inventory (Boudreau, 1991; Riggio, 1986) in an attempt to demonstrate that social factors like social competence affect the global dynamic in addition to physical factors, like the length and mass of pendulums. Subjects were asked to coordinate their movements in such a way that the relative phase between the two pendulums was 180°. Eigenfrequency ratios, required frequency of oscillation, and level of social competence (high or low) were varied; achieved average phase relation and stability of the system (i.e., variance) served as dependent variables. It was found that although physical determinants of phase relation were strongest, the social factor affected the behavior of the global system as well. High–high competence pairings had the most difficulty maintaining the intended phase relation of 180°, whereas high–low pairings were the most stable. It was hypothesized that highly competent subjects were most intent on maintaining their own preferred period; in other words, they demonstrated the maintenance tendency to the exclusion of the magnet effect. Therefore, when subjects who scored low on competence were paired with them, the system was the most stable because one person naturally led the tempo while the other followed. Further analysis revealed that the rating of competence was most highly correlated with the social control subscale of the Riggio Social Skills Inventory. In future research, dominance might be more properly considered the social variable at work in this experiment. The most important implication from this line of research, however, is that more traditional social variables can be shown to affect interperson coordination in ways consistent with a dynamical systems perspective.

D. Attractor Dynamics

Before considering how the study of social relations might be further influenced by a dynamical systems perspective, we will address some key concepts not yet emphasized. First of all, why are we considering pendulums and a person's legs to be dynamical in nature? We have already discussed the self-organizing and lawful aspects of systems like these, but we can also argue that the system's behavior is both periodic in nature and constantly evolving in regard to preferred trajectories. If we observe the movement of these systems over time, we would notice that although neither the pendulum nor the leg follow the same exact pathway each time they complete a full swing, the pathway they do form is consistent; because each swing completes a cycle by coming back to its starting point, it is called *periodic*, or *cyclical*.

If we were to map the trajectories of the system's movements over time, we would find that they all fall around an "ideal" pathway for the system. This ideal pathway is the one formed out of the self-organizing aspects of the system (as discussed earlier) and is dynamically termed an *attractor*, or the cycle toward which all nearby trajectories tend (F. D. Abraham et al., 1990, p. V-1; C. D. Abraham &

Shaw, 1982).[2] Given a specific pendulum, then, each swing would fall on or around that attractor because of the global dynamic that emerges from the properties of the pendulum's local components. The attractor is the most stable option available to the system, so that even if a pendulum is erratically set into motion, it will settle onto its attractor over time. In other words, it is guided toward its own comfort mode. Furthermore, if perturbed, it will resume its attractor path over time as well. The time it takes to do this is called the *relaxation time* and can be used as a measure for the strength of attraction. Manipulation of certain parameters (called *control parameters*) may affect the attractor layout or the potential landscape in such a way that an abrupt shift in behavior occurs because a previously stable state becomes unstable and the system shifts to another stable mode; this critical point of change is called a *bifurcation point*. As mentioned earlier, the pendulum will exhibit increased fluctuations, called *critical fluctuations*, as it approaches the bifurcation point (phase transition).

E. Order and Control Parameters

Considering the dyadic situation, we find that two pendulums likewise set up a global dynamic that they follow, dependent on their initial conditions. They oscillate consistently along a particular pathway, an attractor, over time. Unlike a single pendulum, however, they can achieve a level of coordination in regard to a particular relative phase, an aspect of the system that dynamically constitutes an order parameter (e.g., Haken, 1987; Turvey, 1990). An order parameter serves two basic functions. First, it is a quantitative measure of the coordination, coherence, or cooperativity among interacting components (Kelso & Jeka, 1992). For example, in physical systems, order parameters are 1 when the subcomponents of an entity are in their proper location or phase and 0 when a state of disorder exists (Turvey, 1990). Order is also relevant to proper function; thus, for walking, a 180° discrep-

---

[2]The theory of nonlinear dynamics knows four different types of attractors: (1) Point attractors consist of equilibrium points with zero dimension, where the solution for the system at any given time is a constant (and so the vector field [the field of trajectories of the system's movement over time] vanishes). (2) Periodic attractors are those for which the solution for the system is one of periodic repetition; in other words, the system returns to the same points in state space after a cycle of a certain length and duration. Because the resulting limit cycle is a line, periodic attractors have dimension of one. The pendulum paradigm is an example of a periodic solution. (3) Quasiperiodic attractors are similar to periodic attractors. Their cycles are of a fixed length and duration, but the system never precisely revisits points in state space because the periods contained in quasiperiodic attractors are related in noninteger fashion; they are an irrational number. The dimension of a quasiperiodic attractor is an integer number of minimally two because minimally two periods are required to constitute one. (4) Finally, chaotic attractors are highly irregular, but dynamically driven, solutions for a system; although similar in appearance to random noise, they have a deterministic structure with finite but fractal dimensions.

ancy represents the proper phase relation between two legs, and its order parameter when this occurs is 1. Second, in addition to indexing the order of the component parts, order parameters give orders to those components. This should sound familiar given that our discussion of pendulums was geared toward understanding how the local pendulum systems both influence and are influenced by the global system.

Dynamically, the order parameter also serves as an index of phase transitions, which are brought about by manipulations of the control parameter. The control parameter is the variable that drives the order parameter through its respective stable states such that manipulations of it have the ability to cause qualitative changes in the order parameter; that is, as the value of the control parameter is changed, there comes a critical point at which the system undergoes a phase transition. For example, one of the variables manipulated in Christianson's (1992) study was frequency of oscillation. When the frequency at which pendulums are forced to oscillate is increased and when the system is not already at its most stable, a temporary breakdown in the structure of the system occurs and the system eventually, but automatically, falls into a more stable pattern. To reiterate, if two pendulums are being oscillated at 180° relative phase, they will continue to do so as long as the driving frequency remains within certain bounds; if they are forced to oscillate at higher and higher frequencies, however, they will first demonstrate decreased stability, then critical fluctuations, and finally, they will fall into the pattern at which they are oscillating at 0° relative phase, which, as you will recall, is more stable than 180° relative phase. The manipulation of the control parameter, frequency of oscillation, causes a phase transition in the order parameter from 180° to 0° relative phase. Thinking back to the discussion of attractors, the increased deviation from the ideal frequency for maintaining 180° causes decreased stability to the point at which it necessitates falling into a different attractor region. If the system were merely perturbed, however, and if the frequency is only momentarily and noncritically increased, then the pendulums eventually resume their 180° relative phase mode during the critical slowing down period.

In sum, there is a synergistic relation between control and order parameters that allows us to distinguish between linear accelerations and phase transitions. Specifically, if the relative phase between two limbs is the order parameter, there are certain criteria, termed *catastrophe flags* by Gilmore (1981) that indicate that genuine phase transitions are occurring. These criteria operate both just prior to a transition, as observable behaviors of the system (critical slowing down and critical fluctuations), as well as during the transition, in the form of sudden jumps and hysteresis.[3]

---

[3]As defined by Turvey (1990), paraphrasing Gilmore (1981), sudden jumps occur when slow changes in the control parameter bring about rapid changes in the order parameter, and hysteresis occurs when a phase transition in one direction (as indexed by the order parameter) does not occur at the same value of the control parameter as a transition in the opposite direction.

III. Extension to Social Psychology

Just as a dynamical systems perspective has been used to explain purely bio-logical behavior and physical coordination in a social context, we hope to make clear the extension into strictly social realms, specifically, into the field of interpersonal relations. In selecting a system to model using tools from nonlinear dynamics, we look for a phenomenon that is both synergistic and cooperative, whose components change over time in ways that reflect coordinations among them. Moreover, we look for systems whose evolution over time ". . . can be gradual most of the time, but be punctuated by these dramatic bifurcations as the control parameter passes through critical thresholds" (F. D. Abraham et al., 1990, p. 11). In the following section, we examine two social systems phenomena, the evolution of close relationships and the socialization of group membership. Because they can be viewed as complex, self-organizing systems whose behavior is both emergent from interactions of and involves nonlinear reorganizations of its components over time, we propose that such social systems are dynamical in nature. The possibility of viewing them in this way opens wide the field for new understandings of social phenomena at two levels, the weaker metaphorical level and the stronger empirical one. The weak form of such modeling is to view our treatment as metaphorical in the sense that we are laying the conceptual groundwork for the possibility of using the mathematical tools of dynamical systems analyses to study social coordination-type phenomena. To advance our analysis beyond metaphor, however, we will indicate some possibilities, within each of our substantive sections (dyads, groups), for how to turn conceptual control and order parameters into empirical, quantitative dynamic variables.

A. Modeling Close Relations

In modeling close relations, we plan to look at dynamical effects in regard to two of Levinger's close relation models: his intersection model of pair relatedness (which, although largely intended for cross-sectional comparisons, can also be taken as describing the evolution of relationship closeness; Levinger & Snoek, 1972) and his ABCDE model of the long-term development of a relation (Levinger, 1980). Both models have two essential properties: (1) they view relations as undergoing systematic changes over time that refer to states of organization of a social system (i.e., they are dynamical in the basic sense) and (2) they are reciprocal in the sense that they involve coordinations among components that involve mutual influence. That is, there is both a balancing out of local competitive and cooperative tendencies and a trend toward mutuality and global dynamics, where there is an emergence of mutual entrainment such that the relation can be characterized by an attractor.

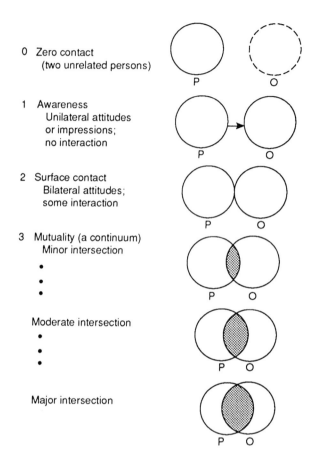

0 Zero contact
   (two unrelated persons)

1 Awareness
      Unilateral attitudes
      or impressions;
      no interaction

2 Surface contact
      Bilateral attitudes;
      some interaction

3 Mutuality (a continuum)
      Minor intersection

Moderate intersection

Major intersection

Figure 1 Levels of relatedness. [From "Toward the analysis of close relationships" (p. 514) by G. Levinger, 1980. *Journal of Experimental Social Psychology, 16*, 510–544.]

We begin such an analysis by examining the Levinger and Snoek (1972) paired relatedness model (described in Levinger, 1980), which we will first describe and then view in coupled oscillator terms.

1. The Paired Relatedness Intersect Model

Levinger (1980) defined his problem space in terms that are congenial to a dynamical analysis (see Figure 1). Specifically, in discussing the development of pair mutuality, he went from informational coordination, in which mutuality of self-disclosure involves an exchange of intimate information, to an aspect of "mutual discovery," invoking shared awareness in which two people not only know much about each other but each one knows what the other knows about him or her and so on. Thus, we have a kind of global level of awareness at the level of the relationship. This is a product of the evolution of the relationship from earlier "self-awareness only" stages.

A second process focuses on what Levinger (1980) referred to as *behavior coordination* and *emotional investment*. Shared emotional investment involves each partner taking increased pleasure from the other's satisfaction. Moreover, as the partners increase in mutuality, the intersection between two people's lives grows, the distinction between "I" and "you" lessens and merges into the larger "we." Behavior coordination refers to how each person learns to accommodate the other's responses and preferences. This behavior coordination can be viewed in exchange terms, which Levinger utilized in this early version. Specifically, there is a shift from focusing on individual outcome matrices to a focus on a dyadic outcome matrix that represents the relationship. In the terminology of this chapter, there is a shift from local to global dynamics.

Mutuality as coupling   The intersect model proposes that levels of mutuality, or interdependence, are marked by mutual responsibility for one another's outcomes, a factor we take to be indicative of commitment to the relationship. What then is self-organization in this context? We believe that the organization of the relationship as a whole evolves out of the extent to which the components reciprocate self-disclosure as well as positive, as opposed to negative, partner expressive and instrumental responses (cf. Gottman, 1979). That is, the global mutuality feeds off the "healthy" feedback of the interaction components.

Before beginning more formal analyses, it should be noted that we face two difficult problems if we are to move beyond a metaphorical level of modeling. First, we need to choose the control variables that act as driving forces for the order variable dynamics that occur in regard to the social systems we are modeling. Fortunately, it appears as if both the evolution of close relationships and group socialization (discussed later) share a common order parameter, levels of commitment (viewed as an index of level of social coordination). Second, we need to demonstrate that the system to be modeled reflects stage-type changes in an order parameter rather than continuous linear shifts. Within recent work on interlimb movement coordination, both within and between individuals, this task has been simplified by treating the components of the movement system, the swinging limbs, as nonlinear oscillators with nonlinear couplings between them. Therefore, one possibility is to model close relationships in dyads as such a pair of oscillators seeking to balance their own interests, or maintenance tendencies, with their efforts to cooperate by means of a magnet effect. Variables, such as personality and differences in life experience, might be considered a part of the local dynamic that each person tries to hold onto at the same time as wanting to enter into a global dynamical system that has a potentially different trajectory or preferred rhythm or attractor. In principle, it is possible to work out the pendulum model beyond the level of the dyad and to include the group situation, but such an elaborate exercise adds little to our present argument.

The oscillating pendulum model may do a good job of modeling how one may "distinguish among close and not-so-close relationships at any single point in time" (Levinger, 1980, p. 541). Here, Levinger offered a treatment of mutuality that could be reconstrued in terms of the coupling function underlying the coordination of two paired oscillators: In Figure 1, mutuality is depicted in terms of Venn diagram types of intersection, ranging from separate, noncontacting circles to highly overlapping circles with large areas of intersection. Here, increasing mutuality involves moving from (1) mere awareness of the other component to (2) unilateral awareness to (3) surface contact, interaction, and bilateral interest to (4) mutuality of interaction involving levels of mutuality. Operationally, Levinger looked for indices of shared territoriality and indices of shifts from public to private norms, including increases in confiding (shift from surface to mutuality) and exclusivity of dating (shift from low to high mutuality). More broadly, he looked for evidence of increased affective and/or behavioral interdependence or coordination. Indeed, Gottman (1979) found evidence of entrainment of both expressive behavior (short-term fast-moving reactions such as smiling and frowning) and mood in dating couples. It is only with mutuality of concern, the highest level of intersect, that the coordination of local dynamics or maintenance tendencies takes place. It is at this highest level of mutuality that interdependence deepens in regard to "intimate disclosure, knowledge of each other's personal feelings, joint development of pair norms, and mutual responsibility for one another's outcomes, not to speak of strong mutual attraction" (Levinger, 1980, p. 513). This description nicely fits Beek and Hopkins (1992) proposition that in dynamical models, "the informational basis for action becomes apparent as a function of time" (p. 438).

To detail this analysis even further, we clearly need to specify the order parameter and the variables that drive it through its respective stable states. The dyadic case may be viewed as a coupling of two people, each with their own local dynamics, into a stable social system such as marriage, which runs on a global dynamic. Perhaps the best candidate for an order parameter for Levinger and Snoek's (1972) intersection model is a quantity that expresses commitment to a global dynamic, as opposed to a local dynamic or maintenance tendency. Specifically, oscillators become entrained in the sense that they "bring each other into the same phase, or into an orderly succession of phases, as in the case of traveling waves" (Garfinkel, 1987, p. 195). Viewed thusly, the order parameter would be the degree of discrepancy in commitment to the relationship that existed between partners, for example, the extent to which Jim's mood of happiness depended on Mary's, versus Mary's on Jim's, that is, the coordination of their investment in each other. To the extent that there is a discrepancy in commitment to the relationship, asymmetrical coupling functions will have to be introduced in modeling this property.

If commitment drives the emergence of a global dynamic or relationship, what controls commitment? What, for example, is comparable to frequency of oscillation for interlimb coordination? Perhaps the most general candidate is reward-ingness or need satisfaction. Specifically, we move from competition between local units to cooperation between local units when people "cannot improve their payoffs by making changes just in their own strategies" (see Garfinkel's, 1987 use of Nash's equilibrium criterion, p. 205). Other candidates for control parameters include the reciprocity of the communication of intimate information as well as increasing levels of affect intensity (arousal).

2. Levinger's ABCDE Model of Long-Term Dyadic Relations

The second close relationship model we consider is Levinger's long-term ABCDE model (Levinger, 1980). In this model, depicted in Figure 2, one can treat the shifts from *attraction* to *building a relation* to *continuation* to *divergence* to *exit* as a dynamical system. Levinger specifically treated continuation as a bifurcation point, which can lead to one of three qualitatively different equilibrium states: grow-ing, satisfying continuation, placid, static continuation, or unstable, conflictful continuation. The latter two are clearly phase changes leading appropriately enough to what Levinger refers to as *divergence* or *decoupling*. He viewed the different phases as having what he referred to as *transition points* that signify *switch points*. For exam-ple, continuation to divergence (C to D) "signifies a switch point between try-ing to maintain an established relationship and letting it go downhill" (Levinger, 1980, p. 536).

What is missing in Levinger's model is the specification of a measure for the observed patterns of behavior, an order parameter needed to index the coordina-tion changes that occur whenever there is a phase transition. Here, we again propose that commitment, or degree of involvement, serves this purpose, where, by *com-mitment*, we mean an investment in the relationship that raises "barriers" around the relationship and, in terms of Levinger and Snoek's (1972) earlier mutuality model, increases the mutuality intersect, the social coordination, between couples. The term *commitment* is further operationalized by mutuality of emotional involvement such that in a good relationship, positive responses are reciprocated, whereas in a poor relationship, negative responses are reciprocated. Levinger suggested that in-volvement (what we refer to as *commitment*) is the key mediator of whether an established relationship will deteriorate or maintain itself. Moreover, "any drop or rise in involvement is the complex resultant of changes in one or more of the following characteristics: the couple's frequency, duration, and diversity of interac-tion; its synchrony of behavioral accommodation; its positivity and intensity of affect; its openness of communication; its trustfulness; its commonality of plans and

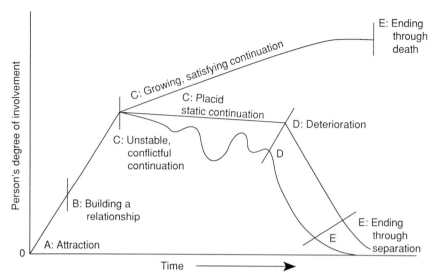

Figure 2   The longitudinal course of a partner's involvement in three contrasting couple relationships. [From "Toward the analysis of close relationships" (p.522) by G. Levinger, 1980. *Journal of Experimental Social Psychology, 16,* 510–544.]

outcomes" (Levinger, 1980, p. 537). These factors all become candidates for control parameters, with intimacy, frequency of interaction, and affect intensity particularly good ones. It can then be argued, for example, that the continuance "trifurcation" reflects gains or losses in, for example, intimacy, affect intensity, and the like. In such a view, these factors are control parameters and commitment an order parameter. For example, "if intimacy rises, so should commitment; if intimacy descends, commitment is expected to do likewise" (Levinger, 1980, p. 537).

   a. Exclusivity as a dynamic order parameter   Commitment fits Garfinkel's (1987) interpretation of an order parameter in that it is a quantity that expresses the cooperativity of coupling in regard to the level of entrainment that exists; in Levinger's terms, what brings the relationship from attraction to building is an increase in the symmetry of involvement. Similarly, what describes the phase shift from building to continuance is an increase in level of commitment in terms of both increased mutuality of investment to a joint pledge to maintain the relationship and increased exclusiveness in regard to placing a barrier around the relationship.
   To shift from a conceptual to an empirical treatment of order and control parameters, we must clarify how the conceptual order parameter of mutuality of investment to the relationship (commitment) can be indexed in terms of a quantity that both changes continuously and can readily be observed and measured (the

dynamic variable). That is, we must answer the question of what is being ordered in dynamical terms. A number of converging sources can be interpreted to suggest that a good dynamical index is the coordination of people's preferred allocation of time for leisure–volitional social encounters. That is, the empirical order parameter is the joint exclusivity of free-time investment in the other person, with complete interchangeability of time investment between target and alternative other partners anchoring one end of a continuum and nonsubstitutability anchoring the other end.[4] This approach is analogous to Premack's (1965) treatment of the reinforcement value of different activities as being indexed by the duration of time for which animals spontaneously engage in particular behaviors or activities when no time or response restrictions exist; it also corresponds to Berlyne's (1974) treatment of aesthetic preferences as being indexed by spontaneous allocation of looking time. Operationally, we could observe a series of weekends for each partner to see if each is shedding social encounters with other people at the same rate, beginning with their refusal to date other people. Finally, for college students, possible observable control parameters for such exclusive time investment could include length of relationship in general and closeness to graduation in particular.

b. Phase transitions Levinger tried to derive three levels of modality change in the transition between B and C shown in Figure 2: ideal, passive, and conflicted trajectories. First, initial conditions or maintenance tendencies (including personality, history, etc.) may prevent a stable coordination; that is, past maintenance tendencies may conflict with forming a new, stable relationship with global attraction (see the "Frankie and Johnny" example below). Second, the interpersonal system may be unstable in regard to level of mutuality achieved (level of intersection regarding shared self-disclosure or mutuality of affective involvement or lack of shift from individual to dyad-level payoff matrix).

At issue in the continuance to deterioration phase transition is the trajectory of "marital" (or long-term involvement) satisfaction over time. In regard to Levinger's danger signal hypothesis, the idea is that if close partners in the middle of the relationship worry about the fairness of the relationship, it indicates that one or both may no longer be receiving adequate rewards or benefits from being in the relationship. This equity hypothesis fits our earlier interpretation of rewardingness as a control parameter. At issue at this point is whether a trajectory of deterioration to exit will occur or whether there will be an attempt to repair the relationship. Attempts to repair the relationship can be modeled as an hysteresis phenomenon.

[4]A related way to view this problem that is more molecular is to use Newtson, Hairfield, Bloomingdale, and Cutino's (1988) cooperation data as a model. Here, what is found is that initially different wave forms for two individuals (local dynamics) merge into a common wave form as cooperation deepens over time. These two approaches can be merged if we assume that as exclusivity increases, the two partners will engage in more activities that share a common wave form.

c. Hysteresis   We expect hysteresis in both a metaphorical and literal sense. Thus, at the level of analogy, whatever leads to a shift from building to maintenance (commitment) or a shift from individualistic exchange to a communal caring relationship (Clark & Mills, 1979)—be it increased intimacy of disclosure, affect intensity, or the like—will not readily allow for relationship repair once deterioration occurs. For example, if a certain amount of intimacy of self-disclosure or rewardingness led to the phase transition from individualistic to communal the first time around, that same amount will not repair the relationship so that it can be communal again; instead, more rewardingness will be needed. If we could quantify rewardingness or intimacy as a control parameter and could demonstrate a drop when building deteriorates to loss of maintenance, this hysteresis hypothesis could be tested (recall the treatment of exclusivity discussed earlier).

Assuming that repair fails, we can model the deterioration to exit path in dynamical terms as follows: The global dynamics, at this point, are no longer functioning as a "virtual system"; that is, local maintenance tendencies are reemerging as dominant over the magnet effect that brings the couple together under a global coordination. At the level of observables, drops in degree of involvement/commitment created by changes in control parameters are indicated by (1) lowered frequency, duration, and diversity of interaction; (2) a drop in synchrony of behavioral accommodation; (3) positivity and intensity of affect; (4) openness of communication; (5) trustfulness; and (6) commonality of plans and outcomes. This signals the path from deterioration to exit. In sum, continuance is based on mutual reinforcement and a shift from "I" to "we" bases for relations. Termination rests on alternative attractors and/or a drop in rewardingness leading to loss of a commitment to the global dynamics of this relationship. In effect, the attractors of this relationship are annihilated because more powerful attractors exist in alternative relationships.

d. Frankie and Johnny   We close this section on dyadic relationships by considering how the presently developed dynamical argument can be applied to a recent movie about close relations, "Frankie and Johnny." We can formalize the Frankie and Johnny analysis in the following way. These two characters, a male cook with a prison history and a desire for intimacy (Johnny) and a waitress with a failed love affair and a fear of intimacy (Frankie), represent the generic conflict between maintenance preferences and cooperation/magnet-type pressures in service of coordination, where the maintenance tendencies (competitive forces) are the local dynamics and the cooperative pressures move toward a globally dynamic relationship. In effect, we begin with different attractor preferences and then move toward a shared preference for an attractor region expressing mutual entrainment, be it absolute (magnet effect) or relative (a new attractor region is established in between or is a [weighted] average of maintenance levels). In the movie, the analogy is the difference between each in terms of their willingness to enter into a relationship. Thus, the phase transition decision to initiate a commitment relationship is what the movie is all about, given the man's eagerness and the woman's reluctance. In regard to fitting a dynamical model, we need to look for appropriate control parameters (e.g., affect intensity or stress) that will create momentarily (i.e., prior to the transition) critical fluctuations (e.g., an increase in mood shifts) but eventually lead to another stable level of social coordination. In the movie, Johnny's sleeping with another female co-worker might have been indicative of such a disequilibrium. Once this occurs, we still need to demonstrate an organization process to get from building into a continuance phase. At issue is shared information (self-disclosure) and shared emotional investment. Frankie's problem can be treated as an issue in hysteresis. That is, having been hurt in a relationship, she needs more affective intensity (control parameter) to get her committed (order parameter) this time around than she needed previously (see our discussion of hysteresis). For her not to slip back into a maintenance mode, the global dynamics of the new relationship must feedback and modify the local dynamics. Unless this occurs, prospects for continuation are not good.

In sum, Levinger's degree of involvement, or commitment, may be treated as an order parameter, with A, B, C, D, and E as the phase transitions that express its modality. He also assumed there are transition decisions; for example, the path from A to B (A→B) refers to a decision to initiate a relationship; B→C refers to a commitment to a more permanent bonding; C→D is a bifurcation point at which the decision is made to either maintain the relationship or let it deteriorate; finally, D→E refers to a judgment to terminate a relationship. These shifts involve divergence and sudden jumps as well as hysteresis if our hypotheses are correct.

B. The Moreland and Levine Group Socialization Model as a Dynamical System

Moreland and Levine (1982) addressed the issue of socialization in small groups, specifically, of temporal changes in individual–group relations (see Figure 3). The common concept between the Moreland and Levine model and the Levinger model is degree of commitment, the proposed order parameter. The issue for a group is similar to that for a dyad: how to instill commitment and avoid disequilibrium in individual and group commitments. Both Moreland and Levine and Levinger dealt with stages in a relationship over time and the importance of a reciprocal or relational perspective of the change. In group socialization, reciprocity takes the form of a focus on coordination in regard to the prospective member's relationship to the group. Moreland and Levine called the passage of individuals through groups a *dynamic perspective*, one that focuses on change over time in the history of an individual's relationship to a virtual system, the group.

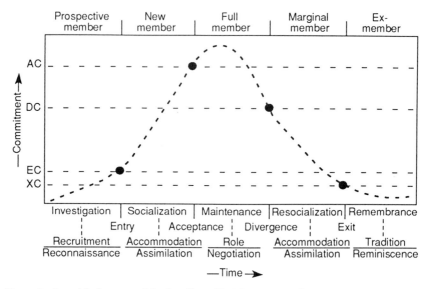

Figure 3 A model of group socialization. (From "Socialization in small groups: Temporal changes in individual–group relations" [p. 153] by R. L. Moreland & J. M. Levini, 1982. *Advances in experimental social psychology 15.* L. Berkowitz, editor. New York: Academic Press.)

We propose that both the building of a dyadic relationship and group socialization embody a stage transition, processes that fit the self-organizational stages of a dynamical system. Specifically, the creation and stability of new forms require the cooperation of two or more subcomponents that follows three stages: (1) component systems interact to form an aggregate or emergent structure; (2) this structure then moves (e.g., bifurcates) from a homogeneous to a more differentiated, complex organization that stabilizes and then, after performing its proper function, (3) may go through a dissolution phase (see Garfinkel's, 1987, discussion of a slime mold). This general model, we claim, fits both Levinger's ABCDE model and Moreland and Levine's group socialization model.

At a more analytic level, we propose that both can be modeled as oscillator-type phenomena, involving issues of entrainment. For example, with regard to coordinations at the dyadic level, we have the tension between components staying at their own preferred space–time behavior, or local dynamics (maintenance tendencies), with the tendency for each oscillator to pull or attract the other to its tendency (the magnet effect). In groups, role transitions, majority versus minority influence, and control of deviants illustrate these processes.

Furthermore, we seek to model the historical evolution of both of these systems in regard to parameters of control and order that jointly produce phase transitions by creating instabilities, characterized by increased fluctuations prior to sudden jumps to another stable mode. Moreover, these fluctuations should be viewed as the system trying out new configurations of attractors as the basis for higher levels of organization (Haken, 1987). We now seek to support these claims by looking at group socialization as the evolution of a self-organizing dynamical system.

1. Group Socialization Phases as Hallmarks of Self-Organizing Systems

The structure of group socialization resembles Levinger's ABCDE model of close relationships both phenotypically, in regard to the types of phase decisions that are at issue, and in regard to a trajectory of increasing commitment that can eventuate in either continuance or deterioration. Genotypically, we argue they are both self-organizing, dynamical systems reflecting the evolution of coordination among components as they interact over time in various patterns of mutual entrainment. In support of this interpretation, Moreland and Levine (in press) claimed that "group membership is both a reciprocal and dynamic relationship; reciprocal because the individual and the group can influence one another [our mutual entrainment], and dynamic because the nature of the relationship changes over time [our claim of phase transitions]." In this regard, one can, for example, treat increases in feelings of mutual commitment as the order parameter that drives the role transitions that take the person into the different phases of group membership. For example, if feelings of commitment become strong enough, then the role transition of entry occurs and the individual enters the socialization phase (the phases are investigation, socialization, maintenance), and if deterioration occurs, resocialization and remembrance (divergence and exit as a person goes from full member to marginal member to ex-member (see Figure 3; Moreland & Levine, 1982, p. 154) Furthermore, during socialization, there is tension between local and global dynamics that varies in the course of time, moving from sidewise during the entry to acceptance process to top–down after acceptance involving majority conformity pressures. Specifically, the group as a whole shows the properties of the magnet effect; for example, the group attempts to change or entrain the entrant's ways (maintenance tendencies) to improve his or her value to the group (shift from individual to group-level attractor or from local to global dynamics), whereas the individual tries to entrain the group to better fit his or her goals or needs (local maintenance attractors). If the cooperative tendency wins out, or in Moreland and Levine's terms, the group influence attempts succeed, feelings of commitment are strengthened and the role transition of acceptance occurs, putting the person into the maintenance phase as a full member.

Basic processes of role change   In overview, evaluation, commitment, and role transition are the key processes that organize the movement of the individual from a prospective member, to a new member, to a full member—a role that either stabilizes and deepens or deteriorates into that of an exmember. The three are linked: Evaluation, which reflects rewardingness for individual and group of social-ization process, is viewed as an antecedent of commitment in the sense that com-mitment is an outcome of perceived rewardingness of individual–group negotiation in past, present, and future. It is in this sense that one could argue that group socialization is a self-organizing system given that internal outputs from antecedent processes drive subsequent states of the system. In particular, commit-ment is the key order parameter, and its values are a function of the rewardingness state of the system (the control parameter). Specifically, evaluation or rewardingness is defined for the person as the group's contribution to need satisfaction, where for the group, the individual has reward value in regard to his or her contribution to group goal attainment. Viewed thusly, increases in rewardingness when they exceed a critical value drive changes in commitment, which in turn can be viewed in terms of a reordering of roles that pass through key bifurcation points during the role transition process (see Figure 3).

In sum, role transition is analogous to phase transitions in the coordination of oscillators. Indeed, alternate to symmetric is not unlike shifts from prospective to new member to full member in regard to increases in stability of the attractor state.

Specifically, we propose that changes in role are driven by changes in com-mitment, the order parameter, that occur as a function of mutual changes in per-ceived rewardingness (control parameter). These self-organizing phase-role transi-tions involve (1) the investigation phase jumping to the socialization phase when the rewardingness exceeds a critical value for entry in regard to binding the individ-ual to the group, (2) commitment of the new member and reciprocally that of the group in regard to a destabilization at the individual level and a stabilization at the group attractor, thereby leading to (3) acceptance as the bifurcation point, leading to full-member status within the maintenance state. One issue at this point is whether we conceive of this phase portrait as having different periodic attractors at the critical points or a single-point attractor of full membership toward which the system is tending. Perhaps factors such as group size, homogeneity, and the like are what determines the nature of the modality changes. Or perhaps, as with Levinger's ABCDE model, the real bimodality occurs at maintenance where either the per-son–dyad or person–group relationship stabilizes into a continuing relationship or diverges and the relationship or group attractor either becomes annihilated (e.g., when an alternative group is oriented toward) or becomes chaotic (e.g., during resocialization, when the group tries to bring a deviant or marginal member back to full-member status). We now take a closer look at the resocialization process viewed as a special case of hysteresis.

2. Hysteresis

It is at this point that we postulate hysteresis occurring in regard to the differences tolerated for the attempts by the group to resocialize a member once divergence occurs. That is, more social influence, more evidence of rewardingness, and the like will be required to resocialize than to socialize an individual, taking the form empirically of more and/or prolonged communications directed at changes. This situation is conceptually analogous to the ABCDE dyadic situation. That is, after divergence, to return to the continuation level of closeness, there is also a possible problem in hysteresis vis-à-vis the need to change the rewardingness or affective intensity as control parameters for commitment to the relationship. If hysteresis is viewed as an index of a group being moved far from equilibrium, it fits current views (Moscovici, 1985) that the minority creates a crisis in confidence in the majority and that minority influence, although more difficult to create, creates deeper and longer change. That is, minority change may model far from equilibrium dynamical process, whereas majority influence may not. Thus, we may observe critical fluctuations and sudden jumps for minority but not for majority change.

Other dynamical processes   Other evidence that group socialization can be modeled as operating in accord with dynamical systems theory is as follows: There is, in catastrophe-type versions of the theory, the postulation of regions of inaccessibility in regard to regions beyond which stable equilibrium attractor states are unavailable (Gilmore, 1981; i.e., the system will become unstable). This type of catastrophe flag seems to match up well with Moreland and Levine's (1982) concept of a group's evaluation of the range of tolerable behavior within which approval is likely to be offered. Specifically, this range defines what a good group member ought to do and is, in effect, the attractor region for the group, either being a single equilibrium point (or point attractor) or perhaps multiple stable points, corresponding to different phases of socialization. For example, Moreland and Levine postulated that a narrower level of deviation from group values in norms is allowed as the membership status moves through socialization to maintenance.

It is interesting, however, that it is likely that it is beyond this range minority groups create the disequilibrium necessary for creating new behavioral modes, with new attractors falling into place and/or old attractors being annihilated. This may explain why minority-produced change is more long-lasting than majority-induced change. That is, minority change may radically alter the attractor layout of the group, thereby defining the nature of long-term change. Majority change, on the other hand, is simply a matter of progressively narrowing the range of toleration in the context of broadening the region of inaccessibility.

3. Commitment Disequilibrium

Central to the Moreland and Levine's (1982) analysis is a concept that gives more precision to our treatment of commitment as an order parameter. This is the idea that there is a discrepancy among commitment relationships they referred to as *commitment disequilibrium*, where the greater the commitment disequilibrium, the less stable the group–individual relationship. For example, potential instability exists in regard to an individual who is negotiating for a position of leadership in the group. Specifically, new members threaten to destabilize a group at a number of levels ranging from their objectivity to their quest for role power. Moreover, if new members band together, they form the basis for minority influence (i.e., a subcomponent that seeks to destabilize a group around alternative goals or attractor organizations). The group, on the other hand, seeks to fit the person into a role instrumental to stabilizing the global group dynamics. This led Moreland and Levine (1982) to assume "a general pressure toward commitment equilibrium between groups and individuals" (p. 149). Viewed in these terms, the coupling between individuals and groups is in terms of coordination of commitment (which, as noted earlier, is a function of perceived rewardingness of each to the other). Finally, there are four major consequences of commitment: (1) acceptance of group goals and values, (2) positive affective ties to the group, (3) willingness to exert effort on behalf of the group, and (4) desire to maintain membership in the group. These consequences are, in effect, indices of the extent to which local maintenance tendencies or dynamics coalesce into a global dynamics, which, in turn, constitutes a virtual system that modifies and is modified by its members.

From metaphor to dynamics Although this description is useful at a metaphorical level, we need once more to ask how to convert conceptual parameter descriptions to continuous dynamic variables that can be observed and measured. Consistent with the dyadic relationship section, we propose that exclusivity of time investment is the key. That is, at issue is the spontaneous allocation of time (e.g., leisure time) to the activities of a targeted group as opposed to other groups or, more generally, to other social encounters including individuals. What is ordered is the exclusiveness of the commitment to a group vis-à-vis allocation of leisure time. Here, however, mutuality of investment is a bit trickier to conceptualize and especially to operationalize in dynamical terms. The present line of reasoning is clearest during the initiation or recruitment period in regard to tracking for the initiant (entrant) the amount of free time spent spontaneously with group members and for the group the amount of time spent with a given initiant relative to other prospective initiants prior to acceptance; emphasis is placed on exclusivity of mutual time allocation as an index of investment regarding group-directed effort. The mutuality of exclusive time investment should increase as the group socialization moves from entry to acceptance as a phase transition. Here, in the extreme case, the individual is so committed (as with a cult), that we can speak of an extreme magnet effect with local maintenance attractors being annihilated.

4. The Nature of Coupling

One issue in group socialization concerns how to model the nature of the coupling between the individual and the group. Earlier, we used the example of the coupled oscillator. Specifically, individuals and groups reciprocally influence each other, most basically in terms of working out a joint rewardingness function that involves individuals seeking groups that allow them to satisfy needs, interests, values, and the like, whereas groups seek new members who are seen as instrumental to the satisfaction of group goals. Up until now, this negotiation has been modeled dynamically in regard to the Von Holst (1939/1973) ideas of coordinating oscillators, each of which has a preferred maintenance tendency leading to reciprocal attempts at entrainment, leading to a global dynamical resolution that either involves absolute coordination (magnet effect) or relative coordination (compromise resolutions).

Coupling as a field dynamic   At this conjuncture, we raise the possibility that this coupling can be treated less as a matter of individually coupled oscillators and more as a field of interdependency related to how individual cells coalesce into a system that functions globally as in the formation of a slime mold (Garfinkel, 1987). In the context of a field view of coupling, the Lotke-Volterra model (1924; 1931; described in F. D. Abraham et al., 1990) prey–predator system becomes relevant as a model of macroscopic coupling. Specifically, there is a vector field between the size of predator and prey populations; that is, they comprise a dynamical system involving coupled rates of change in the size of populations such that the rates of change are reciprocal. Given an initial size of each population, the components follow trajectories of changes that keep cycling back to an optimal ratio of sizes that ensures stability of the populations.

This type of molar coupling model seems well-suited to any coupling wherein extreme size (strength?, power?) of one component of the system is likely to destroy the system, for example, when the predator population is too successful, it destroys its food supply. Similarly, it may be argued that individual versus group commitment requires this balance. That is, Moreland and Levine's (1982) prediction that the greater the commitment disequilibrium, the less stable the group can be viewed in terms of Lotke's (1924) attempt to model interacting biological populations as a dynamical system. For example, the size of the two populations increase and decrease nonlinearly in regard to a joint proportionality related to the product of their sizes. Thus, the short-term advantage in power of the less-committed of the two components is analogous to well-fed predators increasing initially in population size relative to prey populations.

Majority–minority relations can be similarly modeled. That is, if majority influence is too strong, we get the super conformity of groupthink (Janis, 1972), which undermines the proper functions of groups in regard to error correction and/or accommodating to external threats (analogous to adequacy of food supply is adequacy of information about the adaptiveness of group values, goals, etc.). On the other hand, if the size of the minority grows too rapidly, the group loses cohesion, with global dynamics falling apart as old attractors are annihilated before the minority can grow into a new majority. For example, too strong a minority influence can shatter a group into splinter groups with competing attractors. This type of Lotke-Volterra modeling perhaps offers us a general perspective on the meaning of group pathology in regard to the conception that majority and minority groups are a coupled system that needs to be in a certain size ratio for healthy group functioning to occur. For example, groupthink (Janis, 1972) produces information loss, whereas too large a minority undermines the stability of the group phase portrait (e.g., group culture, tradition, values, etc. are undermined). Furthermore, it may be possible to treat ingroup–outgroup relations in regard to a coupled systems model regulated by Lotke-Volterra-like relative size ratios. At issue here is getting outgroup strength to be high enough to increase ingroup cohesiveness given that if outgroup pressure is too weak, internal cohesiveness may suffer. On the other hand, if outgroups grow too powerful, internal cohesion, instead of increasing, may jump in the opposite direction, with members leaving the group. In this example, relative size or strength is treated as a control parameter, with group commitment or cohesion as an order parameter.

IV. Concluding Comments

We close this attempt at doing some of the groundwork for modeling diverse social relations phenomena using tools from nonlinear dynamics by pointing to both specific and general implications of the approach. For social psychologists, there are perhaps two very general principles to be learned. *Social* does not necessarily mean more ambiguous, complex, and disorderly; dynamical systems approaches provide ways to reduce rather than increase degrees of freedom in going from individual to system-level analyses. Furthermore, systems make strange bedfellows; minorities and majorities, ingroups and outgroups, and the like may need each other for optimal functioning. Finally, it is of great interest that with the application of a dynamical systems approach, we, in a sense, come full circle in literally fulfilling Lewin's (1947) vision of there being a group dynamics based on equilibria–disequilibria-type principles, while at the same time raising systems interpretations from loose metaphors to testable models of group functioning.

Acknowledgments

The writing of this chapter and aspects of the research reported were supported by National Science Foundation Grant BNS-8719065 to the first author. Peter Beek's contribution was supported in part by National Science Foundation Grant BNS 91-09880. The authors wish to acknowledge their gratitude to Darren Newtson and Richard Moreland for their helpful substantive comments. Special appreciation is also owed David Kocsis for being a "sounding board" and for assisting at many levels of the preparation of this chapter.

References

Abraham, F. D., Abraham, R. H., & Shaw, C. D. (1990). *A visual introduction to dynamical systems theory for psychology*. Santa Cruz, CA: Aerial Press.

Abraham, R. H., & Shaw, C. D. (1982). *Dynamics—The geometry of behavior: Part 1.: Periodic behavior*. Santa Cruz, CA: Aerial Press.

Beek, P. J. (1989). *Juggling dynamics* (Doctoral dissertation). Amsterdam: Free University Press.

Beek, P. J., & Hopkins, B. (1992). Four requirements for a dynamical systems approach to the development of social coordination. *Human Movement Science, 11*, 425–442.

Berlyne, D. E. (1974). *Studies in the new experimental aesthetics*. New York: Wiley.

Boudreau, L. A. (1991). *Social competence as a determinant of the avoidance of categorization in forming interpersonal impressions*. Unpublished doctoral dissertation, University of Connecticut, Storrs.

Christianson, N. (1992). *Effects of social and physical variables upon between-person visual coordination*. Unpublished senior thesis, University of Connecticut, Storrs.

Clark, M. S., & Mills, J. (1979). Interpersonal attraction in exchange and communal relationships. *Journal of Personality and Social Psychology, 37*, 12–24.

Garfinkel, A. (1987). The slime mold dictyostelium as a model of self-organization in social systems. In F. E. Yates (Ed.), *Self-organizing systems: The emergence of order* (pp. 181–212). New York: Plenum Press.

Gibson, J. J. (1979). *The ecological approach to visual perception*. Hillsdale, NJ: Lawrence Erlbaum.

Gilmore, R. (1981). *Catastrophe theory for scientists and engineers*. New York: Wiley.

Gilmore, R., & Duck, S. W. (Eds.). (1986). Emerging field of personal relationships. Hillsdale, NJ: LEA.

Gottman, J. M. (1979). *Marital interaction*. New York: Academic Press.

Haken, H. (1987) Synergetics: An approach to self-organization. In F. E. Yates (Ed.), *Self organizing Systems: The emergence of order* (pp. 417–434). New York: Plenum.

Haken, H. (1977). *Synergetics—An introduction: Nonequalibrium phase transitions and self-organization in physics, chemistry, and biology*. Berlin: Springer-Verlag.

Janis, I. L. (1972). *Victims of groupthink: A psychological study of foreign-policy decisions and fiascos*. Boston, MA: Houghton-Mifflin.

Kelso, J. A. S., & Jeka, J. J. (1992). Symmetry breaking dynamics of human multilimb coordination. *Journal of Experimental Psychology, 18*, 645–668.

Kugler, P. N., & Turvey, M. T. (1987). *Information, natural law, and the self-assembly of rhythmic movement*. Hillsdale, NJ: Erlbaum.

Levinger, G. (1980). Toward the analysis of close relationships. *Journal of Experimental Social Psychology, 16*, 510–544.

Levinger, G., & Snoek, D. J. (1972). *Attraction in relationships: A new look at interpersonal attraction*. Morristown, NJ: General Learning Press.

Lotke, A. J. (1956). *Elements of mathematical biology*. New York: Dover. (Original work published 1924)

Lewin, K. (1947). Frontiers in group dynamics: I. Concept, method and reality in social science, social equilibria and social change. *Human Relations, 1*, 2–38.

McClintock, C. G. (1988). Evolutional systems of interdependence, and social values. *Behavioral Science, 33*, 59–76.

Moreland, R. L., & Levine, J. M. (1982). Socialization in small groups: Temporal changes in individual–group relations. In L. Berkowitz (Ed.), *Advances in experimental social psychology* (Vol. 15, pp. 137–192). New York: Academic Press.

Moreland, R. L., & Levin, J. M. (in press). The composition of small groups. In E. J. Lawler, B. Markovsky, C. Ridgeway, & H. Walker (Eds.), *Advances in group processes, 9*. Greenwich, Connecticut: JAI Press.

Moscovici, S. (1985). Social influence and conformity. In G. Lindzey & E. Aronson (Eds.), *The handbook of social psychology* (Vol. 2, pp. 347–412). New York: Random House.

Newtson, D., Hairfield, J., Bloomingdale, J., & Cutino, S. (1988). The structure of action and interaction. *Social Cognition, 5*, 48–82.

Paulus, P. B. (Ed.). (1983). *Basic group processes.* New York: Springer-Verlag.

Premack, D. (1965). Reinforcement theory. In D. Levine (Ed.), *Nebraska symposium on motivation* (pp. 123–180). Lincoln: University of Nebraska Press.

Riggio, R. E. (1986). Assessment of basic social skills. *Journal of Personality and Social Psychology, 51*, 649–660.

Rosenblum, L. D., & Turvey, M. T. (1988). Maintenance tendency in coordinated rhythmic movements: Relative fluctuations and phase. *Neuroscience, 27*, 289–300.

Schmidt, R. C., Beek, P. J., Treffner, P. J., & Turvey, M. T. (1991). Dynamical substructure of coordinated rhythmic movements. *Journal of Experimental Psychology: Human Perception and Performance, 17*, 635–651.

Schmidt, R. C., Carello, C., & Turvey, M. T. (1990). Phase transitions and critical fluctuations in the visual coordination of rhythmic movements between people. *Journal of Experimental Psychology: Human Perception and Performance, 16*, 227–247.

Schmidt, R. C., & Turvey, M. T. (1992). *Phase-entrainment dynamics of visually coupled rhythmic movements.* Manuscript submitted for publication.

Turner, J. C., & Giles, H. (Eds.). (1981). *Intergroup behavior.* Oxford, England: Blackwell.

Turvey, M. T. (1990). Coordination. *American Psychologist, 45*, 938–953.

Turvey, M. T., Schmidt, R. C., & Rosenblum, L. D. (1989). "Clock" and "motor" components in absolute coordination of rhythmic movements. *Neuroscience, 33*, 1–10.

Valenti, S. S. (1989). Ecological social psychology: Illustrative experiments on the perception of intention and intercoordination in human social walking. *Perceiving and Acting Workshop Review, 4*(1), 28–32.

Volterra, V. (1931). *Lecons sur la théorie mathématique de la lutte pour la vie.* Paris: Gauthier-Villars.

von Holst, E. (1973). *The behavioral physiology of animal and man.* Coral Gables, FL: University of Miami Press. (Original work published 1939)

Warren, W. H. (1984). Perceiving affordances: Visual guidance of stair climbing. *Journal of Experimental Psychology: Human Perception and Performance, 10*, 683–703.

CHAPTER 7

The Perception and Coupling of Behavior Waves

Darren Newtson
Department of Psychology
University of Virginia
Charlottesville, Virginia

I. Introduction

Dynamical systems theory offers an attractive metaphor for a wide variety of disciplines, social psychology not excepted. The approach consists of a powerful new kind of pattern analysis that is especially adept at identifying temporal regularity in the behavior of systems. It allows the identification of hidden patterns in even apparently random system behavior.

Dynamical systems theory shows how a deterministic system may produce novel, highly adaptive behavior. A dynamical system is simply a bounded set of variables that displays some stability over time in their interrelations. The "white rat" of dynamical systems theory is the simple, friction-free pendulum. Two variables may be identified in its behavior: its displacement of position (we could take the center of its arc as a zero point) and its speed. These variables are interrelated: Speed is maximum at the bottom of the arc and minimum at the extremes of the arc (it stops, then swings in the other direction).

A plot of the behavior of the pendulum would thus require two dimensions, one for each variable. Such a plot for any system is termed its *phase space*. Each variable in the system becomes a dimension in a multidimensional space. Every

Dynamical Systems in Social Psychology

point in that space defines a possible state of the system. The phase space is a wonderfully efficient way of looking at the behavior of a system over time; each point in the phase space is the value of the system variables at a particular time. Thus, the behavior of the system over time can be visualized as a trajectory, or path, in this space. The first step in a dynamical systems theory analysis is the construction of the phase space of the system. *Stability analysis* is simply the demonstration that a specified variable set is bounded within a finite set of values. One variable may be systematically altered and its effects on the system traced by observing how differing values alter the trajectory of the system in phase space. The goal is to specify the range of variable values and the set of initial conditions over which the system is stable.

In the case of the pendulum, we could plot the displacement from the center of the arc against the velocity of the pendulum bob or, equivalently, against the velocity with which the angle of the arm changes. Because velocity must have direction, we might assign motion in one direction positive values and motion in the other direction negative values. When plotted, we could see that the behavior in the phase space of the system traces a circle and that the current location of the pendulum is always a point on that circle. If the pendulum were friction free, we would see that the behavior of the system is constant because all system states fall on the same circle. If we introduced friction, we would see the trajectory in the phase space spiral down, becoming progressively smaller until it stopped. The stopping point would be in the center of the circle, where velocity and displacement are zero.

The phase space may be estimated from observed data or may be explored by means of a theoretical model of the system. In the latter case, a set of equations may be iterated starting from a variety of initial conditions. Thus, we might observe a young child playing in the presence of his or her mother and might measure the distance between them and the proximity of a stranger. We could then trace the relation over time between these two variables; perhaps the child's distance from his or her parent oscillates (it regularly increases and decreases) but variation becomes larger and slower as the stranger recedes and smaller and faster as the stranger approaches. We might then propose a model of the system and explore its properties by trying out varying assumptions and initial conditions (where the child is when the stranger is introduced or how close the stranger is when he or she appears) to see what differing assumptions imply about the behavior of the system over time. Such a plot may add little to understanding for simple, linear models, but nonlinear models become surprisingly complex surprisingly quickly, and a visual representation can be invaluable in understanding the behavior of such a system.

Phase spaces become even more valuable when they show particular sets of values to which systems tend over time. These are discussed in dynamical systems theory as structures, or patterns, in the phase space of a system; a system that tends to a particular set of values is said to have an *attractor set* in its phase space, or more simply, an *attractor*. Systems may also have particular values that they avoid. Such regions of avoidance are called *saddles* or *repellors*. Complex systems may have multiple attractors and repellors in the phase space. Three different kinds of attractors have been identified:

1. *Point attractors*, in which the system tends to a single state or set of values over time. This is the defining characteristic of stable equilibrium systems.

2. *Cyclic attractors*, or limit cycles, which show up in the phase space as a circle. This is the defining characteristic of stable, oscillating systems. A pendulum on a clock, for example, that has a spring mechanism to oppose friction will speed up to its regular cycle after you retard it or will slow down to a regular cycle after you give it a push. A plot of such behavior will show an initial deviation from the circle in the phase space for a few cycles, with a gradual return to the central pattern.

3. *Strange attractors* occur in nonlinear systems and consist of bounded but often irregularly shaped attractors in their phase space. These systems have many intriguing properties.

Linear systems are those in which output is proportional to input. Most of our data analysis models in psychology postulate, for example, that values obtained on dependent or criterion variables are some linear or additive combination of values on independent or predictor variables. In nonlinear systems, however, small changes in critical ranges of a variable may have disproportionate effects. The changes in the properties of water as temperature goes from 33 °F to 32 °F or from 211 to 212 °F are examples of nonlinearity at work. Among the interesting and important properties of nonlinear systems are the following. First, such systems are typically self-organizing. That is, they are capable of producing emergent properties. A system containing a large number of degrees of freedom may, at certain critical values of system variables, spontaneously collapse into a system with only a few degrees of freedom. A common physical example is that of the laser, produced when at certain levels of excitation, all of the atoms of a compound come into phase and emit a single kind of light. Gestalt psychology was at great pains to identify "self-organized" perceptual phenomena.

Second, nonlinear systems may be multistable. That is, the phase space of a system may change spontaneously at certain critical values of one of the system variables. Consequently, the overall behavior of a system, including variable interrelations, may change as a result of a small, linear change in one of the variables. It may appear that some new variable has entered the system or is beginning to affect it, but this is not necessarily the case. Some systems may have point attractors at some values of a system variable, transform into a system with a cyclic attractor, undergo a range of variations in the frequency of oscillation, and finally display a strange attractor. Furthermore, systems may be observed to travel up and down the sequence of phase spaces. Such changes in the organization of the phase space of a system are termed *phase transitions*. Piaget's stages of cognitive development, for example, might be seen as a set of phase transitions within one system, instead of the replacement of successive systems of more advanced organization.

In strange attractors, moreover, the state-to-state transitions in the phase space may become completely unpredictable, although the attractor set remains stable. Thus, novel patterning occurs, but the system remains in a predictable range of values. The weather, for example, is now understood to be governed by this sort of system. This curious mix of unpredictability within predictability is what is termed *chaos*.

A fourth property of nonlinear systems is that, when they are in chaos, they display what is termed *sensitive dependence on initial conditions*. The unpredictability of chaos results not from the emergence of randomness but from a sudden increase in sensitivity of the system to local variables. The system "opens up" to the influence of variables to which it is not normally sensitive. These influences then determine the pattern of state-to-state transitions in a deterministic manner; the unpredictability is the result of the sudden, dramatic increase in complexity of the determinants of the behavior of the system. Thus, a predictable system may become an unpredictable one, and the reverse, as it moves into and out of chaotic regimes.

It is important not to confuse chaos with the merely random nor to see it as necessarily a dysfunctional state. Chaotic systems are capable of creating novel, creative patterns within a fixed behavioral repertoire and put the system into very close coupling with its environment. As a result, the availability of chaotic states may be highly adaptive in many kinds of situations.

Dynamical Systems as Metaphor or Theory

Metaphorically speaking, human behavior has many parallels with the behavior of nonlinear systems. It displays stability; it is sometimes equilibrium seeking, sometimes cyclic, and sometimes flexible, novel, and creative. It may appear random but have an underlying pattern to it. The possibility of emergent properties has a long history in social psychological thinking.

The difficulty in using the theory and its powerful analytic techniques are two: (1) social psychologists are not accustomed to thinking about behavior dynamically, and (2) social psychologists are not accustomed to making models of their phenomena—especially nonlinear models—as a preliminary, rather than final, step in research.

The first problem may be stated most succinctly: Dynamic analysis requires measurement of dynamic variables. A dynamic variable is a variable that is always present, even if zero. Current cognitive analyses treat social behavior almost entirely in terms of categories of cognitive meaning. From that viewpoint, a sequence of actions or interactions is a progression of different categories of behavior, chosen by some decision rule or according to some priorities. All that can be of interest to such an analysis is probabilities or rules of category sequencing. A conversation is simply a sequence of speaking "turns," and the phenomena of interest are those that "signal" the sequence of switches. Imagine trying to deduce the principles of pendulum motion from a categorization of its behavior (e.g., moving right, stopping, moving fast). Such a view does not postulate dynamic regularities in behavior and would not necessarily know what to do with them if they were found. Thus, one requirement for the application of these models to social behavior is the consideration, at least, of alternatives to cognitive models.

Dynamical systems theory has methods and concepts that may be applied to the analysis of such data. Questions concerning the appropriate level of precision for measurement may be asked and answered within the theory. Concepts for describing and confirming the hypotheses as to the nature and dimensionality of attractors underlying system behavior are readily available. At this level, dynamical systems theory, as a theory, may be directly applied.

The second requirement is more problematic. Full application of dynamical systems models requires at least a preliminary model as a basis for evaluation. If a sensible model can be postulated, and that model is nonlinear, and it displays stability within reasonable parameter values, a dynamical systems approach brings tremendously powerful conceptual and analytic tools to bear. Short of this ideal, its application is speculative, although still of reasonable value.

It is here that the value of dynamical systems theory may be more heuristic and metaphorical. If a system shows transitions into differently organized states, does that mean that a new variable has entered the system, or that an intact system has undergone a phase transition? Dynamical systems theory lets one consider the latter hypothesis. Is the organization one observes in behavior an imposed or an emergent property? Dynamical systems theory allows one to ask whether the latter hypothesis is a tenable one. In addition, it can provide clues as to the requirements and limitations of possible theoretical models given that the properties of different assumptions may be readily explored. For example, if, as we shall see, behavior is a wave, does that mean that people must possess a wave-generating mechanism, or could waves occur in behavior as a result of a self-organizing process? If interaction is structured at in-phase or antiphase relations, must that coordination be imposed by cognitive rules, or could it be an emergent property of the joint presence of two wave-generating systems? Exploration of even the most simple models of nonlinear systems shows that these structures may, under certain circumstances, readily occur. As a result, research may be directed along different lines, toward the evaluation of different variables, owing to our knowledge of the possibilities that dynamical systems theory shows may exist.

II. Behavior Is a Wave

Action exists in movement kind of like words exist in sound. Not every sound is a word, nor is every movement an action. This can be misleading in the case of movement given that it is easy to speak of any movement as if it were an intended action, but one can just as easily insert a sound or nonsense syllable into speech. Similarly, as many dimensions of the sound of a word may vary, yet the word retains its identity, so the movement by which the same action is performed may readily vary, yet the action content remain the same. In both cases, some very abstract, as yet unspecified relationship occurs that allows the perceiver to know the content of the event. In both cases, some skill may be required of the observer to comprehend the event. Thus, speakers of a foreign language may seem to speak very rapidly, because we hear them syllable by syllable; if I say the word, *apparently*, for example, a non-English speaker might hear four successive syllables, whereas an English speaker might hear only one word. Similarly, specialized perceptual skills are required to comprehend certain classes of skilled behavior.

As in the case of language, it can be very useful to compare the underlying event structure to the perceptual structure that results. Thus, analysts have examined the acoustic signal that underlies speech and have clarified both the nature of speech comprehension and speech production. Discrete words, for example, are not normally separated by pauses in the underlying acoustic signal; indeed, pauses as long as some between words frequently occur within words, and the existence of pauses is virtually unrelated to word discrimination in the speech signal. In the case of ongoing behavior, such an analysis has required both the development of methods for the assessment of perceptual structure, as well as adaptation of procedures for the analysis of the ongoing behavior stream itself.

A. Segmentation of Ongoing Behavior

The perceptual partitioning of behavior into its component actions may be obtained by asking subjects to press a button whenever, in their judgment, one action ends and a different one begins (Newtson, 1973, 1976). An equivalent instruction is to ask subjects to press the button whenever an action occurs. Both procedures result in the identification of intermittently occurring action unit boundaries, termed *breakpoints* (Newtson & Engquist, 1976). Breakpoints have been found to have many intriguing psychological properties: They are better recognized than are other points in a series, even by children as young as 5 years of age (Newtson, Gowan, & Patterson, 1980). They provide a comic-strip summary of action sequence contents, and they are more readily detected if they are deleted from the ongoing behavior than are nonboundary points (Newtson, 1976, 1980).

In short, studies of the action perception process show that it is an intermittent, sampling process rather than one of low-level movement perception followed by inference.

These results are controversial because the discrimination of breakpoints does not seem to be the result of cognitive activity and does not provide a ready, reliable guide to its cognitive representation (Ebbesen, 1980; Markus & Zajonc, 1985). This has led social cognition researchers to conclude that the measure is an invalid one because they assume that the first step in the perceptual process is the formation of a perceptual representation of the behavior. The alternative view is a Gibsonian one (Newtson, 1990), in which the perceptual process is postulated to provide specification of the environment rather than a topologically similar mapping (or representation). In my view, the formation of representations is a later, optional step in the perception of behavior and is not required for the organization of interaction.

Although this difference in viewpoint is beyond the scope of the present discussion, it is important to keep in mind at this point that there is a third, alternative basis for action perception to those postulated by social cognition analyses. Between lower level movement and higher level cognitive categories, it is possible that another level of organization exists in behavior and that the perceptual process operates on that level of organization directly. Such a proposition requires direct analysis of the stream of behavior for its evaluation.

B. Measuring Ongoing Behavior

One means of behavior analysis widely used in animal research (Golani, 1976, 1992) is based on the Eshkol–Wachmannn movement notation (Eshkol, 1973). As we have adapted it to the analysis of action sequences (Newtson, Engquist, & Bois, 1977; Newtson, Hairfield, Bloomingdale, & Cutino, 1987), a stick-figure tracing is made of each actor in a sequence at ½- or 1-s intervals. Comparisons are then made between each tracing of the figure, and the position of each limb segment or body part is checked for a change in joint angle with respect to its pivot joint. Change is indicated by either a change in drawn angle or in the lengthening or foreshortening of the segment if it moves in the plane toward the camera. Fifteen parts are evaluated as follows: left and right upper arms, lower arms, hands, upper legs, lower legs, feet, head and neck, torso, and pelvis. Two additional features, frontal orientation (to the camera) and weight distribution (forward, equal, back) are also assessed. Same–different judgments are made, assigning 1 to a position change and 0 to no change. The result is an index of position change between each successive coding interval that can range from 0 (position the same) to 17 (position maximally different). Body parts that are not visible are excluded from the comparisons. Reliabilities in the low .90s are readily achieved with only a few minutes of training.

The system is an efficient one for recording position change. If the actor raises an arm, for example, while maintaining full extension of the lower arm and hand, a difference is recorded for change in the coding feature upper arm only given that the other joint angles did not change.

An important issue for any measurement system is, of course, its precision. The question for the application of this system is whether it is precise enough in its measure of position change both in space (i.e., changes in displacement) and in time (i.e., how fine a temporal interval is used). More, however, is not necessarily better when it comes to measurement precision. The appropriate level of measurement depends very much on the use to which the measure is put.

For example, one might think that the best measure of movement would be one at least as fine as human thresholds for movement perception in time. Thus, a temporal sampling density of at least 16–24 frames per s would be ideal given the flicker-fusion limits of human perceivers for motion pictures. Average duration of perceived actions, however, is about 5–8 s, depending on the sequence. If one assumes that action perception is movement perception, then one might want to work to the finer density; if one assumes that structures of longer duration are critical, such fine-grained analysis would be unnecessary or even misleading.

Consider, for example, the ideal measure of length of a mountainous hiking trail. One could measure the trail with a meter stick or with a micrometer. The length one obtains with the micrometer would be far greater than that with the meter stick. The average stride length of a hiker, however, is about 50 cm. The most "accurate" measure to report to the hiker would use a metric of that length; the meter measure would underestimate the trail length, whereas the micrometer would vastly overestimate it.

This would matter, of course, only for an irregular surface. A smooth surface would give the same value for both measures. How irregular is the "surface structure" of the behavior stream? Mandelbrot (1977) gave a means of answering this question. He showed that one may plot the logarithm of an obtained measurement total against the logarithm of the metric used. To the degree that a measured quantity increases with greater precision, the slope of this line will depart from zero. In addition, a linear relation between a measured quantity and precision of measurement implies that the irregularity in a surface does not depend on its scale. Mandelbrot formulated an alternative to Euclidian geometry in which lines can have fractional dimensions, his fractal geometry. Mandelbrot (p. 33) defined the slope of this plot as equal to $1 - d$, where d is the dimensionality of the object of measurement. A Euclidian boundary, such as a straight line, yields a slope of zero (hence, $0 = 1 - d$, $d = 1$), with a dimensionality of one. The measure of d is, in effect, a measure of the degree of departure from this condition and hence is a measure of the degree of irregularity of the object of measurement. He noted that no precise, single answer can be given to the question, How long is the coast of Britain? because coastlines have fractal dimensions, in this case, about 1.5.

If we treat the surface structure of the behavior stream, as measured by the quantity of change from coding interval to coding interval, as analogous to a map of a coastline, we could measure its "length" by summing the amount of change between successive intervals. In this case, the length of the line would be equivalent to the total amount of position change. We could then vary the size of our metric by varying the temporal density of sampling. Accordingly, total position change was measured from codings at successive 1-s, 5-s, 10-s, and 20-s intervals from the seven sequences coded by Newtson et al. (1977). These sequences contained a diverse set of actions, including people shelving books, answering telephones, and setting a table. The log of total position change was then plotted against the log of the metric used.

In addition, Newtson et al. (1977) had three groups of subjects segment these sequences into their component actions under three different instructional sets: fine, large, or "natural" units of action as seemed meaningful to them. Measured total change was taken by assessing the total amount of position change between successive breakpoints. Metric size was taken as the average duration of discriminated actions. This was 3.27, 8.16, and 15.39 s for fine-, large-, and natural-unit instructed subjects, respectively.

Results of this analysis are displayed in Figure 1. Analysis shows a simple, linear component in this graph; obtained slope was $-.82$. Hence $-.82 = 1 - d$, $d = 1.82$. This implies a high degree of irregularity, or turbulence, in position change in the behavior stream. It is also remarkable that the plot is so evenly linear; regression analysis showed a highly significant linear component, with no significant quadratic.

What this means is that the appropriate level of temporal precision in measurement of the behavior stream is highly dependent on the particular application. If one is interested in measuring action, rather than movement, it is simply not the case that a frame-by-frame analysis is better than a second-by-second analysis. If one assumes that action perception consists of a process of automatic movement perception followed by categorization of perceived movement patterns into cognitive representations, then one may want a movement analysis at finer levels. If, however, one postulates higher order structures in movement, then the most precise measurement level is at the level at which such structures may occur. It should be noted, however, that this finding is not inconsistent with findings that particular sequences have particular, clear-cut structures; the implication is analogous to a statement about, say, sentences in general in language.

Another important implication of this finding is that, in general, the structuring principles in behavior may be invariant over scale, or self-similar. That is, the same kind of hierarchical or, to use Turvey's (1977) more accurate term, heterarchical, structures can be expected at larger, action-by-action and episode-by-episode

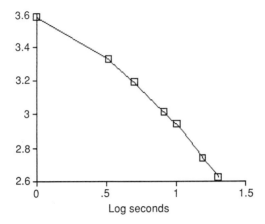

Figure 1 Log of total position change vs. log seconds.

levels of behavior analysis as at lower levels of movement organization. Ongoing behavior is all of a piece, so to speak, and is not composed of qualitatively different systems at different levels. The branching of arteries in the circulatory system follows the same rules as does the branching of capillaries (West, 1990). In terms of behavior organization, the computer model has blinded us to the operation of variables that act slowly in time; those changes that take minutes, hours, and even days may be importantly involved in the structure of everyday behavior.

Fractal geometry is the geometry that is appropriate for the products of nonlinear systems. Strange attractors have fractal dimensions. Mandelbrot (1977) argued that fractal geometry is the "geometry of nature." West (1990) showed that these concepts are necessary to understand basic biological structures, such as the structure of the lungs and circulatory system. Does this mean that behavior structure is necessarily due to nonlinear systems? No, not necessarily. What it does mean is that ideas from dynamical systems theory can be used to give more precise descriptions of our phenomena. The behavior stream is a highly irregular natural object, yes, and most of us knew that. These notions allow us to quantify that statement: The everyday sorts of behavior studied in the Newtson et al. (1977) analyses had a fractal dimensionality of 1.82, which means that any claim that these sequences were excessively simple or repetitive (e.g., Ebbesen, 1980) may be directly addressed and refuted.

A second issue concerns the precision of measurement of the index of displacement, or position change. An actor who raises an extended arm creates more change, in some sense, than does one who sits and crosses his or her legs, yet the sitting action is far more complex than the arm movement. The bias of this approach is be more sensitive to the complexity of position change than the magnitude of movement. One advantage of the Eshkol–Wachmann coding system is that it was developed as a dance notation, to allow choreographers to write dance. It is thus a productive system as well as a descriptive system, and it is possible to recreate action from its codings. The bias toward position change is essential to this feature of the system.

It should be kept in mind that the procedure, as applied, is capable of discriminating 2^{17} (131,072) different positions. It is thus vastly more precise than are categorical schemes of behavior recording. Moreover, when its codings of position changes are factor analyzed, it readily yields groups of coding features that change together. Analyses have yielded from four to six clear-cut feature groupings in the behavior stream of each actor we analyzed (Newtson et al., 1977, 1987). These factors have clear face validity with respect to sequence contents, and one can readily identify which action sequence a given factor structure came from. It is important to note that no "general human movement structure" appears. Instead, body components are variously organized according to the requirements of the task at hand.

These results converge nicely with the concept of "coordinative structures" in research in motor organization. This work has demonstrated that individual action systems (e.g., those used for walking, running, handwriting) are achieved by the formation of peripheral units of body structure. That is, the body is configured into units in which only some of the possible muscle and nerve patterns may occur, and these units are then coupled to forces in the environment to produce stable, dynamical systems (cf. Salzman & Kelso, 1987; Turvey, 1990).

C. Spectral Analysis of Ongoing Behavior

When measured in this way, the behavior stream has a clear-cut, underlying "spike" structure (Newtson et al. 1977, 1987). That is, it consists of periods of relatively smooth, low-magnitude position change, punctuated by spikes of high-magnitude position change. Breakpoints occur at the spikes.

Once one realizes what is occurring, the idea is not at all mysterious. If one sees people playing catch, for example, one sees them adopt a coordinative structure for throwing, cycle that, and then shift to a catching configuration, cycle that, and then reorganize for throwing. Because more joint angle changes occur during the shifts between the two configurations than during the cycling of any one configuration (i.e., reorganization is more complex), the spikes demarcate the boundaries between throwing and catching.

Similarly, the intermittency of behavior perception becomes more understandable. If one can know the action by knowing the coordinative structure in place, information as to the succession of coordinative structures is all that is necessary for knowledge of the action. One can take advantage of the tremendous amount of redundancy in the organization of the behavior. In addition, in most cases, the temporal constraints on the perceiver are not great; one does not need to detect the shift precisely as it is taking place but only immediately in the temporal neighborhood. The process is thus not as demanding as movement perception.

It is important to keep in mind that the "action" is a dynamical event in the interaction of the actor and the environment. Coordinative structures are not cognitive structures; they are particular configurations of the body that require the constraints of the environment to work smoothly. Thus, walking requires a particular coordinative structure and a train of muscle pulses, and the environment provides gravity and the inertial properties of the leg that allow a smooth step cycle. Such systems have readily predictable or knowable outcomes. For example, Runeson and Frykholm (1983), using point-light displays, had actors pick up light or heavy boxes and then pretend that the light boxes were heavy and that the heavy boxes were light. They found that observers could readily discriminate both the actual and the "pretended" weights of the boxes. The dynamic constraints of the actual weight of the boxes showed how heavy they were; the variations produced by the actors who were pretending readily tipped off their intentions. The point-light presentation insured that perceivers could use only dynamical information as a basis for their conclusions.

In terms of dynamical systems theory, then, such systems provide another source of knowledge for the intention of actions. We have assumed that actions are the product of internal cognitive goal structures and hence must be inferred from the perceiver's judgments of the actor's choice of goals (Jones & Davis, 1965; Newtson, 1974). It is also true that, if actions are dynamical systems in the organism–environment interaction, the phase space of those systems is also apparent to an observer, perhaps even including the presence of attractors in those phase spaces. That is, actions are organized in terms of what have been called *mass-spring systems*. A mass, suspended from a spring, will always return to the same point, regardless of the nature of the disturbance. The return does not result from "feedback correction" or choice on the part of the mass but from the enduring pattern of forces present in the system. The equilibrium point is an attractor in the phase space of the system.

If actions themselves are dynamical systems, then, perceiving an action is not different in principle from perceiving a pendulum. As soon as the perceiver sees the dynamics of the system, the "intention" of the system is specified. Consistent with this reasoning, subjects are as ready to discriminate whether an action is intentional or not, action by action, as they are to discriminate its occurrence and are equally reliable in doing so (Newtson, Engquist, & Bois, 1976).

Inspection of plots of position change over time, however, suggested even greater regularity in action (Newtson et al., 1987). These records looked like complex wave phenomena, suggesting that coordinative structures are not only the basis of individual actions but that action sequences are constructed by regular patterning of coordinative structures. Accordingly, spectral analysis techniques suitable for wave analysis were applied to these records.

Results were surprisingly clear-cut. Significant spectral components have been observed in every sequence that we have analyzed, which includes the seven individual sequences analyzed by Newtson et al. (1977), the four interactions previously analyzed by Newtson et al., 1987, 15 pairs of adolescent boys, 16 additional individual Alzheimer's patients analyzed repeatedly over several months (Marcopoulos, Newtson, Horst, & Steiner, 1992), and three additional interactions between undergraduates.

That is, there is empirical evidence for regular waves of position change in every sample of behavior that we have analyzed. These waves have appeared when sequences have been analyzed with the movement notation described above, as well as when analyzed by more traditional, categorical methods (the 15 pairs of adolescents). The assertion that behavior is a wave, then, is at this point an empirical generalization, not a theoretical claim. If one analyzes dynamic variables in everyday kinds of behavior, the kind that occurs in task performances and interaction, one will find statistically significant periodic structures. The important question is whether such waves have psychological significance for the production of behavior or for its perception.

Waves are marvelously organized structures. They have three independent parameters of frequency, amplitude, and phase. The ideas underlying wave concepts are not as distant from conventional ideas of variables in psychological research as might first appear. Many of our basic statistical concepts were derived from the physics of vibrating objects. Thus, a vibrating object has a mean position, just the same as any variable mean. It also has an amplitude of vibration, which is exactly the idea that the standard deviation derives from. If that variation is regular in time, then the frequency of vibration is all that one needs to add to have a wave process. To examine the amplitude of a wave, then, is simply to examine the variance of a process; to examine the frequency of a wave is simply to ask whether that variance occurs regularly in time. If that is so, then any variable that displays variation (amplitude) with temporal regularity is a wave. The phase parameter merely places the starting point of each cycle of variation on a scale, or places the cycles of two waves relative to each other.

Spectral analysis is a powerful technique for the analysis of such phenomena (see Chatfield, 1984, and Gottman, 1983, for introductions to these techniques). It provides a means of testing any time series for the presence of periodic variation against the null hypothesis that periodicity in the series is due to chance, using the estimate of series variance. Its underlying mathematical basis is a deterministic one, with the assumption that an observed series is the product of a finite number of periodic processes plus error variance.

An extension of these procedures may be used to examine the correlation between time series and is termed *cross-spectral analysis* (cf. Gottman, 1983;

Koopmans, 1974). It produces an index of coherence, which is a measure of the correlation between the two series at each frequency. The coherence index is precisely analogous to a squared correlation coefficient. The procedure is exhaustive, so that correlation at each frequency is examined at every phase relation between the waves. Coherence indices are always reported, then, with an accompanying phase relation.

D. Perception of Behavior Waves

Given evidence that action perception is an intermittent sampling process, centered on breakpoints, and evidence that behavior is a wave, it is not unreasonable to suppose that it might operate as a wave-sampling process. There is a theorem, termed the *wave sampling theorem*, that any band-limited waveform (i.e., a wave ensemble with a finite range of frequencies) may be perfectly specified by a sample of amplitudes taken at twice the frequency of the wave (Cherry, 1978). That is, waves have just two independent amplitudes per cycle.

In our investigation of the spectral properties of action sequences, we had expected to find that breakpoint frequencies would be the same as wave frequency and were surprised to find that breakpoint frequencies were always about twice wave frequencies. The wave sampling theorem suggested a reason for the finding, so we proceeded to apply the sampling mathematic to our data. By taking the measured amplitude at each breakpoint (about 8% of the intervals) and using the tabled values of what is termed the *translation function* to estimate the surrounding values, we generated an estimated series (Bracewell, 1986). For comparison purposes, we selected an identical number of series points at random and created a second estimated series.

This was done for seven individual sequences and for four interactions (Newtson, et al., 1987). These were then compared with the observed series in two ways. First, a simple correlation was computed between the series. The estimated series from the breakpoints correlated significantly with the observed series, whereas the series estimated from randomly selected points did not. In addition, correlation was significantly greater for the breakpoint than for the random estimated series. Second, cross-spectral analyses showed high and significant coherence between the observed series and the series estimated from the breakpoints alone.

The observed and estimated series for one interaction analyzed in Newtson et al. (1987) is shown in Figure 2. The sequence was an interaction in which two women unloaded a truck full of large boxes. The values displayed are those for the total behavior of the two women, taken together. As inspection of that figure indicates, overall agreement between the two waves was fairly good. It is worth noting that the procedure, as used, typically overestimates extreme values, and that correction procedures are given in the engineering literature (cf. Bracewell, 1986).

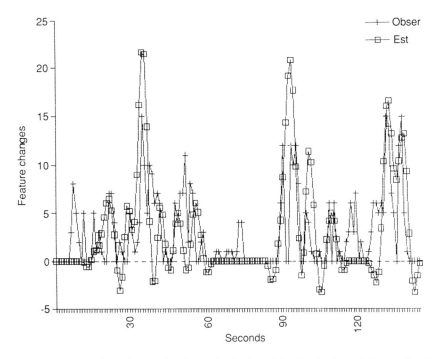

Figure 2   Position change by second as observed and estimated from breakpoints only (summed position change of two women unloading boxes). Adapted by permission.

These results are important because they show that the sampling procedure used in perception of behavior waves contains the information necessary to specify the parameters of the observed waves. They thus speak to the psychological significance of the waves themselves. As I have argued elsewhere (Newtson, 1990), it is not necessary to assume or to demonstrate that the perceiver has a "representation" of a wave but only that the perceiver has available the wave specifications. It is interesting that studies of olfaction, however, show that odors are specified in the olfactory bulb of the brain by wave patterns and that specific smells have specific spectral parameters (Skarda & Freeman, 1987). Thus, wave information is used in a primitive sensory system and in a system with particular relevance for social behavior in infrahuman species.

III. The Nature of Behavior Waves

It is at this point that dynamical systems theory passes from being a metaphor to a being a part of a concrete theory of social behavior. The theory has clear implications for what it is in behavior that behavior waves are made of. If actions are dynamical systems, then each successive action is a physically realized system. The system exists in the relationship between the organism and the environment; that is, it includes variables in the organism and in the environment. Each system has a phase space. The phase space of a system is not only a description of the behavior of the system but is also an objective measure of the information content of the system.

A. The Concept of Information Flow

Consider the phase space of a pendulum, described earlier. The set of all possible states of the system is that set described by the circle in the phase space. When we observe the position of the pendulum, what we are doing is locating a point on that circle with two values, one for its displacement and one for its velocity. This is like laying a grid over the phase space; the more precise our measure of each variable, the finer is that grid, and hence the larger the number of different states we can discriminate. The nominal uncertainty of our observation of the system, then, is simply the log of the size of the state space that we can discriminate (Garner, 1962). Increased precision yields more information in any given measure of the system for this reason.

If we give the pendulum a push, the state space becomes larger because the circle becomes larger; we have not only added energy to the system but also information. When the state space of a system gets larger, its information value is greater, all other things being equal. Information can be said to have flowed into the system. If we introduce friction and let the pendulum spiral down to a stop, its state space shrinks, and hence we have observed not only energy loss but also information loss in the system. These notions (see Shaw, 1981) imply that variation in the phase space of a system may be understood as *information flow*.

A stable system with a constant phase space thus has a constant information value; information flow in the system is thus zero. Think of a repetitive action, such as walking. If we ignore, for the moment, the change in the variable "location," what we see is a stable dynamical system. Each position of the walker is from a phase space of constant size; hence, each position has a constant information value. The specifications of position change, of course, and we might speak of specification flow in the system, but information flow (changes in the information content of the system) would be zero.

This analysis assumes that all system states are equiprobable. If they are not, some flows would occur during the cycling of a system because of its internal structure. Such flows would be likely to be of small magnitude compared with volume of flows induced by changes in the size of the system, as, for example, would occur when a system parameter is changed or a new variable is added to or subtracted from the system.

One way to understand repetitive action, then, is to define it as behavior that occurs within a fixed phase space and, hence, has zero information flow.

A second class of action sequences would be those in which the phase space is stable in its structure (i.e., the same variables are always present) but that is subject to parameter modifications. The pendulum that is given a push is an example of this kind of event. Hollerbach's (1981) analysis of handwriting is a behavioral example. Hollerbach showed that handwriting is produced by means of establishing a dynamical system capable of producing stable loops (as in a succession of script *e*s). Letters are then produced by a series of parameter modifications of this basic system (e.g., to produce a script *l*). Each letter has its particular specification of parameter modifications. We might term such behavior sequences *quasirepetitive action* because the same coordinative structure is used but is successively modified. Information flow would be induced by such modifications in system parameters.

A third and most important class of action sequences are those in which different phase spaces are instituted for each action. We might term such sequences *complex action*. In such cases, one phase space disappears, and a new one comes into being. Such transitions, resulting from shifts in the underlying coordinative structure of action, would produce large information flows at the point of the transition.

It is important to recognize that the existence of information flow in behavior is a fact of its physics, not of its psychology. Consequently, the application of dynamical systems theory to behavior is a direct and not metaphorical one. It is also important to understand that the application of dynamics models to psychology is not a new one. The first systematic attempt to analyze psychological properties in terms of dynamics was that of the Gestalt theorists (Heidbreder, 1933). They argued most explicitly for the understanding of psychological phenomena as emergent properties—we would now say, as self-organizing properties—of the interaction of the organism and its environment. Dynamics then lacked two important concepts that are vital for understanding psychological phenomena: that of information (and, hence, information flow) and that of nonlinear systems.

The central thesis of the present analysis, then, is this: *The flow of information in the organism–environment relation is the central, basic organizing process underlying social behavior. All behavior, directly or indirectly, results from the regulation of information flow in this system.* This assertion follows from the belief that the basic concept for any psychological system is its unit of behavior and that all other concepts in a system depend for their meaning in part on this assumption.

Psychological systems have been constructed on the basis of three such behavior units: the impulse, the reflex arc, and the servomechanism. Dynamical systems such as the coupled oscillator have been shown to exist in animals as well as in humans, to be evolutionarily primitive, and to provide a fourth basic metaphor for psychological theory (cf. Gallistel, 1980).

The assumption that behavior consists of dynamical systems is more than the application of a new method of analysis to old problems. It is a radical step toward a new paradigm. To assert that behavior consists of dynamical systems in the organism–environment relation is to demand redefinition of all the concepts we use to understand behavior (cf. Newtson, 1992). In this view, patterns like coordinative structures, including the sensory systems, interact with the information in the environment to produce dynamically stable systems of specification of the organism–environment relation itself. These stable systems are capable of producing self-organizing, or emergent, structures that, because they consist of information, have extension in space and time. Mental process, properly considered, exists in this interactive information field, not in some dark recess of the brain. Such processes, in order to survive, must produce a stable balance of information flow over time, matching inflows of information that increase complexity to outflows of information that reduce complexity. Such dynamic stability may exist in what have been termed *far from equilibrium systems* (cf. Prigogene & Stengers, 1984). Dynamic instabilities in this flow might be understood as the conditions of emotion and cognitive processes understood as mechanisms that developed to stabilize and maintain temporal stability in information flow.

From this view, the concept of information flow is like that of need in impulse theories, of conditioning in stimulus–response theories, and of representation in cognitive theories. It is the central, explanatory construct for a dynamical systems psychology.

B. The Coupling of Behavior Waves

If behavior consists of waves of information flow in the field of each actor, there are many possible ways that coordination of social interaction might occur. One would be a simple coupling kind of model, where each actor succeeds in organizing interaction by entraining the other at a constant phase angle. Thus, we might see the sequence of "turns" in conversation as the product of two waves coupled at antiphase, such that speech is merely part of the high-amplitude part of the wave. An "ideal" interaction would consist of regular alternation of two waves of equal amplitude and equal frequency at a fixed, 180° phase angle. Because both waves have positive values, with minima at zero, the difference between the waves would also be a wave, with peaks during the speaking turns of one actor and troughs during the speaking turns of the other. The period of all three waves would be the period of the sum of the speaking turns of the participants in the interaction.

We might then understand that so-called nonverbal communicators would be means of adjusting the amplitude of one's wave. Thus, one could increase the amplitude of one's wave by moving closer, as that would increase the degree of change of a constant size motion in the other's visual field; gestures would increase the amplitude by adding complexity to the field; seating angles would affect the ease and degree of overlap of mutual visual fields, and so on. Increasing or decreasing eye contact, or "looking" at the other, would be a means of adjusting the amplitude of the other's wave in one's own visual field. The "substitutability" of different nonverbal "communicators" might then be understood in terms of their common effects on wave amplitude.

Such a model would imply that speaking turns, as the high amplitude segment of each speaker's wave, would be equal for the two speakers. As Jaffee and Feldstein (1970) demonstrated, however, this is rarely the case. They conducted a round-robin study in which each person in a set had conversations with every other person in the set. They found that dyads had stable, characteristic turn lengths for each speaker that were idiosyncratic to the dyad. Equal speaking turn lengths were unusual. These idiosyncratic turn lengths were reliable, however, recurring when the study was repeated several weeks later. These results suggest that each speaker had a "characteristic frequency," which was adjusted in some manner to the frequency characteristics of the conversational partner. No simple weighting scheme, however, was apparent in these adjustments.

Detailed empirical analyses of three interaction sequences have began to clarify the nature of interaction coupling (Newtson, in press). One such interaction was a get-acquainted conversation between a pair of strangers. These individuals were recruited for a study of "film preferences," introduced, and then shown 20 min of clips from three classic films. They were then instructed to talk to each other for 15 min and to try to discover what the other person liked in films and why. The middle 5 min of these conversations were selected for analysis at half-second intervals.

In this conversation, a male and female undergraduate carried on an animated conversation. We analyzed both position change with the behavior coding procedure and vocal intensity. Spectral analysis of both vocal intensity and behavior of the individuals yielded significant components but across broad bands of frequencies. For both speakers, voice and behavior were significantly related, with a peak coherence value of .57 at a 55° phase lag. In other words, vocal intensity and movement were related (equivalent Pearson correlation was .74); they were active speakers and relatively quiet listeners. Voice tended to lead gesture. Mean vocal intensity, on an 8-point scale of relative intensity, was 1.2 for the male and .37 for the female (averaged over speaking and nonspeaking intervals). Mean position change was 1.22 features per half second for the male and .99 for the female.

The structure of this conversation was clearly revealed, however, when the vocal intensity and behavior change measures were summed for each actor and the difference between them was examined. This pattern is shown in Figure 3. As inspection of that figure indicates, a simple alternating pattern emerges; spectral

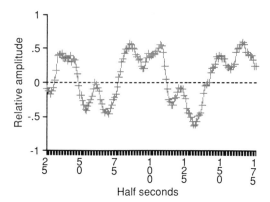

Figure 3   Amplitude difference between summed voice and behavior waves of two people in conversation. From "The Dynamics of Action and Interaction," by D. Newtson. In L. Smith & E. Thelen, *Applications of Dynamical Systems Theory to Human Development.* Copyright 1993 by MIT Press. Adapted by permission.

analysis shows a significant line at the frequency of turn exchange, plus an harmonic. We have dubbed this an "uh-huh" harmonic; at the midpoint of each person's speaking turn, the other emitted either a vocal or gestural interjection.

The wave itself has an intriguingly simple form. The wave has the pattern of the difference between two waves with a frequency ratio of 3:1 at antiphase (and at 60° phase as well). This wave is shown in Figure 4.

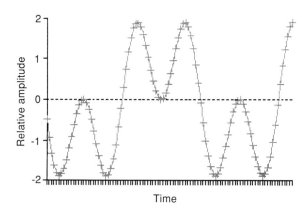

Figure 4   Amplitude difference between two waves with a frequency ratio of 3:1. (Phase angle is 180°.)

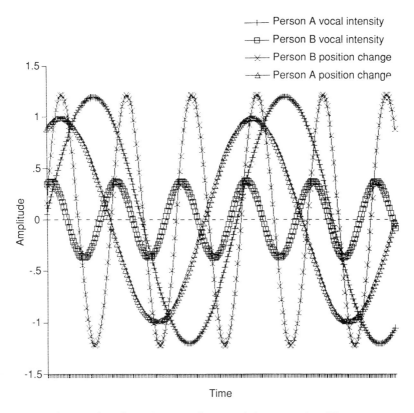

Figure 5   Behavior and vocal intensity waves of two people in conversation. (Waves were generated with observed amplitude, frequency, and phase parameters.)

To understand how this pattern might emerge, the obtained parameters of frequency and amplitude were entered into the canonical wave formula for the four variables measured: the two vocal intensity measures and the two position change measures. Phase angle was set so that voice and behavior waves were at 55°, as observed. These waves, as computed, are shown in Figure 5. The odd result is that a 3:1 ratio occurred between the vocal intensity measure of each actor and the behavioral measure of the other. That is, Actor A had significant frequency values of .046 in vocal intensity and .135 in behavior; Actor B had significant frequency values of .135 in vocal intensity and .046 in behavior. Thus, it appeared that the two actors coupled their behavioral frequencies to each others' vocal frequencies (or the reverse). Combined vocal and behavioral waves are shown in Figure 6 and display a clear 3:1 pattern; the difference between these two waves is shown in

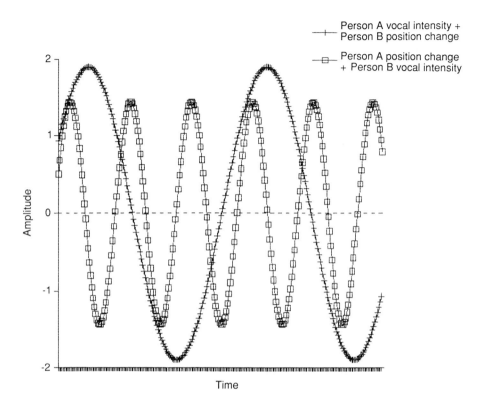

Figure 6   Summed vocal intensity and behavior waves across people (observed parameters).

Figure 7. This difference compares very favorably with the raw pattern obtained in Figure 3.

      These data imply that a simple means of coupling was used in this interaction: Each person coupled his or her gestural movement to the other's voice and relied on the resultant pattern of amplitude differences to coordinate the conversation. Thus, there appeared to be a 3:1 ratio in the "characteristic frequency" of each actor, but we cannot tell from these data which was primary and, hence, which was the "faster." Vocal frequency did lead gesture, suggesting that it was primary.

      It thus appeared that the controlling structure for this interaction was in the relative amplitude of the two voice plus behavior waves. Figure 8 shows the relatively simple manner in which this wave mapped onto speaking turns. Basically, speaking turn changed on the second cusp of the primary cycle wave.

      This analysis is remarkable in that it shows that simple, wavelike organizing patterns emerge in ordinary interaction. Analysis of two other interactions have

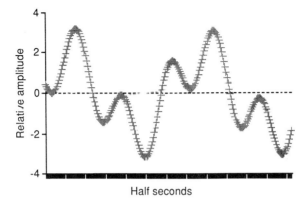

Figure 7   Amplitude difference between behavior waves of two people in conversation calculated with observed parameters.

yielded similarly clear-cut structures (Newtson, in press). These findings allow the formulation of what we have termed the *relative amplitude hypothesis: The regulating pattern for dyadic interaction is the difference in amplitude of the information waves in the behavior of its participants.* As noted, nonverbal behavior may readily be understood as serving an amplitude regulation function. The motivation for such behavior may then be seen as the requirement that a smooth patterning of the relative amplitude wave be achieved to sustain interaction.

Our analysis implies that one way people may achieve such a jointly coupled wave is by coupling their behavior wave to the other's vocal frequency; other ways of achieving coupling in interaction may well be used. The "cross-coupling" of vocal and behavioral waves is, however, an easy and efficient way to achieve patterning in conversation. Results for 2:1, 3:2, 4:1, and 4:3 frequency ratios are given in Figures 9, 10, 11, and 12, respectively, and form a kind of "atlas" of speaking turn patterns that should result from the coupling of speakers with this range of basic frequency ratios. Phase angle for these patterns are at zero degrees; the basic pattern does not change in its fundamental structure at different phase angles. As inspection of those figures indicates, a wide range of complex patterning may emerge; it should be noted, however, that both behavior and vocal recording is required to detect them. Normal speed ranges for behavior are not known, although 2:1 and 3:1 ratios are not unusual. Fast- and slow-motion films typically use speed alterations in the 7:1/1:7 range (Newtson & Rindner, 1979).

Oddly enough, this model will not work for 1:1 frequency ratios; in that instance, an amplitude difference is sufficient to produce simple patterning. If amplitudes are equal, however, a deliberate phase shift is required to produce turn-taking patterning in interaction. Interactions between people with identical wave

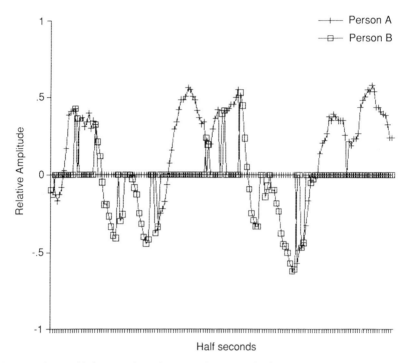

Figure 8 Summed behavior and vocal intensity during speech of two people in conversation. From "The Dynamics of Action and Interaction," by D. Newtson. In L. Smith & E. Thelen, Applications of Dynamical Systems Theory to Human Development. Copyright 1993 by MIT Press. Adapted by permission.

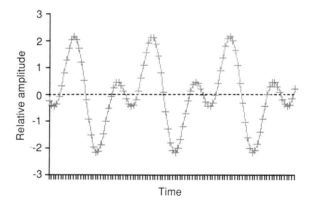

Figure 9 Amplitude difference between two waves with a frequency ratio of 2:1.

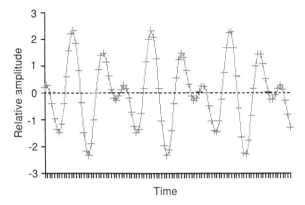

Figure 10 Amplitude difference between two waves with a frequency ratio of 3:2.

parameters are particularly interesting because waves with equal frequencies produce the phenomenon of resonance—a high magnitude boost in the amplitude of both systems. One could speculate, for example, that because wave amplitude is a function of the number of alternative values the wave could take, people in a high-amplitude interaction feel relatively unconstrained in their choice of action. The phenomenon would manifest itself as a feeling that one can find many different things to talk about under such circumstances. In a low-amplitude interaction, by contrast, one might struggle to find things to talk about. Thus, resonance phenomena could be part of the "similarity-attraction" relationship and could provide a concrete basis for the claim that similar others are easier to interact with. Resonance

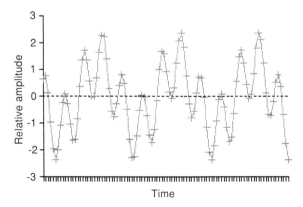

Figure 11 Amplitude diffence between two waves with a frequency ratio of 4:1.

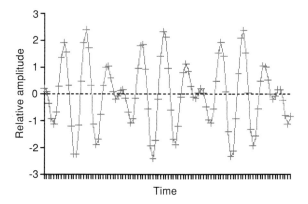

Figure 12 Amplitude difference between two waves with a frequency ratio of 4:3.

phenomena provide a ready basis for selection of interaction participants, as well. (See Newtson, in press, for an explication of this phenomena, as well as data on antisocial adolescents as high-amplitude actors.)

A number of phenomena may be readily understood in light of the relative amplitude hypothesis. One example is that of "shadowing"; coders of interaction have often remarked on the similarity of posture assumed by interactants. If one person in a dyad crosses his or her legs, the other is likely to do so within 10 to 20 s. One could see postural similarity as making amplitude matching or adjustment simpler to achieve. Another example is the occurrence of what we have come to term *bracing postures*. When the interaction is somewhat difficult to follow or understand (e.g., as in teaching), the one having difficulty following the other is likely to assume a motionless posture, often by bracing the body, as with the chin on one's hand. Such braces further simplify the perception of the other's behavior. That is, accurate tracking of the other's amplitude requires subtracting out one's own amplitude; the phenomenon is not different, in principle, from that of using feedback from one's eye muscles to stabilize the visual image during scanning. As in visual tracking, one might simplify the task by holding one's head still, or using a fixed gaze, when the task becomes more difficult. Similarly, in interaction, bracing or freezing simplifies comprehension by eliminating a necessary calculation. In interaction, however, reduction of one's own amplitude has the effect of exaggerating the amplitude of the other; the other is thus forced to simplify his or her behavior to maintain a constant relationship.

Another implication of the relative amplitude hypothesis is that interaction may require "switching signals" only under unusual circumstances. Such circumstances would be those in which relative amplitude information is not available. Short-wave radio communication is notoriously noisy, so it would follow that explicit signaling conventions (e.g., "over" and "over and out") would be required. Similarly, in groups—especially in new groups without well-established social structures—hand-raising conventions may make up for uncertainty as to whose behavior is to be the standard for the establishment of the regulating difference pattern.

Although some form of synchronicity in interaction has long been assumed, it is in fact very rarely demonstrated. One of the most striking aspects of the present findings is that, if these phenomena are measured, such relationships are readily identifiable.

IV. Back to the Future

These empirical findings, then, imply that behavior is a wave, is perceived as a wave, and that behavior waves are coupled in interaction. The relative amplitude hypothesis implies that, in conversation, at least, the relative amplitude of the behavior waves provides the regulating parameter for the behavior of both individuals. Dynamical systems theory adds the consideration that such waves are objectively present and measurable flows of information in the system of organism–environment relations.

Two further questions remain to be addressed. One is how behavior waves are generated, and the other concerns the medium in which they flow. Newtson (in press) addressed the first question, showing that even simple models of information flow can produce waves as self-organizing properties. If one considers the perceptual/action field of the person as a population of specifications (see also Newtson, 1990), then models of population dynamics provide heuristic models, at least, for understanding the emergence of information waves. These models suggest that stable waveforms are just one set of states of a multistable system capable of ranging from steady-state to chaotic regimes. Information flow rate, defined as the net gain or loss of specification action by action, is the critical parameter for such systems. Extensions of these models to those of interacting populations—as under conditions of mutualism, competition, and exploitation—provide some provocative metaphors for the dynamics of interpersonal relationships as well.

The adoption of the dynamical system as the unit of analysis for behavior is a radical step toward a new paradigm, but it is also the occasion for the renewal of an old paradigm in social psychology. It was Lewin (1936) who proposed that social phenomena were the result of a real, measurable "middle-level" organization in behavior and who first proposed that dynamics be used as a basis for its analysis. Indeed, it was the success of his approach in identifying a wide range of phenomena susceptible to controlled laboratory research that gave birth to the field of modern social psychology. The medium in which behavior waves flow can now be understood as an information field that is very much the same as the "life space" that

Lewin postulated. Behavior, then, can be understood as locomotion in that life space, very much as Lewin understood it.

The emergence of dynamical systems theory, as a result, is more than just the appearance of a new set of methodological tools for data analysis and more than just a heuristic set of models with new and exciting possibilities. It sets the stage for the next paradigm in psychology in general and in social psychology in particular. The new psychology is, properly considered, a neo-Gestalt psychology; the new social psychology is a neo-Lewinian social psychology. Physics, at long last, has become sophisticated enough to address psychological phenomena. The challenge is for psychologists to become sophisticated enough in physics *and* in psychology to make use of it.

References

Bracewell, R. N. (1986). *The Fourier transform and its Applications* (2nd ed.). New York: McGraw-Hill.

Chatfield, C. (1984). *The analysis of time series: An introduction* (3rd ed.). London: Chapman & Hall.

Cherry, C. (1978). *On Human Communication (3rd Ed.).* Cambridge, MA: MIT Press.

Ebbesen, E. B. (1980). Cognitive processes in understanding ongoing behavior. In R. Hastie, T. Ostrom, E. B. Ebbesen, R. S. Wyer, D. L. Hamilton, & D. E. Carlston (Eds.), *Person memory* (pp. 46–69). Hillsdale, NJ: Erlbaum.

Eshkol, N. (1973). *Moving, writing, reading.* Tel Aviv: Movement Notation Society.

Gallistel, C. R. (1980). *The organization of action: A new synthesis.* Hillsdale, NJ: Erlbaum.

Garner, W. R. (1962). *Information and uncertainty as psychological concepts.* New York: Wiley.

Golani, I. (1976). Homeostatic motor processes in mammalian interactions: A choreography of display. In P. G. Bateson & P. H. Klopfer (Eds.), *Perspectives in ethology* (Vol. 2, pp. 10–38). New York: Plenum.

Golani, I. (1992). A mobility gradient in the organization of vertebrate movement: The perception of movement through symbolic language. *Behavioral and Brain Sciences, 15,* 249–308.

Gottman, J. M. (1983). *Time-series analysis: A comprehensive introduction for social scientists.* Cambridge, England: Cambridge University Press.

Heidbreder, E. (1933). *Seven psychologies.* New York: Century.

Hollerbach, J. M. (1981). An oscillation theory of handwriting. *Biological Cybernetics, 39,* 139–156.

Jaffe, J., & Feldstein, S. (1970). *Rhythms of dialogue.* New York: Academic Press.

Jones, E. E., & Davis, K. E. (1965). From acts to dispositions: The attribution process in person perception. In L. Berkowitz (Ed.), *Advances in experimental social psychology* (Vol. 2, pp. 220–266). New York: Academic Press, 1965.

Koopmans, L. H. (1974). *The spectral analysis of time series.* New York: Academic Press.

Lewin, K. (1936). *Principles of topological psychology.* New York: McGraw-Hill.

Mandelbrot, B. B. (1977). *The fractal geometry of nature.* New York: Freeman.

Marcopoulous, B., Newtson, D., Horst, S., & Steiner, D. (1992). *Periodicity of agitated behavior in patients with Alzheimer's disease and related dementias: Relationship to circadian change in cognition, physiological variables, and environmental milieu* (Technical Report No 1). Virginia Alzheimer's Association, VA: Unpublished.

Markus, H., & Zajonc, R. (1985). The cognitive perspective in social psychology. In G. Lindzey & E. Aronson (Eds.), *Handbook of social psychology* (3rd ed., Vol. 1, pp. 137–230). New York: Random House.

Newtson, D. (1973). Attribution and the unit of perception of ongoing behavior. *Journal of Personality and Social Psychology, 28*, 28–38.

Newtson, D. (1974). Dispositional inference from effects of actions: Effects chosen and effects foregone. *Journal of Experimental Social Psychology, 10*, 480–496.

Newtson, D. (1976). Foundations of attribution: The perception of ongoing behavior. In J. Harvey, W, Ickes, & R. Kidd (Eds.), *New directions in attribution research.* Hillsdale, NJ: Erlbaum.

Newtson, D. (1980). An interactionist perspective on social knowing. *Personality and Social Psychology Bulletin, 6*, 520–531.

Newtson, D. (1990). Alternatives to representation or alternative representations: Comments on the ecological approach. *Contemporary Social Psychology, 14*, 163–174.

Newtson, D. (1991). What's in an action? *Contemporary Psychology, 36*, 675–676.

Newtson, D. (1993). The dynamics of action and interaction. In L. Smith & E. Thelen (Eds.), *Applications of dynamical systems theory to human development.* Cambridge, MA: MIT Press.

Newtson, D., & Engquist, G. (1976). The perceptual organization of ongoing behavior. *Journal of Experimental Social Psychology, 12*, 436–450.

Newtson, D., Engquist, G., & Bois, J. (1976). Reliability of a measure of behavior perception. *Journal Supplement Abstract Service catalogue of selected documents in psychology*, ms. no. 1173.

Newtson, D., Engquist, G., & Bois, J. (1977). The objective basis of behavior units. *Journal of Personality and Social Psychology, 35*, 847–862.

Newtson, D., Gowan, D., & Patterson, C. (1980, August). *The development of action discrimination.* Paper presented at annual convention of American Psychological Association, Montreal.

Newtson, D., Hairfield, J., Bloomingdale, J., & Cutino, S. (1987). The structure of action and interaction. *Social Cognition, 5*, 191–237.

Newtson, D., & Rindner, R. (1979). Variation in behavior perception and ability attribution. *Journal of Personality and Social Psychology, 37*, 1847–1858.

Prigogene, I., & Stengers, I. (1984). *Order out of chaos: Man's new dialogue with nature.* New York: Bantam Books.

Runeson, S., & Frykholm, G. (1983). Kinematic specification of dynamics as an informational base for person and action perception: Expectation, gender and deceptive intention. *Journal of Experimental Psychology: General, 112*, 580–610.

Salzman, E., & Kelso, J. (1987). Skilled actions: A task dynamic approach. *Psychological Review, 94*, 84–106.

Shaw, R. (1981). Strange attractors, chaotic behavior and information flow. *Zeitschrift fur Naturforschung, 36a*, 80–112.

Skarda, C. A., & Freeman, W. J. (1987). How brains make chaos in order to make sense of the world. *Behavioral and Brain Sciences, 10*, 161–195.

Turvey, M. T. (1977). Preliminaries to a theory of action with reference to vision. In R. Shaw & J. Bransford (Eds.), *Perceiving, acting, and knowing* (pp. 211–266). Hillsdale, NJ: Erlbaum.

Turvey, M. T. (1990). Coordination. *American Psychologist, 45*, 938–953.

West, B. J. (1990). *Fractal physiology and chaos in medicine.* Singapore: World Scientific.

CHAPTER 8

A Family of Autocorrelation Graph Equivalence Classes on Symbolic Dynamics as Models of Individual Differences in Human Behavioral Style

Karen A. Selz
Laboratory of Experimental and
   Constructive Mathematics
Departments of Mathematics and
   Clinical Psychology Center
Florida Atlantic University
Boca Raton, Florida

Arnold J. Mandell
Laboratory of Experimental and
   Constructive Mathematics
Departments of Mathematics,
   Physics, and Psychology
Florida Atlantic University
Boca Raton, Florida

I. Introduction

Much of the work of the biological and psychological sciences centers on the discovery, derivation, or construction of simple but nontrivial mathematical models. In psychology, we traditionally model using distribution functions, and the search for useful models all too often results in the scaling of an observable such that it conforms to a small set of standard distributions (e.g., chi-square or F distributions). Inferential conclusions are drawn using the first or second moment

Dynamical Systems in Social Psychology

(i.e., mean and variance) of experimental groups, assuming the applicability of one of this restricted set of model distributions.

This is in contrast to the physical sciences, in which modeling is focused on the orbits of the time evolution of a system. Here, modeling the influence of specific, idealized independent variables requires the use of ordinary differential equations (ODE) or partial differential equations (PDE) that have (preferably) analytic, algebraic, or numerical solutions. Assuming linearity and the principle of superimposition, this approach involves linear "independent" and "dependent" variable equations, which are added together until a brace of differential equations is considered sufficiently representative of the experiment. This may require many such equations, and the apparent degrees of freedom of the model can become quite large.

A. Equivalence as a Higher Order Observable

Although many interesting physical systems can be modeled in this manner, differential equations are of little help in most real systems that are without the required characteristics of continuity, smoothness, and uniqueness of solutions that allow the extrapolation or interpolation of known data to predicted values. A common example of predictive failure is that of a nonlinear system that demonstrates discontinuities in its solution curves as its control parameter(s) are varied continuously. These discontinuities in the system's behavior are called *bifurcations*. Other examples include nonlinear systems that lose uniqueness and differentiability and manifest behavior that has been called *chaos*. Chaos involves the existence of recurrent orbits with exponential separation of nearby initial conditions (i.e., "stretching") and exponential convergence of initially far apart initial conditions (i.e., "folding") that result in the disordering of the sequence of orbital points.

Analytic evidence that differential equations (as models) have chaotic solutions is limited to cases in which the criteria of Melnikov (e.g., Guckenheimer & Holmes, 1983) or Selnikov (see, e.g., Gaspard & Nicolis, 1983) are met. These require that the "distance" between the underlying expanding ("unstable") manifold and the contracting ("stable") manifold is zero. We can then infer that they must intersect each other at at least one point. When these mathematical conditions are met, they provide justification for the claim of the existence of homoclinic orbits, and therefore the existence of chaotic motions, but little of the individual system's specifics. Most studies of such systems depend on numerical analysis. For the examination of the global structure of the parameter spaces of the mathematical model of an experimental system, we must rely on the *qualitative* study of ODEs and PDEs. That is, we must relax our criteria for saying when two or more systems (or subjects) are or are not equivalent.

This change from analytic to qualitative solutions for ODEs marked Poincaré's departure from the methods of mechanics in the theoretical physics of his day. Through metric-free, "topologizing" of differential systems, he was able to preserve the descriptive and inferential roles of the physical sciences while surrendering a class of unattainable criteria for orbital metric equivalence in favor of attainable qualitative, topological equivalences.

With these new tools in place, it was possible to explore more realistic parameter regimes of model differential systems with large deviations from linearity and resulting global bifurcations (such as those leading to chaos). The study of these kinds of differential equations yielded a finite set of qualitative, topological "types" of solutions. What is lost, however, is the ability to derive specific predictive relations between (ODE or PDE) model system components and system's output. We can no longer decompose our observable into independent, additive processes or modes. This alters the applicability of techniques such as the Fourier transformation of the data. The inference of causality in experimental design is dramatically changed. This gain of global, qualitative information at the cost of predictive specifics cannot be repaired by more tightly constraining our experimental procedures to the observation of a single time scale, as the systems characteristically behave in a single dependent variable across a range of time scales. What, then, can we do?

Topological transformations, preserving continuity, order, and neighborhood properties (here, specifically, symbolic dynamics), followed by statistical approaches to the definition of equivalences protect disconfirmability while providing an heuristic and comprehensive framework on which to explore, model, and test systems of interest. In this approach, we depend strongly on the fact that the abstract dynamical systems that are representative of human behavior possess computable invariants. The ergodic theory of dynamical systems involves invariant statistical measures in the place of asymptotic orbital solutions to differential equations. We assume that these abstract invariant measures can be treated in much the same way that we might treat an experimental observable, but in addition, they may reflect nonarbitrary, deep, global, information about the system over time.

The invariant measures on time series of the observables of interest include "grammatical" or "algorithmic" complexities, entropies, dynamical dimensions, run statistics, and characteristic rates of convergence of these measures with increased sample length (see, e.g., Mandell, 1987; Mandell & Selz, 1991a, 1991b, 1991c; Selz, 1992; Selz & Mandell, 1991, 1992a, 1992b). In lifting a set of empirically computable, abstract descriptive quantities off the particulars of the experimental observable, we automatically reconfigure our definitions of equivalences. In the characterization of real data, instead of the specific, local, metric orbital equivalence of the cartographer, we have access to the global, topological, and statistical dynamic equivalences of a quantifiable artistic impression. As noted earlier, this yields a finite set of categories of behavior.

B. Kinds of Dynamical Equivalence

Many observable phenomena can be grouped into classes characterized by similarity in the behavior of their members. Our theories, manifested in the models that represent them, dictate how we divide up our observations into categories. Furthermore, the existence of a model and/or idealized surrogate system implies that there is some function that can transform our real, behaving system into the behaving surrogate and/or model while conserving the properties of interest. Here, we contrast the equivalence operations of intuitive, verbal analogical relating of observables to theory, as seen in behavioral sciences, to the mathematical notion of topological equivalence through mappings, which define a set of formalisms to accomplish the same goal more quantitatively.

A model implies the existence of a mapping from some aspects of the observable behavior to an alternative symbolic representation (and back again if the mapping is invertible). The formal characteristics of this mapping, as configured by theory, are constrained to a relatively small set of definable types. This is the new element in topological and statistical dynamic predictive methods, using equivalences to model behavior and behavior to predict categories of equivalence. Constraints emerge from the dynamical properties of the abstract formalism itself, which then limit the possibilities in the field of observables to a finite set. The confirmation of these derived constraints through experimental investigations is consistent with these equivalence relations being forms of dynamical laws. What distinguishes these types of mappings from each other can be found in the answer to the question, How much and what type of similarity do we need to say that two things, or two descriptions of the same thing are equivalent?

As noted earlier, although a "map" in lay parlance is a model (i.e., a representation of the original object or system that preserves the qualities and relative quantities that are relevant to the map maker), in the mathematical sense, the map is a function that specifies the relation of the real and model objects to each other. There are three varieties of mappings that we will discuss in order of decreasing "specificity" with respect to the restrictions they place on any statement of equivalences. These types of mappings are isomorphisms, diffeomorphisms, and homeomorphisms.

The most restrictive of these mappings, *isomorphisms*, operate on a metric space and require a one-to-one and "onto" (covered and contained) correspondence between a set of metric (i.e., "ratio data," not relative "ordinal data" or categorical "nominal data") observables or descriptive variables (on a specifiable space) and variables of the model. That is, they require that there is no aspect of the real system that does not correspond to one and only one aspect of the model system (i.e., one-to-one or "injective") and that there are no parts of the model system that do not specify some part in the real system (i.e., onto or "surjective").

These "bijective" (injective and surjective) relations are specific to a metric (e.g., a distance, a weight) and yield numerical equivalences at all points.

Less restrictive, and therefore of more value with respect to generalization, than isomorphic metric relations between observables (as sequential points in the trajectory of the system) and the components of the theoretical system, are the continuous, "in the-neighborhood" relations of manifold topology. These result in equivalences that live through the stretching and shrinking of absolute distances, preserving relative ordering properties, smoothness, continuity, and uniqueness instead. That is, whereas isomorphisms on metric spaces require ratio data, these "diffeomorphic" relations on topological spaces discriminate at the ordinal level.

This sort of "topological" mapping allows equivalence relations between metrically nonisomorphic objects, up to the definitional constraints of the map. On topological manifolds, this equivalence involves the property of smoothness and differentiability of the map. Topological mappings defined on the basis of their differentiability (in C^r topology) are called *diffeomorphisms*. Diffeomorphisms are differentiable mappings that have differentiable inverses. They are one-to-one and onto (bijective) smooth transformations, and given the defined bound on differentiability (i.e., the r in C^r) signify a mapping between observables and theoretic structures such that either system can be smoothly deformed into the other. As examples, phase dynamics on underlying circular manifolds (i.e., tori or invariant circles) are used to model periodic dynamics in biobehavioral processes using these relations.

The limit on diffeomorphic equivalence, exemplified by a cubic curve in the shape of the letter *S*, can be smoothly pulled out into a straight line, " | ", whereas a function with a sharp corner in it (e.g., shaped like the letter *V*), which is not even (C^1) once differentiable at the crease, cannot be smoothly distorted into a line. That is, it has a "singularity" and is C^0, a continuous but not differentiable function, like the tent map of our model discussed later.

It is not uncommon for emergent singularities to destroy equivalence relations in nonlinear systems. In the studies to be reported here, singularities in the forms of fixed points or periodic orbits (limit cycles) destroy equivalence relations between correlation functions of human behavior and their corresponding theoretical structures. We must, therefore, further relax our definition of equivalence.

Homeomorphism is the simplest and most fundamental relation between topological spaces. It is a continuous, one-to-one, and onto (bijective) mapping, which preserves the separateness of points, the compactness of the space, and connectedness. That is, points of observation can be counted (i.e., separateness), they cannot escape the system (i.e., compactness), and they maintain sequential order (i.e., connectedness). Homeomorphic relations allow equivalence relations between orbital dynamics and symbol sequences and will play a prominent role in the description and analysis of our data.

This chapter represents a heuristic demonstration and application of the machinery of homeomorphic, topological equivalence in relating the observables of a human behavioral task with those of a parametrically controlled dynamical system. A commonly used technique in the studies of time series in brain function and behavior, the autocorrelation graph or autocorrelogram, is invoked so that we may make the equivalence relations both categorical and intuitively accessible. This work exemplifies some of the newer modeling techniques derived from the study of chaotic dynamical systems. The methods lie somewhere between the statistical methods of the study of random variables and those involving specific solutions to deterministic differential equations with respect to the underlying ideas about determinism. We feel that these approaches have much to offer those studying complex global dynamics such as those observed in social and cognitive psychologies.

II. Experimental Data

A. Behavioral Style in Experimental Tasks

The present study looks at binarily coded data collected on three related tasks (see Selz, 1992, for a more detailed treatment of tasks and dynamical descriptive variables). The data were collected without the subjects' awareness, in the context of computer-game-like experimental trials.

The proposed model for these data is a family of types of autocorrelation graphs. "Surrogate" data based on the subjects' data is also produced using a piecewise linear map with a single nondifferentiable maximum, a symmetric tent map of the real line. The tent map can be iterated, and, like the subjects' data series, points are partitioned naturally into two states determined by their position relative to the single maximum of the map. This forms a two-state system under the control of a single parameter that controls the height of the tent and, therefore, the steepness of the tent sides.

Our ansatz is that subjects possess a global, signatory quality of time-dependent behavior, which we will call *style*, which allows them to be grouped into exhaustive and mutually exclusive categories on the basis of a wide range of observables. Our choice of a single maximum, "universal" map of the real line (derivable from surface of sections and return maps of phase portraits of generalized second-order ODEs) is consistent with this underlying assumption. Treating people as dynamic information generators and personal style as an aspect of communicative social behavior, pervasive in verbal and "natural language" nonverbal expressions alike, we focus on a simple but universal dynamical model for the symbolic dynamics of the sequential behaviors produced by the subjects.

There were three behavioral tasks performed by subjects in this study. All had a 3-min task duration, at which time the trials automatically terminated, and subjects were given further instructions or dismissed by the appropriate computer text screens. Subjects in all tasks were only instructed as to the structure of the task and that their goal was to "remove" as many blocks as possible from the screen within the 3 min of the experimental task trials. All subjects were verbally debriefed at the completion of their tasks.

Two of the three basic tasks were one dimensional "line" tasks. In both cases, two bars made up of red ¾-in. squares extended from the sides of the computer screen, with a gap of 1⅙ in. between them. At the outset of a trial, the mouse cursor appeared in the middle of this gap as a white "+" enclosed in brackets. Subjects moved the mouse cursor by moving the mouse with their dominant hand (all subjects were right-handed) over the first proximal left or right red square only and "removed" the block by clicking the left mouse key. The movement of the mouse cursor on the screen was restricted to the rectangular region containing the first proximal (medial) left and right squares and the gap between them. Functionally, this restricted subjects' task performance to left and right horizontal mouse movements. Subjects' movements and clicks were coded as "0" for left and "1" for right, and these and the interclick intervals (*ici*'s) were saved to computer files.

The two line tasks differed only in the return time of the "removed" red blocks. In one version, the return time was approximately 40 ms. This was sufficiently brief as to give some subjects the impression that the blocks simply flickered in response to the mouse click. For this reason, subjects were informed in the instruction set that the blocks in these tasks might not seem to disappear entirely owing to the attributes of the monitor, and they were reassured that the number of blocks that they removed was still being recorded by the computer. The short block return time established a situation in which subjects' performance scores would be obviously benefited by a strategy that involved keeping the mouse cursor over a single block and clicking the key as quickly as possible. That is, subjects in this task paid a price for switching from left to right or right to left.

The other line task had a substantially longer block return time (1.3 s). When a block was removed by the click of the mouse key, it did not return for more than a second, forcing subjects to switch to the other side if they were to maximize their (ostensible) scores. Of course, very few subjects developed a perfect point-maximizing strategy, and it is the resulting individual differences in categorical patterns of variability that is the focus of this study.

The third task was a geometrically two-dimensional "triangle task." The task screen had three red ¾-in. blocks, arranged so that they might mark the vertices of an invisible triangle with 3½-in. legs. The virtual triangle was rotated so that no two dots were vertically or horizontally collinear, thus discouraging simple vertical or horizontal mouse movements between any two of the three blocks during the course of an experimental trial. As in the long return time line task, "removed" blocks in the triangle task returned after about 1.3 seconds. Data files generated by this task contained the interclick intervals, cumulative time, block number the cursor was on when a click occurred (i.e., 1, 2, or 3), and whether movement to that block represented clockwise (1) or counterclockwise (0) movement around the invisible triangle.

In both line tasks and in the triangle task, the series of zeros and ones (representing the alternative positions in the line tasks relative to the midpoint of the horizontal mouse window or the direction of relative motion in the triangle task) served as the time series of symbolically coded, $\{0,1\}$, spatial events. Note that the time intervals of this series were determined by the individual subject's behavior. The series of interclick interval events (i.e., the first difference times of sequential spatial events) served as the event series of times. In this report, we will examine only the time series of binarily coded mouse clicks.

Contained in these three tasks are a range of characteristic, intrinsic times, such that the tasks may be ordered. The line fast-return task is the quickest, with a stimulus presentation rate that most "drives" the subject to respond. The line slow-return task is second on this scale of relative lengths of characteristic times, and the triangle task, with its added structural complexity, is the slowest. Because all tasks continued for 3 min, another global measure of the subjects' behavior is the number density of their responses (e.g., the total number of mouse clicks a subject produces in the 3-min trial).

B. Partition of Human Behavior as Support for Equivalence Relations

Although we will be considering a binarily coded data set of human task performance, this is not the only choice of a partition of this data. We could divide up the data into as many states as we like, up to the level of resolution of the recording device. In the present tasks, we could examine subject behavior across spatial states of pixels. In this way, arbitrarily constructed partitions can configure the results of analysis of a measure space. It, therefore, is well-advised to consider data partitions carefully.

Paulus, Geyer, Gold, and Mandell (1990) and Paulus, Geyer, and Mandell (1991) suggested that in applied measure theoretic work, a coding partition should not be chosen a priori on the basis of an idealized physical system but should be dictated post hoc, prior to further analyses, by the context and the content of the particular data set. Such a partition is likely to be nongenerating, with the possibilities of multiply occupied as well as empty cells. Such patterns can be derived from the behavior of the system of interest within the limits of measurement resolution (Selz & Mandell, 1991, 1992a). Such a functional, experimentally determined partition may then be applied in an systematic, experimental manner, following data collection. Unfortunately, although these idiosyncratic partitions allow rigorous comparisons of experimental conditions within individuals or between "ergodic" (i.e., having at least one invariant measure), assumed equivalent subjects, individual differences are "eaten up" in the differing geometries of the partition and are not available for comparisons between individuals within the same experimental conditions (see, e.g., Selz, 1992; Selz & Mandell, 1992a). We, therefore, require an alternative approach.

In the present set of experiments, there are natural candidates for a useful standardized partition of the data that is both constant across individuals (allowing us to locate and compare individual differences) and dictated directly by the natural left/right or clockwise/counterclockwise structure of the experimental tasks. We chose a binary partition as the "coarsest" of the natural ones for coding the experimental computer mouse trajectories. This choice was suggested by both the structure of the tasks and the generator of our "surrogate" data, the tent map, which also produces sequences of data with a "natural" left–right binary symbolic dynamic coding.

Even after this coarse-graining of the observables, a large amount of variability between exact subject sequences was conserved, demonstrating the value of topological equivalences as a modeling technique. Few subjects can be said to be like any other subject if we attempt to match their binary sequences point for point. That is because in n behavioral observations (mouse clicks) there are 2^n possible binary sequences of length n. Experimentally, n ranged from 185 to 993, and if we assume that a subject produced 500 data points (i.e., mouse clicks in 3 mins), then there are 3.2734×10^{150} binary sequences that might represent this subject's behavior! Furthermore, subjects with unequal ns (sample lengths) are automatically unequal.

Demonstrating the usefulness of the techniques of topological equivalence between subjects in discerning the categories of dynamic patterns of the subjects' behavior among these many possibilities is the object of this study. Although similarity of symbol sequences (i.e., shift equivalence) is sufficient to demonstrate the technique, we chose to map the subjects' binary sequences onto a finite set of autocorrelogram types, making the results accessible to visual intuition. We note in passing that all of the available autocorrelation graph types are represented in the behavior of the subjects. At the same time, we used another set of transformations to produce a one-dimensional "dynamical doppleganger" for each subject sequence. These "surrogate" data do not share the specific binary sequence of the subject but share the subject's parity sequence and autocorrelation type. It is in this way that topological equivalence serves as an invariant dynamical law for each subject, who, in turn, can be assigned to membership in a category.

III. Mapping of Subject Data to the Model

The Autocorrelation Graph (Autocorrelogram)

The autocorrelation function of a data series describes, generally, the dependence of the data value produced at one time of observation on data values at other times of observation in the same series. Such analyses have a long history in modern psychology, most notably in early psychophysical research, an area of psychology with established paradigms for the assessment of time series data (see, e.g., Senders, 1953; Verplanck, Collier, & Cotton, 1952; Wertheimer, 1953).

The autocorrelation function is computed in a manner similar to that of standard product-moment correlation coefficients, except that it is computed on pairs of observations from the same series that are separated by some number of intervening observational points. If we call the number of intervening observations τ and call the index of the first observation in any pair t, then we compute $C(\tau)$ between observation $x(t)$ and the observation $x(t + \tau)$. For example, if we have a series of observations $x(t)$, taken at times t ($t = \{1,2,3, \ldots ,n\}$) and we wish to estimate the autocorrelation of one observed value $x(t)$ with another $x(t + \tau)$, we take the product of the two observed values and average over the observation time. This average approaches the exact autocorrelation function as the observation time becomes infinite. That is,

$$C(\tau) = \lim_{T \to \infty} \frac{1}{T} \int_0^T \left[x(t)\, x(t + \tau) \right] dt.$$

Real data from experimental tasks only approximate this quantity owing to the finitiness of the time series.

The computed autocorrelation function is always a real-valued function, may be negatively or positively valued around a zero mean, and is symmetric about $t = 0$. In the graphs in Figures 3, 4, and 5, only the physically real $t \geq 0$ plots are shown. When the lag $\tau = 1$, we compute the correlation (much like a Pearson correlation) of each data point with the next data point, down the length of the series. This is a first-order autocorrelation. We then plot $C(\tau)$ by the lag over increasing τ to produce the autocorrelogram.

This study's focus on characteristic patterns of variation of time dependencies in relation to behavioral style, with the purpose of examining the topological equivalences between the task behavior of the subjects and that of the matched, λ-specified tent map. The autocorrelogram, $C(\tau)$, serves to graphically capture parity-based topological equivalences between the data and the parametric model as well as providing an informal set of categories for behavioral classification.

IV. The Model

We can describe a finite set of "types" of autocorrelation function graphs (i.e., $C[\tau]$, autocorrelograms) that reflect different "types" of topologically transformed behavior. Some idealized examples include the $C(\tau)$ of a series composed of a constant value (i.e., a fixed point). It is always positive and does not decay for the length of the series; the C(τ) of a sine wave is periodic with the same period as that of the data from which it is computed and is nondecaying; the C(τ) of idealized white noise (i.e., random data with "energy" uniform across all frequencies) shows a single spike ("Dirac delta function") at $t = 0$ only. The autocorrelation graph of white noise after the lower frequency components have been removed, however, oscillates over positive and negative values while decaying in a (generally) slower than exponential fashion. An exponential decay of C(τ) with periodic fluctuations, on the other hand, has been associated with wide band passed random data. Note that band-passed random data have autocorrelograms that look somewhat periodic but that decay to zero. The autocorrelogram of the exponential $e^{-\alpha|t|}$ (see, e.g., Bendat & Piersol, 1971) decays with t without oscillatory behavior.

Finally, we might include in our zoology of model autocorrelograms an idealized version of the C(τ) of data on Ce^{4+} concentrations in the Belousov–Zhabotinsky (BZ) stirred chemical reaction (the time-dependent observable in this complex chemical reaction whose recurrent, aperiodic orbit signals the existence of temporal chaos). Such an autocorrelogram of a data sequence, corresponding to the onset of chaos characterized by recurrent aperiodicity (as the generic orbits of chaos return to the neighborhoods of unstable fixed points), manifests relatively symmetric positive and negative amplitudes of correlation (around a zero mean) for adjacent, sequentially lagged observations, with fluctuations as well on longer time scales (see, e.g., Schuster, 1989). We describe similar records from human subjects' data as demonstrating aperiodic recurrent trajectories that are expanding and folding (i.e., sensitive to initial conditions). Real, finite data series (like those of the experimental subjects) often manifest "hybrid" forms of these idealized autocorrelograms.

We can divide all C(τ)s into 10 categories based on 5 experimentally derived patterns of autocorrelation graph decay and whether that decay oscillates (i.e., $e^{-i((t/\tau)^\alpha)}$) or is monotonic (i.e., $e^{-(t/\tau)^\alpha}$). More generally, we may qualitatively categorize the decay of the autocorrelation functions by their rate of decay and the structure of the decay, as below.

Rate of decay	Structure of Decay
1. Faster than exponential ($e^{-(t/\tau)^\alpha}$, $> \alpha$ 1)	Oscillatory or monotonic
2. Exponential ($e^{-(t/\tau)^\alpha}$, $\alpha = 1$)	Oscillatory or monotonic
3. Stretched exponential ($e^{-(t/\tau)^\alpha}$, $0 < \alpha < 1$)	Oscillatory or monotonic
4. Power law/algebraic ($t/\tau^{-(1+\alpha)}$, $0 < \alpha < 1$)	Oscillatory or monotonic
5. Nondecaying/constant ($k = $ constant)	Oscillatory or monotonic

If we had a stationary time series and an infinite number of observations, we might be able to reduce our categories by half, looking only at the rate of autocorrelation decay and ignoring the fine structure (unless, of course, a nearly periodic pattern persisted). In the present case, we would choose not to do this even if it were possible because it is these long transients rather than equilibrium structures that are characteristic of real human data.

The pattern of decay of the autocorrelation functions, $C(\tau)$, and their Fourier transformations, $G(\omega)$, are strictly related to the unstable singularities and mixing properties of the underlying dynamical system (see, e.g., Eckmann & Ruelle, 1985, or Pollicott, 1993). They do *not* reflect some (unknown) underlying mode structure for which one could imagine "causative" control parameters. This change in interpretation of $C(\tau)$ and $G(\omega)$ is central to the application of the tools of chaotic dynamical systems to human behavior.

Singularities in the power spectral representation of these time series represent characteristic dwell times, escape rates, and/or return times, which involve the (unstable) fixed points of the system. The global (averaged) eigenvalues of the system, called the *Lyapounov characteristic exponents*, reflect the "stickiness" of these points, their neighborhoods, and the characteristics of the flow around them. These dynamics serve as "support" for the patterns observed in the $C(\tau)$ and $G(\omega)$. A positive leading Lyapounov characteristic exponent, $\overline{\lambda}_1$, suggests that with an initial value, $x0$, for the system and some small imprecision in measurement, ϵ, $x0 + \epsilon$ will reflect "error growth" that goes like $\epsilon \exp(\overline{\lambda}t)$. Nearby initial conditions separate exponentially over observations *and* initially distant points converge exponentially, as orbits mix on the attractor, generating sensitivity to initial conditions and an exponentially decaying $C(\tau)$ in some systems.

When singularities are present in the system, and we would suggest that these are almost inevitable in biological and psychological systems, we have a case of nonuniform mixing. The result is inhomogeneity in the $C(\tau)$ decay times of the system, which show up as a varied but finite set of autocorrelation graph types.

The existence of a finite set of autocorrelation graph types computed on the output of the homeomorphic symbolic dynamical transformation of the behavior of a dynamical system implies the existence of a generator with a finite set of dynamical states. The geometric theory of such systems on finite dimensional, smooth manifolds allows reductions in the dimensionality of the system such that the single maximum one-dimensional map as used here is topologically equivalent to the original differential system (see, e.g., Guckenheimer, 1980). Smooth, continuous time behavior (flows) in three-dimensional real space can be mapped to smooth, discrete-time behavior (sampled events) in two-dimensional real space as a return map to a Poincare section. This Poincare section (plane) can then be mapped to a topologically equivalent one-dimensional ("line") system (as discrete time semiflows in $\mathbb{R}^1$, the real line).

In addition to its property of dynamical universality and its intrinsic ordering properties, the real line, $\mathbb{R}^1$, is a suitable representation of the $\{0,1\}$, left/right behavior of our subjects. We view our model as both data driven and a "coarse-grained," information preserving reduction from three dimensions to one dimension. We have chosen to do this using a one-dimensional, symmetric tent map of the real line to itself as parametrically matched (using initial condition selection) to each subject's parity sequence associated with the behavioral sequence of that subject. We chose to vary initial conditions rather than using parameter variation to demonstrate how changes in information input can be encoded in "style" without changing the basic character of the map.

V. Creation of Surrogate Data

A. The Tent Map

Figure 1 illustrates the phase space of the one-dimensional tent map. If we let the map

$$\mathscr{T} = x_{n+1} = f(\lambda, x_n) \equiv \begin{cases} \lambda(x_n) & \text{if } 0 < x_n < 1 \\ \lambda(2 - x_n) & \text{if } 1 < x_n < 2 \end{cases}, \text{ then}$$

the function $f(\lambda,x)$ maps the $(0,2)$ interval to itself when $1 < \lambda < 2$. $\mathscr{T}$ is called a *tent map* because of its shape, with two monotonic legs joined at the $(1,\lambda)$ single, symmetric discontinuity. Because $x_n = 1$ as an initial condition generates a stable period two orbit and therefore lacks the required complexity of the human observables, it is not included in this definition of the map.

In our studies, the absolute value of the derivative of f (i.e., $|f'|$) is never less than one when $\lambda > 1$, so the tent map has no stable periodic orbits in this parameter region. Because this is a piecewise linear map, we can calculate an invariant distribution on the $[0,2]$ interval exactly (see Grossman & Thomae, 1977, or Lasota & Mackey, 1985). It has an asymptotically stable stationary probability density distribution (i.e., invariant measure), the same condition implied in the assumption that our subjects (in the practically unachievable limit) can be represented as ergodic message sources, a necessary condition for the computation of many dynamical descriptive variables.

To state the chain of equivalences another way, the tent map as a one-dimensional surrogate for the experimental subjects' behavior is topologically conjugate to a universal class of maps. It can be invertibly mapped, one-to-one, conserving the order of points and their relative positions, onto generic three-dimensional dynamical systems, so that many of the results here can be generalized to more realistically complicated dynamical systems.

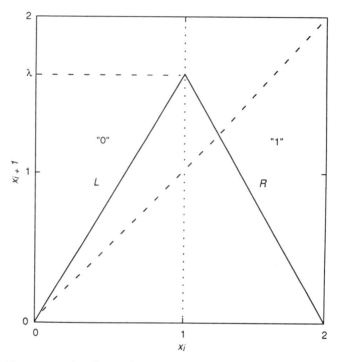

Figure 1 The tent map plotted as its value at observation x_i versus its value at the next observation, $x_i + 1$. (The single parameter of the map, λ, is equal to the height of the tent when the map is depicted in this manner. All points, x_i, in a time series from the map are coded as "0" if $0 < x_i < 1$ and "1" if $1 < x_i < 2$.)

Specifically, the one-dimensional tent map can be shown to be topologically equivalent to the one-dimensional logistic map, which in turn can be shown to be topologically equivalent to a two-dimensional return map of the plane, constituting a surface of section of the three-dimensional attractor generated in phase space by a continuous, nonautonomous, nonlinear second-order differential equation of the sort used to realistically model many biological and psychological processes (e.g., oscillators such as the Hodgkin–Huxley equations or periodically driven van der Pol differential equations). We note that because nonequivalence is possible in this development, disconfirmability is conserved with respect to experimental design. It is in this way that predictive hypotheses may still be tested with "relaxed" but rigorous definitions of equivalence. We can also claim that, by means of topological conjugacy, any findings using the tent map model are generalizable to other members of the same equivalence class representing real systems in higher dimensions.

B. Symbolic Dynamics on Two Letters

Symbolic dynamics is an algebraic approach to labeling and ordering the orbits generated by dynamical systems. This approach was developed conceptually in 1917 in the thesis of Marston Morse (1921), although Procaccia, Thomae, and Tresser (1987) suggested that its use dates back to 1851. The application of symbolic dynamics as it is used here is explained in detail by Hao (1989); Metropolis, Stein, and Stein (1973); and Derrida, Gervois, and Pomeau (1979). Because of the binary character of the experimental tasks, we will concern ourselves with symbolic dynamics on two letters.

Symbolic dynamics, by preserving the ordering property of orbits, can be seen as a way of describing the coarse-grained behavior of a dynamical system over time. Just as we watch subjects' $\{0,1\}$ behavior evolve over the course of an experimental trial, we can code the behavior of the tent map into $\{0,1\}$ and watch the map evolve over time. To do this, we divide the phase space of the map (i.e., the interval of the mapping) into two regions and assign a symbol to each region.

As with the subject data, we know that a natural partition of the tent map divides the interval into two sections in accordance with the monotonic branches of the map, separated by critical (i.e., folding) point(s) (where the derivative of f with respect to x goes through zero) and by the end points of the interval (if they are not already considered as critical points) (see, e.g., Hao, 1989).

In our construction of the tent map on the $(0,2)$ open interval, there are two linear segments separated by a single discontinuity at $x_n = 1$. As with our subject files, a natural partition divides behavior on the map into left, encoded "0," and right, encoded "1." We then move down the series of values produced as we iterate the tent map and at each step assign to the series a symbol "0" if $0 < x_n < 1$ and "1" if $1 < x_n < 2$. The branches of these mappings correspond to the symbols as "1"$(y) = 2 - (y/\lambda)$ and "0"$(y) = y/\lambda$.

We proceed by using an inverse mapping to solve for the λ of a subject's binary behavior and a forward mapping of the tent map at that λ value to generate the surrogate sequences of "0"s and "1"s that can be compared with those produced by the experimental behavior of subjects to which they are matched.

As in the case of the subject data, we can create a functionally infinite number of binary symbol sequences (we are assuming that the map, unlike the subject, can generate an arbitrarily large number of data points). But not every possible sequence corresponds to a sequence such that when its parity is encoded in the inverse mapping (called the λ *auto-expansion*, see below), the expansion converges onto a λ value of the parity-matching forward mapping (e.g., Derrida et al., 1979). The sequences that do converge are called *admissible*, and they imply that the behavior is in the parametric neighborhood of an unstable periodic orbit and therefore has the potential for the emergence of unstable ("transient") periodic behavior of a $\{0,1\}$ symbol sequence. We conjecture that the observed "jitter" around these orbits is the result of multiple, competing, attractive unstable periodic orbits vying for the observable behavioral trajectory of the subject. We have speculated elsewhere that this jitter is the hallmark of all healthy biological systems that require adaptive flexibility in the face of new information input. In our deterministic approach, *jitter* does not mean the "noise" of "randomness."

In the tent map, as in all single maximum maps of the real line, it has been proven that there are an infinite number of competing unstable periodic points (see Jakobson, 1978). In a related approach, one-dimensional maps are often encoded with respect to their sequences of "turning points," which underlie the formation of the parity sequences used in this study (see, e.g., Milnor & Thurston, 1988).

With our subject data, the inverse mapping, from the model back to the subject sequences, is not unique. Many x_n sequences in real-valued observations will correspond to a single binary-coded symbol sequence because of to the coarse graining of the two-letter code (i.e., an infinite number of real values of x_n correspond to either $\{0,1\}$ code symbol). The formal structure of such a selective strategy allows us to consider as topologically equivalent all numerical sequences that correspond to a given symbol sequence. This step represents the essence of the use of topological, homeomorphic equivalences as a research tool with relaxed predictive criteria and conserved disconfirmability. For example, all numerical sequences that have the binary coded representation [0100011] are considered to be equal to each other. This equivalence relation is based on the premise that equivalent orbits are under the neighborhood control of the same unstable periodic points. Current work in dynamical systems in higher dimensions also suggests that the neighborhoods of unstable periodic points serve as "organizing centers" for otherwise very complicated behavior (e.g., Ott, Grebogi, & Yorke, 1990).

In contrast with predictive strategies that result from more restrictive equivalence criteria, the admissibility of a symbol sequence is not dependent on its correspondence to a stable periodic orbit of the iterated unimodal map earlier because these do not exist. Note that they are equally absent in the data. Rules for selection are, nonetheless, well-defined and are concerned with whether the sequence is "maximal." This condition is combinatorial and somewhat technical (see e.g., Hao, 1989). Every binary data sequence, x_i, of n points has an associated parity sequence, a_i, of n points, that depends on the number and order of (contracting) "1"s in the binary transformed data series.

Generally, to be admissible, the tent map binary sequence must begin on the right (descending) side of the map (i.e., $x_1 > 1$, a_1 must equal $+1$) and, as the sequence grows, it must also demonstrate an asymptotic approach to a limiting ratio of lefts and rights. As we will discuss later, the number of values of x_n that fall on the "contracting" ($f' < 0$) right side of the map determines the behavior of the sequence. As we shift the sequence to the left, dropping off the leftmost symbol and appending a zero to the right, we can compare the shifted sequence with the original sequence. The ordering of these sequences on the basis of their parities and sequence order determines admissibility. Admissibility is required for the success of parameter finding using the λ auto-expansion. We note that all of the subjects' data files were admissible.

Recall that the tent map has no stable periodic orbits, but then, as discussed earlier, neither do the files of our human subjects. Instead, we have a collection of subject files with aperiodic, recurrent behavior including transient periodicity (of period ≥ 1) in both our human subject files and in the dynamical model. This suggests that our subjects, like our map, organize their behavior in the neighborhoods of unstable fixed points and unstable periodic orbits. This allows us to take full advantage of the styles of "transient behaviors" of the map in producing matched human-map sequences.

Having relaxed our criteria for predictability to that of topological equivalence, we quantifiably model the behavior characterized by unstable fixed points, aperiodic recurrences, and long transients found in experimentally observable human behavior. This represents a major break from the asymptotic solutions to fixed points or limit cycles, or the statistical distributions with strongly attractive mean values that we have traditionally assumed.

As in the experimental data, we can demonstrate the presence of low-period transient periodic behavior in the bifurcation plot of the tent map without preiteration (Figure 2a) and the disappearance of these unstable fixed points in a similar plot of as many points but with preiteration of 2,500 points (Figure 2b). Recall that the λ parameter controls the height of the tent (and the size of $|f|$) and that we are only using tents in which λs satisfies the inequality $1 < \lambda < 2$.

C. Orbits as λ Expansions

Although somewhat technical, we think that it is important that the λ-finding technique be demonstrated by example so that the reader will not see it as either magical or arbitrary. To get from the binarily coded trajectory of our subjects to a similar trajectory produced by the map, we use a variation of Hao's (1989, 1991) "word-lifting" procedure to find the appropriate value for the parameter λ. Hao used the method of a power series expansion in λ, representing the inverse map of the tent map generator.

If we are looking for a number $1 < x < 2$ as a sum of the inverse power series in $1 < \lambda < 2$, we can begin with $x = 1 + (1/\lambda)$, and if $\Sigma\, 1 + (1/\lambda)$ exceeds the value x, we can subtract the next power (i.e., $-(1/\lambda^2)$) and check again. Of course, if $\Sigma\, 1 + (1/\lambda)$ is less than x, we add the next term in the power series (i.e., $+(1/\lambda^2)$). It is thus clear how an appropriate series will converge on the correct value for $x = \lambda$ by means of its own inverse powers. The λ expansions use the binarily coded data to construct a power series expansion and locate the associated λ. For example, the sequence $[1011] \equiv [101^2]$ in the notation of sequence

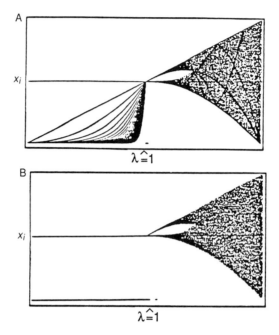

Figure 2 The bifurcation plot of the tent map from $\lambda = 0$ to $\lambda = 2$, iterated 2,500 times for each λ value, (A) without preiteration, and (B) with preiteration. [Notice the dense bands of transient clustering of points in (A) that are discarded with preiteration.]

coding and represents a Period-5 orbit. Using the inverse maps, "1"$(y) = 2 - y/\lambda$ and "0"$(y) = y/\lambda$, [101^2] can be expressed as

$$\lambda = 2 - \frac{2}{\lambda^2} + \frac{2}{\lambda^3} + \frac{2}{\lambda^4}.$$

Because $\lambda = 1$ is a nonunique solution to all sequences from this system, we can cancel $\lambda - 1$ from the above expression. [101^2] can then be written as

$$\lambda = 1 - \frac{1}{\lambda} - \frac{1}{\lambda^2} + \frac{1}{\lambda^3}.$$

What this means is that we have two real numbers, a value n and the parameter λ, and we wish to express x as the sum of inverse powers of λ. That is,

$$x = \sum_{i=0}^{\infty} \frac{a_i}{\chi_1},$$

where a_i is the element of the parity sequence of the subjects data, and $a_o = a_1 = 1$, and $a_i = \pm 1$ (or 0 on the critical point). If some $a_b = 0$ (i.e., if the map lands exactly on the critical point), then $a_i = 0$ for all $i > b$, and the sum is finite. We, of course, have a data-driven truncation of the expansion. That is, our λ expansions are finite because our original, subject-generated data sequences are finite, of length n

The sequence of coefficients, a_i, are coded not on the basis of "0" or "1" but on the basis of the "parity" of the 0 or 1 of the x_i corresponding to each a_i, with $i = \{1,2,3, \ldots ,n\}$. The rules for creating a parity sequence will be discussed later.

With a finite sum, Hao (1989, 1991) showed that if the sequence is admissible as above (i.e., "shift maximal"), then λ can be written as an autoexpansion

$$\lambda = \sum_{i=0}^{n-2} \frac{a_i}{\lambda^i}.$$

That is, λ corresponds to the sum of a sequence of $n - 1$ ratio (i.e., a_i/λ^i) letters.

Because not all sequences are admissible sequences, not every set of a_i will correspond to the autoexpansion of some $1 < \lambda < 2$ (see Derrida et al., 1979). For the sequence of a_i to be the coefficients of an autoexpansion of the tent map, the sequence $(a_o,a_1, \ldots ,a_n)$ must satisfy all of the inequalities $\pm(a_t,a_t+1, \ldots) < (a_o,a_1, \ldots)$ for all $t > 1$, with "0" $< x = 1 <$ "1", with $f' = 0$ at $x = 1$. Pairs of sequences (the original and the shifted ones) are compared term by term, from left to right. Based on parity and sequence, the first appearance of inequality in the sequences determines the valuative ordering of the sequences relative to each other.

Generally then, we can use subject data files of "0"s and "1"s as the initial sequences. Using these, we can define a convergent (iterative) λ autoexpansion representing the inverse tent map and identify a parameter value, λ, of the forward tent map that will produce a sequence matched to the subject's parity sequence. We can, in effect, assign a single parameter value to each subject based on his or her binary behavior on a given task. The sequence of "0"s and "1"s produced by the map at this parameter value should closely approximate the parity-dependent properties of the subject's task dynamics in the surrogate data. We have chosen to graphically demonstrate these homeomorphic topological equivalences through comparisons of the visually discriminable, finite set of geometries of the C(τ)s, the autocorrelation graphs, of the map and subject sequences. We do not claim that C(τ) serves to quantify the property of decay of correlations in the behavior of the map, but rather use it to portray its qualitative type.

D. Assigning Parities and Creating a_is

Any one of our symbol sequences will contain a certain number of "0"s and a certain number of "1"s. The sequence is said to be of odd parity if it contains an odd number of "1"s and of even parity if it contains an even number of "1"s. As noted earlier, this reflects the "turning" behavior that is a parameter-dependent, defining characteristic of one-dimensional, single-maximum maps (see Milnor & Thurston, 1988). The symbol "1" is associated with the negatively sloped (i.e., descending, $f' < 0$) leg of the tent map. So, the parity of the sequence is dictated by the number of descending (contracting) "turns" involved in the orbit of the map or subject. When parity is odd up to $i - 1$, we assign the value $a_i = -1$ to $x_i = 1$s and the value $a_i = +1$ to $x_i = 0$s. When parity is even up to $i - 1$, we assign the value $a_i = +1$ to $x_i = 1$s and the value $a_i = -1$ to $x_i = 0$s (see, e.g., Hao, 1989).

Consistent with the surrogate generator, the tent map, all subjects files began in the center of the mouse-task interval, and the first $\{0,1\}$ symbol in all subject files is assigned as 1. To create the parity sequence that serves as the a_i sequence in the autoexpansion of λ, we take a subject data file, and because $x_1 = 1$, assign the value $+1$ to a_1. Because we have only a single 1 at this point, the sequence has odd parity, so if the second symbol in the subject's file is 1, then $a_2 = -1$, and if the second symbol is 0, then $a_2 = +1$. If the second symbol is 1, then the parity switches to even for the evaluation of the third symbol. If the second symbol is 0, the parity is unchanged. The computer algorithm continues the computation in this way, symbol by symbol, assigning coefficient values of ± 1, referring always to the parity of the sequence up to but not including the data point being coded. When we reach the end of the data file, we have a sequence of $n - 1$ coefficients, $a_i = \{\pm 1\}$.

E. Obtaining a λ Value for a Subject

Using the a_i sequence, we create the λ − autoexpansion series

$$\lambda = 1 + \frac{a_1}{\lambda} \pm \frac{a_2}{\lambda^2} \pm \frac{a_3}{\lambda^3} \pm \frac{a_4}{\lambda^4} \pm \dots \pm \frac{a_{n-1}}{\lambda^{n-1}} .$$

When this equation is treated as an iterated function, we get

$$\lambda_{n+1} = 1 + \frac{a_1}{\lambda_n} \pm \frac{a_2}{\lambda_n^2} \pm \frac{a_3}{\lambda_n^3} \pm \frac{a_4}{\lambda_n^4} \pm \dots \pm \frac{a_{n-1}}{\lambda_n^{n-1}}$$

which converges to a value of λ, the choice of initial λ satisfying $1 < \lambda_{ic} < 2$.

VI. Mapping and Modeling the Surrogate Data

Finally, we calculate and graph the autocorrelation functions of each subject's $\{0,1\}$ data file and of the $\{0,1\}$ file created by the tent map at the λ value assigned to the subject for visual comparison. The results of the modeling procedure will be presented by task, in order of decreasing intrinsic temporal forcing: short-delay and long-delay line tasks and the triangle task. Although the λ parameter equivalent models do not duplicate the specific binary sequences of the subjects, they conserve the parity sequences of the data series. The $C(\tau)$s of the λ-matched maps were geometrically similar to those of the subjects.

VII. Results

A. Correspondence of Subject and Surrogate Models by Task

The homeomorphic, topological equivalence of data and theory is illustrated by the autocorrelograms produced by the coded parameter-matched tent map sequences, which are consistent with the autocorrelogram "types" of the corresponding subjects. In comparisons between subjects and the tent map-generated series, often even the fine structures of the autocorrelation graphs were found to be quite similar.

B. Line Fast-Return Task

There were a finite variety of morphological "types" of $C(\tau)$ observed in the subject files of the line fast-return task. Autocorrelograms of their parity-matched tent map surrogate sequences duplicated not only the type of autocorrelogram of the subject's file to which they were parity matched but often were strikingly similar in their fine structure as well (See Figure 3). This finding is consistent with our hypothesis that specific sets of underlying dynamics, rather than coarse graining of the observables, are responsible for the parity-matched, topological equivalences in the data.

Subjects (examples shown in the left-hand column of Figure 3) and matched tent map sequences (parity-matched examples shown in the right-hand column of Figure 3) demonstrated autocorrelograms that ranged from those with a slowly varying, nearly periodic pattern (see Figure 3a), to sharp "delta" functions like those of "uncorrelated" white noise (see Figure 3b), to nearly periodic, relatively quickly varying, nondecaying patterns (see Figure 3c).

The parity matching procedure on symbolically coded sequences was successful in producing a tent map binary sequence for the subject $C(\tau)$s of quickly varying, regular patterns (see Figure 3d). Also present were intermittent, aperiodically recurrent autocorrelograms, somewhat reminiscent of those produced by the chaotic BZ chemical reaction mentioned earlier (see Figure 3e). Finally, several subject autocorrelograms and those of the parity-matched tent map demonstrated simple exponential decays of correlation (see Figure 3f).

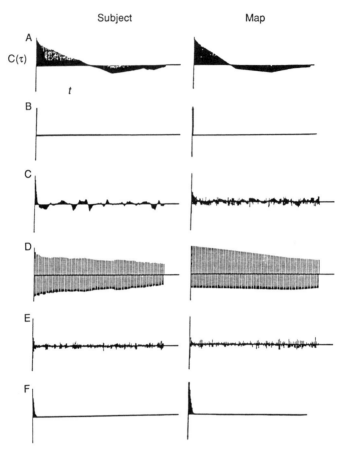

Figure 3 Autocorrelograms of subjects (left) and their corresponding tent-map surrogates (right) representing the finite set of types of autocorrelation graphs observable in the line fast-return task.

The λ value (found by λ autoexpansion) and then used in the tent map binary sequence generator resulted in autocorrelograms that matched both the gross type of the subjects' autocorrelation functions and often their fine structure as well. This analysis was performed on all subject files.

C. Line Slow-Return Task

There were only two related types of autocorrelograms in the entire subject sample on the slow-return line task. Subjects, in performing the line slow-return

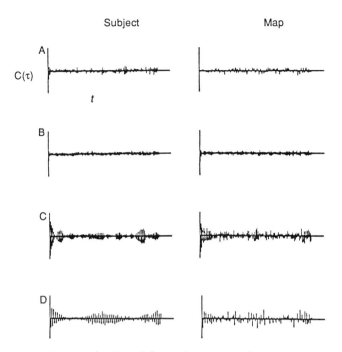

Figure 4   Autocorrelograms of subjects (left) and their corresponding tent-map surrogates (right) representing the finite set of types of autocorrelation graphs observable in the line slow-return task.

task, produced autocorrelation functions without much intersubject variability. All of these were of the "hybrid" recurrent and "intermittent" variety. Again, examples of subject file $C(\tau)$s on the left side of Figure 4 are shown with their parity-matched surrogates $C(\tau)$ on the right. It was these hybrid patterns, with some variability, that their λ-equivalent tent map autocorrelograms emulated. Some were more intermittent and nondecaying, jumping erratically between modest positive and modest negative values (see Figure 4a,b), whereas others had more features in common with near-periodic transition to chaos shown earlier in the context of the BZ reaction (see Figure 4c,d).

D. Triangle Task

There was a greater variety of autocorrelogram types computed on subjects' performance of the triangle task. This increase in complexity across subjects might have been anticipated given that this task is realized in two rather than one physical dimension. Autocorrelation graph types observed ranged from "sinusoidal" slowly

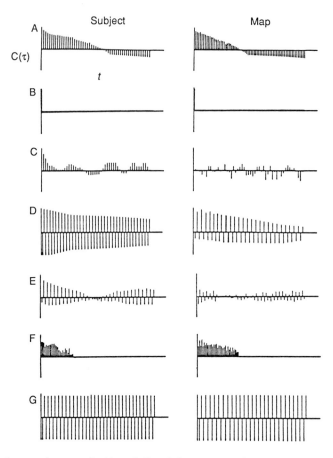

Figure 5   Autocorrelograms of subjects (left) and their corresponding tent-map surrogates (right) representing the finite set of types of autocorrelation graphs observable in the triangle task.

varying patterns (see Figure 5A) to the exponential decorrelation patterns of white noise (see Figure 5B); BZ–type autocorrelation functions (see Figure 5E); (stretched) exponential decay of correlation (see Figure 5F); quickly varying, near-periodic, very slowly decaying patterns (see Figure 5D); slowly decaying oscillatory patterns (see Figure 5C); and very quickly varying periodic behavior that is nondecaying within the sample length, n (see Figure 5G). This latter pattern was not observed in the subject files from the two other tasks. In the strictly periodic cases, we could find an exact parity match, but here differences in the specific symbol sequences altered the results, making the search more difficult. In this case, the one-to-many parity sequence, symbol sequence, and fine structure relations of the autocorrelogram can be lost.

The parity-matching λ expansions were again successful in producing λ values that as parameters of the tent map produced sequences that were often quite different in exact sequence structure but that, following transformation, captured the qualitative geometry of the subjects' autocorrelograms. This lack of specific sequence regularity leads naturally to a finite set of parity-constrained, categorical families of autocorrelograms. As noted, even the fine structure of the $C(\tau)$ function is preserved through the set of data transformations in most cases.

VIII. Discussion

An important issue with respect to the methods of modern dynamical systems theory as applied to experimental design in psychological research is addressed in this study, and an integrative strategy is developed to answer the question, Can the data reduction and transformation methods used by those studying mathematical dynamical systems theory be applied to behavioral data without violating the assumptions or limitations of either. We have shown that they can be if we allow the relaxation of the criteria for establishing relations between experimental data and surrogate data from those of metric equivalence to those of topological equivalence.

Poincaré's break with the physics of his era rested largely on his acknowledgement that all but a few of the differential equations used to represent physical systems were not analytically solvable. He demonstrated that the representational and predictive role of differential theory could be preserved, however, through the use of qualitative (geometric/topological) methods.

The introduction of the tools of differential topology on manifolds to the analysis of differential equations yielded a finite set of topological types of solutions. These types were applicable to a wide variety of specific systems that were subject to quite general constraints. These constraints involve conditions such as the differentiability and dimension of the manifold and the number of control parameters of the system. Specific relations between physical controls and metric observables were not obtainable. The decomposition of these complex dynamical systems into independent, additive modes; the adiabatic elimination of "nonrelevant" time scales; and solutions in the form of Fourier expansions or LaPlace transformations were found to be neither proper nor meaningful in this context.

What then can be the basis for establishing relations between models and observables or surrogate observables under these circumstances? What kinds of criteria for the disconfirmability of theory can be used to maintain the scientific method once we can formally grasp more of the real systems that confront us?

It seems natural to pursue the topological and statistical approaches to the definition of equivalences. Developed in the context of modern dynamical systems theory, these are represented in the work of Smale (1967) among others. It has been found generally that forced-dissipative systems generate a finite set of attractive mathematical structures that produce behaviors that are neither fixed points nor stable periodic orbits but in phase space assume unusually recognizable geometric identities. We see persistent "styles" of behavior that, although somewhat unpredictable in detail, can nevertheless be characterized by the statistical properties of their dynamics and topological equivalence relations between theory, and experimental observables can be created.

We can visually summarize the structure of data/surrogate, data/model, surrogate/model relations constructed in this chapter with the following diagram:

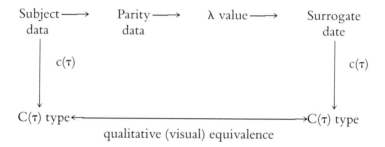

We can place this set of relations in a more general form if we let the letter O represent any subject's binary data series from this study and let T represent the λ-inverse tent generated surrogate series. Similarly, we can represent the autocorrelation graph transformation by $C(\tau)$ and the parity matched λ autoexpansion as $\phi(\lambda)$. O' and T' are the autocorrelation functions of O and T, respectively. Finally, we will denote the human visual assessment of autocorrelation geometric category membership by the letter $\mathscr{E}$. Following a variant of the standard method for the graphical depiction of a topological homeomorphic equivalence, we have

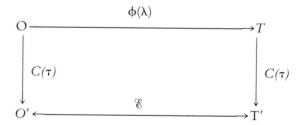

Then, making the prediction (for example) that increasing behavioral forcing in the experimental task would change the parametric height of the λ value associated with the surrogate data series, T, we could test this hypothesis using the methods described here and diagramed above.

We have found that consistent individual differences in task-related parities are conserved under time-forcing conditions, leading to characteristic families of autocorrelation types. Going beyond these qualitative, geometric successes in the parametric modeling of the subjects' behavior on the experimental tasks to the inclusion in a multivariate program of research relating these persistent individual differences to other psychological indices is the future of this work.

Acknowledgments

The authors wish to acknowledge the support of the Office of Naval Research, Biological Intelligence and Systems Biophysics Programs.

References

Bendat, J. S., & Piersol, A. G. (1971). *Random data: Analysis and measurement procedures.* New York: Wiley.

Derrida, B., Gervois, A., & Pomeau, Y. (1979). Universal metric properties of bifurcations and endomorphisms. *Journal of Physics, A12,* 269.

Eckmann, J. P., & Ruelle, D. (1985). Ergodic theory of chaos and strange attractors. *Review of Modern Physics, 57,* 617–656.

Gaspard, P., & Nicolis, G. (1983). What can we learn from homoclinic orbits in chaotic dynamics? *Journal of Statistical Physics, 31,* 499–518.

Grossman, S., & Thomae, S. (1977). Invariant distributions and stationary correlation functions of the one-dimensional discrete processes. *Z. Naturforsch., 32a,* 1353–1363.

Guckenheimer, J. (1980). Bifurcations of dynamical systems. *Progress in Mathematics, 8,* 115–232.

Guckenheimer, J., & Holmes, P. (1983). *Nonlinear oscillations, dynamical systems, and bifurcations of vector fields.* New York: Springer Verlag.

Hao, B. (1989). *Elementary symbolic dynamics and chaos in dissipative systems.* New Jersey: World Scientific.

Hao, B. (1991). Symbolic dynamics in the characterization of complexity. *Physica, D51,* 161–176.

Jakobson, M. V. (1978). Topological and metric properties of one dimensional endomorphisms. *Soviet Physics Dokl., 19,* 1452–1456.

Lasota, A., & Mackey, M. C. (1985). *Probabilistic properties of deterministic systems.* New York: Cambridge University Press.

Mandell, A. J. (1987). Dynamical complexity and pathological order in the cardiac monitoring problem. *Physica, 27D,* 235–242.

Mandell, A. J., & Selz, K. A. (1991a). Heterochrony as a generalizable principle in biological dynamics. In S. E. Stanley & N. Ostrowsky, (Eds.), *Propagation of correlation in constrained systems* (pp. 281–316). New York: Plenum Press.

Mandell, A. J., & Selz, K. A. (1991b). Is the EEG a strange attractor? Brainstem neuronal discharge patterns and electroencephalographic rhythms. In C. Grebogi & J. Yorke, (Eds.), *Impact of chaos on society.* Tokyo: United Nations University Press.

Mandell, A. J., & Selz, K. A. (1991c). Nonthermodynamic formalism for biological information systems: Hierarchical lacunarity in partition size of intermittency. In A. Babloyantz (Ed.), *Self-organization, emerging properties and learning* (NATO Advanced Research Workshop Series, pp. 255–266). New York: Plenum Press.

Mandell, A. J., & Selz, K. A. (1992). Dynamical systems in psychiatry. *Biological Psychiatry, 32,* 299–301.

Metropolis, N., Stein, M. L., & Stein, P. R. (1973). On finite limit sets for transformations of the unit interval. *Journal of Combinatorial Theory, A15,* 25–36.

Milnor, J. & Thurston, W. (1988). On iterated maps of the interval. *Lecture Notes in Mathematics, 1342,* 465–563.

Morse, M. (1921). A one-to-one representation of geodesics on a surface of negative curvature. *American Journal of Mathematics, 43,* 33–51.

Ott, E., Grebogi, C., & Yorke, J. A. (1990). *Physics Review Letter, 64,* 1196–1199. (Erratum: *64,* 2837).

Paulus, M. P., Geyer, M. A., Gold, L. H., & Mandell, A. J. (1990). Application of entropy measures derived from the ergodic theory of dynamical systems to rat locomotor behavior. *Proceedings of the National Academy of Sciences, 87,* 723–727.

Paulus, M. P., Geyer, M. A., & Mandell, A. J. (1991). Statistical mechanics of a neurobiological dynamical system: The spectrum of local entropies ($S(\alpha)$) applied to cocaine-perturbed behavior. *Physica A174,* 567–577.

Pollicott, M. (1993). *Lectures on pesin theory and ergodic theory on manifolds.* Cambridge, England: Cambridge University Press.

Procaccia, I., Thomae, S., & Tresser, C. (1987). First return maps as a unified renormalization scheme for dynamical systems. *Physics Review, A74,* 1884.

Schuster, H. G. (1989). *Deterministic chaos: An introduction.* New York: VCH.

Selz, K. A. (1992). *Mixing properties in human behavioral style and time dependencies in behavior identification: The modeling and application of a universal dynamical law.* Unpublished doctoral dissertation, University of Manuscripts International.

Selz, K. A., & Mandell, A. J. (1991). The Bernoulli partition equivalence of intermittent neuronal discharge patterns. *International Journal of Bifurcation and Chaos, 1*(3), 717–722.

Selz, K. A., & Mandell, A. J. (1992a). Bursting intermittency and microwave popcorn: Comments on the "reporting out" of neuron-like firing behavior. In P. Meakin (Ed.), *NATO Advanced Research Workshop on growth patterns in physical sciences and biology.* San Diego, CA: Academic Press.

Selz, K. A., & Mandell, A. J. (1992b). Critical coherence and characteristic times in brainstem neuronal discharge patterns. In S. McKenna, J. Davis, & S. Zornetser (Eds.), *Single neuron computation* (pp. 525–560). New York: Academic Press.

Senders, V. L. (1953). Further analysis of response sequences in the setting of a psychophysical experiment. *American Journal of Psychology, 66,* 215–228.

Smale, S. (1967). Differential dynamical systems. *Bulletin of the American Mathematical Society, 73,* 747–817.

Verplanck, W. S., Collier, G. H., & Cotton, J. W. (1952). Nonindependence of successive responses in measurements of visual threshold. *Journal of Experimental Psychology, 42,* 273–282.

Wertheimer, M. (1953). An investigation of "randomness" of threshold measurements. *Journal of Experimental Psychology, 45,* 294–303.

CHAPTER 9

Toward a Dynamic Conception of Attitude Consistency and Change

J. Richard Eiser

Department of Psychology
University of Exeter
Exeter, England

In this chapter, I argue for a radical revision of our concept of attitude, which, traditionally in social psychology, has been seen as a point on a linear continuum of favorability. The chapter will be organized in three parts. In the first, I describe some familiar areas of attitude research, not with any pretence at giving an up-to-date review of the current literature, but rather so as to identify a few key issues with respect to which the adequacy of a dynamical systems approach can be assessed. In the second part, I suggest what a dynamical systems view of attitudes might look like. In particular, I argue that attitudes need to be regarded as attractors within a particular kind of phase space. The characteristics of this phase space include multiple dimensions, multiple attractors (of different strengths and ranges), and nonlinearity. In the final section, I argue that the cognitive processes capable of producing such a space are consistent with connectionist principles in cognitive science.

Dynamical Systems in Social Psychology

I. Some Traditions in Attitude Research

A. Attitude Measurement

We take it for granted nowadays that attitudes can be measured. Opinion polls seem indispensable to much political commentary, market research questionnaires a basis for planning far-reaching commercial decisions. But are attitudes simply what attitude scales measure? When we talk of people acquiring, defending, and changing their attitudes, can the processes to which we refer be adequately described by reference to scores on these standardized instruments, or do we need to search for something more fundamental that such simple scores may conceal?

This question was recognized, perhaps even more clearly than now, when techniques of attitude measurement were being first developed. Thurstone (1928) put this well:

> It will be conceded at the outset that an attitude is a complex affair which cannot be wholly described by any single numerical index. For the problem of measurement this statement is analogous to the observation that an ordinary table is a complex affair which cannot be wholly described by any single numerical index. Nevertheless, we do not hesitate to say that we measure the table. The context usually implies what it is about the table that we propose to measure . . . Just in the same sense we shall say here that we are measuring attitudes. We shall state or imply by the context the aspect of people's attitudes that we are measuring. (p. 530)

The principal question that Thurstone himself addressed was that of how favorable or unfavorable an individual or group of people could be said to be on a given issue. He was not especially concerned with a person's reasons for holding a given position but simply with locating that position on an "attitude continuum" ranging from extreme unfavorability (anti) to extreme favorability (pro). The assumption of continuity here is very important. It leads us to think in terms of degrees of favorability rather than look for dividing points between different "sides." It implies, in short, that attitudes are linear.

With the techniques that Thurstone and others developed, we can derive (interval) scores to specify quantitatively the extent to which, say, a sample of fundamentalist Christians are more opposed to abortion than are a sample of atheists or the amount by which an audience's approval for a politician has increased or decreased following a televised speech. Attitude favorability is regarded as something you can have more or less of, much like money in the bank or feelings of hunger before a meal. This is not just simple, it is extremely useful. But, as I argue, it does not tell us what attitudes are, why we have them, or why they mean as much to us as they do.

B. Multiple Dimensions

Not all attitude measurement restricts itself to Thurstone's single continuum of opposition/support. Multidimensional scaling techniques have been developed to take more account of the "complex affair" that Thurstone acknowledged people's attitudes to be. These techniques attempt to locate a person' attitude in a space of multiple dimensions, over and above mere approval/disapproval. In many cases, these additional dimensions are defined empirically with regard to a specific context or set of attitude objects. However, there have also been more ambitious attempts to define dimensions of measurement that are applicable to any attitude context, most notably the classic work on the "semantic differential," described by Osgood, Suci, and Tannenbaum (1957) in their book *The Measurement of Meaning*.

Osgood et al.'s (1957) central claim was that, despite the many thousands of adjectives to be found in any dictionary, factor analysis could identify a very limited number of factors, or underlying dimensions, that define a highly stable—if not universal—"semantic space." Of these dimensions, the three most important are evaluation (e.g., good–bad), potency (e.g., strong–weak), and activity (e.g., active–passive). Osgood et al. equated their dimension of evaluation with the favorability dimension of conventional attitude measurement, considering that potency, activity, and other minor dimensions captured other aspects of "meaning." Like Thurstone's scales, the semantic differential (as well as the many kinds of more "free-style" rating scale procedures that it spawned) assumes linearity.

C. Attitude Change

If we can measure something, we can see if it changes. The development of attitude measurement techniques thus offered opportunities for experimental research on attitude change, exploited fully the Yale University program of the 1950s (e.g., Hovland, Janis, & Kelley, 1953). Although this was arguably persuasion research's golden period, the conceptual basis of this work was limited. Although the possible mediating role of cognition was not denied, persuasion was seen essentially as producing a change in response along a unitary dimension.

D. Attitude Organization

Rivaling the Yale program in its seminal influence is Heider's development of the notion of "cognitive balance." The basic idea of all balance or cognitive consistency theories is that people have a disposition or motivation to see the world as consistent and hence predictable (perhaps to a greater extent than it "really" is). For social psychology, the most important manifestations of this drive for consistency are in the ways we tend to evaluate other people and events. Attitudes, according to this approach, are a form of evaluation. Crucially, though, we are supposed to organize patterns among these evaluations so that they may be grouped together into higher order cognitive structures. These structures are regarded as having the properties of perceptual *Gestalten*, in particular, symmetry and completeness.

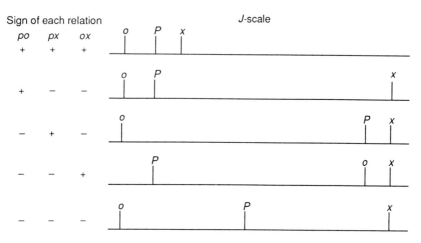

Figure 1   Preference space representation of Heiderian triads.

Best known of these structure are the Heiderian "triads," wherein the relations between a "perceiver", p, another person, o, and an issue, x, are summarized in terms of triangles, the points of which represent p,o, and x, and the lines of which represent the relations between them (from p's perspective). These relations are viewed as either positive (like, approve, feel attached to) or negative (dislike, etc.). Heider (1946) hypothesized that triads with three positive relations or with one positive and two negatives would be "balanced" and therefore more stable, predictable, easy to learn, and preferable. The point is sometimes missed that this kind of consistency has no roots in logic. On the contrary, pressed to the extreme, Heider's balance principle assumes nothing more commendable than an intolerance of ambiguity and a horror of ambivalence—that is, a drive toward a crudely simplistic value system. Put differently, balance theory assumes what Jaspars (1965) termed a *unidimensional preference space*. The argument goes like this.

According to the "unfolding" theory of preference judgment proposed by Coombs (1964), the evaluation given to any single object of judgment will be a function of its distance from some ideal point P along some descriptive dimension, or J-scale. If the J-scale is then "folded" around P (i.e., if raw scores are replaced by absolute differences from P), it will result in a measure of relative preference, with smaller discrepancy scores representing greater preference. Let us now try to map the Heider triads onto a Coombs J-scale, making the following two assumptions. First, Heider's P takes the place of Coombs's P; this essentially involves saying that p has a positive self-concept, which turns out anyway to be one of balance theory's limiting conditions. Second, small distances between objects of judgment on the

J-scale represent positive relations between them; this is already assumed in the case of po and px relations, the additional assumption being that a smaller ox distance is needed to represent a positive ox relation. What is the consequence of this? Remarkably, we find that the only triads that can be mapped onto a unidimensional J-scale are those that Heider regarded as "balanced." Additionally, the three-negative triad (which Heider saw as "ambiguous") can be mapped onto a single J-scale if p occupies the middle point (like some version of a political moderate) and o and x occupy the opposite extremes (see Figure 1).

The message is clear. The "rationality" of balance is no more than a flight from complexity, the "purity" of its gestalt no more than the elimination of diversity. Balance theory demands the mapping of preferences along a single dimension, but in a multidimensional world, this can only be achieved through a selective definition of one's context or frame of reference. Such consistency is relative, not absolute: It depends on what interrelations we choose to attend to and on the criteria we use to make comparisons. Another way of expressing this is to say that cognitive consistency principles presume that the frame of reference has been defined in terms of salient dimensions (Eiser, 1971; van der Pligt & Eiser, 1984).

E. Attitudes and Behavior

Salience is also relevant to the problem of attitude–behavior relations. The "theory of reasoned action" (Fishbein & Ajzen, 1975), now modified as the "theory of planned behavior" (Ajzen, 1991), began as a solution to the problem of attitude–behavior discrepancies. Their insight was that such discrepancies are largely attributable to a mismatch in the levels of specificity/generality between self-reported attitudes, on the one hand, and behaviors, on the other. All versions of the model make strong assumptions about the causal dependence of different kinds of thoughts (intentions, attitudes, norms, specific expectancies, and values) on one another.

As was true of balance theory, we have an apparently "rational" model of decision making that depends on individuals' selective definition of their frame of reference. If we are seeking to predict voting choice, say, why should some facts or assumptions about a candidate be more influential than others? Fishbein and Ajzen (1975) addressed this problem through introducing the notion of "salient beliefs." Beliefs are salient if they are regarded as particularly important by the individual. Because of the limitations of our capacity for holding different pieces of information simultaneously in short-term memory, we are unlikely to consider more than about seven such salient beliefs at any one time in arriving at a global evaluation of an object or behavior. But which beliefs? I have argued elsewhere (Eiser, 1986; van der Pligt & Eiser, 1984) that individual differences in salience (i.e., in the selection of a particular attribute, e.g., likely support for legal abortions, as personally important) may be systematically related to the very attitudes one is seeking to measure and explain. For instance, supporters and opponents of nuclear energy attach different importance to different aspects of the issue, such as economic and technological as opposed to health and safety considerations (Eiser & van der Pligt, 1979).

The point I wish to make here, though, is more general. Attitudes require some internal structure or pattern, not least if they are to predict behavior, but even more generally because otherwise we would be left with a random pile of thoughts and feelings that we would not experience as attitudes at all. All credible theories of attitude make this assumption in some form or other. However, what has not been sufficiently emphasized in more conventional approaches is the dependence of this structure on personal and selective definitions of the frame of reference within which attitude judgments are made. Attitudes are not simple. They are as complex as any other thought and are more complex than most. Yet, this complexity is an emergent property of extremely simple dynamic processes, already at least partly understood in other contexts. By studying the dynamics of attitudes, we are not taking attitude theory away from mainstream psychology but toward it—not out of science, but into it.

II. Patterns of Attitudes

Attitudes are habits of thought involving an association of value with actual or imagined properties of an object or issue. But how are such patterns of association to be represented? Can we account for the flexibility of attitudinal expression and experience in terms of the inflexible linear models on which we have relied since the time of Thurstone? I believe that we cannot and that the time has come to look for new conceptual tools and metaphors.

Let us remind ourselves of what attitudes are supposed to look like, according to the traditional view. The conventional (Thurstone) approach is to regard an individual's attitude as a kind of point on a line (see Figure 2). This line goes from the extreme of unfavorability or opposition to some specific object or issue through to the extreme of favorability of support. It is a well-behaved line. It lies perfectly flat and straight. It stays in one rigid piece, without any gaps. It is unaffected by whoever uses it or looks at it. It also makes no prediction about where a person's attitude is more or less likely to lie. If we think of the point in Figure 2 as something like a marble or a ball bearing rolling along backward and forward along a flat,

Figure 2   A linear attitude space.

frictionless track, then it could come to rest anywhere or nowhere: All positions on the line are equally probable and improbable, equally stable and unstable.

A reputed advantage of this model is that it allows for measurement of change. However, it does not tell us what changes are more or less likely to occur. There is nothing in the model to restrain any change whatsoever, subject to the important restriction that any change would have to take the form of a continuous movement backward or forward along the line: Jumps are against the rules, as are the "catastrophic" changes described in Chapter 10. For example, if we were measuring attitudes before and after group discussion, we would expect (under most conditions) an effect of increased polarization (i.e., movement away from the scale midpoint toward the nearest extreme; Moscovici & Zavalloni, 1969). There also is no way of showing that movement from one attitude position to another is restrained by anything other than the distance between them on the continuum (e.g., by whether the source of a message is categorized as similar to or different from the subject; Lange & Fishbein, 1983). Furthermore, there is no representation of attitude stability—a critical concept in theories of attitude organization given that consistent attitudes are supposed to be more stable or resistant to change in any direction. Organization consists of departures from equiprobability, but no such departures are represented in this simple diagram.

One might respond that the model is only a technique of measurement. It does not claim anything about the forces acting on a person's attitude. If we find that attitudes are especially resistant to change in certain directions or in certain positions, or if we know that pressures for change exist in particular directions, then we can expand our representation to take account of the various extraneous forces at play. For instance, we could add various arrows to the diagram to represent forces of different strengths and direction (see Figure 3). This, however, would be a purely ad hoc exercise that would leave the form of the underlying continuum unchanged. Our ball on the track would be subjected to various pushes and pulls, sucks and blows, but the track itself would stay unmoved.

A. Attitude Space

It is important to see diagrams, maps, and even pictures and sculptures not as literal reproductions of any object that they depict but as summaries of relevant information about that object. If the object has more or less of some feature, then

Figure 3   A linear attitude space with extraneous forces.

it can be said to occupy a position on a dimension where information about that feature is recorded. It is arbitrary whether we draw that dimension from left to right, back to front, or however, just as it is arbitrary that we draw geographical maps with North to the top. Likewise, we need by no means be restricted to the three dimensions of visualizable space. Physicists use the term *phase space* (or *state space*) to refer to a statement, using the "spatial" language of positions on dimensions, to describe the state of a physical system at any point in time. (A corollary of this is that the evolution of a system over time can be described as a trajectory through that space.) Because the amount of information required to describe a system completely is immense, so is the number of dimensions. In fact, given that any single particle requires six dimensions to describe it, the number of dimensions required to describe an entire system will be six times the number of separate particles within it. In theory, it is possible to characterize the entire state of the universe as a single point in a phase space with an infinite number of dimensions. Popular texts on cosmology are full of very simple diagrams, of fuzzy cubes and cones on wavy stalks, to illustrate the universe's evolution—that is, to say, its phase-space trajectory.

However complex a state of affairs may be, we can represent it as a point in space. We can handle extra complexity by adding dimensions to the space, and we can allow for a multitude of dimensions beyond those we can visualize at one go. Another approach is to find appropriate order and control parameters and replace the multiplicity of variables with them (see Chapter 2). In place of the physicists' phase space, we can think of a multidimensional "attitude space" in which a person's attitude at any time can be represented as a single point and attitude change as a trajectory through that space over time.

B. Mental Geography

Diagrams of attitude space are therefore just particular ways of describing important features of a person's state of mind. But we have seen that the conventional straight-line diagrams do not provide answers to some important questions. What keeps attitudes, or states of mind, where they are? What makes it easier for them to change in some directions rather than others? What are the effects of habit and experience? What are the effects of selective attention and information processing? Traditionally, as I have said, these questions have not been regarded as problems of measurement or even problems for measurement. These have been questions for theory and experimentation, and theory, traditionally within much social psychology, has been seen as able to exploit measurement while standing above it. My view is that this tradition has not served us well. Any theory must involve assumptions about its objects of study, and these assumptions necessarily have implications for how these objects are to be measured. Conversely, acceptance of a particular view of measurement can mean that one has adopted theoretical assumptions without being aware of having done so.

This is not at all the complaint of a statistical purist objecting to some detail of a complicated method of analysis. My argument is not at all technical. It is quite simply that, when we obtain measures of attitudes, thoughts, feelings, or anything else, we should be alert to the (psychological) processes by which these measures have been generated. If we are not, we can find that we have implicitly accepted a theoretical view of how these processes operate that we would never have accepted explicitly if this view had been spelt out to us. Frictionless straight-line continua, flat surfaces, cubes, and hyperspaces with no quasigravitational forces within them all carry the same implicit fallacy: that any position in the space that they define is as probable as any other and that any nonzero force in any position and in any direction will be enough to send a person's attitude skidding off to the extremities of that space. We are not offered a mappable or readable space, merely an infinitude of singularities, which effectively is to say, no space at all. This is not a theoretical position that any of us would willingly accept.

But surely (someone might object) maps need coordinates, and these traditional models of measurement are doing nothing worse than applying the techniques of coordinate geometry that have been familiar since the time of Descartes. True, but to be able to interpret such coordinates, we need some fixed reference points, and the difficulty with the kinds of psychological maps I have described is that we do not have any. To use a (two-dimensional) map, we need a little more than a system of coordinates. We need a compass and a landmark. If we do not have a compass, then a second landmark will do just as well. But for all this to work, these landmarks must be identifiably different from their surroundings. There must be something qualitatively distinguishable about them. In fact, both Thurstone and Osgood implied in their writings that their measures involve some kind of pivoting around a neutral point (i.e., the midpoint of the attitude continuum or the origin or zero of the semantic space). This neutral point is assumed to be qualitatively distinct in that it is the point of maximum indecision and ambiguity (according to Thurstone) or "meaninglessness" (according to Osgood). Both would argue too that there is something primary about the direction of the evaluative dimension of approval–disapproval.

This is all reasonable enough, although in a different context I would argue against the notion of an absolute neutral point that can be identified in the same way irrespective of the attitude of the perceiver (see Eiser, 1990). But there is still the difficulty that such assumptions about the special status of the neutral point are extra to the map itself. There is nothing in the map itself that tells us that the neutral point is supposed to be special, still less what it feels like to be there. And there is a very good reason why this is so: If all we are dealing with is a form of coordinate geometry, what matters ultimately are the relative positions and orientations, the choice of origin being arbitrary.

Much the same holds for the primary status of the evaluative dimension. It is easy to accept intuitively that some kind of good–bad distinction is fundamental to many of the judgements we make. But if we take Osgood's cube as a map of semantic space, there is nothing in the map that defines this dimension as more primary and less arbitrary than any other—not, that is, until the space starts to get filled with concepts that stretch out along a particular projection; not, in other words, until we introduce something of meaning. By all means, let us treat the good–bad distinction as special, but let us not expect its special status to be revealed to us by a map of this kind.

If all we mean by a dimension is a line on a map, then any line can be primary if we agree to treat it as such. The problem is rather like taking a trip to the Greenwich Observatory to work out what is special about the Greenwich Meridian. About all that is special when you get there is a brass strip on the ground. The nearby buildings by Sir Christopher Wren are much more memorable. We get by with ordinary geographical maps because the "special" places and directions, although arbitrary to greater or lesser extents, have been agreed on by convention.

But most of this is only dimly related to how most of us use maps. Suppose that you are trying to find the Greenwich Observatory. An atlas of the world would be of hardly any help at all, or at least it might be of some use if you are setting off from Orlando, but it would be quite useless in helping you find your way out of Heathrow Airport. Eventually, though, you manage to weave your way through South London and arrive at the observatory. You see the line of the meridian running South to North. What next? If you decide that you now want to cross the Thames to North London, you would do much better to ask directions from a local than to expect the meridian to do double duty as a signpost. This is not a trivial example. The kinds of maps that are of most use to us most of the time are not just systems of coordinates. They locate landmarks. They identify routes and obstacles, rivers and bridges, and hills and valleys. They tell us how to find places and how to get from one place to another. Navigational maps are likewise far more than sheets of pale blue with lines of longitude and latitude printed on them. To be really useful, these maps need precise details of coastlines, of deeps and shallows, of tides and prevailing winds. The framework of the coordinates needs filling in through experience. If we want to map the mind in such a way as to reflect experience, we must be more like geographers than geometrists. We are not playing with pure forms within some abstract rule system. We are describing something that has both meaning and a physical reality.

C. Curves and Contours

Let us now consider what it would mean to add "geographic" content to the kind of maps we might need to describe a person's attitude. The problem I have

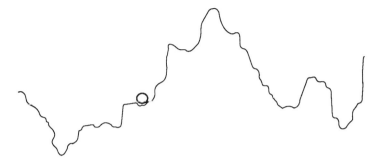

Figure 4 A nonlinear attitude space.

been stressing is that conventional straight-line models contain no infomation about the influences that keep a person's attitude or state of mind where it is. Figure 3 is no better than a clumsy illustration of how some of these influences might operate. We have a linear attitude space, and we have some influences, but neither the space nor the set of influences depends on the other. There is no hint of relativity. How might this space be changed so that the information about the influences is contained in the map itself? A possible answer is shown in Figure 4.

The marble or ball bearing that represents a person's attitude is kept in place not by extraneous arrows but by the contours of the landscape. Being in a deep valley, it needs more energy to climb the hillside. If it were in one of the lesser valleys, it would need less energy to move, and if it were balanced on top of a ridge, it would take very little energy at all to push it one way rather than another. All this, of course, relies on the fact that we interpret such bends and curves on the analogy of real hills and valleys, with a gravitational pull acting downward. We know that it is less easy to push things uphill than downhill and that this is related to the height and steepness of the hill. We know that things tend to roll down to the bottoms of valleys. All I am doing is using a familiar kind of spatial knowledge to communicate a specific piece of psychological knowledge: that someone's attitude can be more stable in some positions than others and will be easier to change in some directions than others. Thus, we can communicate stability and instability, departures from equiprobability, and the relative likelihood of alternative states. In short, we can illustrate the dynamic processes on which the space depends.

D. Dynamics and Attractors

This way of communicating dynamical structure is by now in fact quite familiar in other sciences. The most general way of mapping a dynamical process is by combining several repeated measures of an object within a single phase-space diagram. More simply, we define the axes of our diagram in terms of the distinguishing attributes we regard as important and mark in a dot to represent how much of each attribute the object has at time t_1. Then we move on to time t_2 and record the new characteristics of the object by another dot. And so on. If we draw lines from one dot to another in the order in which they appear, our diagram will reveal the trajectory of the object through phase space over time.

One of the main characteristics of such maps is the presence of attractors. An attractor is simply any position or projection in phase space toward which the various data points appear to be pulled or attracted. For example, if one plotted the trajectory of the tip of a simple pendulum in "ordinary" space, it would converge over time toward a point vertically below its pivot, where it would eventually come to rest (because of the loss of energy to friction). Plotting the same trajectory in phase space, with one axis representing position and another velocity, would produce a spiral converging on a central point, representing zero velocity and the lowest vertical position.

A closely related concept is that of basins or wells of attraction. This reflects a very simple idea, namely that attractors may only be dominant over a limited field or area of phase space. Thus, the plug hole in a bath tub will "attract" the bath water, but it will exert no "pull" at all on the water in a flower vase on a table in another room. Thus, a well of attraction is the range, or set of limiting conditions, within which an attractor has an influence. If an event falls within the well, it will tend to converge on the attractor that defines the well's base or center. This enables us to fill in the phase-space map with a kind of contoured landscape in which unequal conditional probabilities are represented by wells or valleys in different regions. Under these initial conditions, this attractor will dominate; under other conditions, other attractors will exert their influence. Figure 4 can be read as a two-dimensional map of just such conditional probabilities. The different kinds of attitudes that could be taken to correspond to the different dips in the line are attractors of different strengths (depth) and ranges of influence (width). In that these contours represent potentials for, and constraints against, particular mental events, they can be said to constitute an *energy surface*, with the wells representing states of lower potential energy. Viewed another way, the ridges may represent the limits of the context within which attractors have their influence.

E. Stability and Instability

What applies to attitudes can apply to anything in a creature's behavior or experience wherein there is some recognizable pattern of recurrence. Killeen (1989), a behavioral psychologist expressed this eloquently:

Some attractors are fixed from birth, and are called reflexes. Others are acquired early in life; under special circumstances these are stabilized quickly, and the stabilization is called imprinting. Others acquired throughout life are more malleable, and are called habits. The confusion and clumsiness that attend new ways of seeing and doing act to repel innovation, even as "habit" attracts variant behaviors toward old patterns . . . The pull of attractors may be inexorable (categorical perception), strong (persistence in a career or in personality styles) or trivial (techniques for opening a door). Each of these attractors are called fixed points, because while under the control of the attractor, the system stays at or near a fixed point in its space, locked into that pattern by negative feedback. (p. 56)

Negative feedback, adaptation, homeostasis, assimilation, and accommodation are the stuff of most psychological theories. We stay in control by correcting for excesses, by returning to the familiar, and by becoming familiar with the new. Change occurs, but within bounds: Our moods may swing, but like the swinging of a pendulum, they return to their resting place. According to much attitude theory, we strive for consistency, abhor contradiction and ambivalence, and reappraise our thoughts and behavior to protect a stable evaluative simplicity. Psychological processes—like many in fields as diverse as physiology, evolution, and meteorology—appear to find their own level, or so it seems to be for most of the time. But there is another side to the story. There is choice as well as conditioning. There is the ability to imagine alternative states. There are other attractors in the field beyond the well in which we find ourselves if somehow we can make it to the ridge. Most important of all, the pull of an attractor depends on our starting point, that is, on prevailing initial conditions or context.

Consistency and stability depend on the context in which we find ourselves and on our selective definition of it. If we look beyond the ridge, we will see a different landscape. If we resume our journey from the top of the ridge, slight changes in direction will take us into different valleys. We will be subject to the pull of multiple attractors, rather than one. In other words, we will be on the path to chaos. As other chapters in this volume illustrate, however, chaotic processes do not reflect mere randomness but the evolution of natural dynamic systems to the point at which tiny changes in some parameter can produce either complex patterns and rhythms or unconstrained variability. I contend that the interaction of our experience with our environment is just such a system. Consciousness demands the recognition of patterns and rhythms in our experience, and within the category of conscious thought, attitudes reflect patterns of a special kind.

But what kind of patterns—not, from my earlier arguments, a mere point on a line, as in Thurstone's scheme, nor the frozen architecture of Heider's triads? We are dealing with thoughts in constant flux, with evaluations that involve continuous categorization and recategorization of events according to multiple criteria. But within this complexity, there are still local resting points and equilibria. The presence of such equilibria accounts for why traditional theories (of attitude measurement, organization, and change) work as well as they do. The fault of such models and theories lies not in asserting the existence of equilibria as such but in neglecting their multiplicity and their dependence on context. A representation of attitude space therefore requires multiple attractors.

Such attractors will appear differently, though, depending on the angle from which they are viewed—in cognitive terms, the dimension in terms of which the situation or problem is appraised. A cliff that is impossible to scale may be easy to walk around. Viewpoints that seem sharply separated if one dimension is salient may seem compatible with each other if another criterion is used as the basis of judgment. Take any of the dips in Figure 4. The outline of the valley suggests a stable attractor—a balanced attitude. Such balance or consistency, however, is indicated only in terms of one dimension or frame of reference. Take a cross-sectional slice in a different direction or replace it with a contoured surface, and we may see quite a different picture. What we took to be a region of stability might be revealed as no more than a pocket on a precariously narrow ridge. What we see as a narrow indentation might be the gateway to a gorge that runs long and deep in a different direction.

This brings us to yet another meeting point between social cognition and the science of dynamical systems. The curve as drawn in Figure 4, although complicated, can be regarded as "rectifiable," that is, it could be bent back to a straight line of a definite length. If, on the other hand, we want to draw a landscape that allows people, albeit with effort, to climb a hillside, we need to find extra contours and indentations, extra length and surface area, with increased magnification. This means that the effective dimensionality of our landscape or energy surface must be, in Mandelbrot's (1983) terms, *fractal*. To say that an attitude is fractal means that if one looked into greater detail of the attitude space, the more contours and shapes one would find. So, in addition to large hills and valleys, there are smaller ones that are invisible on a macroscopic level. Within them, in turn, an even finer structure could probably be identified.

F. Attitudes as Attractors

Before considering how an energy surface of this kind might come about, let us pause and consider some of the advantages of such a representation for attitude theory. First and foremost, we can infer that attitudes involve selective information processing. The way things are interpreted will depend on the perspective from which they are viewed. The ease of passing from one thought to another will depend on the paths by which they are associated. This is precisely what is meant by saying that different people can regard different aspects of an issue as salient. In a multidimensional universe, the scope for individual differences in interpretation and association is, in principle, infinite.

Another advantage of this approach is that both overt actions, on the one hand, and verbal expressions of attitude, on the other, can be represented as attractors within the same space. Attitude–behavior consistency will thus depend on the ease of passing from an attitudinal attractor to a behavioral attractor or vice versa. In other words, it will depend on the strength of association, without any requirement that such association be unidirectional rather than reciprocal. What is important is that attitudes and behaviors can be distinct (to the extent that they are reached from different starting points, i.e., are activated by different sets of inputs) or closely tied to one another (to the extent that the same initial conditions can lead to both being shown together). In terms of the map, consistency will be reflected in terms of the attractors being linked by a valley and distinctiveness by their separation by a ridge.

The same approach allows for the fact that attitudes can be reappraised, in the light of previous behavioral decisions, much as cognitive dissonance theory would predict. This is a simple consequence of the reciprocal nature of the paths of association between attitudinal and behavioral attractors. To account for standard effects of cognitive dissonance experiments, we need to assume that individuals have a range or repertoire of potential attitude positions that they might endorse on any issue. These different positions can be represented by more or less shallow wells of attraction within the same general region of the space. In the absence of any special influence, an individual's expressed attitude (or preferred position) will tend to gravitate toward the deepest of these wells. However, the effect of "forced compliance" manipulations (e.g., Festinger & Carlsmith, 1959), where people are induced to perform an act inconsistent with their previous attitude, is to "start the ball rolling" from a different part of the space. This starting point will correspond to a new attractor representing (thoughts about) the behavior that the individual has just exhibited. The design of such experiments rests on the intuition that it will be difficult to return from this new behavioral attractor to the original "preferred position" but easy to reach alternative, albeit initially shallower, attitudinal attractors.

III. A Connectionist View of Attitudes

A. Neural Networks

Let us remind ourselves of the job we expect any phase-space map of attitude to do. What we need is a representation of deviations from equiprobability, something that allows us to say which attitudinal events are more or less likely to occur. Precisely this question is addressed by contemporary connectionist work on neural networks. Without attempting a full account of the principles of this approach (see, e.g., Bechtel & Abrahamsen, 1991), the basic ideas are as follows.

A neural network is a computing device, modeled on an extremely simplified picture of the functioning of the human brain, which depends on many simple (neuronlike) units operating in parallel and interacting to produce many different kinds of cognitive events, such as the retrieving of a word from memory, recognition of a familiar object, categorical judgment, and by extension, the evaluation of some attitude object. These events are the outputs of the system. The inputs are, as one might expect, stimulus information. What is crucial, though, is that the system receives this information through a bank of simple receptors or input units, each of which responds to a different specific stimulus feature. Thus, any stimulus object will produce a configuration or vector of activation levels across the bank of input units. In simple networks, any input unit is potentially connected directly to any output unit. However, whether a given output unit will fire (and lead to a particular cognitive event) depends on the total (net) activation it receives from the input units (and on how this compares with the total activation received by other output units). This in turn depends on the input activation levels (already mentioned) and on the strength of the connections (which can be either facilitatory or inhibitory) from each input unit to the output units. Formally, the interconnections between the bank of input units and alternative outputs form a matrix (hence, a "net"), and output activations are calculated by multiplying the input vector by the matrix of connection weights (which can be positive or negative).

Refinements to this scheme involve the introduction of threshold functions and, most importantly, the introduction of multiple layers, or banks of hidden units between the input and output layers. In other words, input information is fed forward to a bank of units that perform preliminary processing operations before feeding this reprocessed information forward (in the form of a transformed vector of activation levels) to the next layer. In such cases, there will be a series of matrices of connection weights, connecting each layer with the next. Although most current simulations of cognitive activities make do with a very limited number of hidden unit layers, this characteristic of neural networks allows the possibility of their being applied to much more complex tasks than hitherto.

The single most distinctive feature of neural networks affecting their ability to solve cognitive tasks is that the connection weights need not be specified in advance. Instead, a net can "learn," from experience with a specific task, what connections are needed to generate a satisfactory standard of performance. The most common way this happens is through a computer simulation procedure known as *supervised learning*. The connection weights are initially set at random; the net is fed some input pattern and produces a (choice of) output. Feedback is then provided to the net in terms of a measure of the discrepancy between this output and some solution defined as correct for the input in question. The net then recalculates the connection weights, and the procedure is rerun until the point at which the outputs show an adequate match with the correct answers. When this is so, the net will continue to be able to make "correct" discriminations between different kinds of input. This procedure requires that the correct answers are specified in advance.

Somewhat less researched, but especially important for our discussion here, is another procedure known as *unsupervised learning*. Here, no feedback is provided, and the modification of connection weights is achieved by the use of a principle postulated by Hebb (1949) that when any two units are simultaneously activated, the connections between them (and hence their ability to activate one another) are strengthened. Simultaneous activation is what is more familiar to social psychologists under the name of *covariation*. Remarkably, neural networks are able to detect covariation in the stimulus environment (i.e., in the patterns of input with which they are presented) and produce a record or representation of such covariation in terms of modification of connection weights. This principle has very general implications. Applied to covariation between different input features, it accounts for a wide swathe of phenomena traditionally explained in terms of associative learning and classical conditioning, as well as many aspects of pattern recognition and categorization. Applied to covariation between input and output, it accounts for the increase in habit strength through repetition. As for the effects of feedback and reinforcement, these are of course handled by the supervised learning procedure.

Connectionism is thus not just an approach with wide applicability. It is one that fits in with a theory that complex cognitive capacities are *emergent properties* of large numbers of simple processes operating together, a theory that in turn fits in with the metatheory that all natural complexity is an emergent property of dynamical systems. But its immediate value in the present context is that it provides an explicit account of how a particular pattern of input can lead to particular forms of output, be these recall of memories, discriminations, behavioral choices, or attitudes. As an account of learning, it also describes the evolution of the system over time. Such evolution consists of modifications to initial patterns of connection weights, so that the probability of a preferred "solution," given a specific stimulus input, is increased at the expense of nonpreferred alternatives or "errors" and so that events that are associated with each other in the real environment also come to be associated in memory.

B. Connectionism and Dynamical Systems

The end point of all of this is a change in the output vector, that is, in the relative probabilities of different outputs. The acquisition of "knowledge" by the system produces more or less stable departures from equiprobability across the configuration of outputs. This process is equivalent to the introduction of one or more attractors into the system's phase space. More probable outputs can be defined as more powerful attractors. Outputs that are likely to occur to any of a number of input configurations can be regarded as attractors with a wider range (i.e., wells of attraction that take up a larger surface of the space). The greater the difference in connection weights leading to alternative cognitive outputs, the greater will be the difference in strength between attractors and/or between any single attractor and its surrounding field. Add the by-now-familiar representation of attractors in terms of vertical depth, and learning can be regarded as the carving of wells and valleys from an initial phase space.

The link between connectionist learning processes and the concept of attractors in physical systems was first noticed by Hopfield (1982). Hopfield, himself a physicist, remarked that, in physical systems, stable attractors, such as orientations in a magnetic field or vortex patterns in a fluid flow, can emerge from the collective interactions of elementary components. He then related this to the issue of content-addressable memory. This is where input relating to some partial characteristic of an object allows one to recall the object as a whole. Hopfield likened this to a physical system in which there is a flow in phase space "toward locally stable points from anywhere within regions around those points (p. 2554)." In other words, having one's full store of information about an object "triggered" by some partial cue is like moving toward an attractor from the perimeter of a well. A useful memory system, however, requires that different items are recalled as a consequence of different inputs. The system must respond discriminatively. Hence, one needs multiple attractors that are each dominant over smaller regions (input configurations). As Hopfield puts it, "Any physical system whose dynamics in phase space is dominated by a substantial number of locally stable states to which it is attracted can therefore be regarded as a general content-addressable memory" (p. 2554).

The process of recall can thus be seen as a flow through a phase space pockmarked by numerous smaller and larger wells of attraction. The bottoms of these wells represent points of local minima as far as the potential energy of the system is concerned. Thus, flow toward an attractor results in lower potential energy. When the attractor is reached (as when some output is produced), there is less available potential energy to move the system into a different state. It is important that the dynamics of this flow can be nonlinear.

Hopfield (1982) proposed an algorithm according to which the flow must always be in the direction of lower potential energy, that is, greater "goodness of fit" between the output and a solution. A computationally inconvenient, but psychologically appealing, by-product of this algorithm is that systems can get stuck in "local minima" or suboptimal solutions, equivalent to dips halfway down a hillside, as in Figure 4. This is generally fixed by raising the "temperature" of the net (i.e., introducing randomness into the resetting of connection weights and activations of the output units). In many respects, this may be regarded as driving a locally stable system into a state of chaos (cf. Killeen, 1989). Another intersting feature of Hopfield nets is that, although they tend toward stability, they can also show more chaotic variations. When testing his model with different starting parameters, Hopfield found that outputs might oscillate between alternative solutions, depending on the size of the net and the relative closeness of different attractors to one another.

Although I have concentrated on Hopfield's work, the main conclusions I wish to draw are not specific to his formulations. Decision making, discrimination, and recall are dynamic processes that may be represented as flows through a particular kind of phase space. One of the most important characteristics of such flows is that they are nonlinear. This is not just a consequence of treating units as binary ("on–off") switches (which may anyway prove an oversimplification). An even more important feature is the stipulation that the firing of a hidden or output unit will depend on the (weighted) activations of *all* the units in the preceding layer that are connected to it. If too few of these preceding units are activated, so that their total activation is too low, then the hidden or output unit will not fire. Any randomness or noise in the distribution of activation levels of individual units within a given layer can lead to further nonlinearity. And then there is the control mechanism of the matrix of connection weights themselves. The lower their value, the more "resistance" is introduced into the network. In other words, there is no one-to-one relation between a change in input and a change in output, as a model of linear flow would demand. The relation depends on the interactions defined by the matrix of connections.

IV. Conclusions

I have proposed that attitudes should be regarded as attractors in a multidimensional phase space, or "attitude space." The configuration of this space is established through experience and interaction with the environment and is an emergent property of the parallel processing of multiple, but relatively simple, features of our social environment. The various contours, ridges, and valleys define the nature of these attractors, their strength (depth), their range of convenience (width), and their accessibility from different prior states (proximity to each other). Resistance to change in a given direction can be defined in terms of the steepness and height of any hillside that needs to be climbed. The stability of an attitudinal position can be defined in terms of its closeness to the bottom of a well (or point of minimal potential energy).

These definitions exploit a spatial metaphor, but behind this metaphor, familiar processes are at work that establish the departures from equiprobability that these spatial inequalities portray. What establishes the strength and scope of an attractor? The consistency of previous associations and the generality of the stimulus context. More stable attitudes are those supported by stronger and more widespread patterns of association. At the same time, many attractors will be relevant only to very limited contexts, that is, will not be activated except under very specific input conditions. This approach in no way claims or needs to cut the ground from under the empirical conclusions of previous attitude research.

But where there is a difference, and an important one, is in terms of what we can expect a theory of attitude to do. Any picture of attitude space can never be more than a snapshot of a moving thing. As William James (1890) put it, thought is in constant change. Attitudes are a special subclass of thought, and although previous research has treated them as static, they also show fluctuation and movement. The more often a viewpoint is expressed, the more likely it will be to be expressed again. The more often aspects of an issue are seen as related to each other (e.g., through argument), the more closely tied they will be to each other thereafter. This is simply a social psychological version of the fundamental Hebbian principle (that when two cognitive units are activated together, the connection between them is strengthened). What happens with a strengthened connection? Future cognitive activity will be likely to travel along that same connection, making it even stronger, and widening its field of attraction to cover yet more units that are simultaneously active. There is a drive toward the strengthening, the overlearning, of habits (and hence attitudes) that are already formed. Initially rather weak or shallow, attractors become stronger and deeper through being repeatedly approached.

The power of a dynamical systems view is that an attitude can be seen as a process, not just as a point. What matters is not just the position you adopt now, in response to this or that item on a questionnaire, but the potentialities for moving to different positions, through different routes, from different starting points. Attractors, by definition, exert a force over a narrower or wider area, so that the same attitude may be elicited by more or less different informational input. We do not simply hold attitudes, we are drawn back to those we hold.

How automatic is this process? This is an intriguing question for future research and one that may relate to more general issues of consciousness, free will, and their neuronal and computational correlates. For what it is worth, my own view is that much attitudinal processing is far more "automatic" than many of the more rationalistic traditional theories imply. We often do not have insight into why we hold the attitudes we do, which is like saying that we do not have introspective access to the connection matrices that translate an input to an output. Connectionism is a model of automatic thought *par excellence*. But we do not simply express our attitudes; with some effort, we can talk about them, reflect on them and on why others might take a different point of view; we can engage in cognitive "elaboration" (Petty & Cacioppo, 1986) and see where different arguments might lead us. All this is intensely conscious and, I suspect, very difficult to simulate on any neural network. It is also difficult to do (which may be partly why many attitudinal differences lead to conflict). But it is possible, and this possibility cannot be denied just because it is difficult to explain.

Thought is a flow through a particular kind of phase space, and the contours of that space undoubtedly influence that flow. The question is whether that flow must be entirely deterministic or whether we can direct it consciously to some extent. If we are to do so, it may be that we require some representation of the structure of our thoughts and memories if we are to loosen the pull they have on us. Perhaps this is what insight or self-awareness means. The effect of this would not be to change the landscape of the part of the attitude space in which we find ourselves but to take us to a different part. Maps can help us climb mountains, not of course because they make them any flatter, but because they help us find a way up from the valley. It is time for attitude theory to get some new maps.

Acknowledgments

A more extended presentation of the argument in this chapter is to be found in Eiser, J. R. (1993). *Attitudes, chaos, and the connectionist mind.* Oxford, England: Blackwell.

References

Ajzen, I. (1991). The theory of planned behavior. *Organizational Behavior and Decision Processes, 50,* 1–33.

Bechtel, W., & Abrahamsen, A. (1991). *Connectionism and the mind: An introduction to parallel processing in networks.* Oxford, England: Blackwell.

Coombs, C. H. (1964). *A theory of data.* New York: Wiley.

Eiser, J. R. (1971). Categorization, cognitive consistency, and the concept of dimensional salience. *European Journal of Social Psychology, 1,* 435–454.

Eiser, J. R. (1986). *Social psychology: Attitudes, cognition and social behaviour.* Cambridge, England: Cambridge University Press.

Eiser, J. R. (1990). *Social judgment.* Buckingham, England: Open University Press.

Eiser, J. R., & van der Pligt, J. (1979). Beliefs and values in the nuclear debate. *Journal of Applied Social Psychology, 9,* 524–536.

Festinger, L. & Carlsmith, J. M. (1959). Cognitive consequences of forced compliance. *Journal of Abnormal and Social Psychology, 58,* 203–210.

Fishbein, M., & Ajzen, I. (1975). *Belief, attitude, intention and behavior: An introduction to theory and research.* Reading, MA: Addison-Wesley.

Hebb, D. O. (1949). *The organization of behavior.* New York: Wiley.

Heider, F. (1946). Attitudes and cognitive organization. *Journal of Psychology, 21,* 107–112.

Hopfield, J. J. (1982). Neural networks and physical systems with emergent collective computational abilities. *Proceedings of the National Academy of Sciences, USA, 79,* 2554–2558.

Hovland, C. I., Janis, I. L., & Kelley, H. H. (1953). *Communication and persuasion: Psychological studies of opinion change.* New Haven, CT: Yale University Press.

James, W. (1890) *Principles of psychology.* New York: Holt.

Jaspars, J. M. F. (1965). *On social perception.* Unpublished doctoral dissertation, University of Leiden, The Netherlands.

Killeen, P. R. (1989). Behavior as a trajectory through a field of attractors. In J. R. Brink & C. R. Haden (Eds.), *The computer and the brain: Perspectives on artificial intelligence* (pp. 53–82). New York: Elsevier.

Lange, R., & Fishbein, M. (1983). Effects of category differences on belief change and agreement with the source of a persuasive communication. *Journal of Personality and Social Psychology, 44,* 933–941.

Mandelbrot, B. B. (1983). *The fractal geometry of nature.* New York: Freeman.

Moscovici, S., & Zavalloni, M. (1969). The group as a polarizer of attitudes. *Journal of Personality and Social Psychology, 12*, 125–135.

Osgood, C. E., Suci, G. J., & Tannenbaum, P. H. (1957). *The measurement of meaning.* Urbana, IL: University of Illinois Press.

Petty, R. E., & Cacioppo, J. T. (1986). The elaboration likelihood model of persuasion. In L. Berkowitz (Ed.), *Advances in experimental social psychology* (Vol. 19, pp. 123–205). New York: Academic Press.

Thurstone, L. L. (1928). Attitudes can be measured. *American Journal of Sociology, 33*, 529–554.

van der Pligt, J., & Eiser, J. R. (1984). Dimensional salience, judgment, and attitudes. In J. R. Eiser (Ed.), *Attitudinal judgment* (pp. 161–177). New York: Springer-Verlag.

CHAPTER 10

Attitudes as Catastrophes: From Dimensions to Categories with Increasing Involvement

Bibb Latané
Department of Psychology
Florida Atlantic University
Boca Raton, Florida

Andrzej Nowak
Institute for Social Studies
Faculty of Psychology
University of Warsaw
Warsaw, Poland

I. Introduction

Attitudes may be the single most interdisciplinary concept in the social sciences. Economists devote a great deal of attention to consumer attitudes, attributing the economic crisis of the early 1990s not so much to structural problems as to a failure in consumer confidence. Political scientists use attitudes as their main measure of political preferences and as a predictor of voting behavior. Sociologists characterize society by means of attitude distributions, with changes in such distributions indicating social change. Finally, social psychologists have focused on attitudes since the early days of this scientific discipline. In 1935, Allport claimed that attitude is social psychology's most indispensable concept, and, with some variation, it has continued on center stage ever since (McGuire, 1986).

We believe two features of the attitude concept explain its popularity among social scientists. First, the concept describes in a rather global way the relationship of a person to her or his environment. Allport's (1935) classic definition of it as "a mental and neural state of readiness, organized through experience, exerting a

Dynamical Systems in Social Psychology

directive or dynamic influence upon the individual's response to all objects and situations with which it is related" (p. 810) captures this key feature of attitudes, although it is now seen as lacking sufficient emphasis on evaluation. Likewise, Krech, Crutchfield, and Ballachey (1962) defined attitudes as "enduring systems of positive or negative evaluations, emotional feelings, and pro or con action tendencies with respect to social objects" (p. 139), whereas Fishbein and Ajzen (1975) defined them as "a learned predisposition to respond in a consistently favorable or unfavorable manner with respect to a given object" (p. 6). Attitudes are thus presumed to be precursors to and predictors of action, and, although their success in predicting behavior has long been open to question, they are central to most theories of action.

Second, the attitude concept may be used to relate different levels of social reality. Through the concept of attitude, individual preferences may be related to group action and social pressures to individual behavior. The concept of attitude may thus be regarded as an interface linking individual cognitive and emotional processes to the social and cultural environment. This relationship is bidirectional. The interactive product of individual attitudes may lead to such group-level consequences as the development of norms, socially shared beliefs, public opinion, and social action. On the other hand, exposure to such norms and opinions is one of the strongest determinants of individual attitude change.

The first feature has motivated psychologists to be interested in attitudes, whereas the second has drawn the attention of other social scientists. In this chapter, we discuss how attitudes are determined by both individual and group level processes. We distinguish two conceptions of attitudes: the traditional view that they represent points on a dimension and a more modern view that they act like categories. We suggest that these views can be linked in terms of catastrophe theory, with involvement as a "splitting" factor. We present evidence consistent with this description showing that distributions of attitudes increase in variance and become bimodal with increasing strength of feeling or judged importance and discuss internal and external mechanisms leading attitudes to change their character with increasing involvement. Finally, we discuss implications of the catastrophe model for predicting when social interaction will lead to consensus and when it will lead to spatial clustering and polarization and suggest that we may soon have the tools for understanding the dynamics of public opinion and the emergence of something like a group mind.

II. Two Conceptions of Individual Attitudes

Next, we discuss the two prevailing approaches for conceptualizing individual attitudes.

A. Attitudes as Points (or Regions) on a Dimension

Ever since Thurstone (1931) applied psychophysical techniques to create attitude scales, psychologists have assumed that attitudes can be represented as points on a continuum and that the problem of attitude measurement is one of locating where an individual stands on an evaluative dimension with respect to an issue (as Eagly & Chaiken, 1993, pointed out, this does not imply that people necessarily represent their own attitudes as points on a dimension).

McGuire (1985) described attitudes as "responses that locate objects of thought on dimensions of judgment" (p. 239), most notably evaluation. Most approaches to psychological measurement rely on some such conception of judgment dimensionality. In the Thurstone technique of attitude measurement, for example, an attitude is located on a dimension according to how many positive as opposed to negative statements regarding an object the respondent has checked as corresponding to her or his opinion. Guttman scaling relies on the idea that the statements concerning a given object can be ordered on a scale where acceptance of one item higher on a scale implies the acceptance of the items below it (Guttman, 1944). Attitude can be thus characterized as a breaking point between accepted and rejected items. Items on Likert scales, probably the most common form of attitude measurement in psychology, take the notion of a dimension literally. The respondent is simply asked to indicate on a scale (usually from 1 to 7) either his or her attitude toward some object or agreement with some evaluative statements, and these ratings are summed to provide the attitude score.

Of course, attitudes may be seen as involving more than one dimension—Osgood, Suci, & Tannenbaum's (1957) semantic differential can be used to ask people to locate objects of judgment on dimensions of potency and activity as well as the more traditional evaluation. In addition, one's location on a dimension does not need to be represented as a point—it may also be represented as a region. Sherif and Hovland (1961) labeled this idea *latitudes of acceptance*, whereas Wieczorkowska (1990) defined attitudes as intervals rather than points.

However, regardless of how we define attitude or whether we locate it in a narrow or a wider region of a scale, the basic result of years of study is that scaling works. It is possible to develop reliable measures that array individuals along a dimension of evaluation, and these measures lead to useful predictions.

B. Implications of the Dimensional View

How are different cognitive and evaluative elements combined to form an attitude? In the traditional view, attitudes are multiply determined by a variety of factors, including personal experiences and information received from others. Anderson (1981a, 1981b) provided the ultimate extension of this often implicit assumption by developing his elegant information integration theory, which suggests that attitudes can be formed by the algebraic combination of numerous independent items of information, which can be assumed to be sampled from some population of facts. Specifically, Anderson suggested that attitudes represent a weighted average or mean of the stimulus values of the various bits of information to which an individual is exposed. Anderson's work in cognitive algebra has been an exemplary contribution to research and theory in social judgment, allowing explicit quantitative predictions from a variety of well-specified models.

Most work with information integration theory has been conducted in laboratory settings, presenting participants with carefully controlled sets of information. To apply the theory to real world settings, one must consider the population of information that individuals sample in forming their own views and the rules that determine the resulting distributions of opinion. The central limit theorem of statistics, introduced in 1810 with major contributions by LaPlace and Gauss (see Stigler, 1986, for a detailed history of its early development), provides a good basis for this consideration. In conjunction with the simplest version of information integration theory, the central limit theorem allows us to make predictions about the distribution of attitudes in a population.

Although the analysis is complex, it has now been thoroughly proven that if a population has a finite mean μ and variance σ^2, the distribution of the means of samples of n independent observations from this population will approach a normal distribution with mean μ and variance σ^2/n as n increases. This theorem applies whatever the form of the population distribution.

According to information integration theory, each person's attitude represents the weighted average of the items of information he or she has been exposed to relevant to that topic. That is, each person's attitude can be considered as a sample of the information available in the population. But what is n? What is an "item" of information, and how many constitute a typical attitude? If your spouse gives you three arguments about an issue, is this one item of information or three? If your mother-in-law adds another argument, is this another independent item of information? Clearly, the number of independent items of information does not grow as fast as the total amount of information to which one is exposed. Nonetheless, in pluralistic societies, increases in the total amount of information are likely to lead to increases in the number of independent items.

Of course, there may be several sources of bias in the process by which people sample or weight information from the population of available information. Internal biases may arise from tendencies toward selective exposure, interpretation, and weighting of incoming information, whereas external biases may arise from one's location in social space. If such biases exist (and we suspect they do), they need to be explained because the traditional view by itself tells us neither what biases may exist nor how they operate. We shall claim that these sources of bias can best be explained in terms of a categorical conception of attitudes, and we defer fuller discussion until later. Here, however, we can note that the most commonly assumed bias is toward similarity—people may selectively seek, find, or weight information that is evaluatively consistent with their current attitudes. Such a bias would be manifested as a primacy effect, stabilizing attitudes at their initial values. The operation of such a bias should reduce the within-individual variance among the evaluative values of encoded items of information, likely increasing subjective confidence. On the group level, such a bias would be manifested by increased variance in the distribution of the attitude in the population because each individual's sample of information is effectively reduced in size.

Applying the central limit theorem to information integration theory, we can expect that to the extent that items of information are independent, the greater the amount of information people have about a topic, the more stable their attitudes should be, the lower should be the variance among people, and the more closely the distribution of their means should approximate a normal distribution. Thus, Anderson's (1981a, 1981b) well-articulated theory has, in our view, at least three strong implications for populations of people when considered in conjunction with the central limit theorem: We should expect (1) attitudes to show set size effects in individuals, (2) decreasing variance, and (3) closer approximations to normal distributions across individuals with increasing exposure to information on a topic. Unfortunately, as we show below, although the evidence supports one implication, it refutes the others. Let us examine each of these implications in more detail.

1. Set–Size Effects

A major way of testing information integration theory has been through studies of "set-size" effects–assessing the effects of the amount of information one has on a topic on subsequent change. As the sample gets larger, the sample mean should more closely reflect the population mean and thus become more stable. It follows, thus, that the more information one already has about a given object, the less one's attitude should change as a result of new information.

This implication has been well supported by studies showing that added information has less effect on changes in impressions of others as the number of previous descriptions grows larger (Anderson, 1967; Sloan & Ostrom, 1974). Although it does not invoke the central limit theorem, Anderson's model does a good job of fitting such data. However, although this phenomenon provides good support for the traditional view, it can also be explained in terms of social impact theory (Latané & Wolf, 1981), which would interpret the results as due to the marginally decreasing impact of information coming from increasing numbers of people. In our view, whatever interpretation one prefers, the set-size phenomenon does not conclusively prove the correctness of the information integration view, although evidence showing set-size effects with information from a single source would reduce the plausibility of the alternative explanation.

2. Decreasing Variance

A second implication of the central limit theorem as applied to information integration theory is that if a group of people, initially differing in opinion, is exposed to the same large amount of new information about a topic, their attitudes should become more similar one to another. If each person's attitude is conceived to be a weighted mean of the available information, the variance of the distribution of such means should be proportional to the variance of the population of information items divided by the number of items in each sample. In other words, the variance in attitudes among people should decrease as a function of shared experience. However, data recently reported by Harrod and Sapp (1992) contradicted this prediction. They had 74 people watch an hour-long television show on food irradiation in which all saw the same set of facts, opinions, myths, and emotions expressed by a variety of experts and nonexperts, whereas another group of 76 did not see the show. All were asked to express their opinion on food irradiation on a 20-point Likert scale. Contrary to the dimensional information integration view, variance increased as a result of this common experience, with viewers exhibiting the full range of 1–20 and a standard deviation of 5.1, compared with a range of 5–18 and an standard deviation of 3.2 for nonviewers ($F = 2.52$, $p < .0001$). Results showing increased variance after exposure to balanced information about a topic have also been reported by Lord, Ross, and Lepper (1979) and by Lord, Lepper, and Preston (1985).

3. Normal Distributions

The third and most direct implication of the central limit theorem as applied to simple information integration theory is that attitudes on a given issue should be normally distributed. Again, if each person's attitude is regarded as the mean of a sample of bits of information drawn from the environment, the distribution of these attitudes should be normal regardless of the distribution of items in the population. Even a very skewed or bimodal distribution of information should, under these assumptions, approximate a normal distribution of attitudes, and this approximation should improve as the sample size increases (as people acquire more information about the issue). Given these assumptions, it is hard to see how attitudes could be distributed nonnormally and especially how such a theory of attitudes could account for a bimodal, U-shaped distribution. Even if we assume strong biases in favor of information that is evaluatively similar to one's initial opinion, we should expect normal distributions of attitude given that the initial opinions themselves are based on information samples. As we shall see, however, bimodal distributions are predicted by the conception of attitudes as categories and are found, under specifiable circumstances, in empirical data.

Thus, as we have shown and shall further demonstrate, each of three major implications of perhaps the most clearly specified traditional attitude theory either can be given an alternative explanation or simply does not square with available evidence. Although it is true that alternative versions of this or other dimensional theories may lead to different outcomes (or, most often, to no clear predictions), we are led to consider an alternative conception of attitudes as categories.

C. Attitudes as Categories

Although psychologists have concentrated on developing scales for locating individuals on an attitudinal continuum, sociologists and political scientists most frequently measure attitudes with simple categorical questions (Schuman & Presser, 1981; Schwarz & Sudman, 1992). Political surveys much more often ask "Who will you vote for?" than "How much do you prefer Candidate X?"

The idea that attitudes are best conceived not as dimensions but as categories can be grounded in cognitive psychology, which deals with how knowledge is mentally represented. Under such rubrics as schemata (Bartlett, 1932), categories (Rumelhart & Ortony, 1977), and frames (Minsky, 1975), cognitive psychologists usually assume that knowledge about classes of objects is organized into hierarchical structures composed of cognitive elements (usually conceptualized as propositions) and relations between them. Whether the organization is based on similarity (Rosch, 1978) or on more abstract reasoning (Murphy & Medin, 1985), the category structure organizes disparate elements into a perceived whole. The relations among elements may be of various kinds, such as subordinate versus superordinate, part–whole, and, most important, relations among attributes (Smith, 1990). Such relations allow us to infer missing information by, for example, "filling in" information about the hidden part of a perceived scene.

The idea that attitudes encompass beliefs, evaluations, and behavioral predispositions toward classes of objects makes an attitude position quite similar to the definition of a category—that is, there may be a prototypical set of beliefs, evaluations, and behaviors that identify a particular attitude position (Rosch, 1978) or a theory underlying these correlations (Murphy & Medin, 1985) that provides the basis for the cognitive organization. This conception of attitudes as categories is similar to holding stereotypic views (Katz & Braly, 1933) or having cognitive schemata, and has empirical consequences. For example, Ostrom (1988; Ostrom & Gannon, 1991) suggested that rating scales can be interpreted as consisting of prototypical categories located at their endpoints and, consistent with this view, reported reaction times that were faster for items at the extremes of scales than for those in the middle.

D. Implications of the Categorical View

Although items of information encountered in our environment may be independent, once they have been encoded into mental representations and organized as categories or schemas, by the very definition of *category* they will not be independent but connected through a network of implications. Such an organization is conducive to the development of bimodal distributions of attitudes.

For example, if the elements in a schema are in a balanced equilibrium with respect to each other (Heider, 1958), changes in the value of a single element in a cognitive version of the domino phenomenon must lead to changes in the other pieces of the schema in order to maintain a balanced equilibrium. The attitude may then rapidly change from a value corresponding to all the elements being in one orientation to a value corresponding to all the elements being in the opposite orientation (e.g., all the propositions concerning an object that were treated as true would be reversed to being false, and vice versa). In extreme cases of organization, only two attitude positions may be possible. Although this may be a rare idealization, some stereotypes do seem to exhibit such a rigid structure. For example, if you believe all Slobbovians are dishonest, suddenly learning that an associate is a Slobbovian may lead to a complete reinterpretation of his prior behavior and a dramatic reassessment of your attitude.

In this model, it is natural to assume intermediate levels of organization in which substructures of various sizes are organized. Then, an incoming bit of information, if accepted, will change the values of only some other items, leaving others intact. Such an attitude will then react with only some degree of nonlinearity, where the change will be disproportional to the cause to the degree to which the attitude is organized. Nonorganized collections of independent pieces of information will then lead to a dimensional representation of an attitude and a linear change rule, intermediate levels to some nonlinearity in the change process, and the highest levels of organization to categorical, binary attitudes. As we can see, the same underlying information can be the basis of either dimensional or categorical attitudes, characterized by either a linear or nonlinear change pattern, depending on whether and how pieces of this information are organized.

Thus, to the extent that attitudes represent organized bodies of knowledge, they should develop an underlying structure like such other cognitive entities as categories and schemata. We suggest that the more the organization, the greater the tendency toward bimodality, and whatever cognitive processes lead to greater organization should also contribute to making attitudes act as if they were categorical. In particular, we suggest that as people become more involved with an issue, their position will become more extreme.

The view of attitudes as complex entities having internal structure is advanced by a "systems" style of research that McGuire (1985) predicted would dominate social psychology in the 1980s and 90s: "The system stylist starts with a set of interacting variables among which he or she attempts to trace the multiple, often bidirectional pathways of causality by using an inclusive research design" (p. 238). The links occur not only inside an attitude but also connect attitudes into attitude systems. According to McGuire, "sets of attitudes operate as connected and coherent systems to the extent that there are structural relations between them" (p. 214).

III. So Which Is It—Dimensions or Categories?

Here, we suggest that both views have merit, but in different circumstances. We believe the dimensional view provides a good approximation for relatively unimportant or noninvolving issues, whereas a number of internal and external processes lead people to develop categorical representations as issues become important. This idea, which has many roots in previous discussions of attitudes, can be represented mathematically as a catastrophe.

Attitude Changes as Catastrophes

Fifteen years ago, the mathematician Zeeman (1977) presented the hypothesis that attitude change may be well described in the language of catastrophe theory (see also Flay, 1978). First proposed by mathematician René Thom, catastrophe theory deals with discontinuous responses of systems to smooth changes in external input.

According to Zeeman's (1977) analysis, opinion y is a joint function of two control factors: c_x, representing information, and c_z, representing involvement. Sources of "information" may include self-interest, heredity, and environment, as well as political persuasion. Involvement, or issue importance, may be voluntary or involuntary. The probability of opinion y given control factors $c = (c_x, c_z)$ can be described as a potential function: $P_c(y)$, with the maxima rather than the minima being important.

In the present case, information can be considered a "normal" factor, helping determine how far left or right a person's opinions fall. Zeeman's (1977) basic hypothesis is that involvement is a "splitting" factor. In other words, the more involved individuals are, the more strongly they are likely to adhere to their chosen opinion and the less likely they are to be neutral, even though the information available to them may be relatively unbiased. This hypothesis can be expressed graphically as a cusp catastrophe surface, as depicted in Figure 1, which diagrams the expected attitude as a two-dimensional manifold in 3-dimensional space. The vertical (y) axis represents the attitude as a function of the net positivity/negativity

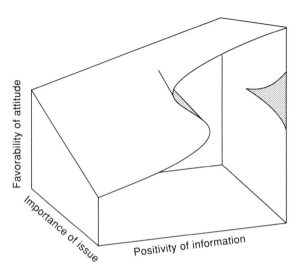

Figure 1   Favorability of attitude as a function of information and involvement: A catastrophe theory perspective.

of the information one has about the topic (shown on the x axis) and the importance of the topic or how involved one is with it (shown on the z axis). By hypothesis, people's attitudes will be located on the catastrophe surface.

Figure 1 expresses the following hypotheses:

1. For uninvolving issues (rear plane of Figure 1), one's attitude (y) will be a direct, linear (with appropriate scaling) function of the positivity of relevant information (x).

2. When information is predominantly positive (right plane of Figure 1), one's attitude (y) will be a direct, linear (with appropriate scaling) function of one's involvement with the issue (z).

3. When information is predominantly negative (left plane of Figure 1), one's attitude (y) will be an inverse linear function of issue involvement (z).

4. With increasing involvement, a "cusp" develops such that even with information of intermediate positivity, people will tend to have either very positive or very negative attitudes (front plane of Figure 1). There is increasing commitment to one's position such that one resists change in response to new information, but at some point, consistently favorable or unfavorable new information will lead to a catastrophic change in attitude.

Several consequences for attitude distributions follow from these hypotheses in conjunction with the central limit theorem:

5. As discussed above, for uninvolving issues (rear plane of Figure 1), the distribution of attitudes should be normal.

6. For involving issues (front plane of Figure 1), the cusp creates a region of inaccessibility such that intermediate attitudes are not possible, leading to a bimodal distribution of attitude.

While recognizing the "unpredictability of the free choice of individuals," Zeeman (1977) suggested some qualitative insights to be gleaned from even this crude model:

> We may regard the individuals as a cloud of points clustered in the neighborhood of the catastrophe surface. As the issue is such that more and more people become involved, for instance as in a Dreyfuss affair or the Watergate affair we can investigate this as a slow drift of the points along the surface in the direction of the c_z-axis. Unbiased individuals find themselves caught into taking sides, and even families are liable to split. Those most involved find themselves sharply divided in opinion along the c_z-axis; in the same time there is a continuous change of opinion along a path going round the top of the cusp through the less involved, and a split overlap amongst the most involved due to individuals near the center, who might have changed their bias yet paradoxically remain entrenched in the old opinion. Both latter features are common to "polarized" populations, but seldom exhibited so clearly in a model.
>
> Suppose that we now change the bias of individuals by propaganda and persuasion moving the points parallel to the c_x axis. The uninvolved will hardly register any change of opinion, the slightly involved will change their minds smoothly, and the more involved will tend to suddenly switch opinion after some delay, not uncommonly to the surprise of both friend and foe, while the fanatics will be very hard to change, but once persuaded will tend to become fanatical and irreversible converts. (p. 629)

Catastrophe theory originated in the study of dynamical systems whose properties depend on several control parameters and attempted to describe the changes in dynamical behavior near points of stable equilibrium as the parameters pass through certain critical values. It later evolved into the study of the singularities of maps (loosely speaking, singularities are points where mapping is not smooth). In less precise terms, catastrophe theory describes how discontinuities may appear in low-dimensional systems.

This theory was very popular in the late 1970s and was expected to lead to new mathematical models for the social and natural sciences. However, leading mathematicians such as Smale (1978) criticized the theory for being overambitious and overpublicized. Feeling that mathematics should be only a tool for expressing knowledge or theory emerging from a deep study of natural phenomena, Smale criticised catastrophe theory's lack of input from actual data. In the light of this and other strong criticism, the popularity of catastrophe theory plummeted. Mathematicians now seem dubious about its scientific usefulness, and other approaches such as bifurcation theory and chaos theory have captured public attention.

Despite these criticisms, catastrophe theory provides a convenient geometrical description of how a continuous function may change into a discontinuous one and allows us to predict a number of associated phenomena. Here, we use the cusp catastrophe or fold singularity primarily to provide a geometric description of the transition from continuous to discontinuous attitudes, rather than using the equations of the theory to derive precise predictions (this would require the explicit specification of equations and parameters). As we show, we can directly interpret mapping parameters for catastrophe theory with social psychological data and can specify plausible underlying psychological processes.

IV. Attitude Distributions Indicate the Nature of Attitudes

One of the strongest predictions following from the distinction between linear (dimensional) and nonlinear (categorical) attitude change rules concerns the difference in the distribution of attitudes in a population. Linear change rules imply that attitudes will be distributed normally. Nonlinear, especially binary (you switch or not), rules predict bimodal distributions. The pressure toward categorization will be evidenced by a gradual shift from a normal inverted-U distribution of attitudes when the issue is seen as unimportant to an upright-U distribution as involvement increases.

This prediction can easily be verified empirically if we measure both the importance and extremity of attitudes. Two sets of data, one old and one new, provide direct evidence about the relation between issue involvement and the extremity of attitudes.

A. Data Set 1: A Classic Study of the Distribution of Attitudes

During WWII, the Research Branch of the Information and Education Division of the War Department conducted thousands of interviews of U.S. soldiers, not only trying to determine their attitudes but to develop techniques for scaling them (Stouffer et al., 1950). For example, in one series of studies, enlisted men were asked six questions as to their attitudes on each of three topics: the point system for demobilization, postwar conscription, and the Women's Army Corps. In addition, after most questions, they were asked to indicate how strongly they felt about their answer.

One problem was the issue of so-called "question bias." Slightly different questions often led to very different rates of endorsement, and even though their responses would be well correlated, it was hard to determine the "zero" point separating positive from negative attitudes for any given question, important for predicting approach or avoidant response tendencies.

In examining the data, one of the researchers (Suchman) observed that the rated strengths of feelings seemed to be strongest at both ends of the content scale

Table I
Frequency Distributions for Attitudes on Three Issues Combined
by Intensity of Feeling

| Intensity (n) | Attitude (number of questions answered positively) | | | | | | | Mean | σ^2 |
	0	1	2	3	4	5	6		
0 (1574)	3%[a]	11%	24%	29%	26%	6%	1%	2.88	28.2
1 (862)	2%	10%	20%	19%	29%	18%	2%	3.29	42.5
2 (940)	4%	11%	19%	22%	23%	15%	6%	3.18	43.9
3 (1005)	7%	14%	20%	17%	19%	16%	7%	3.02	44.3
4 (862)	11%	17%	17%	11%	14%	15%	14%	3.02	53.4
5 (1574)	19%	18%	14%	8%	10%	10%	22%	2.88	60.7

[a]Percentages are rounded and may not equal 100 percent.

continuum and to decrease as one moved toward more moderate positions. Suchman suggested that the scale position with the lowest intensity could be considered as the neutral cutting point separating true positive from negative attitudes.

Following Zeeman's (1977) hypothesis that attitudes resemble catastrophes, however, we suspect that the relation can best be understood by turning it around. Rather than extremity causing intensity, it may be that involvement leads people to become both more intense and more extreme. People who are affected by or feel strongly about the importance of some issue may tend to develop more extreme attitudes on that issue. Let us reanalyze Suchman's data to see how well this holds up. Table I shows frequency distributions of content scores by intensity level combined for the three issues listed above. Attitudes were scaled as the number of questions on each issue for which a soldier had a favorable response and could range from 0 to 6. Intensity was also scaled as the number of answers about which the soldier felt strongly. Table I represents a total of almost 7,000 attitude scores and is based on more than 75,000 responses to 33 multiple-choice questions.

As would be expected from the central limit theorem and the traditional, dimensional view of attitudes, the distribution of content scores on issues about which soldiers reported not feeling strongly (intensity = 0) is well approximated by a normal curve, with almost a third of the cases in the midmost category and only 4% at the extremes. As rated strength of feeling about the issue increases, however, the distribution gradually changes, so that for those feeling most strongly, only 8% occupy the middle position, whereas 41% are located fully at one extreme or the other. Not only has the variance in attitude increased dramatically but the distribution has become truly bimodal. Far from becoming more normal with increasing intensity (and presumably more underlying information), it has become less normal.

Another way of documenting the same effect is through the variances in content scores, shown in the rightmost column of Table 1. As rated involvement increases, so too does the variance in attitudes, and this increase is not only impressively regular but statistically reliable, $F(1573,1573) = 2.15, p < .001$.

These results also hold for other attitudes studied by the War Department (Stouffer et al., 1950). For example, the variance in the attitudes of 3,614 enlisted men toward their officers steadily increased with increases in the strength of feeling, from less than .75 of their mean content score for those who did not feel strongly at all to over 2.5 times for those who felt most strongly. The identical result held for attitudes toward the army as a whole.

Although not apparent in Table I, which presents a composite picture for three attitudes, increasing strength of feeling was also associated with changes in mean favorability, with those people who felt most strongly being more positive toward the point system and postwar conscription but more negative toward the Women's Army Corps. Likewise, those who felt more strongly tended to be more negative toward their officers and toward the army in general. As with the changes in variance reported above, these changes are consistent with the catastrophe theory view of attitudes if the population of items of information from which individuals sample is assumed not to be exactly neutral.

Taken together, these results provide strong support for the catastrophe model. Before taking them too seriously, however, it would be well to see whether they replicate, especially using different scaling procedures for measuring attitudes and operationalizations of issue involvement.

B. Data Set 2: A Modern Study of the Distribution of Attitudes

We asked 100 students (62 females) in two undergraduate psychology classes at the University of North Carolina (UNC) in the fall of 1988 to complete questionnaires as part of a class demonstration. Because this was an election year, we decided to focus on political attitudes. The questionnaire contained 16 propositions (see Table II for a list) reworded from actual referenda appearing on various state ballots (we thank the National Center for State Governments in Lexington, Kentucky, for providing this listing). In choosing political referenda, we were motivated not only by a desire for practical relevance but by the hope of sampling issues of intermediate acceptability.

Each proposition required eight judgments. First, participants indicated their attitude on a 5-point scale from -2 to $+2$ (the endpoints were labeled *oppose* and *favor*, respectively), and then they rated it for "importance" (using a 5-point scale from 0, *unimportant*, to 4, *important*). Then, using similar scales, participants pre-

Table II

Political Propositions in Decreasing Order of Rated Importance

To initiate a state bond issue to finance housing for the homeless.

To grant the governor power to block the parole of convicted murderers

To initiate a $0.25 per pack hike in the cigarette tax, generating revenues for higher education.

To allow insurance companies to require testing for AIDS.

To restrict the use of state funds for abortions.

To allow a state lottery, with the proceeds earmarked for improving teachers' salaries.

To amend the state constitution to establish a fund for victims of domestic violence.

To allow compensation of "innocent victims of crime."

To impose limits on contingency fees for attorneys.

To allow juries of less than 12 members for civil and nonfelony cases.

To declare English the official language of the state.

To establish an additional tax on beer and cigarettes to help fund state university sports programs.

To stagger the terms of members of the Commission on Judicial Performance.

To allow judges to accept part-time teaching positions.

To remove gender-biased language in the state constitution.

To establish a program of lowered tax assessments on historic buildings.

dicted the responses of their best friend, a male classmate, and a female classmate. Finally, they repeated this process for each of the remaining 15 issues.

1. Frequency Distributions

Lumping together participants' reports about their own attitudes across all 16 propositions into a single set of frequency distributions (Table III), we see that, comparable to the Stouffer et al. (1950) data, judged importance seemed to be related to both the favorability and the extremity of attitudes.

As judged importance increased, so did favorability. Only 14% of respondents favored propositions that they rated as 0 in importance, whereas about 80% favored propositions they rated as 4. This finding may be specific to political referenda given that one might be inclined to vote against a change in law simply because one considers it to be insignificant. Alternately, it may be related to the overall tilt toward favorability of the set of propositions, 80% of which were rated positively. Finally, it might be an artifact of making both ratings at the same time—participants may have simply ticked both scales at the same relative locations.

Table III

Frequency Distributions of Favorability toward Political
Propositions as a Function of Their Judged Importance[a]

	Attitude scale value				
Importance (n)	−2	−1	0	+1	+2
0 (178)	30%[a]	7%	50%	7%	7%
1 (177)	7%	25%	31%	29%	8%
2 (377)	4%	10%	41%	32%	14%
3 (405)	11%	12%	6%	48%	23%
4 (454)	16%	2%	3%	7%	72%
Total (1591)	13%	10%	21%	26%	31%

[a]Percentages are rounded and may not equal 100 percent.

As judged importance increased, however, extremity also increased. The number of "fence sitters" expressing a neutral 0 attitude decreased regularly from 50% to 3% as judged importance increased from 0 to 4. Likewise, the number of extreme positive opinions increased from 7% to 72%, whereas with the single anomaly of the 0 importance cell, the number of extreme negative opinions increased from 7% to 16%. We do not know quite what to make of this aberrant cell. Perhaps it represents some participants' attempt to completely dismiss unwanted political change.

Table IV provides a simplified representation of extremity (simply the absolute value of attitudinal responses) as a function of importance collapsed into low-

Table IV

Judged Importance and Extremity
of Own Attitudes[a]

	Extremity		
Importance (n)	0	±1	±2
0–2 (732)	40%	38%	22%
3–4 (859)	5%	33%	62%

[a]Rows all sum to 100%.

and high-importance categories and demonstrates this dramatic distributional shift away from the center of the attitude scale as importance increases.

2. Correlations

Overall, those propositions judged most important elicited the most extreme attitudes ($r = .86$, $p < .001$). This relation holds, not just across propositions in the aggregate, but at the individual level—calculating correlation coefficients for each of the 16 propositions separately, we found for each of the 16 propositions a significant relation between importance and extremity. That is, those people who judged the issue as more important took a more extreme position on it. Overall, the average correlation was .42, significant and substantial. There were also less consistent tendencies for importance and favorability (mean $r = .37$) and favorability and extremity (mean $r = .26$) to be related.

3. Response Style

Do these correlations reflect a response artifact such that those respondents who tended to view most issues as "important" tended also to have extreme opinions? Or is it a phenomenon that occurs across different attitudes held by the same individual? To determine this we calculated, for each individual separately, the correlation between issue importance and attitude extremity across the 16 issues.

Of the subset of 77 persons for whom this correlation was calculated, 73 (95%) showed a positive correlation, and the overall average correlation was .48. Clearly, the phenomenon is not a result of any artifact of individual differences in response style, being present at full strength across attitudes held by the same person.

4. Stereotypes of Others

Data presented so far include only participants' own attitudes. Would these relations hold for their perceptions of other people? We compared participants' perceptions of three other people's beliefs (best friend, female classmate, and male classmate) with their own pattern of response.

Our predominantly female participants judged their best friends and female classmates as being similar to themselves with regard to the importance and desirability of these political propositions. In general, they thought male classmates would rate these propositions lower in both importance and favorability. And they judged all three groups of people as being less extreme in their views than themselves. As with self-ratings, however, correlations among importance, favorability, and extremity were significant and substantial and reasonably consistent across the various target persons. Whatever process leads to increased extremity for more important issues, it occurs for one's perceptions of other's attitudes as well as for one's own attitudes.

5. Replication

Sixty-two members of UNC fraternities and sororities (65% females) served as respondents in the spring 1989 Computer Administered Panel Study (CAPS). CAPS required a commitment of 1 hr per week for 8 weeks, during which time participants completed a variety of different response modules presented by computer of which the present study was one. Respondents were paid for their participation based on attendance and special bonus systems.

This experiment incorporated the following alterations to the original paper-and-pencil questionnaire: (1) The mode of presentation and data collection utilized computers, (2) the sequence of presentation was altered so that importance and favorability judgments were separated in time, and (3) the favor/oppose scale was expanded to 7 points.

Despite these differences from the original study, the form of the results was identical (Table V). Clearly, these shifts in attitude distributions are not artifacts of scaling procedures, number of response categories, or the temporal conjunction of rating of importance and evaluation.

C. Summary of Results from Both the Classic and Modern Studies

Data from both the classic (Stouffer et al., 1950) and the modern (discussed here) studies can be described as following two basic rules:

Rule 1: Greater involvement, as indexed by the strength of feelings about or judged importance of an issue, may be associated with differences in the mean attitude. For example, in the army, those who felt strongly about their officers, about the Women's Army Corps, and about the army in general tended to be more negative than did those who felt less strongly, whereas those who felt most strongly about the point system for demobilization or postwar conscription were most favorable. With regard to political initiatives, people who regarded them as important tended to be more favorable (perhaps because if not important, they are not worth the trouble of passing).

Rule 2: The more strongly people feel about an issue or the more important they think it is, the greater the variance in their attitudes. People who do not feel strongly will tend toward a normal distribution of attitudes (resulting from the additive combination of independent random variables). On the other hand, people who feel strongly will tend toward a bimodal distribution of attitudes.

Table V

Frequency Distributions of Favorability toward Political Propositions as a Function of Their Judged Importance, Experiment 2

Importance (n)	Attitude scale value						
	3	−2	−1	0	+1	+2	+3
0 (185)	25%[a]	9%	6%	38%	8%	7%	8%
1 (156)	8%	10%	6%	24%	17%	19%	15%
2 (217)	7%	6%	6%	16%	18%	25%	23%
3 (220)	9%	11%	6%	5%	13%	22%	34%
4 (212)	18%	4%	2%	2%	3%	8%	63%
Total (990)	13%	8%	5%	16%	12%	17%	30%

[a]Percentages are rounded and may not equal 100 percent.

Data from both these studies show that extremity increases with involvement with an issue. When people view an issue as unimportant or do not feel strongly about their opinion, attitudes tend to fall into a normal, inverted-U distribution, and a dimensional representation may be appropriate. As people become more involved with issues, rating them as more important or their feelings as "stronger," they become more extreme, creating a bimodal U-shaped distribution with higher variance.

This shift to a bimodal distribution with increased involvement means that attitudes on important issues act functionally more like categories than dimensions. Even though an attitude scale contains middle points, they are rarely used, given that people seem to concentrate on the ends of the scale. Because only two positions are used, such an attitude is, in fact, dichotomous, and each attitude position can be regarded as a category. We believe that these results provide strong evidence for the proposition that attitudes behave in accordance with catastrophe theory, becoming more categorical with increases in involvement. This proposition also leads to other implications.

D. Other Implications of the Idea That Attitudes Are Catastrophic

Although the present chapter is not the place to review them in detail, the idea that attitudes behave like catastrophes has a number of other implications, each of which could be tested empirically. For example, we might predict that by manipulating involvement, we should be able to change favorability; that small initial differences in the positivity of information about an attitude object can have large effects on favorability, especially as involvement increases; that we should expect greater primacy effects (hysteresis) for involving than for noninvolving issues; that attitudes about important issues should be more difficult to change than attitudes about unimportant ones (Krosnick, 1988); and that people are not influenced on important issues with gradual increments of change but rather by flip-flopping between polarized positions. The idea implies that attitude change can occur from either of two processes: (1) Some changes may be the result of new evidence or changes in disposition, or (2) some may take place simply as a result of changes in one's involvement with or the importance one accords an issue. In summary, these considerations suggest that attitudes, especially important ones, have a nonlinear quality to them. As we shall see, this has important implications for the outcome of dynamic social influence processes.

Although these data are clear enough for attitudes toward the army and political propositions, perhaps a more intuitive understanding of the catastrophe view comes from imagining its extension to interpersonal attitudes—feelings about another person. According to this view, the more central another person is in your life, the more warming a smile and the more devastating a betrayal will be for your feelings about that person (the implications of catastrophe theory for close relationships are explored in more detail in Chapter 5).

E. Implications for How to Study Attitudes

The idea that attitudes, at least important ones, act as categories rather than dimensions, if it continues to receive empirical support, will require reexamination of a number of research practices in social psychology, as well as the possible reinterpretation of a good deal of previous research. In particular, one should not thoughtlessly assume that any attitude will form a continuous scale without checking the nature of the distribution, especially for those people who are involved with the issue. Attitude scales, especially for important attitudes, should not use standardized scores unless there is independent evidence that the distribution is normal. Because a major effect of exposure to attitudinal information is an increasing extremity of opinions, one also has to be careful about the robustness of the statistical tests one uses with respect to assumptions about variances.

Although scaling works (people can be induced to provide numbers in response to questions), it may misrepresent the true nature of attitudes. If the view that attitudes are catastrophic turns out to be indeed correct, it may explain why the measurement of attitudes as points on a dimension seems largely restricted to the academic laboratory, whereas applied researchers seem largely to ignore the accumulated wisdom of decades of scale development.

In general, these considerations suggest that it may pay to continue to adapt methods from cognitive psychology, such as thought-listing techniques and reaction-time studies, to elicit the dynamic processes affecting belief structures. For one thing, it encourages the study of attitudes as they form. An initial attempt along these lines was made by Rowan, Vallacher, Nowak and Latané (1991) to study the development of attitudes toward a political campaign by exposing subjects to abstracts of all the news articles that had appeared about that campaign. The results, although interesting from a methodological perspective, did not provide clear evidence for or against the present point of view. Likewise, it would be desirable to study dynamic variations in attitudes in real time. In Chapter 11, Vallacher and Nowak suggest using a computer "mouse" as a way of looking at the dynamic time course of attitudes.

V. Why Does Involvement Lead to Categorization?

In this chapter, we have presented evidence that attitudes seem to follow a normal, inverted U-shaped distribution for individuals who do not feel strongly about an issue or who perceive the issue as not very important, becoming a bipolar, U-shaped distribution as importance ratings rise. These results suggest that as people become aware of or involved with an issue, they may tend to categorize themselves with respect to that issue, discovering correlations among cognitive elements related to the issue and thereby forming an extreme attitude. Two possible mechanisms could lead to a press toward such cognitive organization and self-categorization—one stemming from internal processing and one from external pressures. Each of these mechanisms has the result that the more important an issue to an individual, the more extreme will be his or her response on the corresponding favor/oppose scale. A third mechanism results from the link between attitudes and behavior.

A. Internal Processing

The tendency to become more extreme with increased cognitive investment in a topic (i.e., with increasing importance of the topic) might be an inherent bias resulting from cognitive processing. Tesser and colleagues (Sadler & Tesser, 1973; Tesser, 1976, 1978; Tesser & Conlee, 1975) demonstrated that simply thinking about a person, object, or issue can lead to attitudinal polarization. Tesser's results are consistent with the idea that the decisive factor may be the degree of internal organization of the attitudes, with thinking leading to a greater degree of internal organization as people discover connections among subissues and reinterpret some ideas in light of their ruminations about others. Consistent with this view, Tesser and Leone (1977) reported that thought-induced polarization occurs only on issues for which people have developed schemas.

In addition to being more extreme, attitudes rated as being more important or strongly felt should also be more difficult to change. According to Petty and Cacioppo's (1981) elaboration-likelihood model, individuals process relevant information on important issues by means of the central processing route, which, by definition, results in deeper encoding and thus is more difficult to influence than through the peripheral route (cf. Rokeach, 1964; Rokeach, 1970). In our terms, involving issues lead to increased cognitive organization given that the central processing of information is likely to facilitate the development of cognitive linkages in the form of logical or psychological implications. The formation of such links, as we have indicated before, is likely, in turn, to encourage categorical representation.

The proposed nature of the relation between the degree to which attitudinally relevant information is cognitively organized and extremity finds direct support in experimental results. In an experiment by Judd and Lusk (1984), participants rated the overall mental health and the need for psychiatric care of a number of stimulus persons on a 9-point scale. Participants exposed to cases in which the descriptive dimensions were correlated produced more extreme judgments than did subjects who were exposed to uncorrelated material.

The development of correlation among attitudinal dimensions thus seems to lead to extremity of opinions. These results, taken further, suggest that as issues become important, cognitive elements become more and more correlated into an implicational structure (not just a more elaborate collection of bits of information). Following Murphy and Medin (1985), we can say that one develops an organizing theory, placing attitudinally relevant information into cognitive schemas or categories. This theory leads to the possibility of the self-categorization of attitudes.

Downing, Judd, and Brauer (1992), however, reported three experiments showing that the mere expression of attitudes increases their extremity and suggested an associative learning model to explain this effect. This work, in conjunction with earlier studies in the mere exposure tradition (Harrison, 1977), suggests that polarization effects may not depend on increased cognitive organization or that such organization can occur quite quickly.

Whatever psychological processes are at work (see also Mackie & Gastardo-Conaco, 1988), they appear to lead to an intolerance of ambiguity, wherein individuals are more comfortable identifying with a particular category than being a fence sitter. Because an uncomfortable intermediary attitude makes identification with a categorical opinion more desirable, attitude polarization helps shape one's identity by providing a more-or-less coherent attitudinal framework with which to handle unique experiences.

B. External Pressure

Another mechanism in the press for categorization may be pressure exerted on an individual from the social environment. When a "no preference" person encounters individuals committed to either side of a controversial issue, pressures toward uniformity should ensue (Festinger, Schachter, & Back, 1950). To reduce social tension, our fence sitter has a choice of either leaving the group (but, because this person is undecided on the issue, there is no inherent reason to think that the discrepancy in attitudes will overpower the desire to belong to the group) or changing his or her opinion to match that of the group. Opposing the group would increase conflict and the chance of rejection; remaining silent would be difficult given that groups often focus on converting deviates (Schachter, 1951), making likely a net change to the more extreme position. As described, this external process of polarization appears to be driven by the need for affiliation—changing one's attitude to accord with that of a reference group seems to be a by-product of group indoctrination.

Such a perspective on attitudes is very much in agreement with recent theories that treat attitudes more as a means of group identification than behavioral predisposition (Turner, 1991). It would follow that attitudes that are central for an individual's social identity, and thus more important, would be more organized than those that are peripheral and that people often receive information from their social environment that is already organized. That is, one may encounter correlated information in the world as a result of biased exposure to certain sources of social information. There may be selective self-exposure, not to information, but to social circles. As we shall see shortly, one result of dynamic social influence may be the development of attitudinal clusters of people sharing similar views in a more heterogeneous population.

Abelson (1993) listed 12 processes that can lead to an extremification of attitudes in a situation of group conflict. These include group polarization, insults, thought polarization, expression polarization, belief polarization, salience of group conflict, social modeling and normalization of extremity, the "group-in-the-door" effect, formation of hard-core subgroups, commitment and suffering, anger as a cue to misattributed malevolence, and triggered crowd response. Most of the processes analysed by Abelson seem likely to be more pronounced with regard to more important attitudes, and these processes can be seen as mechanisms leading to the shift between the dimensional and categorylike nature of attitudes with increasing importance.

C. Decisions and Behavior

A third force toward extremity is the press toward action. Every time a person makes a choice, cognitive dissonance (Brehm, 1956; Festinger, 1957, 1964) will lead him or her to devalue the unchosen alternative. If people make consistent choices (as society encourages them to do), these cognitive pressures will lead them to develop more extreme attitudes.

Shallice (1988) argued that, in principle, there is no inherent need for cognition to be consistent; however, consistency is required on the level of action. There is nothing wrong with a voter's thinking at the same time about the relative advantages and disadvantages of each candidate, but when he or she puts his or her ballot in the box, it can have only one choice on it. Because cognitions underlie behavior, organisms need to make cognition coherent in order to avoid behavioral confusion. We might thus expect that those attitudes that are directly connected to behavior are more organized than those that are not.

VI. Why Does It Matter? Implications for Group Dynamics

So far, we have discussed attitudes primarily as properties of individuals. As we indicated in the introduction, however, attitudes also exist on the group level of social reality. Next, we will try to show how the nature of individual attitude change processes is critical for the outcome of processes of social influence operating on the group level. We suggest that whether attitudes are dimensional or categorical has strong implications for the outcome of dynamic social influence processes in large-scale social systems.

A. The Traditional View—Convergence

Using a traditional conception of attitudes as dimensions with the explicit assumption that attitude change in response to the social environment will be linearly proportional to the discrepancy between positions, Abelson (1964) was able to show that in any network of interacting persons, opinions should ultimately converge on a single position. Abelson was quick to note that this result is not descriptive of real-world social systems and explored alternative processes that could moderate the effect. Nonetheless, he seemed to prove, by strict mathematical derivation, that traditional views of attitude should lead to a preponderance of intermediate views, with ultimate unification of the system. We have conducted computer simulations designed to incorporate Abelson's assumptions and have been able to show that he was correct—at least when attitudes are represented as points on a dimension and change is linearly proportional to the social environment (Szamrej, Nowak, & Latané, 1992).

Although Abelson did not consider the matter directly, his arguments would seem to suggest another reason to expect normal distributions of attitudes: Social pressures should lead most people to converge relatively quickly on the mean, with only some relatively isolated stragglers making up the tails of the distribution. In a subsequent paper, addressed to another topic, however, Abelson (1979) identified a reason why such distributions might not be obtained. Specifically, he noted, differing opinions may "cluster" around leaders in different regions of the network. Although he restricted his discussion to the implications for the emergence of correlation among attitudes, this mechanism turns out to be characteristic of nonlinear systems and can also help explain nonnormal, multimodal distributions such as we have found.

B. The New View—Clustering

The theory of social impact (Latané, 1981) suggests that for a wide variety of social processes, each individual in a social situation will be influenced by the others in direct proportion to a multiplicative function of their strength, immediacy, and number. The pressure to change attitudes, then, should be proportional to the strength (S), immediacy (I), and number (N) of individuals with opposing views and in inverse proportion to the SIN of those with supportive opinions, including themselves. Dynamic social impact theory (Latané, 1993; Latané & Nowak, 1993; Nowak & Latané, in press; Nowak, Szamrej, & Latané, 1990) applies this rule to explain the relationship between an individual and a group in a series of models of reciprocal and iterative social influence process, using computer simulation to discover the expected autodynamics of group attitude change processes. These simulations assume that attitudes are categorical and that a person will maintain his or her opinion as long as the balance of social influence favors that position but will change to the opposing position as soon as the balance of social pressures changes.

Compared with the traditional view, these nonlinear, categorical models exhibit very different behavior. Instead of convergence, they lead to a complex dynamics of attitude change resulting in clustering and polarization of attitudes on the group level. Whichever opinion is initially in the minority will tend to decrease, but, most significantly, as people change their views, the minority opinion tends to locate in contiguous minds—resulting in spatially coherent clusters of opinion.

Figure 2 shows the attitudes of 400 spatially distributed people before (a) and after (b) social influence. In comparison with the starting configuration, in the final equilibrium distribution, the minority has shrunk in size from 30% to 16% (the group has polarized), and attitudes have shifted to form locally coherent groups (it has clustered). Polarization and clustering may be considered order parameters of this system (see Latané, Nowak, & Liu, 1993). As a result of the rules of individual opinion change, a complex process of interaction has led to the emergence of a

A   B

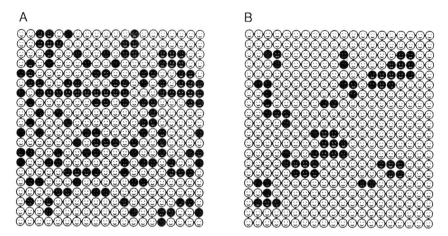

Figure 2   Spatial distributions of attitudes before (A) and after (B) social influence. (The faces represent 400 people, each holding one of two attitudinal positions. Social influence has caused the group to polarize [the initial 30% minority has dwindled to 16%] and cluster.)

stable spatial self-organization of group attitudes. This simulated process takes place without any external influence and may be described as an evolution toward an equilibrium describable by the differential equations of mean field theory (Lewenstein, Nowak, & Latané, 1992). This equilibrium consists of clustered groups in which minority members are shielded from the prevailing majority influence, finding themselves in local neighborhoods wherein their view is in the majority.

People located in the interior of minority clusters are protected from exposure to the majority position. People on the border are not. Latané and Nowak (1993) showed that it is the nonlinear change rule associated with categorical attitudes, in conjunction with individual differences in persuasive strength and self-supportiveness, that protects those on the border of minority islands from eroding into the majority sea. Rather than gradually shifting toward the majority position, strong-willed people on the border can maintain their views, allowing the less committed people with whom they communicate to believe that they are in the majority.

Clustering is reminiscent of many real-world phenomena such as spatial grouping of languages and dialects, dressing styles or cooking habits, popularity of political candidates, and so on. Group polarization (although usually measured in a somewhat different manner) has also been found in a variety of social settings (Moscovici, 1976, 1985; Moscovici & Zavaloni, 1969; Myers & Lamm, 1976). These phenomena are not just figments of a crazed computer simulation: Latané and L'Herrou (1993) demonstrated empirically that even when subjects are rewarded for being in the majority, clusters develop and the group does not unify in opinion as long as information about others' positions is limited to neighbors in some well-defined space. The dynamics of this process and the equilibrium state depend strongly on the geometry of the social space.

C. Feedback of Group Outcomes to Individual Processes

Clusters result from tendencies for attitudes to act like categories, but they may also amplify these tendencies, providing another explanation of why attitudes become categorical. These clusters represent a source of external bias in the information available to an individual about a given issue. As a result of these dynamic social influence processes, people in different regions of social space are likely to find themselves exposed to monolithic rather than mixed attitudinal environments. As discussed earlier, this may enhance the tendency toward adopting extreme attitudes, especially on those topics that promote active group discussion.

D. When Convergence? When Clustering?

The traditional and the new model lead to very different predictions about the fate of attitude change: The group will either unify or cluster depending on whether a linear or nonlinear model is used to predict attitude change. For attitudes that are not very important, linear models of change should be applicable. In this scenario, total unification is only a matter of time because, in linear models, groups always come to agreement. If the attitude is important, however, nonlinear models of the kind proposed by the dynamic theory of social impact should be applied to model the attitude change process. Total agreement is then unlikely, and we may expect that the group will organize itself such that coherent islands of minority opinion will become entrenched in the majority sea. Importance or involvement may then be recognized as a control parameter of the dynamics of opinion change in groups.

A nonlinear theory of opinion change may help explain the prevalence of diversity in our world, despite increasing contact. Although it is easy for groups to achieve agreement concerning unimportant issues, agreement on important issues may be impossible. Such rules of attitude change may promote group coordination concerning the less important matters of daily routine yet preserve diversity on important issues. The adaptive value of such mechanisms would require deeper analysis, but, following arguments from evolutionary theory, the preservation of diversity may allow societies to maintain cadres of minority opinion holders in reserve, ready to become opinion leaders when changing circumstances cause their views to be socially more adaptive than those of the majority.

E. Individual Attitudes and the Group Mind

Wegner (1986) discussed how people extend their internal memory not only with external storage devices such as notebooks and calendars but by relying on other people to remember key facts. A group of people may depend on one another for the enhancement of their personal memory stores, and this interdependence produces a larger and more complex knowledge-holding system than any individual could manage on his or her own. According to Wegner, transactive memory uses individual minds to form a group information-processing system that serves to expand dramatically each person's expertise. Although Wegner restricted his discussion to such relatively small-scale social systems as couples and work organizations, these ideas seem to provide a potentially useful basis for understanding how cultural knowledge grows out of, but is the source of, information in individual minds. According to Wegner, transactive memory provides one basis for the revival of an ancient concept—the group mind—but with one difference. Unlike traditional theories of group mind that emphasize the uniformity of individual mental processes, "transactive memory incorporates the system of interconnections that exists in individual's communications of information and, hence, places direct emphasis on the social organization of diversity" (p. 206) rather than on its destruction.

The present line of research can be seen as a first halting step toward a theory of "transactive attitudes." Like systems of transactive memory, the results of the dynamic self-organization of attitudes in social groups leads to organized diversity (Latané, 1991) and may justify the faith of all those social scientists who have looked to attitudes to bridge the so-called micro–macro interface, explaining how individual action is driven by social forces, which, in turn, derive from individual behavior. From accepting the view that individual attitudes can be seen as catastrophes, shifting according to degree of involvement from dimensions to categories, we can build a dynamic account of how individual attitudes interact to create public opinion. According to this account, although dimensional attitudes may converge to some social consensus, categorical attitudes will not, instead leading to clustering and polarization. Although this new view of the nature of individual attitudes may require the painful reexamination of the very nature of attitudes, resulting in the possible need to reinterpret the results of innumerable academic studies, the payoff may well make this worthwhile.

Acknowledgments

Preparation of this chapter was supported by National Science Foundation Grant BNS9009198. John Martz helped collect Data Set 2. Although we thank Robert Abelson, Jurgen Beckman, Frank Boster, Alice Eagly, J. R. Eiser, Jerry Harnett, Helen Harton, William Lawless, Thomas Ostrom, Anthony Pratkanis, Howard Schuman, Seymour Sudman, and Abraham Tesser for their extremely helpful comments, they should not be held responsible for the ideas and opinions expressed here.

References

Abelson, R. P. (1964) Mathematical models of the distribution of attitudes under controversy. In N. Fredericksen & H. Gullicksen (Eds.), *Contributions to mathematical psychology* (pp. 142–160). New York: Holt, Rinehart & Winston.

Abelson, R. P. (1979). Social clusters and opinion clusters. In P. W. Holland & S. Leinhardt (Eds.), *Perspectives in social network research* (pp. 239–256). New York: Academic Press.

Abelson, R. P. (1993). Dynamics of attitude extremity. In R. E. Petty & J. A. Krosnick (Eds.), *Attitude strength: Antecedents and consequences.* Hillsdale, NJ: Erlbaum.

Allport, G. (1935). Attitudes. In C. Murchison (Ed.), *A handbook of social psychology* (Vol. 2, pp. 798–844). Worcester, MA: Clark University Press.

Anderson, N. H. (1967). Averaging model analysis of set size effects in impression formation. *Journal of Experimental Psychology, 75,* 158–165.

Anderson, N. H. (1981a). *Foundations of information integration theory.* New York: Academic Press.

Anderson, N. H. (1981b). Integration theory applied to cognitive responses and attitudes. In R. E. Petty, T. M. Ostrom, & T. C. Brock (Eds.), *Cognitive responses in persuasion* (pp. 361–397). Hillsdale, NJ: Erlbaum.

Bartlett, F. C. (1932). *Remembering.* Cambridge, England: Cambridge University Press.

Brehm, J. (1956). Post-decision changes in the desirability of alternatives. *Journal of Abnormal and Social Psychology, 52,* 384–389.

Downing, J., Judd, C., & Brauer, M. (1992). Effects of repeated expressions on attitude extremity. *Journal of Personality and Social Psychology, 63,* 17–29.

Eagly, A. H., & Chaiken, S. (1993). *The psychology of attitudes.* Orlando, FL: Harcourt Brace Jovanovich.

Festinger, L. (1957). *A theory of cognitive dissonance.* Evanston, IL: Row, Peterson.

Festinger, L. (1964). *Conflict, decision, and dissonance.* Stanford, CA: Stanford University Press.

Festinger, L., Schachter, S., & Back, K. (1950). *Social pressures in informal groups.* New York: Harper.

Fishbein, M., & Ajzen, I. (1975). *Belief, attitude, intention, and behavior: An introduction to theory and research.* Reading, MA: Addison-Wesley.

Flay, B. R. (1978). Catastrophe theory in social psychology: Some applications to attitudes and social behavior. *Behavioral Science, 23,* 335–350.

Guttman, L. (1944). A basis for scaling qualitative data. *American Sociological Review, 9,* 139–150.

Harrison, A. A. (1977). Mere exposure. In L. Berkowitz (Ed.), *Advances in experimental social psychology* (Vol. 10, pp. 162–202). San Diego, CA: Academic Press.

Harrod, W., & Sapp (1992). *Social representations and amateur science: Food irradiation.* Paper presented at the 25th International Congress of Psychology, Brussels.

Heider, F. (1958). *The psychology of interpersonal relations.* New York: Wiley.

Judd, C., & Lusk, C. (1984). Knowledge structures and evaluative judgments: Effects of structural variables on structural extremity. *Journal of Personality and Social Psychology, 46,* 1193–1207.

Katz, D., & Braly, K. W. (1933). Racial stereotypes of 100 college students. *Journal of Abnormal and Social Psychology, 28,* 280–290.

Krech, D., Crutchfield, R., & Ballachey, E. (1962). *Individual in society.* New York: McGraw-Hill.

Krosnick, J. A. (1988). Attitude importance and attitude change. *Journal of Experimental Social Psychology, 24,* 240–255.

Latané, B. (1981). The psychology of social impact. *American Psychologist, 36,* 343–356.

Latané, B. (1991). Dynamic social impact and the group mind. Paper presented at the annual meeting of the Society for Experimental Social Psychology, Columbus, OH.

Latané, B. (1994). *Strength from weakness: The fate of opinion minorities in spatially distributed groups.* In J. Davis & E. Witte (Eds.) *Understanding group behavior: Consensual action by small groups.*

Latané, B., & L'Herrou, T. (1993). *Social clustering in the conformity game: Dynamic social impact in electronic groups.* Unpublished manuscript.

Latané, B., & Nowak, A. (1993). *The causes of clustering in self-organizing social systems.* Unpublished manuscript.

Latané, B., Nowak, A., & Liu, J. (1993). *Measuring emergent social phenomena: Dynamism, polarization, and clustering as order parameters in dynamic social systems.* Unpublished manuscript.

Latané, B., & Wolf, S. (1981). The social impact of majorities and minorities. *Psychological Review, 88,* 438–453.

Lewenstein, M., Nowak, A., & Latané, B. (1992). Statistical mechanics of social impact. *Physical Review A, 45,* 1–14.

Lord, C. G., Lepper, M. R., & Preston, E. (1985). Considering the opposite: A corrective strategy for social judgment. *Journal of Personality and Social Psychology, 47,* 1231–1243.

Lord, C. G., Ross, L., & Lepper, M. R. (1979). Biased assimilation and attitude polarization: The effects of prior theories on subsequently considered evidence. *Journal of Personality and Social Psychology, 37,* 2098–2109.

McGuire, W. J. (1983). A contextualist theory of knowledge: its implications for innovation and reform in psychology research. In L. Berkowitz (Ed.), *Advances in experimental social psychology* (Vol. 16, pp. 1–47). New York: Academic Press.

McGuire, W. J. (1985). Attitudes and attitude change. In G. Lindzey & E. Aronson (Eds.), *Handbook of social psychology* (pp. 233–346). Hillsdale, NJ: Erlbaum.

McGuire, W. J. (1986). The vicissitudes of attitudes and similar representational constructs in twentieth century psychology. *European Journal of Social Psychology, 16,* 89–130.

Mackie, D., & Gastardo-Conaco, M. (1988). The impact of importance accorded an issue on attitude inferences. *Journal of Experimental Social Psychology, 24,* 543–570.

Minsky, M. (1975). A framework for representing knowledge. In P. H. Winston (Ed.), *The psychology of computer vision.* New York: McGraw-Hill.

Moscovici, S. (1976). *Social influence and social change.* London: Academic Press.

Moscovici, S. (1985). Social influence and conformity. In G. Lindzey & E. Aronson (Eds.), *Handbook of social psychology* (Vol. 2, pp. 347–412). Hillsdale, NJ: Erlbaum.

Moscovici, S., & Zavaloni, M. (1969). The group as a polarizer of attitudes. *Journal of Personality and Social Psychology, 12,* 125–135.

Murphy, G. L., & Medin, D. L. (1985). The role of theories in conceptual coherence. *Psychological Review, 92,* 289–316.

Myers, D., & Lamm, H. (1976). The group polarization phenomenon. *Psychological Bulletin, 83,* 602–627.

Nowak, A., & Latané, B. (in press). Simulating the emergence of social order from individual behavior. In N. Gilbert & J. Doran (Eds.), *Simulating societies: The computer simulation of social processes.* London: University College London Press.

Nowak, A., Szamrej, J., & Latané, B. (1990). From private attitude to public opinion: A dynamic theory of social impact. *Psychological Review, 97,* 367–376.

Osgood, C. E., Suci G. J., & Tannenbaum, P. H. (1957). *The measurement of meaning.* Urbana, IL: University of Illinois Press.

Ostrom, T. (1988). *Judgments as categories.* Paper presented at the Nags Head Conference on Social Cognition, Kill Devil Hills, NC.

Ostrom, T., & Gannon, K. (1991). *The meaning of rating scale extremities: A categorical perspective.* Paper presented at the annual meeting of the Midwestern Psychological Association, Chicago.

Petty, R. E., & Cacioppo, J. T. (1981). *Attitudes and persuasion: Classic and contemporary approaches.* Dubuque, IA: William C. Brown.

Rokeach, M. (1964). *The three Christs of Ypsilanti: A psychological study.* New York: Columbia University Press.

Rokeach, M. (1970). *Beliefs, attitudes, and values: A theory of organization and change.* San Francisco: Jossey-Bass.

Rosch, E. (1978). Principles of categorization. In F. Rosch & B. B. Lloyd (Eds.), *Cognition and categorization,* Hillsdale, NJ: Erlbaum.

Rowan, M., Vallacher, R., Nowak, A., & Latané, B. (1991). *The dynamics of political judgment: Attitude formation and change during an election.* Paper presented at the annual meeting of the American Psychological Society, Washington, DC.

Rumelhart, D. E., & Ortony, A. (1977). The representation of knowledge in memory. In R. C. Anderson, R. J. Spiro, & W. E. Montague (Eds.), *Schooling and the acquisition of knowledge.* Hillsdale, NJ: Erlbaum.

Sadler, O., & Tesser, A. (1973). Some effects of salience and time upon interpersonal hostility and attraction during social isolation. *Sociometry, 36,* 99–112.

Schachter, S. (1951). Deviation, rejection, and communication. *Journal of Abnormal and Social Psychology, 46,* 190–207.

Schuman, H., & Presser, S. (1981). *Questions and answers in attitude surveys.* New York: Academic Press.

Schwarz, N., & Sudman, S. (Eds.). (1992). *Context effects in social and psychological research.* New York: Springer-Verlag.

Shallice, T. (1988). *From neuropsychology to mental structure.* Cambridge, England: Cambridge University Press.

Sherif, M., & Hovland, C. (1961). *Social judgment: Assimilation and contrast effects in communication and attitude change.* New Haven, CT: Yale University Press.

Sloan, L. R., & Ostrom, T. M. (1974). Amount of information and interpersonal judgment. *Journal of Personality and Social Psychology, 29,* 23–29.

Smale, S. (1978). Review of Zeeman (1977). *Bulletin of the American Mathematical Society, 84,* 128–136.

Smith, E. E. (1990). Concepts and induction. In M. J. Posner (Ed.), *Foundations of cognitive science* (pp. 501–526) Cambridge, MA: MIT Press.

Stigler, S. M. (1986). *The history of statistics: The measurement of uncertainty before 1900.* Cambridge, MA: Bellknap.

Stouffer, S. A., Guttman, L., Suchman, E. A., Lazarsfeld, P. F., Star, S. A., & Clausen, J. A. (1950). *Measurement and prediction.* Princeton, NJ: Princeton University Press.

Szamrej, J., Nowak, A., & Latané, B. (1992). *Self-organizing attitudinal structures in society: Visual display of dynamic social processes.* Paper presented at the 25th International Congress of Psychology, Brussels.

Tesser, A. (1976). Thought and reality constraints as determinants of attitude polarization. *Journal of Research in Personality, 10,* 183–194.

Tesser, A. (1978). Self-generated attitude change. In L. Berkowitz (Ed.), *Advances in experimental social psychology* (Vol. 11, pp. 289–338). New York: Academic Press.

Tesser, A., & Conlee, M. C. (1975). Some effects of time and thought on attitude polarization. *Journal of Personality and Social Psychology, 31,* 262–270.

Tesser, A., & Leone, C. (1977). Cognitive schemas and thought as determinants of attitude change. *Journal of Experimental Social Psychology, 13,* 340–356.

Thurstone, L. (1931). The measurement of attitudes. *Journal of Abnormal and Social Psychology, 26,* 249–269.

Turner, J. C. (1991). *Social influence.* Milton Keynes: Open University Press.

Wegner, D. (1986). Transactive memory: A contemporary analysis of the group mind. In B. Mullen & G. R. Goethals (Eds.), *Theories of group behavior* (pp. 185–208). New York: Springer-Verlag.

Wieczorkowska, G. (1990). The range of perceived variability of the object and its representation in cognitive structure. *Polish Psychological Bulletin, 2,* 105–115.

Zeeman, E. C. (1977). *Catastrophe theory.* Reading, MA: Addison-Wesley.

CHAPTER 11

The Stream of Social Judgment

Robin R. Vallacher
Department of Psychology
Florida Atlantic University
Boca Raton, Florida

Andrzej Nowak
Institute for Social Studies
Faculty of Psychology
University of Warsaw
Warsaw, Poland

I. Introduction

In the endless debates over the nature of human cognition, two things should be kept in mind. First, thoughts do not exist in a vacuum. To the contrary, every thought is embedded and experienced in the context of other thoughts. Second, thoughts do not stand still. Even in our most quiescent moments, our thoughts tend to unfold and drift over brief periods of time, so that any one element of thought gives way to myriad other elements. These two features of thought are nowhere more apparent than in thoughts about social stimuli—other people, events, oneself. Thus, a particular thought about someone calls to mind other thoughts relevant to the person, and the whole ensemble of activated thoughts tends to change over time. Our impressions, opinions, and feelings about social objects, in short, tend to be both structured and dynamic.

The structure of social thinking has been dutifully acknowledged within mainstream social psychology. Theorists and researchers from a variety of persuasions have documented the interconnectedness of thoughts within cognitive struc-

Dynamical Systems in Social Psychology

tures. The basic idea is that a domain of thought (a social role, a particular person, an ethnic group, oneself, etc.) consists of specific elements (traits, behaviors, characteristics, etc.), and these elements are coordinated in some fashion to represent one's thoughts about the domain. Concepts such as schema (e.g., Rumelhart, 1980; Taylor & Crocker, 1981), category (e.g., Rosch, 1978), prototype (e.g., Cantor & Mischel, 1979; Posner & Keele, 1968), network (e.g., J. R. Anderson & Bower, 1973), script (e.g., Schank & Abelson, 1977), and implicit theory (e.g., Wegner & Vallacher, 1977) have been used to capture this feature of thought. Thus, the cognitive structures (schemas, etc.) relevant to, say, a professor and a tennis pro are each associated with a unique set of fairly specific cognitive elements that together are said to define how one thinks about these roles.

Unfortunately, psychologists have not been so dutiful in investigating the dynamic nature of thought–its tendency to evolve and otherwise change over various time scales. Indeed, the relative lack of explicit attention to the flow of thinking leaves one with the impression that the cognitive structures detailed by psychologists are rather like fixed architectures in which all the elements fit together like so many pieces of stone in a pyramid. Left to its own devices, then, the "true" state of the cognitive system is assumed to be a stable equilibrium, with all the cognitive elements coexisting in quiescent harmony. So, for example, when the professor or tennis pro role is made salient, a stable configuration of specific elements and an overall evaluation are said to characterize one's thoughts about someone occupying that role. In this view, if change does occur, it is attributed, implicitly if not explicitly, to the receipt of new information or to the experience of social pressure (e.g., persuasion, social comparison). In the absence of external instigations, variability over time in impressions or opinions is considered a result of noise in the system or an artifact of one's measurement tools.

Of course, everyone—cognitive and social psychologists included—knows that this view of social thinking has to be wrong. Thought is inherently a highly dynamic process—a veritable flow of sensations, images, episodic memories, inferences, concerns, and so forth—that virtually never stands still. Even during sleep (Hobson, 1988) and under conditions of sensory deprivation (Zubek, 1969), the mind remains quite active, producing a rapid turnover in output despite the lack of environmental input. Whether thinking about oneself, an intimate friend, or a perfect stranger, our thoughts seem to have a trajectory of their own, changing from one set of elements to another on a rapid time scale, even when no new information is provided and there are no external pressures for updating our thoughts. James (1890/1950) coined the term *stream of consciousness* to convey this idea, noting that thought is continuous and ever-changing, a succession of different states that, although forming a coherent pattern, never replicate exactly earlier states.

This chapter pays homage to the Jamesian metaphor by providing a conceptual and operational scheme for exploring the intrinsic dynamics of social judgment. By *intrinsic dynamics*, we mean internally generated patterns of temporal variation that occur in the absence of external forces. We begin by developing a rationale for this exploration, suggesting why social judgment is inherently dynamic and why it may be important to consider it in these terms. In the second part, we consider the factors that have stalled work on social cognitive dynamics, at least within mainstream psychology, and we present a paradigm intended to circumvent these problems. In the third part, data are presented that attest to the viability of this approach for extracting meaningful information from people's moment-to-moment judgments of social stimuli. In a concluding section, we develop what we feel to be some noteworthy implications of this perspective for theory and research on social thinking.

II. Intrinsic Dynamics

The suggestion that thoughts about social objects are inherently dynamic, changing in a seemingly spontaneous manner over relatively short intervals of time, is hardly controversial. What is less clear is how to connect this idea to more comprehensive models of cognitive process and structure. In what follows, we attempt to provide such a connection. We first suggest how best to characterize the social judgment system so as to gain insight into its underlying dynamics. We then depict the relation between dynamics and structure and ground this relation in the context of network approaches to cognition.

A. Order Parameters

Like any complex dynamical system, social judgment can be characterized in terms of an *order parameter* (Haken, 1984; Landau & Liftschitz, 1968; see Chapter 2). When we think about someone, after all, we are not left with a bundle of separate, unrelated elements (e.g., images, event memories, trait ascriptions). Rather, our thoughts tend to have a "bottom line" to them, some sort of provisional integration that reflects our general sense of the person. Evaluation is an obvious candidate for this role (N. H. Anderson, 1981; Fiske & Taylor, 1991; Wegner & Vallacher, 1977). The specific issue may be impression formation, political attitudes, or assessments of responsibility, but in each case, the broader issue can be framed in terms of how people feel about the person or topic at stake. Sometimes, of course, more specific dimensions of judgment are of interest (e.g., fairness, intelligence, social skill), but even here it is hard to identify dimensions that are entirely devoid of evaluation (Kim & Rosenberg, 1980).

Evaluative integration of diverse cognitive elements is possible if one assumes that each element (i.e., thoughts, attributes, and emotions concerning the target of judgment) is valenced and that a summary judgment—an evaluation—at each iteration represents some computed function (e.g., weighted average) of the valences associated with the activated elements (e.g., N. H. Anderson, 1981). It follows that as the configuration of elements changes over time, there is a concomitant potential for change in one's overall evaluation of the target of judgment.

Consider, for example, the succession of thoughts that come to mind concerning one's spouse on the heels of a contentious discussion concerning respective contributions to the household.[1] Clearly, there is an overabundance of information concerning the spouse and household maintenance, only some of which is likely to be activated as a result of the discussion, and these bits of information are connected to one another in certain ways. One may think of the spouse's workload outside the home, for instance, and this may call up his or her education, income, and stress tolerance. Each of these elements may then activate other thoughts about the spouse (e.g., stress tolerance calls to mind his or her vacation fantasies), while inhibiting consideration of myriad others (e.g., his or her physical appearance, musical tastes). The newly activated pattern of cognitive elements then calls to mind other associated thoughts (e.g., vacation desires call to mind his or her capacity for fun, sexual desirability, and so on). At each iteration of this process, the activated elements are integrated in some fashion to give rise to a global judgment about the spouse. Thus, within a remarkably short period of time, one can oscillate between judgments that run the gamut from highly negative (resentment, frustration) to exceptionally positive (empathy, lust).

To capture the intrinsic dynamics of social judgment, then, it may not be necessary to track the rise and fall in salience of individual cognitive elements. In fact, the attempt to track a particular element of thought may prove fruitless because it may disappear from thought altogether as one subset of elements gives way to another subset. Of course, a particular element of thought may have clear theoretical or clinical significance (e.g., memory of a traumatic event from childhood, an unwanted thought), and one may therefore have good reasons to track its appearance over time in consciousness (e.g., Pennebaker, 1989; Pope & Singer, 1978; Uleman & Bargh, 1989; Wegner, 1989). But if one's concern is with the dynamics of the social judgment system as a whole, it may be necessary to track the global output of the system over time. The stream of social judgment, in short, can be characterized in terms of the variation over time in some index of overall evaluation of the target of judgment.

B. Structure and Dynamics

It might seem that emphasizing the dynamics of social judgment undermines the assumption that thought is structured. After all, to say that thoughts about

---

[1] We wish to thank everyone we have ever met for suggesting this example to us.

social stimuli have structure is tantamount to saying that there is a more-or-less fixed architecture of social judgment. A group stereotype, for instance, is defined as a fairly stable mental representation, one consisting of many specific attributes that are rather rigidly linked in some manner (e.g., covariation, superordinate–subordinate). Can one then turn around and argue that thoughts about social stimuli drift and otherwise change over time? Does this not suggest that whatever structure exists in social judgment is not all that stable? How can thoughts about ourselves, other people, and social groups be both structured and dynamic?

The apparent inconsistency between structure and dynamics is more illusory than real. Tracking the temporal trajectory of thinking, in fact, is important precisely because it provides information about the structure of the underlying system (cf. Eckmann & Ruelle, 1985; Grassberger & Procaccia, 1983). To appreciate this idea, consider how different rules of organization of judgmental systems might be reflected in temporal trajectories of interpersonal evaluation. Imagine first a simplified case in which each set of positively valenced elements calls to mind other sets of positively valenced elements. If any of these sets of elements were activated, more and more positive elements would become simultaneously activated. The overall evaluation would become increasingly positive until a plateau in evaluation was reached and maintained (unless, of course, some external influence were to change the state of the system). A symmetrical situation would occur with negative elements calling to mind other negative elements. In both cases, there would be a monotonic increase in evaluative polarization.

A more elaborate description of this scenario is provided in Tesser's (1978) research on thought polarization, which constitutes perhaps the best documented case of intrinsic dynamics in social judgment. This research has shown that with the passage of time, subjects' evaluations of an attitude object (e.g., a stranger) tend to become more extreme: An initial positive impression becomes more positive, whereas an initial negative impression becomes more negative. This is particularly true if judges have well-developed schemas concerning the attitude object, such as men evaluating a football play or women evaluating fashion (Tesser & Leone, 1977). Polarization is said to reflect the addition of evaluatively consistent cognitions and the suppression or reinterpretation of inconsistent cognitions about the target. If dynamics of this kind were observed, one could infer that the underlying representation is evaluatively consistent or is in the process of becoming so. This scenario would promote subjective certainty in evaluation because each encountered element would strengthen the interpretation of other elements.

Notwithstanding the press toward evaluative consistency in thought (Festinger, 1957; Heider, 1958), over time one's thoughts can become increasingly differentiated and complex as opposed to increasingly unified and global (e.g., Bartlett, 1932; Haken & Stadler, 1990; Harvey, Hunt, & Schroder, 1961; Linville, 1985; Piaget, 1971; van Geert, 1991; Werner, 1957). Differentiated structures can give rise to more complex dynamics, at least for time spans of relatively short duration (i.e., before integration is attained). To see why, consider a contrived example in which each positive element calls to mind a negative element and vice versa (assume that only one element is called to mind at a time). We would then observe regular oscillations of the overall evaluation, such that the evaluation at each point in time would be indicative of whether a positive or negative element is currently activated.

Now consider a somewhat more complex example in which negative elements are activated only after a certain number of positive elements, and vice versa. The oscillations between positive and negative evaluation in this instance would obviously be much slower. In everyday life, this type of judgment tendency would seem to capture the changes in evaluation associated with two conflicting perspectives on a social target. Of course, in reality we may expect considerably more complex rules of organization in social judgment systems and hence more complex temporal trajectories. If the structure has very low integration and the temporal sequence of elements coming to mind approximates randomness, for instance, we would expect very irregular changes in evaluation, a state of affairs likely to be experienced as confusion, ambivalence, or uncertainty (cf. Scott, Osgood, & Peterson, 1979).[2] The point is that the resultant temporal trajectory can be used as a basis for inferring what the rules of organization are.

The relation between structure and dynamics can be cast more formally in network terms (Amit, 1989; J. R. Anderson & Bower, 1973; Hopfield, 1982; McClelland & Rumelhart, 1986; see also Chapter 9).[3] Specifically, we can portray the judgment system as a set of elements interconnected by functional relations. Each element represents a node in such a network. Depending on the architecture of the system and the rules of activation for different subsets of connections, the system will display different types of temporal behavior. When the connections are symmetrical and all are simultaneously activated, for instance, the system will quickly evolve toward one of its possible equilibrium states. When different sets of connections are activated at different times, however, the system may show more complex dynamics, such as regular oscillations or chaotic change (e.g., Amit, 1989; Barinaga, 1990; Carpenter & Grossberg, 1987; Hopfield, 1982; Labos, 1987). In other words, the structure of the system and the rules of propagation of signals in the system set constraints on the types of behavior that a system can exhibit. So by observing the temporal trajectory of the system, we can eliminate at the outset certain possible rules of underlying structure and, by the same token, gain insight into the most probable rules of underlying structure.

---

[2]Rather than reflecting randomness, irregular evolution of this kind may be indicative of deterministic chaos (cf. Schuster, 1984) produced by the nonlinear interactions of a few cognitive elements (see Chapter 2).

[3]A system composed of information elements is clearly a higher level system than one composed of neurons, but the rules of neural networks have been shown to be applicable to higher levels of organization (cf. Sejnowski & Churchland, 1989).

It is also the case, however, that the information value of dynamics is lost when the system is at or close to a stable equilibrium state. This is because the dynamics of the system slow down dramatically in the vicinity of an equilibrium. In attractor neural networks, for example, the rate of change in the system has been shown to be a powerful indicator of distance to an equilibrium point (Lewenstein & Nowak, 1989). Even for systems that are evolving toward an equilibrium state, though, the characteristics of the approach toward the equilibrium may still be revealing about the system's structural characteristics when the system is relatively far from equilibrium.

III. Measuring the Stream of Social Judgment

At first blush, gauging the ebb and flow of people's stream of social thinking would seem to be a simple task. People can reflect on their thoughts, after all, so in principle the task is simply one of getting people to verbalize their reflections as they occur. On closer examination, however, obtaining valid self-reports of this kind is fraught with difficulties, some of which are sufficiently intractable to derail the whole enterprise. Next, we indicate what these difficulties are and then introduce a paradigm designed to circumvent them.

A. The Problems with Self-Report

Reflecting on one's own thoughts as they unfold is a well-documented paradox (e.g., Hofstadter, 1979; James, 1890/1950; Polanyi, 1969; Ryle, 1949; Wegner & Vallacher, 1981). The essence of the paradox is simple: to track what is going on mentally as one thinks about, say, a new acquaintance is tantamount to changing what one is thinking about. Instead of thinking about the acquaintance, one is now thinking about one's thinking. If one then decided to reflect on *that* set of thoughts, the focus of thought would again change—from how one is thinking about the acquaintance to how one is thinking about thinking about the target. In short, there is a potential for infinite regress in trying to report on one's thoughts as they unfold, with the likelihood of success no greater than that associated with trying to catch one's own shadow. One cannot both be in a mental state and know what it is like to be in that state any more than one can simultaneously sleep and know what it is like to be asleep. This, then, is the terrain we enter when we ask people to report on their thoughts as they occur.

One solution is to let the thought process unfold naturally and then ask subjects to report from memory what their intervening thoughts and feelings were. Unfortunately, there are problems here as well. For one thing, because of the press toward cognitive consistency, there is a danger that once an overall attitude or sentiment has been expressed, subjects will be inclined to reconstruct their inter-vening thoughts to make them appear evaluatively consistent with the expressed attitude (e.g., Lingle & Ostrom, 1979).[4] Beyond that, there is reason to think that people simply are not very insightful into the workings of their own minds (e.g., Mandler, 1975; Nisbett & Ross, 1980; Nisbett & Wilson, 1977). A person may readily report his or her feelings about a target person, for example, but draw a blank or provide a rationalization when probed for the intervening steps leading to the resultant feeling. Moreover, even if people were fairly cognizant of the moment-to-moment feelings associated with their evaluation of some target per-son, they might not provide an inquisitor a faithful account of these feelings, pre-ferring instead to describe their thoughts in personally flattering or socially desirable terms (cf. Crowne & Marlow, 1964; Edwards, 1957). Such tailor-made accounts are particularly likely when it is obvious how various accounts are likely to be evaluated by the inquisitor (Rosenberg, 1965).

A final issue concerning the information value of self-reports on ongoing thought is a very practical one involving limitations in the timing associated with traditional assessment techniques. The temporal patterns associated with social judgment can operate on different time scales, perhaps even those involving milli-seconds. Clearly, tracking self-reports on such time scales is unreasonable. One can readily assess an attitude on a questionnaire on a given occasion and perhaps do so again a few minutes later. But it is simply impossible to assess judgments in this way every few seconds, let alone several times a second.

At the outset, then, there seems to be fundamental restrictions on what one can hope to learn about the flow of thought from people's self-reports. They may tell you what they think but when probed for the intervening thoughts on their way to their current state, they may provide answers that are fraught with paradox and lack genuine insight, revealing more about their intuitive theories of cognitive process, or perhaps their particular concerns over personal evaluation, than about the process that actually transpired (cf. Ajzen, 1977; Nisbett & Ross, 1980). From this perspective, the stream of consciousness makes for a poor reflecting pool.

B. The Mouse Paradigm

Gaining access to the flow of social judgment is clearly not a simple task. The trick is to get people to express their feelings continuously but to do so without reporting on them. This itself seems somewhat paradoxical, but with the aid of

[4]The reverse effect could also occur: Recounting one's specific thoughts relevant to an attitude can affect the attitude being reported, bringing the attitude into line with the specific thoughts (e.g., Bem & McConnell, 1970), for example, or perhaps undermining the attitude altogether (Wilson, 1990).

modern computing technology and a classic idea in social psychology, we have recently attempted this trick.

The classic idea was provided by Hovland, Janis, and Kelley (1953). They suggested that evaluation can be considered an implicit approach-avoid response. In literal terms, this idea implies that a judge's preferred proximity to a target represents an expression of his or her current feeling about the target. The closer the judge's preferred distance from the target, the more positive his or her feeling. By extension, movement toward or away from the target represents change in the judge's feelings about the target. With this general and intuitively reasonable idea in mind, the task then becomes one of finding a means of sampling a judge's preferred distance from a target continuously, so as to ascertain the moment-to-moment fluctuations in his or her feelings about the target.

The feature of modern computing we used for this purpose was simply a computer mouse used to control a cursor on a computer screen. The paradigm we developed around the mouse is straightforward. Two symbols are presented on the computer screen: an arrow reflecting the position of the cursor and a small circle positioned in the middle of the screen. The arrow is said to represent the subject, and the circle is said to represent a particular target of judgment. Subjects read a description of a target person or of an event involving themselves and a target person and are asked to think about the target. As they do so, they adjust the arrow in relation to the target circle (by moving the mouse) so as to express their moment-to-moment feelings about the target over a 2-min period. The mouse is positioned on the side of the keyboard corresponding to subjects' dominant hand.

In introducing the task, the experimenter informs subjects that if they feel positive about the target, they should move the arrow toward the circle by moving the mouse; by the same token, if they feel negative toward the target, they should move the arrow away from the target. The experimenter then informs subjects that if their feelings about the target change, they should move the arrow toward or away from the target to express these changes. Subjects are free to adjust their position relative to the target as often and as much as is necessary to reflect their feelings about the target as they continue to think about him or her.

After a 20-s practice session in which subjects moved the mouse and observed the corresponding movement on the screen, the screen cleared and a description of a particular target person appeared. Subjects then began the 2-min mouse procedure. The location of the arrow was assessed 10 times per second for a total of 1,200 potential data points. Research to date reveals that all subjects spend the first few seconds moving from the initial position (immediately adjacent to the target) to a "safe" starting position. For this reason, subjects' movements during the first 3 s were not included in subsequent analyses. The program preserves the Cartesian coordinates of each data point, although for purposes of our initial investigations (described below), only the absolute distance from the target was considered. This distance provides a measure of subjects' moment-to-moment feelings about the target.

IV. Variation in Intrinsic Dynamics

By itself, the suggestion that social judgment shows temporal variation in the absence of new information or social influence, and that this variation can be measured, does not mean that such variation is necessarily meaningful. One could argue, after all, that the mind is simply a busy place and that the turnover in thought that people experience when considering someone results simply from so much noise obscuring a more stable signal. In this section, we want to establish that temporal variation in judgment is indeed meaningful. First, we look for and attempt to characterize patterns underlying the temporal variation in social judgment. If patterns corresponding to those obtained in other areas of science (e.g., periodic evolution, catastrophic change) are found, this would bolster our suggestion that social judgment is a dynamical system. Second, we attempt to establish empirical connections between properties of temporal dynamics and established criteria of social judgment and thereby demonstrate that dynamics convey meaningful information about a person's consideration of social stimuli.

A. Temporal Patterns in Judgment

The emergence of temporal patterns is a universal property of all biological systems, and the characterization of patterns is one way of understanding the underlying dynamics (e.g., Haken, 1984; Kelso, Ding, & Schoner, 1991; Chapter 4). Assuming social judgment to be a dynamical system, then, we would expect to find evidence of temporal patterns in people's moment-to-moment feelings regarding a target of judgment. Depending on the particular target and the structure of the underlying system, a wide variety of patterns might be observed, some of which might correspond to motion on an attractor for the system (e.g., convergence on a fixed point, periodic oscillations, chaotic evolution). If so, this would provide a new basis for characterizing social judgment, one that would supplement and perhaps complement characterizations based on valence, content, and structure.

Our initial study using the mouse paradigm was an attempt to uncover temporal patterns in social judgment (Vallacher & Nowak, 1992). Nine subjects performed the mouse task for each of four hypothetical event descriptions (presented in random order). Each description was designed to engender some ambivalence in subjects so to maximize the likelihood that their moment-to-moment feelings would show temporal variation (i.e., fluctuation between positive and negative feelings). The descriptions can be summarized as follows.

1. The subject meets an attractive person of the opposite sex at a party and arranges to date the person the following weekend. Later, the subject overhears another person tell someone else that the subject's future date had once dated someone who had tested positive for HIV but had broken off the relationship once he or she had discovered this.

2. The subject is discussing marriage plans with his or her prospective spouse. The marriage partner discloses that there is a history of a potentially fatal genetic disease in his or her family and that the odds are 1 in 4 that any offspring they have will develop the disease.

3. The subject is having an increasingly heated argument with his or her marriage partner concerning their relative contributions to the household. One of them (unspecified) storms out of the room.

4. The subject learns that a close friend once stole money from another of his or her friends. The close friend never admitted to the theft or tried to make amends to the victim.

In thinking about each description, subjects were instructed to indicate their moment-to-moment feelings about the event and/or target (i.e., the date, the impending marriage, the spouse, the close friend).

Results revealed intrinsic dynamics in all cases, with judgment corresponding to one of several distinct temporal patterns. To illustrate the sorts of patterns obtained, Figure 1A–D presents the raw data generated by four subjects. The x axis in these figures represents time (0–120 s), the y axis the absolute distance from the target in pixels. Figures 2A–D and 3A–D show the autocorrelations and Fourier transforms, respectively, associated with the data in Figure 1a–d. Visual inspection of Figure 1a suggests that the subject's judgments alternated between two values. The periodic nature of this pattern is revealed by the autocorrelations in Figure 2A. The autocorrelations gradually decrease in value, becoming negative after about 80 lags—a pattern that is indicative of simple low frequency periodicity. Fourier analysis reveals one dominant low frequency (Figure 3A), confirming again the simple periodicity in the raw data.

In contrast, Figure 1B shows gradual change (increasing positivity) for the first minute, followed by a catastrophic change (sudden positivity), and finally some slight correction toward the end of the two-min period. The corresponding autocorrelations (Figure 2B) show only a slight decrease in value over 120 time lags, a pattern indicative of slow dynamics, such that a judgment at one point in time is a good predictor of a long series of judgments. The Fourier transforms of the subject's data (Figure 3B) reveals only a dominant zero frequency, confirming the lack of periodicity in this subject's judgments.

Visual inspection of Figure 1C shows seemingly irregular oscillations with decreasing amplitude, as if judgment were converging on a stable attractor. The

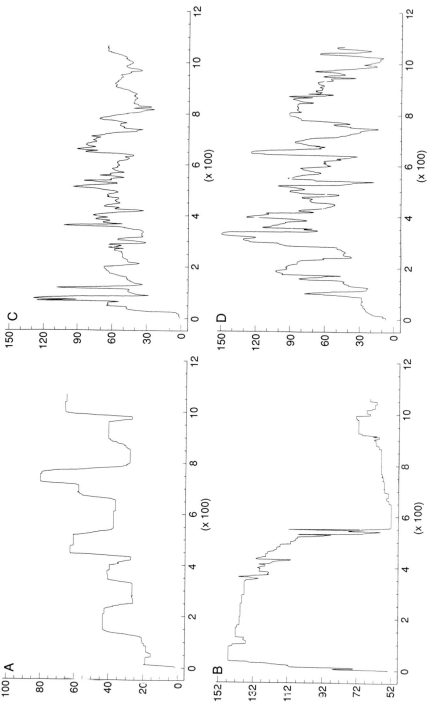

Figure 1A–D Absolute distance from target over 2-min period for each of four subjects. (The x axis represents time [0–120 s]; the y axis represents absolute distance from target in pixels.)

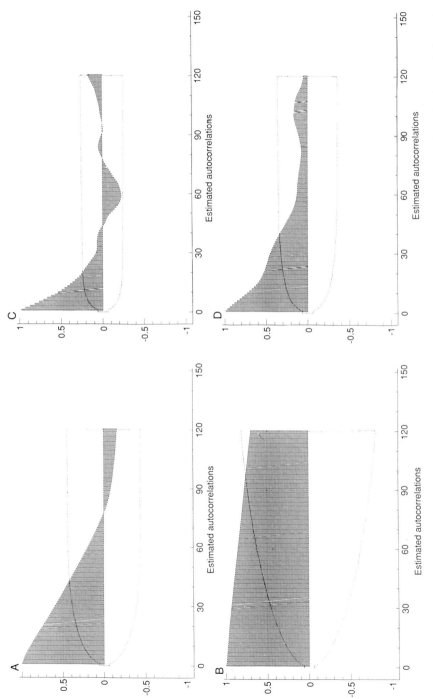

Figure 2A–D Autocorrelations as a function of time lag for raw data presented in Figures 1A–D. (The x axis represents number of time lags [0–150 s]; the y axis represents correlations coefficient [−1.0–+1.0].)

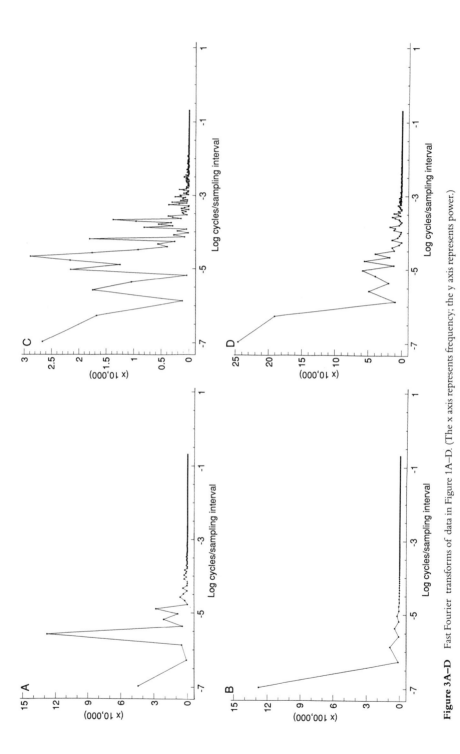

Figure 3A–D Fast Fourier transforms of data in Figure 1A–D. (The x axis represents frequency; the y axis represents power.)

corresponding autocorrelations (Figure 2C) drop rapidly to zero, become slightly negative, and then become negligibly positive with increasing lags. The inability to predict far into the future from a given judgment suggests the operation of dynamics on a short-time scale. The Fourier transform data (Fig. 3C) reveals many frequencies in this subject's judgments, none of which are dominant.

Finally, Figure 1D is similar to Figure 1C in demonstrating irregular oscillations but different in that there is less pronounced decrease in variance associated with these oscillations over time. It is interesting that the autocorrelations associated with this subject's judgments (Figure 2D) remained positive for up to 120 time lags due to dominant very low frequency periodic oscillations, which are revealed in the Fourier transform data (Figure 3D). However, the irregular shape of the autocorrelation function indicates complex underlying dynamics, which is further confirmed by the presence of many periodic components in the Fourier transform data. This pattern suggests that the dynamics may have a chaotic nature.

These results suggest the importance of identifying the temporal patterns in people's judgments of social entities. One can collapse patterns across time to reveal an average assessment of a target, but such an approach may fail to characterize appropriately the stream of social thinking. This is clearly the case for ambivalence, which can be described as repeated fluctuations between positive and negative evaluations. The targets used in the Vallacher and Nowak (1992) study were intended to generate ambivalence, and the data indicate that several discernible patterns other than simple oscillation (catastrophic change, polarization, etc.) characterized subjects' moment-to-moment feelings regarding the targets. Being able to identify these patterns is essential for the prediction of a person's judgments in the future. The knowledge that there are periodic oscillations between positive and negative judgments, for instance, enables one to predict that a positive judgment at one time will be followed by a negative judgment some time later. The relaxation time of the autocorrelation function, meanwhile, indicates how far into the future one can predict a person's judgment of a target person.

Thus, the variation in thought that people experience is not simply noise obscuring a "true" signal but represents the essence of the thought process itself. In the same way that actions unfold on identifiable time scales (Chapter 7) and relationships tend to undergo a sequence of phase transitions (Chapter 6), thoughts transpire in accordance with temporal patterns that suggest the operation of an underlying dynamical system.

B. Dynamics and Information

In social judgment, the primary concern always centers in one way or another on how the target of judgment is evaluated. Although the valence of evaluation (positivity vs. negativity) is of foremost concern in this regard, attention is occasion-

Table I
Relationship between Self-Report and Dynamic Measures[a]

Dynamic	Self-Report				
	Liking	Stability	Good–Bad	Strong–Weak	Active–Passive
Mean distance	−.82**	.03	−.26*	−.19*	−.03
Speed–close	−.40**	−.23*	−.25*	−.08	−.15
Speed–far	.18	.15	−.11	−.17	−.27*
Acceleration–close	−.34**	−.22*	−.27*	−.10	−.19*
Acceleration–far	.02	.13	−.17	−.14	−.27*
Time at rest–close	.51**	.21*	.07	.10	.17
Time at rest–far	−.48**	.22*	.03	−.00	−.09

[a]$N = 24$ in each target valence group. Results for Liking are first-order correlations; results for remaining self-report measures are correlations with Liking partialed out. *$p < .05$; **$p < .01$

ally given to the certainty of people's evaluations as well. What, if anything, do the intrinsic dynamics of judgment reveal about each of these established parameters of evaluation?

A study within the mouse paradigm provides some insight into this matter (Vallacher, Nowak, & Kaufman, 1992). Subjects in this research were asked to think of a same-sex professor from whom they had taken a course during the past year and to form a vivid image of him or her for 30 s. In addition to completing the 2-min mouse procedure with respect to this target, subjects responded to a set of questions on the computer screen concerning the target. Specifically, they were asked how positively they felt about the target, how negatively they felt about him or her, how stable their feelings were, and whether they had mixed feelings (ambivalence) about the target. They were also asked to indicate how certain they were of their responses to the positivity and negativity questions. On completion of these general questions, a new screen appeared that instructed subjects to rate the target on each of 15 trait dimensions intended to sample the basic dimensions of semantic space (Osgood, Suci, & Tannenbaum, 1957).[5]

Factor analyses were performed on the general questions and on the trait ratings. Two factors were obtained for the general items: *liking*, consisting of the positivity and negativity items, and *certainty*, consisting of the stability item, the ambivalence item, and the two certainty items. For the trait ratings, three factors were observed: *good–bad* (e.g., sincere vs. insincere, warm vs. cold), *strong–weak*

[5]Half the subjects responded to the general questions and the trait items prior to the mouse task; half did so after the mouse task. Subsequent analyses revealed this variable to be of negligible importance, and hence it is not discussed further

(e.g., independent vs. conforming, timid vs. forceful), and *active–passive* (e.g., excitable vs. calm, lazy vs. energetic). Subjects were assigned scores on each of these five factors reflecting their average responses (reverse scored when necessary) to each item loading on that factor.

With respect to mouse movements, we developed simple and intuitive measures to capture basic and general properties of judgmental dynamics. Our most basic measure was distance from the target (in pixels), which provided an indicator of overall evaluation. To characterize changes in evaluation, we measured the average speed (pixels per 0.1 s) and acceleration (changes in the number of pixels traversed in 0.1 s) of mouse movements. The speed measure indicates the average rate of change in evaluation, whereas the acceleration measure indicates changes in this rate and thus more variable dynamics. We also measured the time at rest (seconds without mouse movement). The speed, acceleration, and time at rest measures were computed separately for distances relatively close to the target and for distances relatively far from the target. The close versus far distinction was normalized for subjects by dividing in half the range of distance (i.e., the span from the minimum to the maximum) used in each subject's mouse movements. There were thus seven variables for each subject: distance, speed–close, acceleration-close, time at rest–close, speed–far, acceleration–far, and time at rest–far.

The mouse paradigm rests on the assumption that distance from the target and the pattern of changes in this distance reflect global evaluative responses to the target. Working from this assumption, we expected that mean distance would be associated with liking and perhaps with the more specific dimensions of evaluation (good–bad, strong–weak, active–passive) as well: The less the mean distance, the more favorable the evaluation. We also expected that relatively volatile dynamics— greater speed and acceleration and less time at rest—would be indicative of a system that has not reached equilibrium. Two more specific hypotheses follow from this expectation. First, with greater positivity in evaluation, there should be slower mouse movements and more time at rest when subjects are relatively close to the target but faster mouse movements and less time at rest when subjects are relatively far from the target. Second, with increasing uncertainty, instability, and ambivalence in evaluation, there should be greater speed and acceleration in mouse movements and less time at rest.

Correlational analyses were performed to test these hypotheses. Because liking tended to be correlated with the other self-report measures, we computed correlations between liking and the dynamic measures and between each of the other self-report measures and the dynamic measures with liking partialled out. The results of these analyses provided support for the hypotheses (Table I). The less distance subjects maintained from the target, the more positive their general evaluation of him or her and the more positive their ratings of him or her with respect to good versus bad and strong versus weak traits. Positive evaluation was also reflected in the speed, acceleration, and time at rest measures: As predicted, the more positive the evaluation, the less the speed and acceleration when close to the target, the more time at rest when close to the target, and the less time at rest when far from the target. Finally, the more certain, stable, and unambivalent the evaluation, the less the speed and acceleration when close to the target and the more time at rest when both close to and far from the target.

These data suggest correspondence between the stability of a social judgment system and the system's internally generated dynamics. At one extreme are opinions, attitudes, and impressions generated by a system lacking a stable equilibrium. The output of such a system is likely to be characterized by relatively volatile dynamics, with judgment oscillating in some fashion between different unstable equilibria (e.g., positive/favorable and negative/unfavorable). At the other extreme are opinions, attitudes, and impressions generated by a coherent, internally consistent system. The output of such a system may display temporal variation, but over time judgment should gravitate toward a relatively stable equilibrium. The research on polarization discussed earlier is consistent with this idea. Thus, if a well-developed schema exists for a target of judgment, there is a tendency for positive judgments of the target to become more positive and negative judgments to become more negative as the judge continues to think about the target (e.g., Tesser & Leone, 1977).

To explore these purported dynamic differences between stable (internally consistent) and unstable (internally inconsistent) judgment systems, Vallacher, Nowak, and Kaufman (1993) asked subjects to think about one of three people: someone they liked, someone they disliked, or someone about whom they felt ambivalent. As subjects thought about the target, they used the mouse to express their moment-to-moment feelings about him or her. We expected to find gravitation toward a stable equilibrium for the univalent targets. Over the two-minute judgment period, this would be apparent in decreased distance from the liked target and increased distance from the disliked target. For both of these targets, we expected to observe a decrease in speed and acceleration of mouse movements as the judgment system converges on a relatively stable (polarized) evaluation. Polarization was not expected, however, for the target promoting ambivalence (cf. Liberman & Chaiken, 1991). Because this target is not associated with a stable equilibrium, we anticipated that distance from the target should neither increase nor decrease, and that the speed and acceleration of movement should remain relatively high throughout the two-minute period. To test these hypotheses, we computed the values for distance, speed, and acceleration during the first 40 seconds and again during the final 40 seconds of the judgment period. We then performed a repeated measures analysis of variance on these scores as a function of target.

Results confirmed our expectations. Subjects induced to think about a well-liked acquaintance showed a reliable decrease in distance from the target, those induced to think about a disliked acquaintance showed a reliable increase in distance, and those induced to consider a mixed valence acquaintance showed no change in distance from the first to the last portion of the judgment period. Meanwhile, for speed and acceleration, subjects in both the liked and disliked target conditions showed a decrease over time, whereas subjects in the mixed valence condition tended to maintain a relatively rapid and variable rate of change in their moment-to-moment feelings about the target (see Vallacher et al., 1993, Expt, 1, for details concerning procedure and results). To provide a feel for these differential effects, Figures 4A C display the temporal trajectories observed for a typical subject in each of the three target conditions. Each figure shows the absolute distance from the target sampled 10 times per second during the judgment period. Note the change in distance and loss of dynamics for the univalent targets, but the maintenance of initial distance and dynamics for the mixed valence target.

V. Rethinking Social Thinking

Focusing on the intrinsic dynamics of social judgment may come to represent something of a phase transition in both a theoretical and methodological sense. Theoretically, the perspective we have forwarded in this chapter offers a new way to think about issues and topics in attitudes and social cognition. Methodologically, a focus on intrinsic dynamics alerts us to the importance of incorporating time into our research designs and data reduction techniques. These related sets of implications are discussed briefly in turn.

A. Implications for Theory

The way we think about people is often complicated, sometimes confusing, and never static. Even a person who we see in consistently glowing terms generates a succession of different memories, trait inferences, and concerns as we think about him or her. Each set of thoughts relevant to someone, in turn, is associated with a different overall feeling about him or her. Such temporal variation in social judgment can be understood theoretically in terms of the relation between structure and dynamics described in Section II, B. When a representation consists of both positive and negative elements, for example, and if these elements are not easily integrated, there will be relatively rapid fluctuation over time in one's summary feeling about the target, as each set of elements rises and falls in relative salience. Lacking integration, such a representation also lacks a stable equilibrium, so that it is unlikely that a more or less stationary evaluation of the target will evolve over a reasonably short period of time.

Volatility in intrinsic dynamics is associated with the subjective experience of ambivalence. Although ambivalence is commonly considered to be unpleasant, at least when sustained over a long period of time, there is reason to think that this mental state and the internally generated dynamics it reflects may be adaptive rather

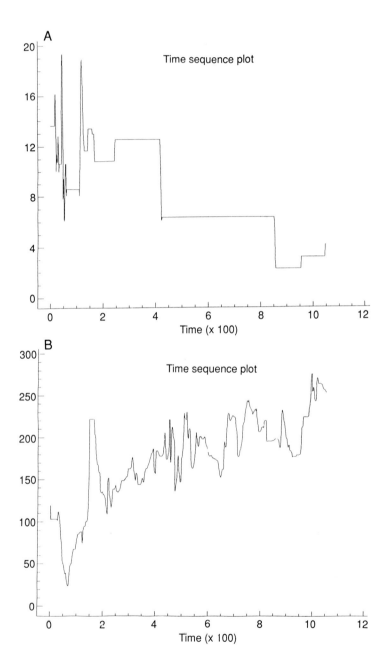

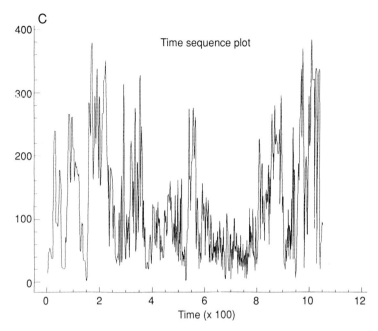

Figure 4A–C (A) Absolute distance from target over a 2-min period for target promoting liking. The *x* axis represents time (0–120 sec). The *y* axis represents absolute distance from target in pixels. (B) Absolute distance from target over 2-min period for target promoting disliking. The *x* axis represents time (0–120 sec). The *y* axis represents the absolute distance from target in pixels. (C) Absolute distance from target over 2-min period for target promoting ambivalence. The *x* axis represents time (0–120 sec). The *y* axis represents absolute distance for target in pixels.

than dysfunctional. In particular, ambivalence represents a condition wherein the cognitive system is not ready to settle down on a stable equilibrium but rather samples different evaluative states. This may be adaptive in much the same way that a degree of instability in EEG activity (e.g., low-dimensional chaos) enables the brain to respond to changing demands and provides a critical precondition for sensory discrimination and learning (Kelso & DeGuzman, 1991; Skarda & Freeman, 1987; see also Chapter 3). Thus, moment-to-moment variation in feelings about someone enables diverse information to be absorbed and consequently provides a spectrum of evaluative states from which the perceiver can develop a differentiated representation. And if the various perspectives can be integrated, movement between different evaluative states can be seen as setting the stage for the evolution of a representation that is coherent as well.

Knowing the temporal trajectory of subjects' social judgments may prove useful in predicting behavior. There is evidence that the correlation between people's attitudes and overt behavior is disappointingly low (Schuman & Johnson, 1976). In response, many theorists have concluded that attitudes are in fact a poor predictor of behavior and have proposed alternative, less direct causal connections between attitudes and action. It may be, however, that attitudes and other endpoints of social judgment find expression in behavior but that such expression is masked when only the central tendency of the attitude is assessed. An emotionally charged behavior (e.g., aggression), for example, may be associated with fluctuations in the relevant attitude (e.g., disliking) that exceed some threshold rather than with the value of the attitude averaged over time. A pattern of rapid oscillations between extreme maxima and minima, meanwhile, might predict frequent behavioral expression of the relevant judgment (i.e., expression each time a maxima occurs). More generally, insight into the feedback mechanisms between social judgment and behavior may be forthcoming from examination of the covariation over time between intrinsic dynamics and indices of behavioral expression.

The intrinsic dynamics of social judgment may also have relevance for interpersonal relationships. One of the more consistent findings in the relationship literature is the tendency for people with similar attitudes and beliefs to be drawn to one another (e.g., Byrne, Clore, & Smeaton, 1986). Conceivably, the coordination of temporal patterns in social judgment may be as important, if not more so, than the correspondence in attitudes and opinions collapsed across time. This idea is reflected in the everyday observation that people who like each other are "on the same wavelength" or "resonate with each other." Thus, whether two people come to like one another may depend on their ability to synchronize their patterns of social thinking. Even if they disagree regarding some topic, they may still enjoy interacting with each other if their respective rates of change in thought are similar or if they show similar tendencies toward convergence. If confirmed empirically, the coordination of intrinsic dynamics in thought between two people would provide a counterpart to the tendency for the actions of two people to develop phase relations in the service of joint action (see Chapter 7).

B. Implications for Research

In the prototypical attribution or impression formation paradigm, information about some target person or event is provided and then at some arbitrary time later, subjects' attributions or impressions are assessed. The intervening processes are not assessed directly but are inferred from the pattern of outcome measures in the experimental design. In such research, moreover, virtually no attention is given to the time scale on which the inferred processes might operate. With a few notable exceptions (e.g., Tesser, 1978), it is also commonly assumed that change in the output of social judgment occurs only in response to some sort of external factor— new information, perhaps, or some sort of social pressure. When change is observed in the absence of external "causes," then, it is commonly ascribed to random variation or perhaps to regression to the mean, habituation, or forgetting.

As we noted at the outset, of course, there are formidable methodological and operational difficulties inherent in the measurement of ongoing thought processes (see, e.g., Eiser, 1990; Fiske & Taylor, 1991). In bypassing self-reports, however, the mouse paradigm provides a way of circumventing some of the more vexing of these problems. And because this approach enables subjects to express their feelings without having to provide conscious reports of them, it would seem to be immune to issues of introspective access (Nisbett & Wilson, 1977) and cognitive versus affective primacy (Zajonc, 1980). In short, this approach provides a means of gaining insight into social judgment as it unfolds without disrupting it in the process. As such, it holds promise of enabling researchers to explore explicitly what they know to be true implicitly—namely, that social judgment unfolds over time and can do so without informational or social pressures from the outside.

In the research conducted thus far within the mouse paradigm, we have been concerned with establishing correspondence between summary self-reports and moment-to-moment temporal variation. Thus, we have attempted to minimize likely instigations to the suppression or editing of subjects' verbal reports (social desirability, evaluation apprehension). Such instigations, however, are inherent in many real-world situations. A person might have serious doubts about someone, for example, but nonetheless express moderate liking for the person if he or she feels that his or her assessment would somehow be made available to the person. Expecting to interact with the target of judgment can also promote inflated judgments of him or her, presumably out of a concern for having a pleasant rather than an unpleasant encounter (e.g., Knight & Vallacher, 1981). In these and no doubt other instances, the information contained in people's moment-to-moment evaluations of a target would likely provide a more accurate reflection of their feelings about the target than would their summary verbal self-reports and would perhaps would provide better prediction of their subsequent behavior toward the target as well (e.g., nonverbal indication of affect, attempts to pursue vs. avoid subsequent contact).

Although we have emphasized internally generated temporal variation, the mouse paradigm could investigate external influences on people's attitudes and impressions. To expose the dynamical underpinnings of influence, for example, one could simply provide new and inconsistent information regarding a target person at some point during subjects' moment-to-moment consideration of the target. Presumably, if such information had the intended effect of changing subjects' opinion regarding the target, it would do so by perturbing the existing dynamics, thereby creating the precondition for a different dynamic pattern to emerge that would accommodate the new information. A change from a positive to a negative opinion of a target person, for example, might be revealed in increased distance from the target, increased speed of movement, and so on. By tracking subjects' feelings on a moment-to-moment basis, one could document the timing of the phase transition from one pattern to another as subjects' thoughts became reorganized.

In like manner, the mouse paradigm could be extended to such diverse topics as self-evaluation, attitude formation, the mind sets associated with different action phases, group stereotypes, moral evaluation, action identification, and causal attribution. Beyond documenting the dynamic concomitants of known outcome effects (e.g., attitude change, emergent action identification, switch from person to situation attribution), research of this kind might reveal new insights into the cognitive processes associated with each of these phenomena or perhaps establish basic commonalities among them (e.g., hysteresis associated with transitions from one mental state to another). The investigation of different phenomena within a common paradigm, in short, enables us to identify both what is unique about each and what is invariant across them and thus representative of social thinking generally.

We hasten to note that we have barely scratched the surface in exploring the dynamics of social thinking. To date, the data we have collected within the mouse paradigm have been analyzed primarily in only very intuitive ways (speed, time at rest, acceleration, etc.). There are, however, powerful analytical and statistical tools used in the investigation of nonlinear dynamics and complex systems, each of which provides unique information about the pattern of temporal variation and the structure of the underlying system that produced it, and these may someday become indispensable elements in the analysis of social judgment dynamics. Several of the chapters in the book develop the rationale for these and other dynamical measures (see Chapters 2, 3, 4, 7, and 8), and all of the chapters provide clear hints as to how such measures can be brought to bear on the personal and interpersonal dynamics of thought and action.

VI. Conclusions

Thinking is inherently a dynamic process generated by a complex system of interconnected cognitive elements. Once initiated by a social stimulus, the judgment system takes on a life of its own, generating a continuous stream of output that can be characterized in terms of reliable patterns and dynamic properties. Variation in these patterns and properties, in turn, can be mapped onto the content and structural features of the underlying representation of the social stimulus. On this view, there is no necessary incompatibility between structural and dynamic models of social thinking. Quite the contrary, structure and dynamics provide interrelated means of description of the social judgment system.

In a broader sense, a focus on the intrinsic dynamics of thought represents an attempt to integrate the study of social cognition with other areas of scientific inquiry that are being recast in terms of dynamical systems. This attempt reflects our conviction that there are principles of dynamics that cut across the usual scientific boundaries (physics, chemistry, biology, psychology, etc.) and that a complete theory of social thinking must be built on these principles. Mind, after all, is inarguably a complex system, and like any complex system, it has the potential for rich dynamics. Cognitive processes, including processes underlying social judgment, can thus profitably be conceptualized in terms of the same ideas that capture the essence of physical systems. From this perspective, it is no longer necessary to invoke artificial systems—computers in particular—to depict the nature of human thought. Instead, virtually every natural system provides a metaphor for mind. This means that we can—and should—look to streams, clouds, and even the stars to unravel the mystery of the system that enables such looks.

Acknowledgments

Portions of this chapter were prepared while the first author was a visiting scholar at the Max Planck-Institute for Psychological Research, Munich, Germany. We wish to thank Peter Gollwitzer and L. F. von Seidler for their helpful comments on an earlier draft of this chapter.

References

Ajzen, I. (1977). Intuitive theories of events and the effects of base rate information on prediction. *Journal of Personality and Social Psychology, 35*, 303–314.

Amit, D. J. (1989). *Modelling brain function: The world of attractor neural networks*. Cambridge, England: Cambridge University Press.

Anderson, J. R., & Bower, G. H. (1973). *Human associative memory*. Washington, DC: Winston & Sons.

Anderson, N. H. (1981). *Foundations of information integration theory*. New York: Academic Press.

Barinaga, M. (1990). Neuroscience models the brain. *Science, 247*, 524–526.

Bartlett, F. A. (1932). *A study in experimental and social psychology*. New York: Cambridge University Press.

Bem, D. J., & McConnell, H. K. (1970). Testing the self-perception explanation of dissonance phenomena: On the salience of premanipulated attitudes. *Journal of Personality and Social Psychology, 14*, 23–31.

Byrne, D., Clore, G. L., & Smeaton, G. (1986). The attraction hypothesis: So similar attitudes affect anything? *Journal of Personality and Social Psychology, 51*, 1167–1170.

Cantor, N., & Mischel, W. (1979). Prototypes in person perception. In L. Berkowitz (Ed.), *Advances in experimental social psychology* (Vol. 12, pp. 3–52). New York: Academic Press.

Carpenter, G. A., & Grossberg, S. (1987). Discovering order in chaos: Stable self-organization of neural recognition codes. In Koslow, S. H., Mandell, A. J., & Schlesinger, M. F. (Eds.), *Annals of the New York Academy of Science*, Vol. 504. *Perspectives in biological dynamics and theoretical medicine* (pp. 33–51). New York: New York Academy of Sciences.

Crowne, D. P., & Marlowe, D. (1964). *The approval motive*. New York: Wiley.

Eckmann, J. P., & Ruelle, D. (1985). Ergodic theory of chaos and strange attractors. *Review of Modern Physics, 57*, 617–656.

Edwards, A. L. (1957). *The social desirability variable in personality assessment and research*. New York: Holt.

Eiser, J. R. (1990). *Social judgment*. Pacific Grove, CA: Brooks-Cole.

Festinger, L. (1957). *A theory of cognitive dissonance*. Palo Alto, CA: Stanford University Press.

Fiske, S. T., & Taylor, S. E. (1991). *Social cognition* (2nd ed.). New York: McGraw-Hill.

Grassberger, P., & Procaccia, I. (1983). On the characterization of strange attractors. *Physical Review Letters, 50,* 346–350.

Haken, H., & Stadler, M. (1990). *Synergetics of Cognition.* New York: Springer.

Haken, H. (1984). *The science of structure: Synergetics.* New York: Van Nostrand Reinhold.

Harvey, O. J., Hunt, D. E., & Schroder, H. M. (1961). *Conceptual systems and personality organization.* New York: Wiley.

Heider, F. (1958). *The psychology of interpersonal relations.* New York: Wiley.

Hobson, J. A. (1988). *The dreaming brain.* New York: Basic Books.

Hofstadter, D. R. (1979). *Godel, Escher, Bach.* New York: Basic Books.

Hopfield, J. J. (1982). Neural networks and physical systems with emergent collective computational capabilities. *Proceedings of the National Academy of Sciences of the United States of America, 79,* 2254–2558.

Hovland, C., Janis, I., & Kelley, H. H. (1953). *Communication and persuasion.* New Haven, CT: Yale University Press.

James, W. (1950). *The principles of psychology.* New York: Dover. (Original work published 1890)

Kelso, J. A. S., & DeGuzman, G. C. (1991). An intermittency mechanism for coherent and flexible brain and behavioral function. In J. Requin & G. E. Stelmach (Eds.), *Tutorials in motor neuroscience* (pp. 305–310). Dordrecht, The Netherlands: Kluwer.

Kelso, J. A. S., Ding, M., & Schoner, G. (1991). Dynamic pattern formation: A primer. In A. B. Baskin & J. E. Mittenhal (Eds.), *Principles of organization in organisms* (pp. 397–439). New York: Addison-Wesley.

Kim, M. P., & Rosenberg, S. (1980). Comparison of two structural models of implicit personality theory. *Journal of Personality and Social Psychology, 38,* 375–389.

Knight, J. A., & Vallacher, R. R. (1981). Interpersonal engagement in social perception: The consequences of getting into the action. *Journal of Personality and Social Psychology, 40,* 990–999.

Labos, E. (1987). Chaos and neural networks. In H. Degn, A. V. Holden, & L. F. Olsen (Eds.), *Chaos in biological systems* (pp. 195–206). New York: Plenum Press.

Landau, L. D., & Lifschitz, E. M. (1968). *Statistical physics.* New York: Pergamon Press.

Lewenstein, M., & Nowak, A. (1989). Recognition with self-control in neural networks. *Physical Review A, 40,* 4652–4664.

Liberman, A. & Chaiken, S. (1991). Value conflict and thought-induced attitude change. *Journal of Personality and Social Psychology, 27,* 203–216.

Lingle, J. H., & Ostrom, T. M. (1979). Retrieval selectivity in memory-based impression judgments. *Journal of Personality and Social Psychology, 37,* 180–194.

Linville, P. W. (1985). Self-complexity affective extremity: Don't put all your eggs in one cognitive basket. *Social Cognition, 3,* 94–120.

Mandler, G. (1975). *Mind and emotion.* New York: Wiley.

McClelland, J. L., & Rumelhart, D. E. (Eds.). (1986). *Parallel distributed processing: Explorations in the microstructure of cognition* (Vol. 2). Cambridge, MA: MIT Press.

Nisbett, R. E., & Ross, L. (1980). *Human inference: Strategies and shortcomings of social judgment.* Englewood Cliffs, NJ: Prentice-Hall.

Nisbett, R. E., & Wilson, T. D. (1977). Telling more than we can know: Verbal reports on mental processes. *Psychological Review, 84,* 231–259.

Osgood, C. E., Suci, G. J., & Tannenbaum, P. H. (1957). *The measurement of meaning.* Urbana: University of Illinois Press.

Pennebaker, J. W. (1989). Stream of consciousness and stress: Levels of thinking. In J. S. Uleman & J. A. Bargh (Eds.), *Unintended thought* (pp. 327–350). New York: Guilford Press.

Piaget, J. (1971). *Biology and knowledge.* Chicago: University of Chicago Press.

Polanyi, M. (1969). *Knowing and being.* Chicago: University of Chicago Press.

Pope, K. S., & Singer, J. L. (Eds.). (1978). *The stream of consciousness.* New York: Plenum Press.

Posner, M. I., & Keele, S. W. (1968). On the genesis of abstract ideas. *Journal of Experimental Psychology,* 77, 353–363.

Rosch, E. H. (1978). Principles of categorization. In E. Rosch & B. B. Lloyd (Eds.), *Cognition and categorization* (pp. 27–48). Hillsdale, NJ: Erlbaum.

Rosenberg, M. J. (1965). When dissonance fails: On eliminating evaluation apprehension from attitude measurement. *Journal of Personality and Social Psychology, 1,* 28–42.

Rumelhart, D. E. (1980). Schemata: The building blocks of cognition. In R. J. Spiro, B. C. Bruce, & W. F. Brewer (Eds.), *Theoretical issues in reading comprehension* (pp. 249–291). Hillsdale, NJ: Erlbaum.

Ryle, G. (1949). *The concept of mind.* London: Hutchinson.

Schank, R., & Abelson, R. (1977). *Scripts, goals, and understanding.* Hillsdale, NJ: Erlbaum.

Schuman, H., & Johnson, M. P. (1976). Attitudes and behavior. *Annual Review of Sociology, 2,* 161–207.

Schuster, H. G. (1984). *Deterministic chaos.* Vienna: Physik Verlag.

Scott, W. A., Osgood, D. W., & Peterson, C. (1979). *Cognitive structure: Theory and measurement of individual differences.* Washington, DC: Winston.

Sejnowski, T. J., & Churchland, P. S. (1989). Brain and cognition. In M. I. Posner (Ed.), *Foundations of cognitive science* (pp. 301–356). Cambridge, MA: MIT Press.

Skarda, C. A., & Freeman, W. J. (1987). How brains make chaos in order to make sense of the world. *Behavioral and Brain Sciences, 10,* 161–195.

Taylor, S. E., & Crocker, J. (1981). Schematic bases of social information processing. In E. T. Higgins, C. P. Herman, & M. P. Zanna (Eds.), *Social cognition: The Ontario Symposium* (Vol. 1, pp. 89–134). Hillsdale, NJ: Erlbaum.

Tesser, A. (1978). Self-generated attitude change. In L. Berkowitz (Ed.), *Advances in experimental social psychology* (Vol. 11, pp. 85–117). New York: Academic Press.

Tesser, A., & Leone, C. (1977). Cognitive schemas and thought as determinants of attitude change. *Journal of Experimental Social Psychology, 13,* 340–356.

Uleman, J. S., & Bargh, J. A. (Eds.). (1989). *Unintended thought.* New York: Guilford.

Vallacher, R. R., & Nowak, A. (1992). [Temporal patterns in the intrinsic dynamics of social judgment.] Unpublished research data.

Vallacher, R. R., Nowak, A., & Kaufman, J. (1992). [Intrinsic dynamics and self-report measures of social judgment.] Unpublished research data.

Vallacher, R. R., Nowak, A., & Kaufman, J. (1993). Intrinsic dynamics of social judgment. Manuscript submitted for publication.

van Geert, P. (1991). A dynamic systems model of cognitive and language growth. *Psychological Review, 98,* 3–53.

Wegner, D. M. (1988). *White bears and other unwanted thoughts.* New York: Viking.

Wegner, D. M., & Vallacher, R. R. (1977). *Implicit psychology.* New York: Oxford University Press.

Wegner, D. M., & Vallacher, R. R. (1981). Common-sense psychology. In J. P. Forgas (Ed.), *Social cognition: Perspectives on everyday understanding* (pp. 225–246). London: Academic Press.

Werner, H. (1957). *Comparative psychology of mental development* (3rd ed.). New York: International Universities Press.

Wilson, T. D. (1990). Self-persuasion via self-reflection. In J. M. Olson & M. P. Zanna (Eds.), *Self-inference processes: The Ontario Symposium* (Vol. 6, pp. 43–67). Hillsdale, NJ: Erlbaum.

Zajonc, R. B. (1980). Feeling and thinking: Preferences need no inferences. *American Psychologist, 35,* 151–175.

Zubek, J. P. (Ed.). (1969). *Sensory deprivation: Fifteen years of research.* New York: Appleton-Century-Crofts.

CHAPTER 12

Toward a Dynamical Social Psychology

Andrzej Nowak
Institute for Social Studies
Faculty of Psychology
University of Warsaw
Warsaw, Poland

Robin R. Vallacher
Department of Psychology
Florida Atlantic University
Boca Raton, Florida

Maciej Lewenstein
Institute for Social Studies
University of Warsaw and Center
    for Theoretical Physics
Polish Academy of Sciences
Warsaw, Poland

I. Introduction

In the natural sciences, models of dynamical systems are widely used as a conceptual tool in theory construction. This approach, however, has been traditionally rejected as inappropriate for modeling complex phenomena in the social sciences. Two major obstacles in particular have commonly been identified: (1) the apparent lack of deterministic causal laws governing social phenomena and (2) the inability to measure adequately the phenomena to be modeled. As we know today, linear (as well as "integrable" or analytically solvable) models of dynamical systems are not adequate to model much beyond the simplest physical phenomena. It should come as no surprise, then, that they cannot deal with the considerably more com-

Dynamical Systems in Social Psychology

plex nature of the social world. In other words, the impossibility of applying the tools developed in mathematics and physics to the domain of social sciences can be partially attributed to the weakness of those tools and their associated models, not necessarily to the weakness of social sciences as was traditionally done.

The new developments in the theory of nonlinear dynamical systems enable one to describe complex phenomena often with quite simple models. In fact, as our understanding of qualitative properties of various models grows, it is possible to construct and verify models on the basis of much more specific measurement than had been possible before. The theory of dynamical systems also points out the kinds of data that can be used to verify dynamical models. In social psychology, we were often not aware of the potential usefulness of certain types of data, such as time series measurements of a single variable.

We believe that this volume demonstrates the enormous potential for applications of dynamical systems theory in social psychology. The subject matter of social psychology is either the individual mind, the dyad, or the social group. All of these may be considered dynamical systems because they all consist of mutually interdependent, interacting elements whose interaction may be described, at least in theory, by differential or difference equations. To apply fully the theory of dynamical systems, however, we must modify how we go about doing social psychology. Our aim in this chapter is to suggest how this can be accomplished. In particular, we develop the main implications of dynamical systems theory with respect to the field's philosophical underpinnings, theoretical concerns, methodological approaches, and statistical techniques.

II. Implications for Philosophy of the Social Sciences

A. Determinism

The most important philosophical implication of dynamical systems theory concerns the concept of determinism. In the Laplacean model of determinism, the state of the world in any given instant determines uniquely its future. Theoretically, if one knew the states of all the elements in the universe at a given moment, one could predict all future states of the elements. The applicability of such a strong version of determinism to the social sciences has been questioned over the years, in large part because it ran counter to the possibility of free will on the part of humans. The observation of weak relations between variables was taken as evidence that an underlying deterministic order simply did not exist, at least in the sense that Laplace had in mind.

In light of the contemporary notion of chaos, both sides of the determinism debate outlined above are to some extent inadequate. Laplacean determinism does not have any practical relevance for chaotic systems. Even the smallest changes in initial conditions or the smallest perturbations of the dynamical equations may lead to sudden, large, and completely unpredictable changes in the dynamics of the system. A lack of predictability and the existence of weak correlations between variables therefore cannot be taken as proof that the variables in the system lack an underlying mathematical relations.

Although chaotic dynamical systems are not predictable in the classical sense, this does not mean that nothing can be said about the properties of chaotic dynamics. On the contrary, dynamical systems theory allows one to characterize chaotic dynamics quite precisely using appropriate statistical tools, such as, for example, the Grassberger–Procaccia analysis (Chapter 2). and theoretical concepts such as attractors. If we know what the attractors of the dynamics of a social system are, we can make some predictions concerning the future state of the system, even when we do not know the system's present state. Namely, regardless of the initial state of the system, in the future the system will be close to its attractor. As a trivial example, we can predict with confidence that a pendulum will hang down motionlessly some time after it has been pushed (because there is friction in the system). For this prediction, we do not need to worry about how strongly and in which direction the pendelum was pushed.

B. Causal Laws

Cause and effect acquire a new meaning from the dynamical systems perspective. In particular, the notion that theories should consist of causal laws specifying that an independent variable at time t_1 leads to change in the dependent variable at time t_2 needs to be reconsidered. The division into independent and dependent variables assumes an asymmetric, one-directional relations. Quite often in psychology, however, we deal with symmetric relations in which each variable both influences and is influenced by the other. So although it is certainly possible to document empirically a cause–effect relation between a pair of variables, it is conceivable that in some instances the converse causal connection might characterize the relation as well. Indeed, bidirectional causality may turn out to be a fundamental feature of social psychological phenomena that have been explored primarily in terms of asymmetric causal relations among putative independent and dependent variables. More generally, the dynamical systems perspective raises the possibility that social psychological variables may display relations that conform to a variety of different feedback mechanisms. The traditional view in psychology of unidirectional cause and effect is simply not the best conceptual tool to capture this idea.

There is another sense in which traditional canons of causal inference do not fit well in the science of dynamical systems. In particular, a change in the value of a variable in the system does not necessarily imply the action of any causal agent because such change may reflect the system's internal dynamics. As a system evolves naturally by virtue of its internal dynamics, it tends to produce a pattern (see Chapter 4) that persists over time. It is when this pattern changes that one should think in terms of causal agents—but causal agents of a particular kind. Specifically, when a change in pattern occurs, it may often be attributed to a change in the system's control parameters.[1] Such a change in control parameters can then be considered a causal factor in changing the pattern of the system's behavior. For example, if a person takes a step, we do not need to look for a causal factor that produced this step. If, however, the person had been walking and then starts running (a change of pattern), we should look for a causal agent—that is, we should identify what control parameter has changed.

In this fundamental sense, the goal of contemporary social psychology should change: Instead of trying to find one-way causal relations between variables, social psychology should attempt to find regularities or patterns. Causal relations in the form of a distinct cause leading to a specified effect represent just one kind of pattern. A vastly different kind of relation is observed among dynamical variables, wherein the time evolution of each variable is determined by values of other variables in the system. In such a relation, each variable is both a cause and an effect at the same time. This kind of relation is often observed and precisely specified in the physical sciences, but it is not often discussed in terms of cause and effect. Another form of regularity might be represented in the form of coordination among the different parts of a system leading to the emergence of patterns. The change of patterns with the passage of time (such as when the system is converging on an attractor) or as function of change of some other variables in the system (such as control parameters) are other examples of regularity. Sometimes the regularity might be visible only at certain stages in the system's evolution. For example, a system that has fixed-point attractors may be characterized quite precisely at late stages in its evolution but not necessarily in the early stages. Schroeck (Chapter 4) discusses more precisely different possible types of regularities and various ways of identifying them.

C. Unpredictability of Human Behavior

From the dynamical systems perspective, the unpredictability of human be-havior acquires a possible new interpretation, regardless of whether it results from free will or other factors. Specifically, unpredictable behavior can be modeled ac-cording to rules of deterministic chaos. The consequences of such unpredictability are very different from the traditional view, both on the individual level and the social level. Patterns of individual behavior, although unpredictable, may still be well characterized using appropriate methods such as those mentioned above. On

[1] Of course, a change in a system's pattern may instead reflect the system's intrinsic dynamics.

the other hand, the unpredictability of individuals does not necessarily lead to the unpredictability of group behavior. When we heat a pot of water, we are unable in practice to predict (and do not care about) the behavior of individual water molecules. Still, we can precisely describe what is going on using global concepts, such as the temperature and pressure of the water. From this perspective, although individual behavior may be impossible to predict, we might be able to predict the course of change of global parameters in a group or society. As an example, individual decisions to marry may be totally unpredictable, but in general the number of marriages in a society may exhibit some properties of a chaotic low-dimensional system (Nowak, Kús, & Napiórkowski, 1993).

III. Implications for Theory in Social Sciences

There are three important implications of dynamical systems for theory construction in social psychology. First, the dynamical systems approach suggests new structures to identify in social psychology and indicates the kinds of data to collect. Second, the dynamical systems approach tells us how to construct "ambitious" quantitative models. Last but not least, this approach tells us how to construct less ambitious but nonetheless extremely useful models. Of course, the latter possibility should be exercised with great care because of the possibility of misuse and misinterpretation and because of the danger of creating pseudoscientific results.

A. What to Identify and Measure

1. Intrinsic Dynamics

A general prescription is to analyze the intrinsic dynamics and/or the stability of systems. Note that such an approach requires a completely new paradigm for the social and behavioral sciences. Traditionally, in social psychology, we have assumed that a change in thought or behavior is only a reaction to some stimulus. Although systems obviously do react to stimuli, it is also the case that they undergo significant intrinsic changes. To identify and measure such changes, one should observe the behavior of the system in the absence of external stimuli or at least under conditions in which the influences of external stimuli are somehow minimized.

Within psychology, intrinsic dynamics have been observed on the neurophysiological level. Examples of intrinsic dynamics include reverberation in the brain and attractors in neural networks. In a series of recent experiments on monkeys, for example, Miyashita and Chang (1988) demonstrated the existence of such attractors governed by intrinsic dynamics in the absence of any stimuli. There is reason to think that intrinsic dynamics exist at higher levels of human information processing as well. Vallacher and Nowak (Chapter 11), for instance, suggest that our global evaluations of a target person show reliable and meaningful moment-to-moment variation, even when no new information regarding the target is provided. Work by Nowak, Szamrej, & Latané (1990), meanwhile, indicated that intrinsic dynamics are exhibited at the social level of information processing (see Chapter 10).

2. Patterns

The identification of patterns of spontaneously occurring changes in a system often constitutes the first step toward understanding the system's dynamics. Although a change in the system's behavior does not necessarily indicate the influence of external factors, changes in the patterns themselves typically do result from external causes.[2] As noted earlier, the cause in this case is associated with changes in the system's control factors. It is clearly essential, then, to identify factors (i.e., the control factors) responsible for changes in a system's pattern of behavior. Kelso's (e.g. Kelso, Ding, & Schoner, 1991) program of research on the synergetics of motor behavior is a good example of this approach.

3. Stability

Another important aspect of the dynamical approach is a new understanding of stability versus readiness for a change or, from a different perspective, an analysis of equilibrium behavior. A system may rest in either a stable or an unstable equilibrium. If a system rests in unstable equilibrium, then even a slight external influence may cause a dramatic change in the behavior of the system. If the system rests in stable equilibrium, however, even a relatively strong external influence will not significantly influence the system. If the equilibrium is superstable, then regardless of the strength of an external influence, the system will return to this equilibrium after some time. Thus, by perturbing the system in a controlled way and determining whether it returns to its original state or instead jumps to another state, we may learn about the degree of stability in the system.

Another way to analyze equilibrium behavior is to look at the distribution of variables in the system. If there are point attractors in the system, then the observed values will usually be concentrated around those attractors. This means that after a period of time, the system will converge on one of its attractors. In sum, the description of equilibrium states provides a means of characterizing a dynamical system. The behavior of stable equilibria in systems can sometimes be conveni-

---

[2]Note that we use here the notion *external* to describe factors external to the dynamical system in question. This does not imply that such factors are necessarily external to the considered organism or social group as a whole.

ently described by catastophe theory (cf. Thom, 1975), which is discussed in the present volume by Tesser and Achee (Chapter 5) and by Latané and Nowak (Chapter 10).

In investigations of dynamics, it is essential to look for signatures of nonlinear behavior. The identification of such phenomena as hysteresis, period doubling, critical slowing down, Hopf bifurcation, and so forth allows us to gain qualitative insight into the mechanisms underlying the behavior of a system. Sometimes, on the basis of such knowledge, we may strive toward a construction of a model in the form of mathematical equations. The construction of a precise model is an ultimate goal in science. Unfortunately, in social psychology, we often are unable to acquire precise enough measurements to enable the construction of such models. However, as we discuss later, considerable insight into the phenomena in question may be achieved even without the construction of precise models because our understanding of the phenomenon may be facilitated by models of qualitative understanding.

A specific case of nonlinear behavior is deterministic chaos. As noted earlier, chaos can be distinguished from purely random behavior, and there are methods available for making this distinction. Such methods should be used when dealing with a social (Nowak et al., 1993) or behavioral (Skarda & Freeman, 1987) system that is apparently chaotic. Time series analysis is an essential tool for this purpose.

B. "Ambitious" Models versus Qualitative Understanding

In some situations, one can proceed according to the orthodox rules used in the natural sciences. For instance, if we know patterns of behavior and the way they change and if we can identify relevant dynamical variables and control parameters, we may then build a precise mathematical model of the system. Usually values of the control parameters for such models have to be fitted, but when this done, the model may serve to reproduce and predict empirical data quantitatively. Such an approach is successful in very clean and rare cases (e.g., Kelso et al., 1991). More commonly, such an approach is too ambitious for social psychology; it is more reasonable to look for qualitative agreement and qualitative understanding. Most social scientists, in fact, might scoff at the suggestion that theories should be formulated in terms of differential equations. One of the reasons for this is a disbelief in the possibility of predicting the behavior of individuals. As indicated earlier, however, unpredictability is a fact of life in dynamical systems theory and thus is not necessarily incompatible with building ambitious models. The real reason for seeking qualitative understanding is the lack of precision associated with social phenomena.

Physics, chemistry, and engineering are perceived by most people as quantitative sciences, in contrast to such sciences as psychology or sociology, which are perceived as qualitative. Social scientists themselves might question the appropriateness of mathematical models for qualitative analysis. It should be stressed, however, that physics and other natural sciences also use a qualitative approach. It is simply not true that all models in physics are built to obtain exact agreement with experimental data. There are many models that are constructed to gain qualitative understanding of physical phenomena. The simplest model of a ferromagnet—the Ising model—is a good example. This model, built to explain magnetic phenomena, assumes that each particle of a magnetic material may have only two orientations of its magnetic moment, which are usually represented as arrows pointing either up or down. This model has really very little in common with physical reality where any particle may have any orientation in three-dimensional space but nevertheless serves as a paradigm for understanding phase transitions and other collective phenomena. Simple systems of differential equations, such as the Lorenz model, similarly serve as paradigms for our understanding of multiple phenomena in meteorology, hydrodynamics, nonlinear optics, and so forth.

The application of qualitative methods in physics is well represented in statistical physics. Statistical physics deals with large systems consisting of many interacting elements and, as the name implies, uses statistical methods. Within statistical physics, one can describe collective phenomena, the emergence of patterns, self-organization in systems, and so on. One of the main insights of statistical physics concerns the universality of qualitative mechanisms and phenomena. The qualitative behavior of large systems often does not depend a great deal on details involving the behavior of individual elements. This observation is of major importance for researchers. To achieve qualitative understanding, it is often possible to build very simple models that capture only essential properties of the interactions in the system. Such simple models nevertheless allow for the proper description of aggregate behavior.

A similar kind of universality holds in dynamical systems theory. Here, we speak about universality of types of behavior, types of changes of behavior, and so on. It is possible, for instance, for two sets of differential equations that differ in details to exhibit similar qualitative behavior.

C. Qualitative Models in Social Psychology

The construction of ambitious quantitative models in the social sciences is, with a few exceptions (see Weidlich, 1991), a hopeless task at present. We believe, however, that the construction of qualitative models is possible and that they will lead to fruitful results, just as they have in the natural sciences. First, qualitative models offer fundamental understanding of social phenomena from new perspectives. Even if the model makes predictions that are trivial from the viewpoint of social scientists, the fact that they follow from rules of mathematics is by no means trivial and, in our opinion, has important philosophical consequences. Second, qualitative models not only explain phenomena but also have predictive power. For example, if we observe period doubling in some social system and if we identify the control parameter responsible for it, we may expect that further changes of the control parameter will cause further period-doubling bifurcations, eventually leading to chaos. In another words, from observation of a change in the pattern of behavior and from identification of the cause of the change, we may predict further changes in the pattern of behavior.

Third, certain properties of dynamical systems may be used to understand individual differences in social thought and behavior. Let us assume that certain aspects of the dynamics of individual human behavior may be described by some system of dynamical equations. We should then expect that such a system has the same or at least a similar form for all individuals. Then why do they behave differently? A possible explanation lies in the fact that each individual is characterized by different values of the same control parameters. As a result, different individuals may display drastically different behavior. From this perspective, it is possible that people differ reliably from one another, even though the basic control mechanisms are the same. Such an explanation of individual differences is similar to some concepts developed in modern linguistics (Chomsky, 1981).

Instead of striving for prediction in the understanding of chaotic systems, empirical research attempts to find patterns in data. This holds for all levels of analysis, from individual to group to society. Some patterns may express a causal relation in which one event reliably follows another. Other patterns may express a linear correlation, wherein the values of one variable are directly and uniformly associated with the values of one or more other variables. Many other kinds of patterns are also possible, however, that cannot be subsumed by causation or linear correlation. Examples include the wavelike pattern in the movements of a person or the particular phase relation coordinating the behavior waves of two people (see Chapter 7), the spatial distribution of attitudes in a society (see Nowak et al., 1990), motor coordination (e.g., Kelso et al., 1991; Turvey, 1990), intermittent activity characterizing a person or dyad (see Chapter 4), quasiperiodic oscillation in the evaluation of a target person (see Chapter 11), phase transitions in the evolution of a close relationship (see Chapter 6), the distribution of values on a dimension of judgment (see Chapter 10), and the complexity displayed in a sequence of binary behavioral choices (see Chapter 8).

Once a pattern is identified, the next step is to try to find a system of equations that produces a similar pattern. One should also find out if this system of equations changes its pattern of behavior as a function of changes in the control parameters in a manner similar to that observed in the empirical system being modeled. If it does, then one has hit on a theoretical model that captures important aspects of the phenomenon one is trying to understand.

D. Complexity of Theory

A general rule in science is to strive for explanations of observed phenomena that are as simple as possible. From the perspective of dynamical systems, it is sometimes a nontrivial matter to decide what will make a theory simple and what will make it more complex. Thus, the behavior in an apparently complex system may be accounted for by either a large number of linearly related or a smaller number of nonlinearly related variables (see Chapter 2). We can thus greatly reduce the number of variables at the expense of increased complexity in the relations among variables. On the other hand, very complex relations among some variables might become notably simplified if we introduce a few more variables into the theory (see Chapter 4).

There is no ready recipe for simplifying a theory apart from the general heuristic that one should find the smallest set of variables that will generate a pattern that matches one's experimental data. A more specific heuristic often used in the natural sciences is to decide which aspects of the phenomena are the most important to model and then to build such a model to capture only those aspects. For example, when trying to build a model of crowd behavior, one should not attempt to build a model that will capture everything one might observe in a crowd. Instead, one might concentrate on particular phase transitions, such as a change from rejection to acceptance of a persuasive message or a switch from a mood of aggression to a mood of panic.

IV. Implications for Statistics

A. Nonlinear Relations

The vast majority of statistical methods used in social psychology are based on the assumption of linearity. If the relations among variables are nonlinear, the traditional methods are not adequate to capture them. It is difficult, for instance, if not meaningless, to separate variables into those that are "independent" versus those that are "dependent." We need to go beyond such distinctions, and traditional statistics more generally, to develop methods that can adequately describe the behavior of dynamical systems. Such methods can become extremely complex.

Specifically, we need tools to detect nonlinear relations. One of the most useful tools for such a task is simply visual inspection of data presented in graphical form (see Chapter 4 for a discussion of the brain and pattern recognition). We start by plotting variables as a function of other variables and/or as a function of time. We try various combinations of variables to find one that "works." If instead of a shapeless blob there appears a shape (a pattern), it means that we have found a relation. The shape of a pattern, in turn, may tell us a great about the nature of the relation.

A different approach is to use the sophisticated methods of modern mathematics and physics, such as Fourier transforms, the Grassberger–Procaccia method, the direct test for determinism of a time series, coherent state analysis, or neural networks to detect nonlinear predictors. These methods are well represented in the preceding chapters, so there is no need to develop them here.

B. The Danger of Averaging

Traditionally, the heart of statistical analysis in social psychology is averaging. For example, we average over the attitudes of group members to characterize a group attitude. In experiments, meanwhile, we average to get the mean value of a dependent variable in each experimental condition. If we are dealing with a variable from a dynamical system evolving in time, however, averaging does not make much sense. For example, if somebody alternately hates and loves his or her parent, it is misleading at best to suggest that this person on average mildly likes the parent (see Chapter 11). By averaging over time, one loses considerable information—perhaps the information that is most critical for understanding the phenomenon.

Averaging is also likely to conceal meaningful patterns when we are dealing with an ensemble of different dynamical systems that have the same mechanisms. Imagine, for example, that attendance at a restaurant can in fact be described by the logistic equation (see Chapter 2). Now assume that to test this model, a scientist measures the attendance at each restaurant every week and averages the results. Although each restaurant's attendance is governed by the same equation, each of them is likely to be at a different point in its evolution with respect to this equation. The average attendance clearly would not show meaningful differences as a function of time, and the pattern of individual evolution would be concealed. In short, one can identify the distribution of trajectories in time but still lose all the important dynamic information.

This does not mean, however, that averaging is always inappropriate when dealing with the information in nonlinear dynamical systems. We can, for example, try to classify each individual pattern and then perform statistics using the frequency of types of pattern as the dependent measure. Another approach is to characterize each pattern by a set of parameters and average the parameters rather than raw data. Possible parameters here might include topological and metric entropy (see Chapters 3 and 8), dimension determined by the Grassberger–Procaccia method (see Chapter 2), the relaxation time for autocorrelation (see Chapters 8 and 11), the dominant component in a Fourier transform (see Chapters 4, 7, and 11), or such simple measures as speed and acceleration (see Chapter 11).

Even if we assume that people's behavior in a given domain is governed by the same basic mechanism—that is, the behavior can be described by the same dynamical system—it is quite likely that the values of the control parameters will be different for different people. This would be reflected in very different time trajectories for different subjects, despite the basic similarity of underlying psychological mechanisms.

Finally, it is worth noting that in light of recent developments in dynamical systems theory, the usefulness of mathematical models may be much greater than previously thought. Qualitative modeling is a totally acceptable approach in science and thus enables us to develop mathematical models of many phenomena that are impossible to capture quantitatively. It is also the case that the potential for verification of mathematical models is much greater that once thought. In light of Takens' theorem (Takens, 1981; see Chapter 2), it is not always necessary to measure every variable in the system. Indeed, considerable insight may be gained by monitoring the time evolution of even a single variable in the system. On the basis of such measurement, it is possible in some cases to reconstruct some features of the dynamics of the system as a whole.

V. Summing Up: Social Psychology Reconsidered

The nonlinear dynamical systems perspective is rapidly emerging as one of the dominant metatheories in the natural sciences, and there is reason to think that it will come to provide integrative understanding in the social and behavioral sciences as well. This is not to say that social psychology in its present form is deficient or that it has reached a point of diminishing returns. To the contrary, some of the most exciting and useful notions about human thought and behavior are contained in countless journal articles and books devoted to social psychology, and the growth of such knowledge has become exponential in recent years. One could argue, in fact, that the field suffers from an embarrassment of riches in that it is difficult to establish conceptual coherence with respect to such a diverse set of topics, findings, and ideas. The dynamical systems perspective, we feel, may be able to provide just this sort of coherence.

We wish to emphasize that linear relations, if they can be found, and cause–effect reasoning are not inconsistent with the basic tenets of dynamical models. Social psychological theories and research strategies built on such assumptions thus may well stand the test of time, providing valid insight into important features of interpersonal functioning. At the same time, the dynamical perspective also allows for, and indicates how to conceptualize and measure, aspects of functioning that are nonlinear and embedded in feedback mechanisms that defy understanding in terms of simple models of cause and effect. This means that the concepts and tools of dynamical models create a broad net within which existing theories can be understood and new theories generated.

For a new paradigm to be accepted in social psychology (or in any area of science), it is not sufficient simply to expose limitations of the current paradigm. As Kuhn (1970) and others have noted, punctuation points in the history of science require that a new paradigm become available that can provide a better synthesis of the data generated within the old paradigm. So, although social psychology strikes many as a fragmented field lacking theoretical consensus (see Chapter 1) and thus ripe for self-organization with respect to a new set of integrative ideas and methods, it is essential that the value of the new ideas and methods be made explicit and concrete. With that in mind, we offer the following pieces of advice to those interested in rethinking social psychology in dynamical terms:

1. Look for temporal changes in the phenomenon of interest and give explicit consideration to the time scale on which these changes occur. Let the system unfold according to its own intrinsic dynamics.

2. Analyze the stability versus instability in the phenomenon of interest. Perturb the system in some way and note whether it returns to its equilibrium state and, if so, how readily.

3. Look for signatures of nonlinear behavior in the phenomenon. These include hysteresis, critical slowing down, and bifurcations. The specific form of nonlinear behavior identified (e.g., the type of bifurcation observed) provides insight into the mechanisms underlying the system's behavior.

4. Try to build a model in the form of differential equations. We hasten to add that this strategy may commonly prove to be unnecessary or impractical. When possible, though, it is extremely valuable to do so in view of the substantial precision in understanding it provides.

5. Try to build a model of qualitative understanding. Do not attempt to model the entire complexity of the phenomenon; rather, try to model important qualitative aspects of the phenomenon. Keep in mind that the natural sciences frequently do the same.

6. Look for order parameters. Alternatively (or in conjunction), measure many variables that evolve in time and try to find patterns of dependency among them.

7. Try to identify the control parameters in the phenomenon. Manipulate the values of the control parameters and observe their effect on the pattern of temporal behavior.

8. Play around with different combinations of variables until a clear pattern emerges. Sometimes visual inspection alone with reveal the existence of a pattern.

9. Last but not least, become familiar with recent developments in mathematics and in computer tools and techniques.

Many of these recommendations require the use of analytical and statistical methods developed in physics and mathematics. In this sense, social psychology can be looked on as a new challenge for these disciplines. But although basic models in physics and mathematics are proving to be remarkably general and hence applicable to a variety of topics (e.g., economics, population dynamics), it is still the case that these models must be adapted, or perhaps even replaced with better models, to deal with the nuances of people's mental, emotional, and behavioral dynamics. The analytical tools used to test these models also must be adapted in light of the accumulated knowledge generated by social psychology.

For their part, social psychologists will have to gather new kinds of data, such as time series, that are specifically appropriate to these tools and models. Beyond that, we wish to stress the importance of making use of modern computer technology, which enables powerful methods of data analysis, visualization of results, and exploration of the behavior of models through computer simulation. The rapid development of nonlinear dynamical systems theory simply would not have occurred had it not been for the power of modern computers. For one thing, computer-aided numerical methods are often the only feasible means of solving sets of nonlinear differential equations. Computers have also enabled the visualization of complex processes that would otherwise be opaque to human understanding. And through computer simulations, we can explore the behavior of highly complex systems for which analytical solutions sometimes are not available. Computer simulations are already an important tool in cognitive psychology, and in recent years the importance of simulations in social psychology has become increasingly recognized as well. This trend will help to bring social psychology in line with other areas of science that explore the applications of models of dynamical systems.

We noted at the outset of this volume (Chapter 1) that social psychology has always been sensitive to the complexity and concomitant lack of prediction in even mundane interpersonal functioning but that lacking appropriate concepts and tools, this sensitivity was not always manifest in mainstream theory and research. Now that dynamical systems theory is emerging as the principal player in the natural sciences, and given the natural but largely unexplored fit between this perspective and the subject matter of social psychology, we suspect that in the years to come, physicists and others in the natural sciences will join the ranks of social psychologists in working toward a common goal: imposing theoretical order on the many degrees of freedom in the minds, actions, and interactions of human beings.

References

Chomsky, N. (1981). Principles and parameters in syntactic theory. In N. Horstein & D. Lightfoot (Eds.), *Explanation in linguistics* (pp. 123–146). Cambridge, MA: MIT Press.

Kelso, J. S., Ding M., & Schoner, G. (1991). Dynamic pattern formation: A primer. In A. B. Baskin & J. E. Mittenthal (Eds.), *Principles of organization in organisms* (pp. 397–439). New York: Addison-Wesley.

Kuhn, T. S. (1970). *The structure of scientific revolutions* (2nd ed.). Chicago: University of Chicago Press.

Miyashita, Y., & Chang, H. S. (1988). Neuronal correlates of pictorial short-term memory in the primate cortex. *Nature, 331*, 68–70.

Nowak, A., Kús, M., & Napiórkowski, M. (1993). *Choas in the social sciences.* In press.

Nowak, A., Szamrej, A., & Latané, B. (1990). From private attitude to public opinion: A dynamic theory of social impact. *Psychological Review, 97*, 362–376.

Skarda C. A., & Freeman, W. J. (1987). How brains make chaos in order to make sense of the world. *Behavioral and Brain Sciences, 10*, 161–195.

Takens, F. (1981). In D. A. Rand & L. S. Young (Eds.), *Lecture notes in mathematics* (Vol. 898, pp. 366–381). New York: Springer.

Thom, R. (1975). *Structural stability and morphogenesis.* New York: Benjamin-Addison Wesley.

Turvey, M. T. (1990). *American Psychologist, 45*, 938–953.

Weidlich, W. (1991). Physics and social science: The approach of synergetics. *Physics Reports, 204*, 1–163.

AUTHOR INDEX

SUBJECT INDEX

A

Aggression, 75, 95–97
Ambivalence, 57, 209, 260, 265, 268–269, 271
  adaptive value of, 269, 271
Attitude, 3, 197–217, 219–246, 287, *see also*
    Social judgment
  as attractor, 197, 210–211,
  bimodal distribution, 224–226, 230–231,
    236–237, 239, 243
  category vs. dimension, 219–246
  linear assumption of, 198–199, 202–203,
    220–224
  polarization, 203, 239–241, 245
  semantic space, 199, 205, 221, 266–267, *see*
    also Attitude organization
Attitude-behavior relation, 2, 201–202, 211, 220,
    242, 271–272
Attitude change, 14, 197–199, 220, 226,
    240–243, 245, 273–274
  catastrophic, 219–246
Attitude formation, 11, 220, 239
Attitude organization, 199–201, 203, 225–226,
    239–240, *see also* Attitude, semantic space;
    Cognitive structure
Attitude research,
  traditional, 197–203, 206, 221
  dynamical approach to, 207–216, 238–239,
    246
Attractor, 9, 25–26, 29, 35, 40, 42, 45, 47–51,
    59–62, 79, 101, 118–121, 124, 128,
    131–135, 140–141, 143, 150, 182, 197,
    207–211, 213–215, 257, 261, 281–283
Autocorrelation, 43, 48, 58–59, 62, 76–77, 174,
    177–180, 187–195, 261, 263, 265, 289
Averaging, danger of, 269–273, 289–290

B

Bat echolocation, 76, 87–88
Behavior,
  coordination, 123–124, 156–165, 265, 272,
    287, *see also* Social coordination
  Eshkol-Wachmann movement notation for,
    145–147, 149

pattern, 73, 79, 89, 113, 288–290
  segmentation, 144–145, 149
  surface, 99–100, 107–108, *see also* Catastrophe
    theory
  wave, 139–166, 287
Bifurcation, 14, 17, 19, 35–36, 38–39, 41–42, 55,
    119, 121, 125, 129–130, 132, 170–171,
    185–186, 229, 286, 291, *see also* Catastrophe
    theory; Phase transition
  diagram, 37, 41
  set, 99–102
Biological rhythms, 12, 18, 38, 58, 62, 65
Biological systems, 112–118, 148, 169, 180, 182,
    184, 260
Bistability, 39–40, 42, 102
Brain sciences, 55, 58, *see also* Neurobiology;
    Neuroscience
Broccoflower, 35
Butterfly effect, 8, 17, 31, 57, *see also* Initial
    conditions, sensitivity to (STIC)

C

Canonical/normal social psychology, 95–98, 108,
    see also Mainstream social psychology
Cardiac death, 59
Catastrophe, 95, 99–101, 105–106, 108, 120,
    133, 203, 229, 231, 237, 246, 260–261, 265,
    see also Bifurcation; Phase transition
  attitude change as, 220, 227–230, 237–238
  behavior surface, 99–100, 107–108
  butterfly, 99
  control surface, 99
  cusp, 38, 99–102, 228–229
  fold, 99
  theory, 18, 36, 95–108, 220, 227–230, 232,
    237–238, 284
Central limit theorem, 48, 55, 58, 64, 222–224,
    231
Chaos,
  deterministic, 10–11, 13, 17–19, 29–30, 32–35,
    41–51, 57, 59–61, 71–72, 77–79,
    99, 142, 165, 170–171, 180, 191, 214,
    229, 256, 260, 265, 280–283, 285, 287